Film Genre

Film Genre

Hollywood and Beyond

Barry Langford

Edinburgh University Press

© Barry Langford, 2005

Edinburgh University Press Ltd
22 George Square, Edinburgh

Reprinted 2006, 2007, 2009, 2010 (three times), 2011

Typeset in Monotype Ehrhardt
by Koinonia, Manchester, and
printed and bound in Great Britain by
CPI Antony Rowe, Chippenham, Wilts

A CIP record for this book is available from the British Library

ISBN 0 7486 1902 x (hardback)
ISBN 0 7486 1903 8 (paperback)

Contents

Preface

The concept of *genre* – a French word meaning 'type' or 'kind' – is used throughout film culture: in film production, in the popular consumption and reception of films and in academic film studies. Yet the ways in which genre is understood are anything but consistent across those different constituencies. At a more fundamental level too, genre remains a perplexingly evasive and, philosophically speaking, idealistic entity. On the one hand, no individual genre film can ever embody the full range of attributes said to typify its genre; by the same token – as volumes of frustrated critical effort attest – no definition of a genre, however flexible, can account equally well for every genre film. For newcomers to the field, it must often seem that, as with Gertrude Stein's Oakland, 'when you get there, there's no "there" there.'

This book proposes that, such problems notwithstanding, genre remains an essential critical tool for understanding the ways that films are produced and consumed, as well as their broader relations to culture and society. However, the shifting valences, relations and definitions of the concept of genre pose obvious problems for students, who must additionally balance abstract and/or generalised categories – in 'defining' individual genres and in understanding the underlying principles of generic classification as such – on the one hand against their realisation (or repudiation) in any given film on the other. Rather like the baffled private eye Harry Moseby in the 'revisionist' genre film *Night Moves* (1975), anyone studying genre is prone to encountering an unexpected complexity in apparently common-sense categories where every new turn threatens further consternation. Harry Moseby ends up quite literally going around in circles. Students risk a similar fate.

The aim of this book is to make that dismal outcome less likely. Focusing mainly on the best-known and longest-lived Hollywood genres – those with roots in the classical studio era, even if like the action film they have taken on a different generic character and a hugely expanded industrial importance in the post-classical period – I have tried to show the ways in which film genre theory has informed the most influential accounts of major genres and vice versa. In some cases, students may find that their prior assumptions about what makes films generic, or how individual genres work, are challenged. As disorienting as this might sometimes be, it seems nonetheless an appropriate dimension of learning to understand what are after all complex entities with widely ramified connections to film, social – and critical – history. Such ramifications defeat Harry Moseby, who at the end of the film we leave adrift in a boat named *Point of View*. *Night Moves* leaves it deliberately ambiguous whether Harry himself lacks a point of view or is baffled by too many conflicting ones. The reader of this book will I hope be able to understand the reasons for the controversies and conflicting views of film genre and genre films, and through such understanding develop a critical perspective of their own.

Books, like films, are collaborative productions. Thanks are owed to many colleagues and undergraduate and postgraduate students, and to Royal Holloway, University of London, who have in a variety of formal and informal contexts helped formulate and refine the ideas about film genre explored in this book. I have also had the benefit of airing some of these ideas, notably on Westerns and on Holocaust film, in papers delivered at conferences in the UK and the United States: I am grateful to the conference organisers for those opportunities and, once again, to numerous colleagues for the responses and insights they have volunteered. Some material is based on essays previously published in *Film & History* and the *Journal of Holocaust Education*. My editor at Edinburgh University Press, Sarah Edwards, expertly coaxed the book through the initial proposal and then waited (and waited!) patiently for the eventual arrival of the manuscript. My family had to live with an increasingly reclusive and grouchy author as his deadline first approached, then passed. They did so with a good deal more grace than he did. In particular, without the support, tolerance and keen editorial eye of my wife Carole Tonkinson this book would not have been possible, and it is dedicated with love to her.

About this book

The overall approach of *Film Genre: Hollywood and Beyond* situates genres in their historical – primarily, cultural and (film) industrial – contexts; the overarching context of the book is the transition from the 'classical' Hollywood system to a 'post-classical' mode that extends to the present day. In making this separation, I neither explicitly challenge nor endorse arguments about the extent to which 'post-classical' Hollywood represents a qualitatively different set of visual stylistics in Hollywood film, or is essentially continuous in formal terms with the 'classical' Hollywood cinema (see Bordwell, Staiger and Thompson, 1985; Bordwell, 2002). It is clear enough, as numerous studies have now established, that the relatively standardised mass-production of film entertainment that typified the studio era until shortly after the war has been replaced by a far more dispersed and heterogeneous mechanism (this does not mean of course that the outcomes are equally heterogeneous), and thus the structure of contract artists – stars, writers, directors, set and costume designers, composers, etc. – studio backlots and standing sets, annual release 'slates' and vertically integrated corporate organisations that collectively comprised what André Bazin called 'the genius of the system' and which supported and encouraged genre production, has gone. Some genres, like the musical and the Western, seem for a variety of reasons to have been so much a part of that system that they could not easily survive its passing, while others, like *film noir* and the action blockbuster, are in different ways clearly outcomes of a different order of production than the Hollywood studio system and may usefully be considered in the context of a post-classical cinema. In any event, I have arranged the genres discussed in the book into three categories – classical, transitional and post-classical. Like other boundaries discussed in this book, these too are porous and certainly open to challenge: they are intended as heuristic tools rather than definitive statements.

Each chapter addresses both genre history and some of the principal critical approaches each genre has invited. History and criticism are at every stage interlinked: it is easy enough in genre study to lose the wood for the trees, and so I have not attempted either to cover every major critical approach to every genre (a task in any case undertaken magisterially by Steve Neale, 2000), nor have I aimed to provide in each case a comprehensive genre history, as this can easily end up simply offering lists of insufficiently differentiated film titles. Each chapter does, I hope, give a reasonably clear picture of a genre's historical development while also engaging with those critical perspectives that seem to have the most direct bearing either on the current state of critical understanding of a genre or its location within genre studies as a whole. In citing genre critics and theorists I have maintained a slight bias towards recent research to reflect the current state of play and new critical directions. Each chapter concludes with a brief 'case study' of a genre film or pair of films. These films have not been selected for either their 'classic' or their representative status, but simply as films that can be and have been firmly located within the genre in question, whose more detailed consideration seems to me in useful ways to complement or amplify the issues raised in the main section of the chapter. The account given of the film(s) is not intended to be comprehensive, nor could it be in the space available: the elements highlighted are those that bear most directly on genre history or genre theory.

Genre studies has historically been dominated by analysis of the major Hollywood genres, and this book is principally about Hollywood. However, the subtitle – *Hollywood and Beyond* – reflects firstly my own concern to indicate that Hollywood genres not only colonise the rest of the world, but are and have been open to it; secondly, the stream that in recent years has become a flood of critical studies of the popular cinemas of other nations and their genres; and third, that even American genres are not and have not been exclusively produced by Hollywood. The first concern means that, where relevant (for example, the horror film and *film noir*) influences on Hollywood from other national cinemas and cultures are considered in their proper place in the main body of each chapter. The second is inadequately – for reasons of both space and in many cases the limits of my own expertise – covered in a concluding section to each chapter (bar Chapter 5 on the war/combat film, which, to highlight the interaction of genre and nationhood, proceeds on a comparative international basis throughout) which briefly indicates some of the ways that major Hollywood genres have also figured importantly (sometimes under Hollywood's influence and sometimes wholly separately) in other national cinemas. Non-Hollywood American genres like documentary and pornography are discussed at somewhat greater length in the final chapter.

Note: Films are listed with their year of release on their first citation in any individual chapter: the country of origin is assumed to be the US unless otherwise indicated.

CHAPTER I

Who Needs Genres?

Thinking about why we might 'need' genres means thinking about the uses to which we commonly put genre concepts and the value we derive from doing so. Thus we can focus on genre's role as an active *producer* of cultural meanings and film-making practices alike. The provisional answer to the question 'who needs genres?' is 'Everyone – but in different ways, and not to the same degree'. For film-makers, organising production around genres and cycles holds out the promise of attracting and retaining audiences in a reliable way, so reducing commercial risk. For audiences, genre categories provide basic product differentiation while the generic 'contract' of familiarity leavened by novelty seems to offer some guarantee that the price of admission will purchase another shot of an experience already enjoyed (once or many times) before. For scholars, genre provides a historically grounded method of establishing 'family resemblances' between films produced and released under widely differing circumstances, and of mediating the relationship between the mythologies of popular culture and social, political and economic contexts.

Unlike many topics within academic film studies, the basic concept of genre is readily grasped and widely used in the larger contemporary film culture, as a visit to any video rental store readily illustrates. In my own local outlet in South West London, for example, videos and DVDs are arranged into the following categories: latest releases, action, thrillers, drama, science fiction, horror, comedy, family, classics, cult and world cinema. Such a listing illustrates both the practical utility of genre and some of the problems that genre theory and criticism have always faced. Certainly – perhaps unsurprisingly – for film consumers in this high-street context at least it is genre, rather than other means of grouping films adopted by film scholars, that offers the readiest means of charting a path through the variety of available films to those they are most likely to want to see. Although film history, for example, plays some role in these classifications, the overarching principle is not a historical one. Nor does the notion of the 'auteur' play a terribly visible role: although the identification of (usually) the film director as principal creative agent has become an interpretative norm for broadsheet and specialist magazine film criticism, directors in general feature only marginally in the promotion or classification of videos. This of course tells us nothing about the percentage of customers who enter the store to find a particular film, or a film by a particular director, and are thus uninterested in or uninfluenced by the genre categories: indeed, as we shall see, genre theory generally has found it rather difficult to establish with any certainty how far the film industry's categories map onto, let alone determine, audiences' actual experience of movie-going.

Stars, another major focus of academic film studies, play a much more visible part in the promotion of individual films – 'above the line' talent usually features prominently on video or DVD covers and is clearly a major factor in attracting audiences. Yet stars as such do not comprise generic categories. Film students, indeed, may be surprised to see that star personae – a major force in film production and consumption since the 1910s, when public demand forced reluctant producers to identify their hitherto anony-mous performers (and pay these new 'stars' accordingly inflated salaries) – are also suppressed as a criterion for classification. Industrial change has clearly played a part here: no longer salaried contract players assigned to several different film roles annually within the studio's overall release 'slate', today's film stars are free agents, leading industry players in their own right, and usually have their own production companies to originate film projects and bring them to studios for financing and distribution deals. Actors today are accordingly much freer to diversify and extend both their acting range and their star image; they need not be pigeonholed in just one style or genre of film.

In the classical period the interplay of star, studio and genre was complex and not necessarily unidirectional: Sklar (1992: 74–106) argues that rather than hiring performers to meet pre-established generic needs (let alone compelling actors against their will into restrictive genre roles), having Humphrey Bogart and James Cagney, both actors with 'tough' urban screen personae, as contract players encouraged Warner Bros. to make a speciality of the crime thriller during the 1930s and 1940s. Even the Western *The Oklahoma Kid* (1939) wholly conforms to the template established in other contemporary Cagney and Bogart gangster films like *Angels With Dirty Faces* (1938) and *The Roaring Twenties* (1939). As usual, Cagney (much the bigger star at this point) plays the hero – here in the 'pro-social' gangbusting mould into which his early 1930s gangster persona had subsequently been recast (see Chapter 6) – and Bogart the underworld boss 'heavy' in a narrative that simply transposes the racketeering/syndicate gangland template of *G–Men* (1935) to the 'wide-open town' Western. In general – and with different approaches from one studio to another – the bigger the star the greater his or her opportunity for diversification: thus Cagney in the 1930s played not only gangster parts but musicals (*Footlight Parade*, 1934), aviation films (*Ceiling Zero*, 1937) and even Shakespeare (*A Midsummer Night's Dream*, 1935). Moreover, star personae could transform over time, as with Bogart's own transition from second-lead heavies in the 1930s to the ideal romantic leading man for the war-torn 1940s. But the studio system generally made casting a much more reliable guide to the nature of a film than today: whereas fans of Errol Flynn in *The Adventures of Robin Hood* (1938) could be reasonably confident that *The Sea Hawk* (1941) would offer similar pleasures – and that this would be true even if the generic mode shifted from swashbuckling action-adventure to Western (*They Died With Their Boots On*, 1941) or war film (*Desperate Journey*, 1942) – admirers of Tom Cruise in *Top Gun* (1986) or *Mission Impossible* (1996) may be surprised, disappointed or even outraged by his performance in *Magnolia* (1999). The movement of a contemporary star like Julianne Moore between large-budget popcorn spectaculars like *Jurassic Park II: The Lost World* (1997) and stylised independent films like *Far From Heaven* (2002) offers audiences little clear generic purchase.

Artwork on film posters and DVD jackets typically relies at least as much on sending out generic signals – typically by means of *iconographic* conventions (see below) – as on star personae, which are indeed often modified or generically 'placed' by such imagery. Arnold Schwarzenegger grins goofily in linen lederhosen on the front of *Twins* (1988); on *Kindergarten Cop* (1990) he gurns in exaggerated alarm as he is assaulted by a swarm of pre-schoolers. Both films are comedies and both images knowingly play off the unsmiling, tooled-up Arnie featured on the publicity for the techno-thrillers *The Terminator* (1984) or *Eraser* (1996).

Yet as central an aspect of film consumption and reception as genre may be, another look at the video store's generic taxonomy quickly reveals what from the perspective of most academic genre criticism and theory look like evident anomalies. For example, while some of these genres – action, thriller, horror, science fiction, comedy – match up fairly well with standard genre headings, the video store omits several categories widely regarded as of central importance in the history of genre production, such as Westerns, gangster films and musicals (examples of all of these are dispersed across drama, action, thriller and 'classics') – let alone more controversial yet (in academic discussion) ubiquitous classifications as *film noir* or melodrama. Other categories are uncanonical by any standard: 'latest releases' is self-evidently a time-dated cross-generic category; 'classics' is generically problematic in a different way, since it apparently combines both an evaluative term ('all-time classic', 'landmark', etc.) with a temporal one (the small and seemingly random selection of pre-1975 films available for rental are automatically classified as 'classics', regardless of critical standing). The 'family' category combines G-rated films from a number of conventionally separate genres (animated films, comedies, Disney live-action adventures and other children's films). 'World cinema' is used, not as it is in academic film studies (somewhat reluctantly, given its implicit Euro- or Anglo-centrism) to designate film-making outside of North America and Western Europe, but rather includes any subtitled film, most independently produced US films and British films – for example, the films of Ken Loach – that fall outside recognised and familiar generic categories like the gangster film, romantic comedy, etc. Nor are these categories stable in themselves: all new titles eventually mutate from 'latest release' into one of the other backlist categories; those (English-language) films that last the course may in due course be elevated to 'classics'.

Anomalies of course beset classificatory programmes of any kind. In a celebrated example (much quoted by critical theorists, most famously Michel Foucault, 1970: xv), the Argentinian fabulist Jorge Luis Borges quotes a 'certain Chinese encyclopedia' in which animals are divided into '(a) belonging to the Emperor, (b) embalmed, (c) tame, (d) suckling pigs, (e) sirens, (f) fabulous, (g) stray dogs, (h) included in the present classification ...' and so on, concluding in '(n) that from a long way off look like flies'. The 'wonderment' of this taxonomy, as Foucault puts it, consists less in its sheer heterogeneity per se – since it is precisely the function of conventional lists to enumerate similarities and discriminate differences – than in the epistemological and ontological incompatibility of the categories: 'the common ground on which such meetings are possible has itself been destroyed' (Foucault, 1970: xvi). While film genre criticism would seem to avoid such difficulties, many studies of genre – including the present one – combine within their pages genres with rather different standings: those that have a long and verifiable (for example, through film-makers' correspondence or trade paper reviews) history of usage as production categories within the film industry itself, such as Westerns, musicals or war films; those where industry usage differs markedly from critical usage, notably melodrama (see Chapter 2); and those that are largely a product of critical intervention, pre-eminently *film noir*. The history of early cinema meanwhile reveals that film distributors in moving pictures' first decade tended to classify films under such heterodox (by today's standards) headings as length (in feet of film) and duration rather than the content-based generic categories that emerged by 1910. Even the most uncontroversial categories remain heterogeneous: war films and Westerns are identified by subject matter, the gangster film by its protagonist(s), thrillers and horror films by their effects upon the viewer, *film noir* by either its 'look' or its 'dark' mood. Studio-era producers, in addition to the familiar genre categories (usually referred to in the industry as 'types'), used the *economic* category of the 'prestige picture' to denote their most expensive, high-profile and (hopefully) profitable pictures – which could of course also belong to one or more of the standard types, but whose audience appeal would be expected to break out beyond that type's core market.

Our sojourn in the video store illustrates above all that genre is a *process* rather than a fact, and one in which different perspectives, needs and interests can and do deliver widely varying outcomes. Genres are not born, they are made. The store manager explained to me that the 'classic' category combines individual preference with institutional supervision: that is, while store managers have wide personal discretion in assigning 'classic' status to individual films, corporate policy mandates that if one film in a series is categorised as a 'classic', other series entries must automatically be filed alongside. Thus since *Die Hard* (1988) is (so I was informed) 'an obvious classic', *Die Hard: With a Vengeance* (1995) also has 'classic' status thrust upon it. This bears out James Naremore's (1995–96: 14) observation that 'individual genre has less to do with a group of artefacts than with a discourse – a loose evolving system of arguments and readings, helping to shape the commercial strategies and aesthetic ideologies.' (One might note that the leeway this system affords individual managers brings into play the social categories through which contemporary cultural studies engages popular media texts – race, gender, ethnicity, sexuality, even age. The video-rental business is, as Kevin Smith's microbudget indie film *Clerks* (1994), testifies, dominated by young white males: the 'classics' section abounds in stereo-typically 'male' genres like Westerns, action films and science fiction, with a striking deficit of musicals or family melodramas.)

How might any of this be relevant to genre studies? In relation to the last example, genre critics and theorists have in recent years laid increasing importance on institutional discourses and practices, broadly conceived – what Steve Neale (1993, citing Gregory Lukow and Steve Ricci, 1984) designates the industry's 'inter-textual relay', comprising both trade journalism (*Variety*, *Film Daily* and so on) and newspapers as well as the language of film promotion and publicity – as a means of locating in a determinate if always changing historical context the understandings of generic categories upon which genre criticism in turn bases itself. For such categories, however apparently deceptively solid 'in theory', often prove surprisingly elusive in both industrial, and hence critical, practice. These 'historicist' approaches to genre studies have in some cases – notably the Western and melodrama – significantly extended the historical horizons and cultural contexts for under-standing genres and productively problematised conventional critical accounts. Today's genre-constituting 'relay' includes such venues of film consumption as the corner video store, which occupies an important place in the global and vertically integrated 'film industry' – not in fact the singular and unified entity that term suggests, but a complex network of cross-media enterprises mostly clustered into a few very large transnational corporate enterprises, for whom a film's performance in ancillary (but no longer secondary) markets like home video provides a growing share of its profitable return on investment.

As Christine Gledhill (2000: 225f.) points out, the empirical history of industry relays neither defines nor exhausts the terms on which audiences engage with genre texts. Moreover, film genre studies today itself constitutes its own 'relay': the terms and categories that have developed through decades of analysis and theory about individual genres and genre in general have established meaningful contexts in which genres and genre films are understood today. This process of generic legitimation is the principal reason this book generally cleaves to 'canonical' genre categories like the Western, the combat film, etc. What on the other hand I have tried to avoid is any sense that such categories are more than provisional or that generic identities can be fixed, however critically convenient such fixity would undoubtedly be. If anything, genres may intermittently stabilise in the sense of becoming for strictly delimited periods carriers of particular meanings or vehicles through which specific issues may be negotiated (for example, 'whiteness' in early Westerns (see Abel, 1998), or 'technoscience' in the contemporary science fiction film (see Wood, 2002)).

THE SYSTEM OF GENRES

Genre, as a police detective in a (British) crime film might say, has form. Aristotle opens his *Poetics*, the foundational work of western literary criticism, by identifying it as a work of genre criticism: 'Our subject being Poetry, I propose to speak not only of the art in general but also of its species and their respective capacities' (1911: 3). By 1601–2, when Shakespeare's *Hamlet* was first performed, genre categories – and their abuse – were clearly 'hot' issues. In *Hamlet*, Act II, Scene ii, the busybody courtier Polonius excitedly announces the arrival of a troupe of travelling players. Praising – today we would say hyping – their abilities, he declares them 'the best actors in the world, either for tragedy, comedy, history, pastoral, pastoral-comical, historical-pastoral, tragical-historical, tragical-comical-historical-pastoral, scene indivisible, or poem unlimited' (l. 392ff.).

Shakespeare here is clearly making fun of Polonius' ludicrous attempt to pigeonhole, ratify and standardise the aesthetic realm to within an inch of its life; however, he may also be targeting for satire the abuse of *valid* categories that will ultimately lead to the breakdown of the utility of categorisation itself. Genre, in other words, is a tool that must be used wisely but not too well: defining the individual artefact in generic terms can be helpful but shouldn't be pursued at all costs. Not every aspect of the genre text is necessarily or purely attributable to its generic identity, hence there is no need to invent absurd refinements of generic denomination, or to make the mesh of the classificatory or definitional net so fine as to allow no light through. At the same time, if the concept is to have any critical utility at all, it needs to be able to make meaningful discriminations: 'scene indivisible' or 'poem unlimited' seem unhelpfully broad as workable categories for genre criticism. Polonius seems unconsciously to exemplify Jacques Derrida's (1992) dictum that texts – all texts, any text – neither 'belong to genres' (because texts can always exceed specific expectations and labels), yet nor can they escape being generic (because all texts are encountered in contexts that involve some, often major, measure of expectation on the part of readers in regard to style, identity, content, use, meaning: a text is necessarily 'placed' as a very condition of its being able to be read at all).

However, even if 'there is always a genre or genres' (Derrida, 1992: 230), this merely establishes that the task of film genre studies must be to establish the particular *kinds* of genres that are characteristic of commercial narrative cinema, the varieties of assumptions and expectations that play around and through them, the uses to which they are or have been put, and finally the identities, roles and interests of the different stakeholders (film-makers, film distributors and exhibitors, audiences, critics and theorists) in this process. One approach might be to emphasise those relatively concrete and verifiable aspects of the film-industrial process that historically subtend genre production, above all though by no means exclusively in Hollywood cinema, to demarcate a field of study. At the same time, one might want to look at the ways in which individual films seem either to conform to or to confront and challenge the (assumed) expectations of the spectator.

Douglas Pye ([1975] 1995: 187f.) has described genre as a context in which meaning is created through a play of difference and/in repetition, one 'narrow enough for recognition of the genre to take place but wide enough to allow enormous individual variation'. This combination of sameness and variety is the linchpin of the generic contract. While it may reasonably be assumed that audiences do not wish to see literally the same film remade time and again, considerable pleasure is to be derived from generic narratives through the *tension* between novel elements and their eventual reincorporation into the expected generic model. The confirmation of generic expectations generates what Richard Maltby (1995a: 112) describes as a 'sense of pleasurable mastery and control'. In an analysis of genre films in the 1970s, a period when many traditional genres underwent considerable revision and revamping, Todd Berliner (2001) has argued that even 'revisionist' genre films 'bend' rather than 'break' – that is, manipulate and modify, but do not wholly dispense with – generic conventions as they seek to engage their audiences in a more conscious scrutiny of genre conventions and the values they embody.

For most film genre theorists, the concept of 'genre' has implied a great deal more than simple conventionality. On the contrary, genre was historic- ally an important means for writers interested in popular, and above all Hollywood, cinema – as distinct from, for example, European art cinema (though see Tudor, [1973] 1976; Neale, 1991) – to establish the value and interest of their chosen field of critical enquiry. This was an important move because some mid-twentieth-century critiques of popular/'mass'[1] culture tended to blur the lines between genre, formula, stereotype and simple cliché as part of a critical project to deprecate popular culture generally on grounds of unoriginality and derivativeness. Those popular cultural forms to which genre is most evidently indispensable were on that very account discounted: for early twentieth century modernists, for example, this included such Victorian relics as the bourgeois novel and theatrical melodramas – both of which exerted a strong shaping influence on early cinema and so to speak helped damn it by association.

Such deprecations of the popular/mass may partly be attributed to the cultural privilege attached to 'originality' by post-Romantic literary theory. Whereas earlier ages had judged works of literature according to their up- holding or replication of, and consistency with, pre-existing standards of artistic excellence and 'decorum', from the late eighteenth century onwards aesthetic theory laid increasing stress on the irreducible particularity of the artwork – that is, the ways in which it stretched or transgressed the 'laws' of good taste, craftsmanship, and so forth (see Kress and Threadgold, 1988). In the age of industrialisation, a growing divide grew up between the 'merely' workmanlike or 'well-crafted' artefact – with the implication that such works were the products of apprenticeship and the acquisition of essentially mechanical skills – and the 'true' work of art; the latter was increasingly seen as the product of inspiration not perspiration, of genius not hard graft. Art, in short, was henceforth to stand *outside* rules and conventions: that is what made it art. Writing in the 1930s, Walter Benjamin ([1936] 1970) noted that the work of art had come to acquire an 'aura' born in part of its uniqueness and indivisibility, an 'aura' that facilitated art's institutionalisation as secular cult.

A definition of art that places such heavy emphasis on originality and self- expression will inevitably tend to devalue works that appear to be produced through collective rather than individual endeavour, and along quasi-industrial lines: this will be all the more true when the resulting artefacts themselves seem to manifest qualities of repetition and stereotypicality, or when they seem to have been designed with an existing template in mind. Questions of authorship are implicitly invoked by such critiques of genre – for in the new aesthetic orthodoxy that emerged out of Romanticism, the individual author had become the best guarantee of a work's integrity and uniqueness. So it is wholly logical that it was through the category of authorship that the first serious critical attempt to recover Hollywood genre texts like Westerns and musicals for the category of 'art' was undertaken, in the French auteur criticism of the 1950s. Auteurism seeks to (and claims to be able to) identify submerged patterns of continuity – thematic preoccupations, characteristic patterns of narrative and characterisation, recognisable practices of *mise-en-scène* and the like – running through films with (usually) the same director. Establishing such individuating traits makes a claim for that director's creative 'ownership' of the films he has directed: the director earns a status as a creative originator – an *auteur* – along the traditional lines of the lone novelist or painter. Thus, for example, John Ford's films can be seen to work through a repeated pattern of thematic opposition between wilderness and civilisation ('the desert and the garden'): this is Ford's auteurist 'signature' (see Caughie, 1981).

Although the limitations of auteurism are often correctly identified as an important factor motivating the development of genre studies, without auteurism it is doubtful genre would have made it onto the critical agenda at all. Auteurism proved particularly effective in establishing the serious critical reputation of directors who had rarely if ever hitherto been conceived of as artists because their entire careers had been spent filming Westerns, gangster pictures, musicals and the like – quintessentially disposable US junk culture. The American auteurist critic Andrew Sarris proposed a model of 'creative tension' between the creative drive of the film director and the constraints of the commercial medium in which he worked. Thus, for Sarris, whether a director *could* stamp his own artistic personality and concerns on essentially stereotypical material was in a sense the qualifying test for being awarded auteur status.

Auteurism at least drew genre texts within the scope of serious critical attention. However, within auteur criticism genre itself remained very much the poor relation – since the unspoken assumption in Sarris's schema that auteurs were more deserving of critical consideration than non-auteurs (or as François Truffaut notoriously classified them, mere '*metteurs-en-scène*') relied in turn on the claim that what distinguished an auteur was precisely his transformation of formulaic generic material into something personal. Genre is thus in some measure the culture – like a petri dish – on which genius feeds, rather than meaningful material in its own right. Directors and films that strain against or break the limits of their given genre are thus evaluated as 'superior' to texts that remain unashamedly and unproblematically, even banally, generic. In this way auteurism recapitulated the birfurcation, familiar as we have seen since the early 1800s, of (true) 'artist' and (mere) journey-man. It was the transcendence, not the comfortable inhabitation, of genre that marked the auteur (as *nouvelle vague* film-makers, the original French auteurist critics mostly used genre as a framework for transgressive indivi-dualising gestures).

Obviously, such an approach will discourage sustained attention to the particularity of genres themselves, other than as tedious normative values for the inspired artist to transgress or transcend. The desire to find a means of talking about the things that typified conventional commercial narrative film as well as those that challenged or subverted it, was a governing factor in the emergence of genre studies in the late 1960s and early 1970s. Early genre critics stressed auteurism's inability to explain such important questions as why genres flourish or decline in particular cycles; how spectators relate to generic texts; how genre artefacts shape the world into more or less mean-ingful narrative, moral or ideological patterns – in other words film genre's history, its aesthetic evolution, its social contexts.

The problems facing early film genre theorists were not especially recondite, and indeed have not changed fundamentally in the thirty-five years since Edward Buscombe first tabled them:

> [T]here appear to be three questions one could profitably ask: first, do genres in the cinema really exist, and if so, can they be defined? second, what are the functions they fulfill? and third, how do specific genres originate or what causes them? (Buscombe, [1970] 1995: 11)

Most accounts concur that generic labelling historically preceded organised genre production in early cinema, with distributors prior to 1910 classifying films in a variety of ways including length as well as topic for the benefit of exhibitors. During and after the First World War, with film production in all national cinemas increasingly concentrated in a small number of studios and feature-length narratives becoming the norm, more closely defined and con-ventionalised generic categories started to appear. Altman (1998: 16–23) suggests that the crystallisation of a genre may be traceable in its evolving nomenclature, as the defining term moves from adjectival and modifying (as in 'Western melodrama') to substantival ('*the* Western'). This shift also seems to mark a shift of emphasis in terms of production, as genre concepts move from the descriptive to the prescriptive: a 'Western melodrama' is simply a melodrama (a term generally used by exhibitors before the First World War to describe non-comic dramatic narratives of any type) set in the American West; a 'Western' is a film set specifically in the *historical* West that also involves certain strongly conventionalised types of characters, plots and, rather more debatably, thematic motifs or ideological positions.

Since such a degree of conventionalisation obviously happens over a large number of films, the concept of film genre in turn implies a system for something like the mass production of films. The studio systems that developed in Europe as well as the USA during the 1920s all relied on genre production in some measure, but it was in the American film industry, the world's largest, that genre became most fundamentally important. Most theories of film genre are based primarily on analysis of the Hollywood studio system. Contemporary theories acknowledge Tom Ryall's (1975) argument that genre criticism needs to triangulate the author–text dyad in which auteurism conceived meaning by recognising the equal importance of the role of the audience as the constituency to which the genre film addresses itself. The resulting model recognises genre as an interactional process between producers – who develop generic templates to capitalise on the previously established popularity of particular kinds of film, always with a view to product rationalisation and efficiency – and generically literate audiences who anticipate specific kinds of gratification arising from the genre text's fulfilment of their generic expectations. Thus, as Altman summarises:

> A cinema based on genre films depends not only on the regular production of recognizably similar films, and on the maintenance of a standardized distribution/exhibition system, but also on the constitution and maintenance of a stable, generically trained audience, sufficiently knowledgeable about genre systems to recognize generic cues, sufficiently familiar with genre plots to exhibit generic expectations, and sufficiently committed to generic values to tolerate and even enjoy in genre films capricious, violent, or licentious behaviour which they might disapprove of in 'real life'. (Altman, 1996: 279)

The importance of the audience is worth emphasising here since, as we shall see, in most genre theory and criticism the audience has remained a somewhat elusive presence, notionally an indispensable interlocutor in the generic process but in practice, in the general absence of clear evidence about its historical composition, remaining largely a projected and undifferentiated function of the text (or rather, of the meanings ascribed to the text), its responses 'read' at best largely in terms of the spectator 'implied' by the genre text.[2] The difficulty of verifying the responses conjectured for historical genre audiences helps explain why the unfolding history of film genres and critical readings of genre films have dominated critical discussion.

Broadly speaking, genre criticism has evolved through three stages, each of which roughly corresponds to one of Buscombe's three questions. A first phase focused on classification – the definition and delimitation of individual genres. A second stage, overlapping with the first, focused on the *meanings* of individual genres and the social function of genre in general, within broadly consensual generic definitions and canons – principally, through analyses that understood genre in terms of either ritual or ideology (as we shall see, there is some overlap between the terms). Alongside influential works of genre theory, mostly in essay form, several book-length studies of individual genres, each informed by a distinctive understanding of genre but tending to follow either the ritual or the ideological approach, were produced in this period, including Basinger's (1986) study of the war/combat film, Sobchack's (1980, 1987) study of science fiction, analyses of the Western by Wright (1975) and Slotkin (1992), Doane's (1987) study of the 1940s 'woman's film', Altman's (1987) book on musicals and Krutnik's (1991) study of *film noir*. Finally (to date), more recent scholarship, as part of a generally renewed interest across film studies in understanding film historically and reacting in particular to what has been seen as the second phase's at times essentialist and decontextualised accounts of genre identities, has focused on the *historical contexts* of genre production – the forms inherited from other media like the novel and the popular theatre, and the institutional practices (studio policy, marketing and publicity, modes of consumption, and so on) through which genres become available, in all senses of the term, to audiences.

The very earliest studies of film genres, of which probably the best-known are essays by André Bazin ([1956] 1971] on the Western, and by Robert Warshow ([1943], 1975a, [1954] 1975b) on the Western and the gangster film,[3] were only indirectly concerned to define their novel objects of study: that is, in the very act of arguing for the serious critical consideration of popular film genres they were necessarily performing some basic definitional work. Like many later writers, Bazin set the Western within existing narrative traditions, drawing parallels with traditional 'high' literary forms such as the courtly romance; he indicates core thematic material, proposing the relationship between individual morality and the greater communal good, or the rule of law and natural justice, as the issue which charges the genre; and he makes the first attempt at establishing a genre 'canon', identifying the period 1937–40 as the Western's moment of 'classic perfection' – with John Ford's *Stagecoach* (1939) as the 'ideal' Western – and contrasting this with the postwar period when large-budget 'superwesterns' strayed from the true generic path by importing topical political, social or psychological concerns that Bazin sees as extraneous to the genre's core concerns (although the 'B' Westerns of the 1950s in his opinion maintained the form's original vigour and integrity). Both Bazin and – especially – Warshow based their arguments on a rather small sample of genre films (just three in the case of Warshow's gangster essay), and treated genre history, by today's academic standards, rather casually (Bazin identifies as examples of 1950s 'B' Westerns such major studio releases as *The Gunfighter* (1950), and simply ignores the thirty-five years of Western genre production before *Stagecoach* (for more on problems of sampling and genre history in relation to the Western, see Chapter 3).

Most fundamentally, while Bazin and Warshow both insisted on the integrity and distinctiveness of generic character, their project did not extend to considering the means whereby individual Westerns or gangster films can be identified as such in order to then be periodised, classified or evaluated. Setting the terms for such recognition then became the project of the first wave of genre theorists proper starting in the late 1960s.

PROBLEMS OF DEFINITION

Fairly early in the development of film genre theory, Andrew Tudor succinctly nailed an inescapable and basic crux in trying to define individual genres. Noting that most studies of this kind start out with a 'provisional' notion of the field they are working on that they then set out to define more clearly, he suggests there is a basic problem of circularity:

> To take a genre such as the 'western', analyse it, and list its principal characteristics, is to beg the question that we must first isolate the body of films which are 'westerns'. But they can only be isolated on the basis of the 'principal characteristics' which can only be discovered from the films themselves after they have been isolated. (Tudor, [1973] 1976: 135)

Only very recently has the focus on industrial discourses and 'relays' suggested a means of squaring this circle. Much previous work on genre definitions either ignores the problem or proposes itself as an empirical approach that nonetheless clearly begs the questions Tudor asks.

In his 1970 essay quoted above, Edward Buscombe proposed to identify genres through their *iconography* (a term derived from art theory) – their characteristic 'visual conventions', such as settings, costume, the typical physical attributes of characters and the kinds of technologies available to the characters (six-shooters in the Western, for example, or tommy-guns and whitewalled motorcars with running boards in the gangster film). These iconographic conventions were to be seen not only as the formal markers of a given genre, but as important vehicles for explicating its core thematic material: in a celebrated passage, Buscombe ([1970] 1995: 22–4) analyses the opening of Sam Peckinpah's *Ride the High Country* (UK: *Guns in the Afternoon*) and notes how the juxtaposition of conventional and non-conventional (a policeman in uniform, a motor car, a camel) Western elements, with the non-conventional ones variously signifying progress or at least change, by disturbing the genre's standard iconographic balance communicates the film's 'essential theme', the passing of the Old West. Iconography was also central to Colin McArthur's (1972) *Underworld USA*, a book-length study of the gangster film. Iconographic analysis is as subject to Tudor's circularity charge as any other, but its taxonomic value is apparent: an empirically derived set of generic attributes helps both to establish the dominant visual motifs and by extension the underlying structures of a genre, and to determine membership of that genre. A particular strength, as Buscombe pointed out, is that iconographies are grounded in the visuality of the film medium: they are literally what we see on-screen. Moreover, as the conventional meanings that audiences understood to inhere in iconographic devices (for example, the Westerner's horse) derived not from the genre alone, but from the interplay between common-sense understandings of their valences and their specific generic usage (as Buscombe notes in his analysis of *Ride the High Country*, in Westerns the horse is 'not just an animal but a symbol of dignity, grace and power'), iconography potentially established a porous frontier where the generic/textual and the social interacted with one another – hence a basis for discussing a genre's larger socio-cultural currency. Finally, inasmuch as iconographic analysis took its force from those elements that were repeatedly or consistently present in genre entries, it centred on those very qualities – conventionality and repetition – by which genre as a whole is typified.

One limitation of iconographic analysis was its limited applicability. Buscombe and McArthur focused on the Western and the gangster film, well-established and familiar genres that both lend themselves particularly well to iconographic interpretation. However, as several writers who have tried and failed to discover such well-defined and defining visual conventions in other major genres (comedy, biopics, social problem films, etc.) have noted, the very consistency of their iconographic conventions makes these genres atypical of film genre generally; the Western is particularly unusual in having such a tightly defined physical and historical setting (see Chapter 3). Also, iconography's interest in film as a visual art form, a considerable virtue, stalled in the pro-filmic (the space framed by the camera) and failed to engage with visual style (camera movement, editing, etc.). Nor did it seem to offer a means of identifying and discussing narrative structures, although narrative models – such as the musical's basic 'boy meets girl, boy dances with girl, boy gets girl' template – probably form as or more important a part of the audience's expectational matrix than abstracted iconographies.

An issue to which the discussion of iconography interestingly relates is that of generic verisimilitude, since one function of visual conventions is to establish a representational norm, deviation from which constitutes generic discrepancy (which can of course also be generic innovation). These norms are in turn bound up with our sense of what is likely or acceptable in the given generic context, which may or may not relate to our understanding of

From *Son of Frankenstein* (1939). Reproduced courtesy Universal/The Kobal Collection.

what is possible or plausible in our lived reality. Regimes of verisimilitude are generically specific, and each bears its own relation to reality as such. Many genres include 'unmarked' verisimilitudes – like the laws of the physical universe – whose observance can simply be taken for granted and establishes the continuity of the generic world with that of the spectator. On the other hand, the suspension of those laws (teleportation, travelling faster than light or through time) may form a basic and recognised element of the verisimilitude of an outer-space science fiction film. As discussed in Chapter 4, the classic Hollywood musical has its own quite distinct, specific and readily recognisable verisimilitude. Altman's summary of the genre audience quoted above suggests that the audience's willingness to 'license' certain departures from what would normally be considered desirable and/or believable behaviour constitutes an important part of the generic contract. (For fuller discussions of genre and verisimilitude, see Neale, 2000: 31–9; King, 2002: 121f.)

Considerations of verisimilitude extend iconography's implicit socialisation of genre convention further into the domain of the everyday and this has important implications for discussions of generic meanings (see below). Clearly, too, while iconographic conventions are entailed in verisimilitudes, so are the narrative dimensions iconography leaves out. Yet lifelikeness, even conventionalised lifelikeness, is not the principal agent of generic form. The model for genre analysis proposed by Rick Altman ([1984] 1995, 1987) seems usefully to combine many of the strengths of each approach. Altman argues that genres are characterised, or organised, along two axes which he nominates, employing linguistic terminology, the semantic and the syntactic. If the semantic axis involves the 'words' spoken in a genre, the syntactic concerns the organisation of those 'words' into 'sentences' – into meaningful and intelligible shape. Every film in a particular genre shares a set of semantic elements, or components: these certainly include traditional iconographic aspects like setting, costume and the like, but range more widely, taking in characteristic narrative incidents, visual style and even (as hard as this might be to quantify) typical attitudes. A contemporary action blockbuster like *Face/Off* (1997), then, might number among its semantic components portable armaments ranging from automatic pistols to light artillery, car (or boat or plane) chases, large set-piece action sequences usually involving explosions and/or the destruction of buildings and expensive consumer durables (the aforementioned cars, boats, planes), and a distinct disregard for the value of human life. Genre films' syntactic dimension involves their characteristic arrangement of these semantic elements in plots, thematic motifs, symbolic relationships, and so on. (*Face/Off* shares a recurrent motif of 1990s action films: the hero's defence or reconstruction of the family through, paradoxically enough, ever-greater violence to and destruction of people and objects – see Chapter 10.) Altman (1996: 283–4) adds that whereas semantic elements usually derive their meanings from pre-existing social codes, generic syntax is more specific and idiosyncratic and thus more fully expresses the meaning(s) of a given genre.

The major problem of Altman's interpretative matrix, as Altman himself acknowledges, is knowing where to draw the line between the semantic and syntactic. For example, if as suggested above spectacular action sequences are a semantic 'given' in the action film, it would be highly surprising if at least one of these did not occur at the climax of the film and resolve the central narrative conflict – in other words, enter into the syntactic field.

Questions of definition eventually became somewhat discredited as insufficiently critical and inertly taxonomic, and genre studies started to focus increasingly on the functions of genre. Recently, however, genre definition(s) have been put back into critical play. Collins (1993) and others have argued that postmodern tendencies to generic mixing or hybridity call into question the traditional fixity of genre boundaries.[4] Perhaps partly in response to this, a historicist trend has emerged – Gledhill (2000) compares it to the influential 'new historicism' in literary studies in the late 1980s – that has used the empirical analysis of how genre terms were and are used within the film industry itself (by producers and exhibitors) to reassess traditional understandings of and claims about the historical basis of genres. This has indeed challenged some fundamental assumptions about genre stability and boundaries, and suggests that much of the postmodern preoccupation with generic hybridity relies on a historically unsupported notion of classical genres as far more rigid and secure and much less porous and prone to generic mixing than was actually the case. One does not have to delve very deep into genre history to find examples of generic mixing: for example, a quick scan reveals Western musicals (*Calamity Jane*, 1953; *Paint Your Wagon*, 1969), Western melodramas (*Duel in the Sun*, 1946; *Johnny Guitar*, 1950), *noir* Westerns (*Pursued*, 1948; *The Furies*, 1950; *Rancho Notorious*, 1952), horror-Westerns (*Billy the Kid vs. Dracula*, 1965; *Grim Prairie Tales*, 1990), even science fiction Westerns (Gene Autry in *The Phantom Empire*, 1935).

Neale (2000: 43) argues that the industry's 'inter-textual relay' (see above) must constitute the primary evidential basis both for the existence of genres and for the boundaries of any particular generic corpus:

> ... it is only on the basis of this testimony that the history of any one genre and an analysis of its social functions can begin to be produced. For a genre's history is as much the history of a term as it is of the films to which the term has been applied; is as much a history of the consequently shifting boundaries of a corpus of texts as it is of the texts themselves. (Neale, 2000: 43)

PROBLEMS OF MEANING

As we have seen, early genre studies, in aiming to introduce and identify the core groupings of films in key genres, also made observations about the function of genres; indeed, these played an important part in their argument for the value of genre texts. However, they typically stopped short of theories of genre as a whole. Subsequent critics advanced various theories of the kinds of meanings that could be derived from the genre text. Despite diverse approaches, they commonly centred on an understanding of genre as a form of social practice – as ritual, myth or ideology. All were motivated by the conviction that film genre offered a privileged insight into 'how to understand the life of films in the social' (Gledhill, 2000: 221). And all proceeded from a shared basic assumption about how that insight was generated. Genre films by definition are collective rather than singular objects: their meanings are comprised relationally rather than in isolation. Whereas to attempt to 'read off' social or political debates in the broader culture onto individual films is thus likely to prove reductive and speculative, the sheer number of films in a given genre means that changes in generic direction and attitudes across time may reasonably be understood as responses and/or contributions to the shifting concerns of their mass public. Genre films solicit audience approval through both continuity and variation; audience responses encourage genre film-makers to pursue existing generic directions or to change them.

The closely linked concepts of 'myth' and 'ritual' aim to relate this transaction to the underlying desires, preoccupations and fantasies of audiences and to ascribe these in turn to the social and cultural contexts in and through which film genres and their audiences are equally constituted. In the standard anthropological sense, 'myth' denotes something like an expression of archetypes on the part of a particular community (grounded in that community's social experience of the natural world and/or its collective human psychology). Sometimes 'myth' is invoked in genre criticism in precisely this sense: in his study of the Western, Wright (1975: 187) states that 'the Western, though located in a modern industrial society, is as much a myth as the tribal myths of the anthropologists.' More often, as applied to popular media forms, myth in its most neutral formulation designates forms of (culturally specific) social self-representation, the distillation and enactment of core beliefs and values in reduced, usually personalised and narrative, forms. Myth is also characterised by specific kinds of formal stylisation, for example extreme narrative and characterological conventionalisation. The strongest influence on mythic readings of popular culture is the structuralist anthropology of Claude Lévi-Strauss, which argues that the role of myth is to embody in schematic narrative form the constitutive contradictions of a society – typically in the form of pairs or networks of strongly opposed characters/values – while through the stories woven about these oppositions, and formally in the fact of their integration into mythic narrative, partially defusing their potentially explosive force. Thus in film genre theory, 'myth' broadly designates the ways in which genres rehearse and work through these shared cultural values and concerns by rendering them in symbolic narratives. 'Ritual' meanwhile redefines the regular consumption of genre films by a mass public as the contractual basis on which such meanings are produced.

The ritual and mythological models of genre quickly encounter genre theory's characteristic problems, noted earlier, with the audiences whose participation in generic ritual plays so central a role. Thus although mythological analyses frequently pay scrupulous attention to individual genre texts and carefully differentiate their negotiations of generic conventions, the audience features as a homogeneous and largely notional presence. The prevailing assumption appears to be that audiences seek out, and respond to, the mythological address of the genre film – what the Marxist theorist of ideology Louis Althusser would term their 'interpellation' – in the same ways. There seems little possibility of concretising this claim, at least as regards historical audiences. Box-office popularity – of individual films or of entire genres – is sometimes cited as an apparently objective criteria for demonstrating the popularity of a genre – hence of the values sedimented within it. Yet to purchase a ticket for a film of course does not (as academics studying popular films would certainly have to acknowledge) necessarily prove assent to all or indeed any of a film's ideological content. It is also enormously difficult to compute popularity: Westerns, for example, were by no means universally popular and were shown by audience surveys in the 1930s to be strongly disliked by a considerable proportion of movie-goers. Regular Western fans, however, were dedicated followers of the genre and likely to see most or all the Westerns that made it to their local theatre: thus the reliable market that supported the huge number of 'B' (or series) Westerns produced during the 1930s. Does this narrow but deep audience base make the Western more or less representative of the national temper than a genre with a broader but perhaps less 'committed' following, such as screwball comedy?

To complicate matters further, recent research has shown how even the most apparently orthodox and classical genre films were not necessarily universally perceived in that way at the time of their original release. Leland Poague (2003: 89) demonstrates that *Stagecoach*, partly to counteract the Western's received image at the end of the 1930s, a decade dominated by 'B' Westerns, was publicised in ways that de-emphasised the film's generically 'Western' aspects (which would limit its appeal to exhibitors and audiences, especially in metropolitan areas) in favour of elements of broader appeal such as the dramatic interactions of a disparate group of characters in enforced proximity ('*Grand Hotel* on wheels', as a contemporary review put it) or the (hardly realised) promise of sexual tension among '2 women on a desperate journey with 7 strange men!'. While the expectations created around a film do not of course exhaust its range of possible meanings, such examples indicate that large assertions about the ritual function of individual genres are equally incapable of dealing with the range of responses audiences may bring to bear on any single genre film.

Claims that the Western or the musical articulate dominant or foundational paradigms for American national identity also need to take account of
the presence within the same industry at the same time of genre films that
seem directly to challenge those values: *film noir*, for example.[5] In the most
influential argument for genre as ritual, Thomas Schatz (1981, 1983) partly
addresses the latter question by identifying different genres with different sets
of key American ideas and dilemmas. Each genre has its own 'generic community': thus

> what emerges as a social problem (or dramatic conflict) in one genre is
> not necessarily a problem in another. Law and order is a problem in the
> gangster film, but not in the musical. Conversely, courtship and marri-
> age are problems in the musical but not in the gangster and detective
> genres. (Schatz, 1981: 25)

In so far as these problems are discrete, each genre has its own specific set of
concerns and performs a particular kind of cultural work; in so far as these
issues are generally relevant to American life, the system of Hollywood
genres as a whole enables a kind of ongoing national conversation about such
issues. The classical Hollywood studio system, Schatz argues, was especially
well-suited to this 'ongoing discourse – the process of cultural exchange'
because of its mass production of genre films and domination of the
American popular imagination (1981: 20–8). In the diversified entertainment
markets and weaker generic landscape of the New Hollywood, by contrast, as
Schatz acknowledges in his 1983 book, this conversation and hence the
movies' ritual function is greatly weakened.

In its association of core generic preoccupations with specific ritual functions, Schatz's argument seems to presuppose a degree of generic segregation
and consistency the generic record hardly bears out. The two examples
quoted above – the musical and the gangster film – are rendered as distinct
and their concerns clearly differentiated. It is certainly advantageous to have
a model of genre that allows for the possibility of different 'solutions' to
comparable problems in line with the changing cultural understandings that
subtend such solutions (see, for example, the analysis of *New York, New
York*, 1977, in Chapter 4 below). But where does this leave a gangster
musical like *Guys and Dolls* (1955)? Alternatively, what are likely to be the
'problems' tackled by a series of detective films about a married couple (like
the popular *Thin Man* series, 1934–47)? Schatz also seems to overstate generic
homogeneity – not all musicals, for example, are about courtship and
marriage (backstage musicals, an extremely important sub-genre, may be at
least as much about professional prestige).

Myth-based readings of genre are related to ideological critiques: in a foundational text of semiotic analysis, indeed, Roland Barthes (1957) names the pervasive ideological fictions in contemporary capitalist culture as, precisely, 'mythologies'. Place (1978: 35) states that popular myth 'both expresses and reproduces the ideologies necessary to the existence of the social structure'. Yet in general myth is, as Neale observes, ideological criticism minus the criticism: that is, whereas writers such as Judith Hess Wright ([1974] 1995) identify genre's ideological dimension with its provision of imaginary and bogus resolutions to the actual contradictions of lived experience under capitalism, proponents of genre as myth tend to a more neutral descriptive account of how genres satisfy the needs and answer the questions of their audiences. In other words, they do not stigmatise such satisfactions as delusion designed to maintain individuals and communities in acquiescent ignorance of the real conditions of their oppression. Moreover, the dialectical nature of the Lévi-Straussian schema implies that underlying social contradictions are less resolved away than repeatedly re-enacted and thus – at least in principle – exposed by their mythic articulations.

Initial ideological accounts of genre like Wright's often imputed a somewhat monolithic character to the ideological work performed by genre films. As products of a capitalist film industry, genre films must necessarily produce meanings that support the existing social relations of power and domination: their ideological function, in fact, is precisely to organise perceptions of the world in such a way as to elicit acquiescence and assent to the proposition that this is not only the way the world is, but the way it ought to be – or even the only way it ever could be. In Theodor Adorno and Max Horkheimer's excoriating account of the 'culture industry' ([1944] 1972: 120–67), the standardising imperatives of genre production signified the absolute unfreedom of contemporary mass media forms (and conversely the relative – and only relative – truth-content of their mirror-image counterparts, the recondite practices of high modernist art).

On an ideological analysis, genre closes off alternatives, resists multiple meanings and symbolically resolves real contradictions in imaginary (here meaning illusory) ways. Specific generic outcomes (like the gangster's exemplary fate reiterating that 'crime does not pay') also work to promote a larger pattern of acquiescence in conventional and rule-governed methods of 'solving' problems.

One would have to say that if the genre system is as secure and sealed as this view holds, it is hard to see where the impetus for any kind of change comes from – still less why a genre might be moved to perform the kinds of quite radical self-critique undertaken by numerous Hollywood Westerns, musicals, gangster films and other traditional genre films during the 1970s, a move that moreover encompassed explicit criticism of the violence and racial prejudice of American society (as in such 'counterculture' films as *Easy*

Rider, 1969, or the contemporaneous 'Vietnam Westerns': see also below). Of course, American society and the core ideologies sedimented in its principal cultural forms confronted a major crisis of legitimation in the late 1960s; but with contemporary opinion polls showing a majority of Americans still supporting conservative positions on war, race and sexual/gender issues, genre films ought to have been working harder than ever to sustain rather than to challenge the status quo. Ideological analysis also seems to have difficulty acknowledging the real differences between genres: even if the 'affirmative' nature of Westerns and musicals is granted, this still leaves unaccounted for the strongly critical charge of much *film noir*, to say nothing of the gangster film's historically well-attested ideological ambivalence (see Chapter 6). In this sense, ideological criticism's view of genre is both too reductive – in that all genre films are held to relentlessly promote a singular message of conformity – and not reflective enough – in that it seems not to allow for the possibility of interference in core genre propositions by changes in social and cultural context such as those powerfully at work in American society from the late 1960s onwards. The virtual disappearance of the 'woman's film' since the 1960s, to take another example, seems hard to account for without acknowledging the impact of the women's movement on traditional concepts of gender roles (see Chapter 2).

Ideological criticism in the later 1970s generally started to modify the inflexible model inherited from Althusserian Marxism, inspired in particular by the rediscovery of the writings of the Italian Marxist Antonio Gramsci in the 1920s. Gramsci's concept of 'hegemony' reinscribed ideological domination as an ongoing process in which dominant orthodoxies continually struggled to retain their mastery over both residual (older and outmoded) and emergent (newer and potentially revolutionary) positions. Applying this to the study of popular culture allowed critics to trace the fractures and contradictions in the apparently seamless structure of classical Hollywood, and thus to discover ways in which even the genre film could – perhaps unconsciously – take up positions at variance with dominant ideology. Much contemporary film analysis remains rooted in the critique of ideology, in fact, in the sense that it addresses itself to the ways in which films work through (or act out, to use psychotherapeutic terminology) the values and interests of different groups in society. An increasing dissatisfaction with the older monolithic models of ideological domination, however, as well as the waning of explicit Marxist critical affiliations, means that analyses focused on issues of gender, race, ethnicity or sexuality – and on the ways that the popular media structure attitudes towards minority groupings – are less clearly marked as ideology critique in the older sense.

PROBLEMS OF HISTORY

The 'revisionist' tendency evident across several major Hollywood genres in the 1970s (including the Western, the gangster, private-eye and police thriller, and the musical) impelled several genre theorists to propose 'evolutionary' models of generic development. According to John Cawelti:

> One can almost make out a life cycle characteristic of genres as they move from an initial period of articulation and discovery, through a phase of conscious self-awareness on the part of both creators and audiences, to a time when the generic patterns have become so well-known that people become tired of their predictability. It is at this point that parodic and satiric treatments proliferate and new genres generally arise. (Cawelti, [1979] 1995: 244)

Schatz (1981: 36–41) develops this theory of generic evolution much more systematically – indeed, naming it as such – yet follows the same basic outline, while grounding his account in his 'ritual' thesis. Thus 'at the earliest stages of its life span' a genre expresses its material in a direct and unselfconscious manner – because 'if a genre is society speaking to itself, then any stylistic flourishes or formal self-consciousness will only impede the transmission of the message'. After this experimental stage where its conventions are established, the genre enters its classical stage (a phase beloved of genre theorists since Bazin). This stage is marked by *'formal transparency*. Both the narrative formula and the film medium work together to transmit and reinforce that genre's social message ... as directly as possible to the audience' (emphasis in original). Eventually, the genre arrives at a point where 'the straightforward message has "saturated" the audience': the outcome is that the genre's 'transparency' is replaced by 'opacity', manifested in a high degree of formalistic self-consciousness and reflexivity. Schatz suggests that both the musical and the Western had reached such a stage by the early 1950s, and he cites as examples such 'self-reflexive musicals' as *The Barkleys of Broadway* (1949) and *Singin' in the Rain* (1952) and 'baroque Westerns' like *Red River* (1948) and *The Searchers* (1955). At this stage the 'unspoken' conventions of the genre – the centrality of the courtship ritual to the musical, the heroic individualism of the Westerner – themselves become narratively foregrounded.

From today's perspective, however, the 1950s seems very far from the ultimate developmental stage of either the Western or the musical. *All That Jazz* (1980) and *Heaven's Gate* (1980) are very different from *An American in Paris* (1951) or *The Searchers* (1955), and *Moulin Rouge* (2001) and *The Missing* (2004) are different again. So to be workable the evolutionary model would at least need extending: one would probably want to differentiate a further stage where 'opaque' self-consciousness intensifies yet further and mutates into outright genre 'revisionism': this period may also often be accompanied by a slowdown in the rate of production of genre films. 'Revisionism' implies that traditional genre attitudes may be seen as articulating a world-view no longer applicable, perhaps in changed social circumstances: thus a key aspect of revisionism is that the genre is no longer self-sufficient, but is critically scrutinised for its ability to offer a cognitive purchase on the contemporary world. Yet another 'stage' might involve the re-emergence of the genre under altered (industrial or cultural) circumstances, partially purged of its original ideological or mythic content (or those parts thereof which no longer speak to a contemporary spectatorship). Such texts never recover the unselfconsciousness of the 'classical' period, but equally they are neither as serious as the 'mature' period or as corrosively critical as the 'revisionist' period; rather, they will often display a playful degree of referentiality and generic porosity of the kind frequently regarded as characteristically postmodern, for example by injecting anachronistic elements into period settings (a 'riot grrl' Western like *Bad Girls*, 1994) or highlighting the racial diversity traditionally suppressed by the classical genre text (for example, the transformation of gangster to 'gangsta' in the New Black Cinema of the early 1990s).

Such a model of generic development is appealingly straightforward. However – even if one overlooks the obvious objection that genres, as a form of industrial practice, are not organisms and to propose generic phylogenies of this kind risks a category error – it raises several problems. In the first place, its historical account smacks of special pleading – seemingly designed to justify the critical attention already bestowed on certain groups and periods of genre film. If one accepts the evolutionary model, the allegedly more complex and self-aware films of the 'mature' and 'revisionist' phases are always likely to command more attention than the straightforward presentations of generic material in the 'classical' period. In fact, as Tag Gallagher ([1936] 1995: 237) argues, earlier films are to an extent set up as naive 'fall guys' for later, allegedly more sophisticated, challenging and/or subversive approaches. However, as early film historians are quick to point out, many pictures from the silent and early sound periods in a variety of genres display a surprising degree of generic self-consciousness (surprising, that is, if one assumes as the evolutionary model suggests that these classical phases should be typified by the 'straight' presentation of generic material). In fact, the entire, rather literary, notion of self-consciousness, inwardness and reflexivity as a function of 'late style' seems to bear little relation to the realities of market positioning, a process which is more likely to be typified by a variety of approaches ranging from the steadfast and generically secure to the playful and experimental.

Another problem, as Neale (2000: 214f.) notes, is that the evolutionary model necessarily, despite Schatz's (1981: 36) citation of 'external (cultural, thematic) factors', tends to attribute generic change to intra-generic factors: genre is in fact hypostatised, sealed off from social, cultural and industrial contexts. It is an idealised and implicitly teleological model (that is, its outcomes are predetermined). As Mark Jancovich (2002: 9) observes, 'narrative histories of a genre ... usually become the story of something ... that exists above and beyond the individual moments or periods, an essence which is unfolding before us, and is either heading towards perfect realisation ... or failure and corruption.' Yet one of the most obvious examples of genre 'revisionism' already referred to, the cycle of strongly, even militantly pro-Indian Cavalry Westerns made at the start of the 1970s – such as *Little Big Man*, *Soldier Blue* (both 1970), *Ulzana's Raid* and *Chato's Land* (both 1971) – that depict white cavalrymen or paramilitaries almost to a man as venal, brutal, sadistic and exploitative and thus neatly invert many of the categories of the classic Western (in *Solider Blue* it is the white cavalrymen, not the Indians, who threaten the white heroine with rape, and at one point the soldiers break out in war-whoops while scalping an Indian brave), are transparently intended as allegories of and statements about US military involvement in Indochina: they are not 'natural' or inevitable outcomes of the generic lifecycle.

Genre revisionism thus appears to be a function of larger trends within the American film industry, and in turn within American popular and political culture, as much as, or more than, of evolutionary change in a generic universe closed off from interaction with the world outside. Many critics indeed have found genre a useful tool for mediating large and hard-to-grasp socio-historical issues and popular media texts: rather than simply reading off, say, the cynicism and paranoia of the Watergate era onto bleak mid-1970s Westerns like *Posse* (1975) as a set of one-to-one correspondences, the idea of genre allows social reality to be mapped onto individual fictional texts in a more subtle and indeed plausible way. Robert Ray (1985: 248f.) has suggested that the binary 'reflection' model can helpfully be triangulated by the addition of the audience as the missing link between text and (social) context. Thus the accretion of conventions over the totality of a genre's historical evolution, the film-maker's modulation of these conventions and the role of the audience as both a participant in and in a sense the arbiter of this interactive process, together map the evolving assumptions and desires of the culture.

In fact, research on the American and global film industry in the both its classical and contemporary periods has increasingly tended to suggest that the film studies' preferred notion of genre is likely to need some important modifications. As far as the 'New Hollywood' (broadly speaking, Hollywood since the late 1960s, with an important watershed within that period around 1977) is concerned, new genres (or sub-genres) such as the 'yuppie night-mare film' (see Grant, 1998), the road movie (see Cohan and Hark, 1997; Laderman, 2002) or the serial killer film seem to be differently constituted than those of the classical period. Put simply, earlier generic structures – the individual genres and the system of genre production as a whole – were part of a system for mass-producing films in which regularised production, a carefully managed, monitored and highly centralised machinery of distribu-tion and exhibition, and on the audience's part regular moving-going in a relatively undiversified entertainment market, together enabled the kind of informal yet powerful generic 'contract' Altman describes. A well-known series of events over about 20 years starting in the late 1940s – including the legal ruling that compelled the studios to sell off their theatre chains; the rise of television, itself part of a general transformation of American lifestyles and leisure pastimes; the loss of creative freedoms and personnel as a result of the anti-Communist witch-hunts and blacklist of the 1950s – largely put a end to this system (see Ray, 1985: 129–52; Schatz, 1993; Krämer, 1998; King, 2002: 24–35). Over the course of the late 1950s and 1960s, the deceptively singular term 'Hollywood' masked an increasingly dispersed and decentralised industry in which agents, stars, directors and writers worked with independent producers to originate individual projects conceived outside the assembly-line and economy-of-scale principles of classic Hollywood. The role in this process of the major studios – who by the end of the 1960s had themselves mostly been taken over by larger conglomerates for whom the entertainment sector was merely one part of a diversified business portfolio – was in many cases limited to providing finance and distribution. The armies of craft and technical personnel who under the studio system had contributed so much to the stylistic continuities by which studio identities were defined, and who had made factory-style generic production possible, had long since been laid off. Although the 1980s and 1990s would see further major changes in the American film industry, including the major studios' return to the exhibition sector in a changed regulatory climate as their corporate parents increasingly restructured themselves into dedicated, vertically integrated multimedia businesses (see Prince, 2000: 40–89), neither the majors' ever-greater empha-sis on blockbuster production (see Chapter 10) nor the rise of 'independent' production enabled anything like a return to the generic production of the 1930s. New genres such as those mentioned above are far more likely to appear as relatively short-lived cycles.

The latter may in fact be a good deal less novel than this overview implies. In fact, an argument can be made that the very concept of 'genre' – if understood as it usually has been as a large, diachronic vehicle for producing and consuming meanings across a range of texts – needs radical modification if it is to be made relevant to the practices of an industry that has more often relied on shorter-term series or cycles of films seeking to capitalise upon proven seasonal successes or topical content. The fluctuating patterns of popularity and ideological address in genre films owe as much to contingent industrial factors as they do to generic evolution or the kinds of intra-generic dialectic favoured by critics. Writing in 1971, Lawrence Alloway argued that it was misleading to import into the study of popular cinema approaches to genre inherited from art criticism that sought out thematic continuity and universal concerns, insisting rather that Hollywood production was typified by ephemeral cycles seeking to capitalise on recent successes, hence by discontinuities and shifts in meaning and focus in what only *appeared* (or were critically constructed as) consistently evolving 'genres'. Maltby (1995: 111–12) states flatly that 'Hollywood never prioritised genre as such', instead working in the studio era as today in 'opportunistic' ways to pull together elements from different genres into a profitable whole. Barbara Klinger (1994a) has proposed a category of 'local genres', such as the teen delinquent films of the mid-1950s (*The Wild One*, 1954; *The Blackboard Jungle*, *Rebel Without a Cause*, 1955), marked by clear topical affinities and competing in the same markets, and which comprise a clear and time-limited classification over a particular production cycle.

An added irony is that even as the classic Hollywood system of genre production was disappearing, film genres – newly understood in the light of an industry 'relay' that for the first time included academic film criticism – took on an increasing importance as explicit points of creative reference for emerging New Hollywood film-makers. As is again well established, the writers and directors most strongly associated with the New Hollywood, the 'movie brats' of the 1970s (for example, Martin Scorsese, Paul Schrader, Peter Bogdanovich, Francis Ford Coppola, George Lucas, Brian dePalma) and their diverse successors (James Cameron, Robert Zemeckis, Oliver Stone, Quentin Tarantino), came to professional film-making through pathways (television, film school, film journalism) that equipped them with a different historical understanding of film culture than their classic Hollywood predecessors. Whether or not New Hollywood film-makers are actually more self-conscious and film-literate than (for example) John Ford, Howard Hawks or Nicholas Ray, or whether they simply possess and exploit those qualities in different ways, is an open question. However, as the web of generic inter-textuality that enfolds (some might say constitutes) a film like Tarantino's *Kill Bill* (2003, 2004) amply demonstrates, notwithstanding the end of the system that created and supported genre film production, the historical legacy of classical film genres clearly provides New Hollywood film-makers with a preferred means of establishing not only (in classic auteurist fashion) their own creative identities, but connecting to larger traditions of national identities, social conventions and ideology. In this sense, to adopt Altman's (1996: 277) terminology, while 'film genre' may have become a questionable category, the 'genre film' remains very much alive.

Between the institution(s) of film genre and the genre film text's activation of those institutions are of course the structures of individual genres, each with its individual history, thematic concerns and representational traditions. But underlying and informing those structures there may also be less tangible modalities that can neither be identified firmly with larger ideological categories nor located or contained within individual genres. It is to such a modal form, crucial to the history and in all likelihood the future of American film genre, that the next chapter will turn its attention.

NOTES

1. Though habitually confused, the terms are by no means synonymous and have been hotly debated: see Strinati (1995: 2–50).
2. A problem shared with film apparatus theory, which has some interesting affinities with genre theory.
3. On Warshow's gangster essay, see Chapter 6 *passim*.
4. Staiger (2001), however, argues that 'hybridity' is an inappropriate concept to bring to bear on film.
5. Conversely, as Maltby ([1984] 1992: 57) points out, neither should *noir* be used, as it often has been, to embody the Zeitgeist. Either construction, he suggests, entails 'a process of historical distortion which comes about from the practice of generic identification, and has [I might prefer to say, can have] the effect of imposing an artificial homogeneity on Hollywood production'.

CHAPTER 2

Before Genre: Melodrama

Most of this book is concerned with generic categories that have, over the course of decades of sustained production, established clear generic identities in the eyes of producers, audiences and critics alike. As discussed in Chapter 1, this does not mean that all or any of those groups share the same generic understandings, nor that these identities are in any way fixed or immutable. On the contrary, as Derrida observes, if the 'law of genre' dictates that every text belongs to a genre it also dictates that texts do not belong wholly to any *one* genre, hence that they can and will find themselves serving a range of different interests and put to a range of different uses in a variety of contexts of reception, distribution and consumption. Thus generic identities – those of genre texts, and those of genres themselves as ultimately the sum of the texts that comprise them – are provisional and subject to ongoing revision.

Such observations apply strongly to melodrama. Critical debates in particular have played a governing role in consolidating melodrama's generic paradigm(s). Indeed, no genre – not even the endlessly debated *film noir* – has been so extensively redefined through critical intervention. (On the contrary, as we shall see in Chapter 9, the initially esoteric critical conception of *noir* became naturalised by widespread usage to the point where *noir* eventually realised an autonomous generic existence within the contemporary Hollywood. By contrast, a gulf persists between the film-theoretical and the industrial understandings of 'melodrama'.) By identifying melodrama with the allegedly marginal female-centred and oriented dramas of the studio era, feminist criticism in the 1970s and 1980s successfully overlaid a new definitional framework onto a long-standing industry category – a project that successfully reoriented the gender politics of film theory itself. Feminist criticism located melodrama in the intense pathos generated by narratives of maternal and romantic sacrifice in films such 'women's films' as *Stella Dallas* (1937) and *Now, Voyager* (1942), and has fiercely debated the gender politics of these texts – the gendered social roles created by and for their female protagonists, and the 'viewing positions' they offer female spectators. Melodrama has also been identified with a rather different body of films, the emotionally wrought dramas of family conflict directed in the 1950s by Nicholas Ray (*Rebel Without a Cause*, 1955; *Bigger Than Life*, 1956), Elia Kazan (*East of Eden*, 1955) and above all Douglas Sirk (*Magnificent Obsession*, 1954; *All That Heaven Allows*, 1955; *Written on the Wind*, 1958; *Imitation of Life*, 1959), dubbed 'family melodramas' in the 1970s by such critics as Thomas Elsaesser ([1972] 1991), Geoffrey Nowell-Smith (1977] 1991) and Chuck Kleinhans ([1978] 1991), whose high emotional pitch and 'excessive' visual style are held to effect a subversion of ideological norms.[1] Behind and beyond all of these studio-era films in some way lay the melodramas of the silent era and further back still the legacy of popular nineteenth-century theatrical melodrama, a seemingly separate tradition whose connection to Ray, Sirk, et al. film studies has until recently conspicuously failed to address.

Clearly, to what extent these strains constitute (a) genre(s) is a question that can be needs to be, and is endlessly debated. As in other areas of film genre studies, recent historical research has uncovered new fields of melodrama – notably in pre-Hollywood silent cinema – while problematising prevailing assumptions about others. The exact status of the 'woman's film' as an industry category, for example, is open to question: while Rick Altman (1999: 27–33) labels it a 'phantom genre' (i.e. critically rather than industrially constructed), Steve Neale's (2000: 188–94) research on the film industry's own generic terminologies as reflected in the trade press from at least the 1920s to the 1950s indicates that the term was used from the 1910s onwards, but in neither as localised nor as consistent a way as feminist criticism has suggested. Recent research has also placed a question mark over the woman's film's 'subaltern' status in studio-era Hollywood, an important dimension of its retrieval/construction as a critical object. On the other hand, based on the same research methodology Neale (1993, 2000: 179–86) argues that in studio-era Hollywood at least 'melodrama' was a term which, while it could and did mean many things, rarely meant what 'melodrama' has come to mean in contemporary film studies and in particular meant almost anything *but* 'women's films'; 'family melodrama', meanwhile, is a term Neale declares himself unable to locate anywhere in this 'industry relay' at all. 'Melodrama' seems generally (though by no means exclusively) to have denoted blood-and-thunder dramas of passion, crime, injustice and retribution – in fact the term was widely used to describe films across (in standard genre-critical terms) a wide variety of classical genres, from Westerns to crime thrillers and exotic adventure films. Richard Maltby (1995: 111) notes that of the six major categories used to classify pictures for the Production Code Administration in the 1940s, melodrama was by far the largest, accounting for between a quarter and a third of all production.

A growing body of scholarship, starting with Gledhill (1987, 1994), has argued for the centrality to Hollywood film *in general* of a melodramatic mode that extends back to and derives directly from the popular nineteenth-century stage. While the theatrical inheritance is most clearly visible in silent film, the melodramatic mode in this larger, even capacious conception extends well beyond the silent film-makers most readily associated with melodrama such as D. W. Griffith, into not only studio-era film, but contemporary Hollywood too. Moreover, this melodramatic 'mode' maps directly onto *neither* the earlier gender-based critical constructions of sound-era melodrama (Sirk, Minnelli, the woman's film, etc.) *nor* onto the 'industry relay' explored by Neale. As a set of narrative conventions, affective forms and ideological beliefs present across a wide variety of genres in different periods, melodrama is at once before, beyond and embracing the system of genre in US cinema as a whole. Linda Williams offers perhaps the clearest, as well as the most ambitious and far-reaching recent statement of this reconception of melodrama:

> Melodrama is the fundamental mode of popular American moving pictures. It is not a specific genre like the western or horror film; it is not a 'deviation' of the classical realist narrative; it cannot be located primarily in woman's films, 'weepies', or family melodramas – though it includes them. Rather, melodrama is a peculiarly democratic and American form that seeks dramatic revelation or moral and emotional truths through a dialectic of pathos and action. It is the foundation of the classical Hollywood movie. (Williams, 1998: 42)

Thus any discussion of film melodrama needs to begin not by defining the genre – because if Williams is right there are clear grounds for arguing that melodrama is not a genre in the same, relatively if always questionably well-defined, sense as the other genres described in this book – but by demarcating a field. Williams and several other writers, indeed, suggest that melodrama is a 'mode' or 'tendency' that has been taken up at different times and with different formal and stylistic characteristics in numerous different literary, theatrical, cinematic and more recently televisual genres (for example, soap operas). In her celebrated study of the woman's film, Mary Ann Doane (1987: 72) suggests that, '[W]hether or not the term melodrama is capable of defining and delimiting a specific group of films, it does pinpoint a crucial and isolable signifying tendency within the cinema which may be activated differently in specific historical periods.'

I will be employing this notion of melodramatic 'modalities' in this chapter and elsewhere in this book. In a seminal study, Peter Brooks (1976) speaks of 'the melodramatic imagination', which he finds informing a wide variety of nineteenth-century cultural practices from the popular stage to the novels of Henry James. 'Melodrama' here is something like the specific literary or performative expression of a 'world-view' that can be compared to those of tragedy, comedy or satire. Like those large categories – which are referred to in literary theory as genres but which, as Alan Williams (1984) and others observe, mean something very different from the more localised genres of film studies and film history – the melodramatic finds expression in a variety of contexts, styles and media. If this is starting to sound dangerously amorphous, one way to translate the reified concept of 'the melodramatic' back into the critical practices in film genre theory discussed in the previous chapter might be to suggest that, in Altman's terms, melodrama has a syntax but lacks a clear semantic dimension. In fact, such a proposition may be essential if the term is meaningfully to take in, as it usually does, D. W. Griffith's mostly large-scale historical films of the late 1910s and 1920s (*Broken Blossoms*, 1919; *Way Down East*, 1920; *Orphans of the Storm*, 1922), studio-era 'women's films' such as *Stella Dallas*, *To Each His Own* (1946), or *Letter From an Unknown Woman* (1949), as well as the 1950s films of Ray, Sirk, Kazan and Vincente Minnelli (*The Cobweb*, 1955; *Some Came Running*, 1959). If the notion of melodrama is extended, as Linda Williams (1998) and Deborah Thomas (2000) have recently proposed, to take in either science fiction films like *The Incredible Shrinking Man* (1957) or such contemporary films as *Rambo: First Blood Part II* (1985) or *Schindler's List* (1993), it becomes clearer still that we are indeed talking about a form that, in Thomas's words,[2] goes well 'beyond genre' in the conventional sense.

MELODRAMA AS GENRE AND AS MODE

Altman (1996: 276) states that melodrama was, along with comedy, one of the two foundational strains of the American narrative cinema that formed the basic 'content categories' used by early film distributors in their catalogues to distinguish releases for exhibitors. The later 'substantival' generic categories of Hollywood cinema originated as 'adjectival' modifiers – 'Western melodrama', 'musical comedy' – of these parent genres. But if melodrama was a catch-all category for non-comic films, this does not mean it was either random or unfocused. On the contrary, the strong influence of nineteenth-century popular theatre, in which melodrama was the dominant form, ensured that the characteristic forms of theatrical melodrama – which were unified far more by narrative structures and ideology than by strict iconographic conventions – transferred wholesale to the screen. The question is not *whether* melodrama's established attributes – including stark and simplified oppositions between

From *All That Heaven Allows* (1955). Reproduced courtesy Universal/The Kobal Collection.

moral absolutes personified in broadly drawn characters, eventful narratives packed with sensational incident, a strong scenic element and a powerful emotional address – carried over to US cinema, since even this brief summary makes it quite plain they did and indeed continue to do so. The real question is *when* – if ever – melodrama's grasp on the American cinema's dramatic imagination slackened and gave way, wholly or in part, to a more recognisably 'realistic' mode, and also whether the emergence out of melodrama of substantival genres like Westerns and gangster films leaves behind a distinct generic residue of 'melodrama' that can be identified as a separate generic category in its own right. Neale's research suggests that at least as far as the industry was concerned, melodrama remained a 'live' taxonomic presence throughout the classical period and indeed beyond.[3] The wide-ranging relevance of the term is apparently testified by the industry usage that, as already noted, encompassed or modified virtually every standard generic category and type of genre film used by subsequent critics and theorists (with the notable *exception* of the 'women's films' or 'family melodramas' on which critical debates about film melodrama in the 1980s focused).[4]

A further problem in determining what 'melodrama' might usefully mean in relation to Hollywood film involves the distinctly pejorative qualities the term acquires in some critical usage starting in the early twentieth century. Undoubtedly, the negative associations of the form – including a reliance on stereotypes, cliché and formula, a reductive and gross simplification of complex issues and emotions, and a sensation-oriented appeal to the lowest common denominator of the audience grounded in emotion rather than reason – are bound up with larger debates about mass culture in elite and academic circles from the 1920s on in particular. They also draw on a strongly gendered critical lexicon in which the audience for melodramatic fictions is 'feminised', that is ascribed a 'feminine' sensibility based upon assumptions about femininity itself as 'hysterical': unreflective, irrational, easily swayed and prone to outbursts of violent, excessive and undirected passionate emotion (see Huyssen, 1986). Melodrama thus becomes both a form of representation damned by association with an undemanding if not actually debased audience, and itself the embodiment of the failings with which such an audience is typically afflicted. In fact, one could argue that melodrama becomes the generic text *par excellence*, as the failings attributed to melodrama essentially recapitulate the negative aspects of popular genre generally (as discussed in the previous chapter). To the extent that the (critically) privileged concept of realism became increasingly associated with representational and performative restraint, excessive display in these areas was understood as trivialising or caricaturing the richness of emotional and imaginative experience. This divisions operated not only to separate high from low culture, but to discriminate relatively privileged modes of the latter: thus, that the Western emerged as (white male) America's preferred self-representation may have as much to do with its valorisation of a restrained virile masculine style as with the myth of the frontier.

There is an irony of sorts that this negative association of melodrama with a sexist construction of the 'feminine' was implicitly endorsed by feminist theory which collapsed melodrama into the narrower category of the 'woman's film'. As we shall see, the acceptance of a gendered version of melodrama was motivated by the intention both sceptically to interrogate and also to recuperate for a female subjecthood the terms on which women/'woman' were constructed and/or interpellated by these texts – a polemical critical intervention that is in no way discredited by recent research. A key theme of this book is that genres are not static entities with clearly defined essences and meanings, but rather moving targets – subject to ongoing reappraisal and reconstitution not merely at the level of interpretation but at the level of basic generic identification. Thus the reorganisation of 'melodrama' into a clearly defined generic tradition, even one with a questionable basis in film history or actual industry practice, can itself be historicised without being devalued by that historicisation. Nonetheless, this critical strategy left unexplored the ways in which the melodramatic mode functioned in Hollywood film more generally, possibly to destabilise the apparently secure gender/genre categories of such 'male' forms as the Western, the combat film or the gangster film.

It might be, however, that by bringing the negative cultural construction of the 'melodramatic' to bear upon the (sometimes dismissive, but often straightforwardly descriptive) industry understandings of melodrama unearthed by Neale, we can relate the construction of melodrama as a gendered mode to the expanded field of meanings opening up through current research. Christine Gledhill (2000: 227) suggests that 'if male-orientated action movies are persistently termed "melodrama" in the trade, long after the term is more widely disgraced, this should alert us to something from the past that is alive in the present and circulating around the masculine' – the implication being that this 'something' involves an uneasiness or instability in the apparently secure concept of 'masculinity' that subtends its representation in 'male' genres like the crime thriller, whose presence is 'confessed' through the acknowledgement of 'melodramatic' elements in such films. If we refer back to the thumbnail sketch of melodrama above (personified moral oppositions, conventionalised characterisations, action-packed stories, scenery and emotion) it is after all evident how much the Western continued to owe to its melodramatic origins even as it achieved substantival generic status and hegemonic maleness. In fact, a great deal of critical work has been done on constructions of masculinity in genre films – for example, Mitchell (1996) on the Western, or Jeffords (1989) on the Vietnam combat film – but the identification of melodrama with the woman's film or the family melodrama has generally inhibited considering these issues in light of their melodramatic affinities. In this book, the exploration in Chapter 5 of the paradoxical ways in which the gangster's dominating phallic individualism is bound up with the 'weakness' of reliance on others might seem to bear out Gledhill's observation.

None of this is intended as an argument for radical generic surgery or genre reassignment. Even if *Film Daily* or *Variety* characterised *The Locket* (1946), *Jesse James* (1939) or *Psycho* (1960) as melodramas or 'mellers' (see Neale, 2000: 179–81), this does not mean that their conventional genre designation as *film noir*, Western or horror film somehow becomes either misplaced or redundant. Quite clearly, at any number of levels, semantic and syntactic alike, *Jesse James* has a good deal meaningfully in common with *Stagecoach* (1939) and *Billy the Kid* (1941), and more in common with them than with either *The Locket* or *Psycho*, let alone such 'critically assigned' melodramas as *The Reckless Moment* (1949) or *All I Desire* (1953). Yet by the same token trying to understand what is being said about these films by attributing 'melodramatic' qualities to them may help us understand the operations of horror films, Westerns or *noirs* better – particularly if acknowledging the force of the melodramatic mode encourages us to question our assumptions about realism as a norm in ('male') popular cinema.

REALISM AND EXCESS

The ongoing debate that has both broadened and deepened the understanding of film melodrama has involved a crucial reassessment of some standard thinking about the place of realism in Hollywood cinema, and accordingly the extent to which melodrama and melodramatic 'excess' can or should be seen as a deviation from or a challenge to standard realist codes. To clarify this point, we will need to digress briefly into film-theoretical history.

In the 1970s, a series of essays and articles published in *Screen* identified the dominant representational mode of Hollywood (and other mainstream narrative) film with the 'classic realist text' of the nineteenth-century novel. The proponents of 'classic realism', notably Colin MacCabe, cited certain common discursive properties shared by the novels of, for example, George Eliot and Honoré de Balzac – principally their alleged narrative transparency and avoidance of 'contradiction' in favour of homogenised narratives that reassured the reader with their comprehensive grasp of the narrative situation – and argued that the underlying principles of this brand of literary realism carried over into the classical Hollywood film. Classic realism's most characteristic attribute, its reassuring narrative integrity, was accomplished according to MacCabe by the deployment of a 'metalanguage'. In literary terms this meant the (usually unmarked and impersonal) narrative 'voice' through which all of the other voices in the text – the words spoken by characters, for example, or letters – were placed in a 'hierarchy of discourses'. While individual speakers in a narrative might be characterised as untrustworthy or mistaken, the voice that brought their error or deceit to the reader's knowledge – that declared it to be raining or foggy on a given day, that was in a position to write the words 'he said' before a passage of direct quotation – was not capable of challenge: its absolute competence, even 'omniscience', was a condition of the very readability of the text itself. In Hollywood and other mainstream narrative film, the equivalent of the novelistic 'meta-language' was, so it was claimed, the 'third-person' gaze of the camera (any shot, that is, not explicitly marked as a point-of-view shot).

This account of realism was linked to a larger theoretical project – influenced by psychoanalysis and by Althusserian Marxism – for explaining the conventions of the continuity system and the ways in which the spectator was discouraged from attending to the mechanisms of representation – formal (i.e. textual) or institutional (the studio system) – in favour of a whole-sale illusionistic and identificatory immersion in the unfolding narrative and in turn, by somewhat debatable extension, collusion in the social and ideological norms sedimented in those narratives. Opposed to 'classic realism' were a variety of modernist textual practices that in various ways (and with, it should be said, a wide variety of aims) served to highlight the textuality of the filmic artefact, from the decentred narrative style of Carl Dreyer (for example, *Vampyr*, Sweden 1934) to the didactic dialectical montage of Sergei Eisenstein. Given the clear impossibility of such radical formal experimentation in classical Hollywood, critical attention focused on those texts which seemed through various formal devices gathered together under the category of 'excess' to indicate ironic distance from, and thus call into question, the ideological, aesthetic and generic conventions of their basic narrative material. These 'excesses' might include such 'melodramatic' elements as a high-pitched, extreme or overstated emotional tenor, florid and/or ostentatiously symbolic *mise-en-scène*, an overstated use of colour or of music, and plots featuring a high degree of obvious contrivance, improbable coincidence or sudden reversals. Through such devices, as Thomas Elsaesser ([1972] 1991: p. 85) argued in a hugely influential paper that effectively set the terms for the next 20 years' critical engagement with the genre, melodrama 'formulate[s] a devastating critique of the ideology that supports it'.

The idea of 'classic realism' was challenged almost as soon as it was proposed, in particular by writers who made the obvious point that the nineteenth-century novels invoked as a benchmark and model for the translation of the concept into cinema were themselves far from the stable, monologic artefacts constructed by the theory. The modernist orthodoxies underpinning the argument were also questioned (as neither as wholly original nor as thoroughly subversive of normative categories as was argued to be the case). Ironically enough, Brooks's study of the 'melodramatic imagination' focused on two writers – Balzac and Henry James – who as much as or more than any were (and are) identified with literary realism.

More ironically still, however, the legacy of 'classic realism' is still visible today in (what became) the standard account of melodrama in the 1980s. Many of the most widely cited accounts of melodramatic 'excess' – for example Rodowick ([1982] 1991) – continued to assume the centrality to Hollywood film of a realist mode whose integrity was predicated upon a systematic repression of its own signifying practices. The presence of melodramatic excess could accordingly be read as 'hysterical' symptoms, deformations and effusions on the textual body drawing attention to those 'unspeakable' but fundamental dimensions of American social life – such as class and sexuality – on whose repression the ideological coherence of the realist film relied. This 'symptomatic' reading of the melodramatic text mirrored the understanding of melodrama's generic place within the larger system of realist representation as located at the point where intense ideological overdetermination elicited revelatory confessions – albeit in the coded form of hysterical symptom – of the unacknowledged forces governing the whole.

Yet it may be possible to read these melodramatic symptoms in other ways, not as deviations from or challenges to a normative realism but as the characteristic expressive forms of a different, non-realist order of representation. For instance, the deprecatory identification of melodrama with one-dimensional characterisation, obvious narrative contrivance and so on may indicate, as Elsaesser's essay suggests ([1972] 1991: 75–81), that melodrama above all abjures *interiority*, locating its conflictual content not within the fully realised psychological landscapes of complex individuals but in stylised and acted-out, interactional form. Melodrama evolved a stylised and quite formalised but at the same time flexible set of dramatic structures and characterological conventions that aided the audience's interpretation of their lived realities by rendering those realities and resolving their contradictions in clarified, simplified and emotionally satisfying moral and dramatic terms. Whereas realism often uses an individual character to guide the spectator through a complex narrative towards greater understanding, melodrama is much more likely to situate meaning not as a process but as a *situation*, fixed and externalised in a binary oppositional structure (good/bad, desire/ frustration, happiness/misery, and so on).

Ben Singer (2001: 44–9) identifies five 'key constitutive factors' of melodrama, not all of which are always present in every individual example: pathos, overwrought emotion (which includes pathos but also other highly charged emotional states such as jealousy, greed, lust, anger and so on), moral polarisation, non-classical narrative structure (with coincidence, extreme narrative reversal, plot convolutions and *deus ex machina* resolutions all exacerbating a tendency towards episodic rather than integrated/linear narrative) and sensationalism ('an emphasis on action, violence, thrills, awesome sights, and spectacles of physical peril'). This list certainly suggests the ongoing modal affinity of major Hollywood genres – in particular the contemporary action blockbuster (see Chapter 10) – with the melodramatic, while also clearly allowing room for classic Hollywood 'women's films', which although they largely lack moral polarities and sensationalism are certainly rich in pathos and other overwrought emotions.

Singer's 'constitutive factors' still fall, as he himself acknowledges, into the category of 'excess'. However, 'excess' here is reconceived not in relation to a normative realism that it either knowingly ironises or symptomatically deforms, but to the moral world melodrama seeks to render that simply cannot be bodied forth except under stress. Byars (1991), among the first critics to argue the case for broadening film studies' operative conceptual-isation of melodrama back out from explicitly female-oriented 'weepies', describes melodrama as 'the modern mode for constructing moral identity' and argues, following Brooks, that

> traditionally, melodrama has focused on the problems of the individual within established social structures, and as it attempted to make up for the loss of the categorical but unifying myth of the sacred, melodrama's mythmaking functioned at the level of the individual and the personal, drawing its material from the everyday. (Byars, 1991: 11)

The desacralisation of modern culture – the rise of secular society and the concomitant decline of established religion and its capacity to supply a 'master narrative' for making sense of the world – forms one of the generally agreed contexts for the rise of melodrama. Melodrama takes its cue not from the divine or the ineffable (the traditional domain of tragedy) but from the modern world around it, and aims to enact the key terms for understanding that world. While retaining abstract notions of good and evil inherited from an older, tragic episteme, in the absence of tragedy's sustaining religious framework these concepts are personified in stock characters whose function – moral embodiment – renders them almost equally abstractions.

Byars argues for melodrama as a fundamentally non-contestatory mode, one that insists on the rightness and validity of binding social (but depicted not as social but as universally human) institutions as marriage and the family. Melodrama addresses, and seeks to resolve, conflicts *within* a given order (what Neale (1980: 22) calls an 'in-house arrangement') rather than conflicts of order as such: it seeks to *rectify* the situation – by vanquishing villainy and having virtue and innocence triumph – rather than to transform the conditions upon which that situation of injustice or victimisation has arisen or challenge the terms in which they are conceived. It is the impossibi-lity of this project that generates both the extremity of melodrama's narrative devices and its characteristic affect, pathos. Rainer Werner Fassbinder, the major figure in the 'New German Cinema' of the 1970s and a fervent admirer of Sirk (whose *All That Heaven Allows* Fassbinder transposed to modern West Germany in *Fear Eats the Soul*, 1974), explained that he cried while watching Sirk's *Imitation of Life* because 'both [the film's main characters] are right and no one will be able to help them. Unless we change the world. At this point all of us in the cinema cried. Because changing the world is so difficult' (Fassbinder [1972] 1997: 106). And, he might have added, because melodrama indicates no way of making it happen. Pathos, and the tears that are its trade mark, are functions of helplessness. This does not mean that melodrama is fatalistic; on the contrary, melodrama's huge energies strain violently against their performative contexts, intensifying the sense of entrapment that is also one of melodrama's hallmarks (for example, the rigid social hierachies and prejudices that both Stella Dallas and Cary Scott (Jane Wyman) in *All That Heaven Allows* must battle against).

On this reading, melodrama takes shape as the form that seeks to make moral sense of modernity itself. However, at this stage we have come a long way from the specifics of film melodramas. In order to understand how the issues outlined here 'body themselves forth' in American film melodrama in its various forms, we need to look at the particular performative tradition inherited from the popular stage by early cinema.

MELODRAMA FROM STAGE TO SCREEN

Broadly speaking, melodrama emerged during the late eighteenth and early nineteenth centuries in England and France to supply the need for entertainment and diversion of the burgeoning working class in the rapidly expanding urban centres of the industrial revolution. Since in France the officially licensed theatres enjoyed a monopoly on the spoken word, the new popular theatres relied on music, spectacle and a strongly performative gestural language ('melodrama' literally means 'musical drama', a point noted by Douglas Sirk in a 1971 interview – see Halliday, 1971: 93f.). Over the course of the nineteenth century, these lower-middle-class and proletarian entertainments increasingly intersected with the needs of the new industrial middle class, whose growing economic and political influence seemed as yet unsatisfactorily reflected by the ossified conventions of the neoclassical and aristocratic theatrical tradition. Facing both competition from unlicensed melodramatic performances and the demands of an increasingly socially diverse audience, 'official' theatres responded by appropriating the new popular styles. By the time that theatrical performance was delicensed in the middle of the nineteenth century, melodrama had become the dominant theatrical style across both popular and elite theatre.

Stage melodrama bequeathed both stylistic and institutional legacies to the cinema. An important element of nineteenth century theatrical melodrama, for example, was its stress on visual forms of audience address, to some extent at the expense of spoken dialogue, which became increasingly inert and stylised. As new theatrical technologies of lighting, set construction and scene-shifting developed, new storytelling styles with a strongly pictorial dimension also emerged. In some of the largest-scale late-nineteenth-century spectacular productions, the proscenium arch became a picture frame, establishing pictorial conventions (for example, the elaborate historical or exotic tableau) that would be carried over into early film. The huge expansion of the theatre 'industry' in this period also necessitated a new rationalisation and professionalisation of the processes of writing and producing dramas: the rapid turnover of the melodramatic stage encouraged a promotional emphasis on spectacle and on readily recognisable sub-genres that followed intense cycles.

Melodrama was characterised by a strongly polarised depiction of moral qualities – what has often been termed a 'Manichean' world-view with equally balanced forces of absolute good and evil battling one another in the personalised shape of hero and villain, their contest usually waged over the symbolic terrain of an 'innocent' woman or child. Other classic melodramatic oppositions included those between country and city and (closely related) between the family and the world of work (and money). The melodramatic imaginary was strongly motivated by a nostalgic reaction against the complexification and perceived challenge to traditional models of gender and the family posed by new urban ways of living, a reaction that found narrative expression in plots that obsessively reworked themes of injured innocence.

Towards the end of the nineteenth century, a revival of 'serious' drama (partly reflecting the desire in some sections of the now-hegemonic middle classes to differentiate their culture from that of the petty bourgeoisie and working classes) renewed the scission of popular and elite theatrical forms, with the new topical, political and symbolist dramas of Ibsen, Shaw and Harley Granville Barker reasserting the primacy of speech over spectacle and reflection over sensational action. The emerging modernist reaction against Victorian proprieties found in the pious sentimental clichés of melodrama a ready target for derision and, more importantly, a structure for self-differentiation.

Thus at the moment of cinema's invention, a well-established tradition of pictorial and episodic narrative mass entertainment provided a ready repertoire of both narratives, creative personnel (actors and writers) and representational conventions for the new popular medium to draw on. However, cinema's emergence – as of course a silent medium – coincided with a renewed conviction of the importance of (spoken) discursive reflection and debate in the most advanced serious theatre of the time. High cultural practice was thus recentring itself on a dimension cinema was specifically unable to provide. This further cemented the association between popular narrative cinema and the melodramatic tradition (see Brewster and Jacobs, 1997).

That tradition, however, was itself 'in process' – evolving and dividing – in the late nineteenth century. Thus while the 'ten-twenty-thirty' cent theatres in America offered blood-and-thunder narratives in the traditional earlier nineteenth-century melodramatic vein to a mostly working-class audience – the same audience that would soon crowd the nickelodeons – at the same time modified forms of melodrama and the 'well-made play' offered more respectable pleasures to middle-class audiences alienated by the more boldly experimental and confrontational forms of the realist and social theatre. 'Modified melodrama' mitigated the narrative and pictorial extravagances of the traditional popular model and placed a greater emphasis on character, more nuanced and deeply felt states of feeling, and emotional rather than grossly physical conflict. Neale (2000: 201f.) and Singer (2001: 167–77) suggest that subsequent critical confusions around the valances of 'melodrama' in film may be attributable to inadequate understandings of this prior bifurcation with the melodramatic tradition. Walker (1982: 16–18) suggests that a genealogy of film melodrama distinguish between 'action melodramas' – out of which emerge such film genres as the Western, the war/combat film and the various forms of crime thriller – and 'melodramas of passion, in which the concern is not with the external dynamic of action but with the internal traumas of passion', and which give rise to, among other cinematic genres, the woman's film and the family drama. (As we shall see in Chapter 9, *film noir*, in its classic form at least, might be seen as straddling these forms of melodramatic inheritance in a unique way.)

SILENT MELODRAMA

Melodrama thus offered cinema at least two different popular dramatic traditions on which to build. Initially at least, in the era of the nickelodeons it was the now culturally denigrated forms of working-class theatre that dominated the new medium, and early cinema's strong appeal to urban working-class audiences (and the anxious commentary this provoked in elite opinion circles) has been well documented (see Hansen, 1991; Rabinovitz, 1998; Charney and Schwartz, 1995). However bourgeois spectators certainly did not deprecate the pictorial and episodic. On the contrary, as the success of *Birth of a Nation* (1915) shows, it was primarily the perceived 'excellence' – measured in terms of scale, narrative ambition and historical 'seriousness' – or otherwise of a form that coloured its class reception. Griffith's film owes a great deal more to popular melodrama than to the 'well-made play', but its actual and perceived enhancement of the cheap ephemera of the nickelodeons (actualised not only in the film but in its exhibition contexts, with reserved seating and ticket prices during its premiere run closer to the legitimate theatre than to storefront cinemas) made it – and through it the cinema generally – more attractive and acceptable to a middle-class audience.

The importance of melodrama to silent film has always been recognised, but melodrama's reconception in film theory to denote studio-era domestic and familial dramas has meant that silent melodrama has until recently been comparatively little discussed (an important exception being Vardac, 1949). Two exceptions to this rule are D. W. Griffith and Charlie Chaplin, whose historical importance to cinema's development as a mass medium has compelled consideration of their preferred dramatic modes. As a comedian Chaplin would seem to stand outside the melodramatic tradition, yet his films repeatedly – particularly following his move to features – draw on recognisable melodramatic motifs. In *The Kid* (1920), when the foundling adopted by the Tramp is forcibly removed by the authorities, Chaplin and Jackie Coogan as the child pantomime their anguish in a parade of wretched gesticulations and facial contortions. Both the scenario being played out – the victimisation of the innocent by the heartless and powerful, here as elsewhere in Chaplin's work given a powerful dimension of social criticism by the depiction of Charlie's destitution and the rigidity and indifference of established authority (the medical services and the police) to human misery – and the manner of its performance are unmistakably melodramatic.

Griffith's debt to melodrama is equally apparent and has always been recognised by critics, from his earliest short subjects at Biograph as a specialist in sensational melodramatic narratives to his celebrated features of the late teens and early 1920s. Griffith's films are universally marked by the presence of such melodramatic hallmarks as pathos, the victimisation of innocents (the transhistorical subject of *Intolerance*, 1917), threats to the family and sensational sequences rendered 'respectable' by their integration into carefully developed rather than episodic narratives (such as the climactic ride of the Klan in *Birth of a Nation*, 1915, or the escape across the ice in *Way Down East*). Another 'abduction' scene, in Griffith's *Orphans of the Storm* – when Henriette recognises the voice of her blind sister Louise in the street below, but is prevented from rescuing her from the beggar's life into which a malign beldame has forced her when she is arrested at the behest of an aristocratic father who aims to prevent her marriage to his son – displays a similar stylised gestural intensity to *The Kid*, but in a narrative context that better typifies melodrama's reliance on coincidence and sudden reversal to generate and intensify pathos (on Griffith and melodrama, see Allen, 1999: 42–74; the *Orphans* recognition scene is analysed in detail on pp. 98–103).

The general tendency in early bellelettristic film criticism was to regard the melodramatic aspects of Griffith's and Chaplin's work as flaws that either (depending on the writer's attitude) qualified their artistic achievement or could be set aside in estimating it. The perceived legacy of Victorian sensibilities in Griffith – for example, the model of Dickens, first noted with a different emphasis by Eisenstein – elicits such judgements as:

> [W]hat we have in Griffith is the surface world of Dickens – that which made him so popular because it touched on the surface nerves of the public – but not the wit or the penetration, the insight into complexity and emotional depths that underlay the surface simplicities, the types, the sentimentalities of situation and emotion. What is left is the energetic rendering of the shell: Griffith's cinematic embodiment of exaggerated, sentimental emotionalism, naïve, simplistic conflict and tension, and one-dimensional character stereotypes. (Casty [1972] 1991: 364)[5]

The modernist orientation of much film scholarship in the 1970s encouraged an approach that 'retrieved' Griffith's technical and stylistic innovations from the surrounding Victorian baggage (or reconceived Chaplin in terms of modernist urban typologies). Alternatively, as in Belton's ([1972] 1991) comparative reading of Griffith and Frank Borzage, the 'intensity' of the artist's engagement with a melodramatic 'world-view' can be seen as conferring upon their work an 'integrity' lacking in more routine melodramatic production.

As with several other classical genres to be discussed in this book, the upsurge of interest in silent cinema and the allied historicist trend in recent film scholarship has resulted in studies that aim both to broaden the discussion of silent melodrama beyond the 'canon' of major auteurs and to engage with the historical specificity of the forms of spectatorial address characteristic of silent melodramas. Singer (2001), for example, focuses on the popular sensational melodramas of the 1910s typified by serial adventures such as *The Perils of Pauline* (1914) and *The Hazards of Helen* (1914–17) (films notable not least for their active heroines).

THE WOMAN'S FILM

The woman's film has received the most sustained critical attention of any of the Hollywood genres in the melodramatic genealogy. Whenever the term 'woman's film' became widely used in Hollywood (see Simmon, 1993), it is clear that from at least the late 1910s and probably before, the notion that a certain type of film might have a particularly strong appeal to women was present in the industry 'relay' (Neale, 2000: 191–2). This type of film centred on women's experiences, specifically domestic, familial and romantic (though with romance subordinated to or at least crossed with the domestic or familial rather than carrying the story in its own right); their protagonists were women, and women's friendships often figured importantly (for example, the professional partnership of Mildred Pierce and Ida Corwin). Woman's films were frequently based on literary properties written by women, and female scriptwriters were also often involved (see Francke, 1994). The value of such films to the film industry stemmed from the perception – which by the 1940s had firmed up into something like an orthodoxy – that women comprised both a simple majority of movie-goers and the most reliable and regular viewers, that they often had a more decisive voice in choosing the films they attended with their male partners, and that this important constituency was drawn to films on conventionally 'feminine' subjects.[6]

These last points are worth emphasising because of the sometime assumption in feminist criticism that the women's film was a Cinderella genre, occupying a subordinate position in Hollywood's aesthetic and economic hierarchy. The woman's film's attraction to melodramatic rather than realistic modes of representation – 'realism' being a privileged category in elite (male) opinion (see Gledhill, 1987) – confirmed and exacerbated the general deprecation of the genre. Thus, it was held, like other forms of women's expression, women's films, however numerous and popular, remained subject to masculinist interests and perspectives. In reality, in line with the received industry wisdom concerning female audiences, a woman's film was if anything likely to be a more rather than a less prestigious production in terms of budget, profile and very often critical reception too. As conventional and middlebrow as producers' assumptions about 'quality' may seem today, quite clearly women's films along with other prestigious product like costume dramas, biopics and literary adaptations (all of these could of course be women's films too, though biopics usually featured male subjects), served as advertisements of the 'best' Hollywood could produce. Women's films were almost invariably major studio productions, usually 'A' features, and were assigned top stars and directors. (This industrial prestige need not of course have reflected the personal tastes of male studio heads and indeed, as Gledhill (2000: 226) observes, economic importance is not necessarily an index, even in a capitalist enterprise, of 'cultural value'; but Harry Warner's remark to Bette Davis that he hated her films and only made them because the box office demanded it surely cuts both ways.) As Maltby (1995a: 133–6) notes, the deprecation of the woman's film feminist theory set itself to contest existed far more among the male critics who dominated the early years of film studies and tended to carry through their theoretical propositions through such 'male' genres as the Western and the gangster film. As far as melodrama is concerned, it follows from what has already been said about the general industry usage of the term that, as far as contemporary film-makers and (presumably) viewers were concerned, women's films were *not* melodramas (like thrillers or combat films) and quite likely all the better for it. It does not at all follow from this that it is 'wrong' to focalise critical discussion of such films through the theoretical matrix of melodrama, merely that it is hard to use the melodramatic address of the woman's film to press arguments about its cultural status.

Of the many women's films of the studio era, *Stella Dallas* (1937, following a silent version in 1925) has become perhaps the paradigmatic example. The film tells the story of a working-class woman who, having married 'above her station', eventually drives away her beloved daughter Laurel to be brought up by Stella's estranged husband so she will not be dragged down by association with her mother's vulgarity, and was the focus of an extensive critical debate among feminist film theorists in the mid-1980s that encapsulated the different and frequently ambivalent responses provoked by the female-oriented films of the studio era. Crucially at stake was the extent to which Stella's sacrifice at the altar of bourgeois domesticity represented a submission the film was recommending to its female spectatorship, or alternatively the possibilities for that spectatorship's recovery of a positive sense of female strengths from her story – albeit strengths that Stella's social context and her interpellation by patriarchal ideologies ensure she is unable to actualise. The nature and degree of women's investment in the conventions to which Stella finally surrenders were crystallised in the film's extraordinary final scene, where the rain-drenched Stella fights her way to the front of a crowd of gawkers outside her ex-husband's mansion so that, tearful yet triumphant amid this crowd of strangers, she can view Laurel's wedding – symbolic of her acceptance by the high society that has shunned Stella herself. This pathos-filled scene, which seemed to position Stella as a spectator analogous – in her rapt, teary intensity – to the female cinema viewer herself in ways that made a clear judgement of her choice almost impossible, summarised the woman's film's compelling yet deeply ambiguous attraction.

Another much-discussed woman's film, *Mildred Pierce* (1945), presented a conflict of gender roles articulated through a generic contest between the 'woman's film' and the *noir* thriller. The film's *noir* elements include the extensive use of geometric patterns of light and shade, expressionist lighting, a convoluted narrative presented largely in flashback, and strong strains of pessimism and paranoia; the contrasting 'woman's film' elements include the domestic focus, the centrality of childrearing and specifically motherhood, and a narrative centred on female experiences. *Mildred Pierce* is an unusual and interesting film inasmuch as it straddles the different (contemporary industrial and critical) understandings of melodrama and indeed activates them as its central conflict.

THE FAMILY MELODRAMA

Identifying the part played by the family in American life of course opens up a vast field of enquiry, but as Gallagher (1986) suggests, as a subject the family is often absorbed back into other genres and accommodated to their normative concerns: *The Searchers*, for example, is more likely to be read as a film about white racism or the pathology of masculinity than as a parable of the struggle to envision and constitute or maintain a family. It is also notable that the traditional dramatic construction of numerous genres – including romantic comedy (see Wexman, 1993), the series Western, etc. – locates the moment of familial investment (that is marriage, or at any rate the confirmation of the couple) as the climax and the conclusion of the drama rather than as the central dramatic situation. By contrast, according to Geoffrey Nowell-Smith ([1977] 1991: 268), the family melodrama is inscribed by 'a set of psychic determinations ...which take shape around the family' and takes its subject matter primarily and consistently from the familial domain.

Although of all 'phantom genres' the 'family melodrama' is the most elusive, appearing nowhere in the contemporary relay (see Neale, 1993), it has become as closely identified with the critical construction of melodrama as any, largely owing to the revival of interest in Sirk's 1950s Hollywood films during the 1970s on the ironic terms noted above (strongly encouraged by Sirk himself). Family melodramas intensify, arguably to a parodic degree, the pathos of the woman's film, relocating melodramatic excess to the stylistic domain. The family melodrama is often understood in terms of its contradictory imperatives to reveal and to repress issues, tensions and stresses around the family – the arena in and through which psycho-sexual identity is most importantly constituted – denied either a 'polite' hearing in American society, or direct cinematic representation under the terms of the Production Code, hence its characteristic resort to the fantastic, the highly stylised and the 'contrived'.

Marxism suggests that melodrama's emphasis on conflicts within and around the family enacts a classic bourgeois displacement of problems actually present in the economic and political field onto the personal and domestic scene: morality thus becomes a personal rather than a political issue. Once on that terrain, however, even if class conflict is displaced onto domestic types, nonetheless the unspoken – and socially unspeakable – tensions inside the family matrix within which the individual is formed inevitably push their way to the fore. The family is (in Althusserian terms) a classically 'overdetermined' arena: it is both inadmissably social and political (because bourgeois ideology denies the impact of the economic upon the family, where personal morality reigns supreme), *and* the site of the equally unspeakable desires and drives of the Freudian family romance (Elsaesser, (1972) 1991: 81] punningly describes the family melodrama as 'where Freud left his Marx on the family home').

Sirk's films in particular constitute a repeated investigation of the ways whereby normative social demands are enforced or regulated, and social authority refracted, through the institutions of the family. In *All That Heaven Allows*, the widowed Cary's relationship with her younger gardener Ron Kirby (Rock Hudson) – transgressive in terms of both age and class – is initially curbed by a combination of regulatory methodologies applied by her children: on the one hand her son's forceful, aggressive, punishing and overtly repressive mode, on the other her social worker daughter's therapeutic, cajoling, professionally 'sensitive' approach. *Written on the Wind* (1958) is a dynastic melodrama that associates issues of patriarchal authority in decline with eruptions of sexual and social deviance and further links these domestic pathologies to business and industrial crises: the collapse of one is directly implicated in the breakdown of the other. The apparent triviality of Sirk's subject matter – its consumer magazine romance material – is belied by the promiscuous vitality of his style: an overtly stylised and incipiently reflexive *mise-en-scène* – saturated and non-naturalistic use of colour, elaborate camera movements, the construction of frames within the frame, extensive use of reflective surfaces, etc. – combines with a heightened acting style to manifest 'hysterical' symptoms of repressed thematic material on the textual body of the film itself.

The extended range of familial representations explored during the 1950s may have been in part a response to the normative familial ideology promulgated above all by television in this era. Situation comedies of the era in particular offered an idealised vision of the suburban middle-class WASP family, significantly lacking in major problems or conflicts; possibly television's identity as a domestic medium demanded that it not challenge the consensus forming during the decade around the fundamental importance of the family, and of conventional gender (and age) roles within the family, to American life. (A centrality perhaps never better encapsulated than when Nikita Kruschev and Richard Nixon confronted each other in a US show kitchen at a Moscow trade fair in 1959: their famous 'kitchen debate', amidst gleaming white goods, defined the home as a symbolic arena, the new terrain of the Cold War.) It is surely no coincidence that the 'reward' Carey receives from her children for her compliance with their demands to subjugate her sexuality is a television: a subsequent shot catches her lonely reflection in the blank screen, ironically apposite for the principal medium of the traditional nuclear family's valorisation. Klinger (1994) has identified the ways in which several canonical 'family melodramas' were promoted on the basis of their challenging 'adult' content – in *Written on the Wind*, for example, psychological instability, incestuous desire, homosexuality, alcoholism and impotence – offering audiences sensational material beyond the constrained domesticity of the TV networks.

MELODRAMATIC LEGACIES

Melodrama, at least in the modality that has most preoccupied contemporary film theory – the family drama and the 'women's film' – would appear, as Neale (2000: 195) suggests, to have lost some of its impetus with the disappearance of the productive repressions of the Production Code in 1966 as well as the larger transformations of gender, sexual and familial identities in the wake of the 1960s and consequent broadening of women's personal and professional options. Nevertheless, from *Love Story* (1970) and *Terms of Endearment* (1983) to *Ordinary People* (1980) and *Moonlight Mile* (2002), 'weepies' and generically identifiable family melodramas have continued intermittently to appear. Attempts to fashion modern versions of the 'woman's film', similarly updated to take account of changing social norms, have included *Alice Doesn't Live Here Anymore* (1974), *An Unmarried Woman* (1978), *Starting Over* (1979), *Beaches* (1988), *Stella* (a remake of *Stella Dallas*, 1990), *Fried Green Tomatoes* (1991) and *How To Make an American Quilt* (1995). Maltby (1995a: 124) notes that the psychological romance *The Prince of Tides* (1991) was described by several reviewers as a 'melodrama', suggesting that, as with *film noir*, critical usage may have crossed over to industry and popular generic understandings. In 2003 two films, *The Hours* and *Far From Heaven*, presented themselves quite explicitly as intertexts of the classic woman's film – the latter a quasi-remake (in period) of *All That Heaven Allows*, complete with lush Sirkian *mise-en-scène* and emotive Henry Mancini score, but now using stylistic excess to point up the contrast of mode and previously off-limits content (homosexuality and miscegenation) rather than as symptom of the textually inexpressible.

This diminution of the domestic and maternal melodrama, however, does not mean that melodramatic modes have reduced in their centrality to Hollywood generally. On the contrary, as Chapter 10 will explore, a renovated melodramatic mode combining aspects of both blood-and-thunder and modified melodrama characterises the most important contemporary Hollywood genre, the action blockbuster. Moreover, an understanding of the melodramatic imagination may indeed prove an essential tool for comprehending and responding to the political climate of twenty-first century America (of which the action blockbuster is itself an important gauge) – which is to say for citizens of every nation in the world. In his study of the sensational melodramas of the 1910s, Ben Singer quotes Ludwig Lewishon, a critic for the liberal *Nation* who in 1920 associated melodrama with 'the primal brutality of the mob'; in the age of the 'war on terror' and a successful revival of the Manichean sensibility in American politics, his words have an uneasily prophetic ring:

> [For the average American] his highest luxury is the mass enjoyment of a tribal passion. War, hunting, and persecution are the constant diversions of the primitive mind. And these that mind seeks in the gross mimicry of melodrama. Violence, and especially moral violence, is shown forth, and the audience joins vicariously in the pursuits and triumphs of the action. Thus its hot impulses are slaked. It sees itself righteous and erect, and the object of its pursuit, the quarry, discomfited or dead. For the great aim of melodrama is the killing of the villain ... The melodrama of this approved pattern brings into vicarious play those forces in human nature that produce mob violence in peace and mass atrocities in war. Nations addicted to physical violence of a simpler and more direct kind have cultivated the arena and the bullring. Those who desire their impulses of cruelty to seem the fruit of moral energy substitute melodrama. (Quoted in Singer, 2001: 40–1)

NOTES

1. All of these essays and Schatz's chapter on family melodramas are collected in Landy (1991).
2. Though her own use of the concept of melodrama is in some ways quite idiosyncratic.
3. His examples of films identified as 'mellers' include citations from *Variety* in the 1970s (*Chato's Land*, a Western) and the 1980s (*Missing in Action*, 1984, a Vietnam combat film).
4. Note, however, that as Altman (1998: 72) points out, Neale tends somewhat to collapse the distinction between (trade) film criticism and film production, as if the perceptions of the former necessarily or invariably reflected the creative practices of the latter.
5. Sergei Eisenstein's 1944 essay 'Dickens, Griffith and Film Today' has ensured that the relationship has been the subject of enthusiastic critical discussion. Dickens is of course the novelist who more than any other exposes the bogus claims of 'classic realism': Altman ([1989] 1992) explores Dickens's melodramatic legacy to Griffith (and Eisenstein).
6. It should also be noted that in the 1910s, as the film industry attempted to break out past its core urban working-class audience to the hitherto indifferent middle-class audience (attractive because of its ability and willingness to pay more for a ticket and also because of its political support in the industry's battles with municipal and state censorship bodies), attracting female viewers was an important benchmark of cinema's growing respectability (see Hansen, 1991: 60–89).

Part I
Classical Paradigms

The four genres considered in this section, along with the romantic or 'screwball' comedy, are virtual embodiments of classical Hollywood. These are the genres which, on account of their long production histories – stretching back in each case (bar, obviously, the musical) to the silent era – and exceptionally high degree of generic codification and conventionalisation, are most reliably invoked in support of the various iconographic, semantic/ syntactic or ritual accounts of genre film generally discussed in Chapter 1. Less consideration has generally been given to the ways in which these genres can also be seen as modalities of film melodrama (the musical aside, which as 'musical drama' combines melodrama's basic elements – *melos* [music] + drama – in different ways). All of these genres have in common a preoccupation with how masculine identities – as cowboys and cavalrymen, soldiers, singers and dancers and gangsters (sometimes as singing cowboys or dancing gangsters) – are constructed and portrayed, a concern that might be understood as the specific ways that such 'male melodramas' articulate the melodramatic mode's characteristic concern with gender and family outside the context of the domestic melodrama.

Given the long production histories and the rich and extensive critical literature on all of these genres, these pages do not aim to provide either summary overviews or critical historiography. Rather, each genre is discussed in a specific interpretative matrix: for the Western, its relationship to (generic and social) history; for the musical, questions of form; for the war/ combat film, questions of nationhood and national experiences of modern warfare; and for the gangster film, the relationship between the gangster as an exemplary figure and the social context out of which he emerges and to which he answers. While not pretending to exhaust the relevant issues in any of these genres, these frameworks for discussion and analysis are intended to shed light both on these individual genres and on questions of genre theory and interpretation as a whole.

CHAPTER 3

The Western: Genre and History

More, and larger, claims have been made for and about the Western than any other film genre. It has a fair claim to be the longest-lived of all major film genres, as well as the most prolific. Westerns are immediately recognisable – anybody, even a novice, can identify a Western within a few minutes' viewing time – and almost everyone knows, or thinks they know, what makes a Western a Western. Instantly recognisable 'Western' qualities, including not only the genre's classic iconography – corrals and ten-gallon hats, swinging saloon doors and Colt revolvers, stagecoaches and Cavalry charges, schoolmarms, saloon girls, showdowns and shoot-outs – but its abiding thematic elements – the frontier, 'the desert and the garden', 'dead or alive', ' a man's gotta do what a man's gotta do' – are lodged deep in the American and indeed the global popular imagination. And this despite the fact that with the precipitate decline in production since the late 1970s and *Heaven's Gate* (1980) (only in small measure, however, because of that film, Hollywood folklore notwithstanding), Westerns have increasingly become curiosities, relics of an older age in a film culture dominated by newer technologies of action spectacle like science fiction and techno-blockbusters.

Westerns have long been seen as a kind of master key to unlocking and understanding the most basic elements of American identity. 'Westerns appeal so much to us [i.e. Americans],' according to Joan Mellen (1994: 471), 'because they are explorations of who we are, dramas in which America's soul, the national identity, hangs in the balance'. The particular complex of history, fantasy and ideology clustered around the 'frontier myth' codified in the Western has been assigned a central, even defining, place in the formation of American national identity and national character. This renders Western motifs, in particular the genre's emphasis on ritualised and usually lethal violence as a means to personal and social regeneration, a handy and concise means of commenting (usually negatively) on aspects of American domestic or foreign policy. (Such critiques of course can be and have been mounted from within the genre itself, notably the 'revisionist' Westerns of the late 1960s and 1970s and the highly successful and influential European 'Spaghetti' Westerns of the same period.)

More than any other genre, too, the Western illustrates the use of genre as a means of mapping historical experience onto popular media texts through an analysis of shifts in genre conventions. The exceptionally high degree of codification and conventionality to be found in Westerns makes tracing this process unusually transparent. It is not necessarily true that the Western possesses a more distinctive iconography than other genres – a shot of R2-D2, for instance, sends just as clear a generic signal as John Wayne cradling a shotgun – but its semantic elements generally have remained unusually stable over time. It is these constants, themselves rooted in a clearly defined and limited (albeit heavily fictionalised) historical setting, that in turn make the Western's limited repertoire of narrative situations and thematic preoccupations seem exceptionally condensed. Hence, perhaps, the widespread belief that Westerns are both exceptionally formulaic and, partly as a result, generically 'pure' in a way that genres less fixed in a particular time and space, and less tightly bound by narrative convention (melodrama, say, or action-adventure films), are not. This consistency makes the Western an attractive point of reference for theoretical accounts of genre film but also, as several recent commentators have noted, probably an atypical example of genre film in general: in particular, setting up the Western's unusual degree of (in Altman's terms) semantic/syntactic continuity as a yardstick of generic integrity seems an unduly prescriptive and restrictive critical approach (see Neale, 2000: 133–4).

In any case, even if as Buscombe (1988: 15–16) says the Western's basic generic material displays a 'remarkable ... consistency and rigour', the perception of generic purity is at best only partly accurate. Any viewer with more than a passing familiarity with Westerns knows that the bad guy only occasionally wears a black hat, and that rarely if ever is the only good Injun a dead Injun. As the list of 'hybrid' Westerns in Chapter 1 makes clear, Westerns are as prone to generic mixing as any other genre. Moreover, as we shall see, the genre's syntax (in Altman's terms) has not only varied in some important ways over time but has developed unevenly in different intra-generic strains in the same period.

Nevertheless, it is certainly true that the Western is a 'strong' generic form; Saunders (2001: 6) notes the Western's 'ability to digest and shape almost any source material.' Of all genres it has been perhaps the most reliable to the widest audience for the longest period of time. This long and continuous history of a (notionally at any rate) historical genre makes history itself an appropriate frame for considering the genre. The sections below address, respectively, the history of the genre and ongoing critical debates about that history; the influence of Western historiography on the Western's narrative and thematic material; the particular versions of the 'real' history of the West favoured by the Western at different points in its evolution; and the impact of contemporary historical events upon that evolutionary process.

HISTORIES OF THE WESTERN

The Western's semantic constituents coalesced at a remarkably early stage in the history not only of the genre but of cinema itself. Edwin S. Porter's eight-minute *The Great Train Robbery* (1901), a landmark in the history of narrative cinema and often claimed as 'the first Western', was probably not received as such – rather than, say, a crime film or a train film – by its original audience (see Musser, 1990: 352–5; Altman 1999: pp. 34–8). However, its principal elements would become instantly recognisable iconographic and narrative touchstones for the genre: the masked outlaws, the carefully engineered hold-up, the fight atop the moving train, the posse, the chase on horseback, the climactic shoot-out. Even the structural opposition of civilised/effete East and rugged/savage West emphasised by Kitses (1969) and others is embryonically present in a barn dance interlude where the assembled cowboys torment a 'greenhorn' or 'dude' (immediately identifiable by his derby hat) by shooting at his feet. The film's status has undoubtedly been enhanced by the famous extra-diegetic shot[1] of the moustachioed outlaw shooting directly at the camera, an iconic image that resonates through the subsequent century of Hollywood's most popular and prolific genre (Sergio Leone echoes Porter's act of specular aggression when Henry Fonda fires at the camera in *Once Upon a Time in the West*, 1969).

Out of the very large critical literature on the Western, a fairly standard genre history has emerged whose outlines might be summarised as follows: having established itself as a popular genre if not with Porter then certainly by 1905, the Western thrives throughout the silent and early sound eras. The genre reaches its peak of both popularity and cultural centrality in a twenty–year period starting in the late 1930s. During the postwar decade, the Western is characterised by a self-conscious expansion and 'deepening' of its generic remit and takes in a greater range of psychological, narrative and sometimes political complexities. The 'adult' Westerns of the 1950s – including such classics as *Shane* (1951), *High Noon* (1952), *The Searchers* (1955) and *Rio Bravo* (1958) – are often either ostentatiously mythic (*Shane*) or directly contemporary (*High Noon*, or the cycle of early 1950s 'pro-Indian' Westerns including *Broken Arrow*, 1950, *Devil's Doorway*, 1951, and *Apache*, 1954) in their address. During the 1960s and intensifying in the 1970s, a combination of interrelated factors – generic exhaustion, ideological confusion and shrinking audience appeal – led to the Western's 'demoralisation' (Slotkin, 1998: 6) and ultimately, despite (or, depending on the writer, partly because of) the injection of violent pop energy from the Italian 'Spaghetti Western', its eventual demise as a mainstream Hollywood genre by the end of the 1970s. Although the subsequent decades have seen occasional nostalgic revivals and the genre's core thematic preoccupations – in particular, the myth of the frontier – persist in other genres (notably science fiction), the Western must now be regarded as a largely historical form.

A reliable feature of such histories is the assertion of the Western's centrality to the history of the American film industry, reflected in the enormous number of Westerns produced – more than any other genre – from the early silent period until the 1970s, and the Western's consistent popularity with (some) audiences throughout much of that period. Yet most such accounts involve a striking if unacknowledged anomaly. On the one hand, the sheer scale of Western production, which during the genre's years of peak popularity saw well over a hundred Westerns released each year (Buscombe, 1988: 426–7, estimates some 3,500 films in the sound era alone), importantly sustains the large – sometimes very large – critical claims made for the Western's importance as a cultural document. On the other hand, in pursuing such claims Western criticism has tended to rely very heavily on rather a small selection of this enormous filmography – perhaps two dozen films, almost all of them made after the Second World War II. The most influential and frequently cited discussions of the Western have tended to conduct an internal conversation about a very limited number of films that together form an established Western 'canon': *Stagecoach* (1939); infrequently another late 1930s prestige Western such as *Jesse James* (1940); Ford's *My Darling Clementine* (1946) and his 'Cavalry trilogy' – *Fort Apache* (1948), *She Wore a Yellow Ribbon* (1950), *Rio Grande* (1951); Howard Hawks' *Red River* and *Rio Bravo*; *Shane*; Anthony Mann's series of 1950s Westerns – especially *Winchester '73* (1950) and *The Naked Spur* (1953, both with James Stewart), and *Man of the West* (1958, with Gary Cooper); Ford's *The Searchers*, and perhaps one of the 1950s 'pro-Indian' Westerns, most likely *Broken Arrow*; *The Man Who Shot Liberty Valance* (1962, Ford again); Sam Peckinpah's *The Wild Bunch* (1969). These, plus a few post-1970 films, notably *Little Big Man* (1970), *McCabe and Mrs Miller* (1971), Peckinpah's *Pat Garrett and Billy the Kid* (1973), and the newest candidate for entry into the pantheon, *Unforgiven* (1992), are rewarded with ongoing debate and reinterpretation. 'The Western' thus conceived becomes all but synonymous with a selection of prestige Westerns from the postwar era, with moreover a strongly auteurist slant in the emphasis on Ford, Mann, Peckinpah and most recently Eastwood. *Stagecoach* remains in such accounts – including most recently Coyne (1997) and Saunders (2001) – as it was for Warshow and Bazin, a watershed if not actually a foundational film in which the 'mature' genre's principal motifs and concerns crystallise for the first time. Nobody of course claims that Westerns had not been made prior to 1939; rather, it is asserted that only then was 'the time ... evidently ripe for the Western to take its place as a major Hollywood genre' (Coyne, 1997: 16). Like Wright (1975) before him, Coyne (1997) attempts to construct clear and transparent criteria for producing a representative sample, using either production budgets or box office returns as a useful and, on the face of it, relatively objective measure to identify 'major' Westerns within this 'major genre'.

The question is whether such 'major' works alone – even if one accepts the criteria for selection – necessarily constitute the most appropriate sample for understanding a genre. We encounter here an important problem in genre studies: the process of selection and exclusion through which a generic corpus is constructed. Largely written out of the standard accounts are not only many 'A' Westerns of the 1950s and early- to mid-1960s, but the literally thousands of silent Westerns and the 'B' (or series) Westerns of the 1930s and early 1940s – the overwhelming majority, in fact (at a very rough estimate some 75–80 per cent), of all of the American Westerns ever released.[2] Thus the Western constructed through conventional genre histories is a somewhat inexact mirror of the Western as actually produced and consumed for approximately half its life-span. Of course, the critical construction of almost any artistic field, the Victorian novel no less than the Western, is marked by a process of canon formation through which classics and major artists are established, subsequently drawing the greater proportion of critical attention and defining the key terms of debate in the field. And developing any coherent account of 'the Western' out of a vast field will quite clearly require some degree of selectivity: few critics have been willing to undertake the truly Herculean viewing task a truly comprehensive account of the genre would entail. But this problem of requiring a quite clearly unrepresentative sample – in purely statistical terms at any rate – to 'stand in' for a vastly larger field, and the difficulty of gauging the merit of the claims made for or about that larger field through analysing such a sample, is a long-standing one; it is particularly vexed in the context of popular media studies, where it is compounded by problems of marketplace competition and access to material (infrequently screened on television, rarely featured in genre or auteur retrospectives, even the renewed profitability of the major studios' film libraries during the video explosion of the early 1980s did little to restore the visibility of series Westerns produced by Republic or Monogram).

Beyond the usual questions of bias and ideological preference that canon formation inevitably raises (see Fokkema, 1996; Gorak, 1991), the specific critical problems with such extreme selectivity in relation to Westerns are perhaps twofold. In the first place, a general rule of Hollywood production throughout the classical period was that the larger the budget, the more extended a film's audience appeal needed to be. Whereas routine, low-cost programme Westerns could earn a decent return from the Western's core extra-urban and regional audience alone, bigger stars and higher production values necessarily entailed outreach beyond that core constituency.[3] This requirement of generic amortisation becomes all the more pressing with the spiralling budgets of the New Hollywood: accordingly, when embarking on what eventually became *Heaven's Gate* (1980), the infamous $40 million rangewar catastrophe that would lose most of them their jobs and virtually bankrupt their studio, United Artists' production executives balked at Michael Cimino's script's original title – *Paydirt* – which struck them as 'very western indeed' (and undesirably so, given the genre's long-term declining popularity) (Bach, 1985: 176).[4] This is not simply an issue of marketing – although if box office returns are to be used as sampling criteria, what audiences expected to see in a particular film is surely as important as what modern critics of the Western see today – but also of content. A prestige Western might, for example, include a more fully developed romantic interest to draw in female audiences, as in the Errol Flynn–Olivia de Havilland star vehicle *They Died With Their Boots On* (1941). In short, 'A' Westerns – a category into which most of the canonical films listed above would fall – might well be *less* generically representative in so far as, by design, they feature elements that transcend, and hence extend, the Western's essential generic frame.

Indeed, much of the discussion of these canonical Westerns turns out to focus on just such qualities of generic innovation and extension. The postwar films on which most scholarship has focused are typically distinguished from prewar 'B' Westerns (not to mention the programme Westerns that continued to be produced in significant numbers until the late 1950s) by higher budgets, more complex approaches to character and history, and quite explicit – in many cases highly elaborate and self-conscious – attempts to extend and/or transgress generic conventions and boundaries: all characteristics that naturally recommend themselves to critics frequently schooled in techniques of literary analysis for whom complexity, formal experimentation, etc., are privileged qualities. This in turn raises a second difficulty: for the claim of these films' generic novelty (hence usually, at least by implication, artistic superiority) necessarily relies on their deviation from or adaptation of generic norms which, however, are themselves typically assumed rather than exemplified or explored.

It is timely then that the history of the Western genre is currently the subject of a scholarly range war, or at least a border skirmish. The standard narrative of the genre's evolution is being challenged and the Western's generic map partly rewritten. This inevitably complicates matters for students – not least because it inevitably tends to emphasise films outside the existing canon, many of them difficult to access – but should nonetheless be welcomed as rebalancing a long-standing problem of critical bias. Gallagher (1995) argues that the standard account rhetorically constructs a large, and largely unseen, body of prewar films as naively primitive purely to provide an unflattering comparison with the psychological and ideological complexities and ironies of the postwar Western.[5] Neale (2000) and Stanfield (2001), among others, have also strongly criticised the distortions caused by the obviously partial – both incomplete and also *parti pris* – version of a long and extensive genre history summarised above.

The loss of so many silent films of all kinds, and the extremely limited circulation of all but a few of those that have survived, makes serious study of the silent Western very difficult for all but specialists. Seminal Western stars such as Broncho Billy Anderson, Tom Mix and William S. Hart, although their films established many of the genre's enduring formulae, are for most modern viewers dimly glimpsed figures the other side of a sizeable historical and cultural chasm. However, contemporary scholarship has started to give the silent Western its generic due, as reflected in recent books by Lusted (2003: 67–94) and Simmon (2003: 3–97). Alongside studies of the early Western as an important discourse for mediating and refining American white male identity in the Progressive era, a period in which mass immigration and the spectre of racial pollution troubled the white imagination (Slotkin, 1998: 242–52; Abel, 1998), a growing body of work has paid attention to the unexpected complexities of the representation of Native Americans in pre-First World War Westerns (Aleiss, 1995; Griffiths, 1996, 2002; Jay, 2000). The latter research suggests that some prevailing assumptions about the novelty of canonical postwar 'pro-Indian' Westerns such as *Broken Arrow*, *Devil's Doorway* and *Apache* may need to be re-examined.

The problem posed by the critical neglect of 'B' – or, more accurately, series – Westerns is even more acute, particularly since unlike the silents this body of films is largely extant (and has recently started to find its way onto home video). More than a thousand Westerns were produced during the 1930s. However (following the box-office failure in 1930 of the prestige Westerns *The Big Trail* – the film intended to break John Wayne as a major star, which instead consigned him to series Westerns for the rest of the decade – and *Cimarron*), only a handful of these were 'A' pictures. Not until the very end of decade did the 'A' Western see a renaissance that persisted through US entry into the Second World War at the end of 1941. Yet today, as Peter Stanfield (2001) points out in the introduction to his pathbreaking recent study, the series Western is almost entirely forgotten, consigned to the same memory hole as the silents, treated as juvenile ephemera of interest only to collectors and their numerous buffish enthusiasts. As with Hart and Mix in the silent era, the names at least of some series Western stars remain very familiar – Wayne, of course, and in particular, the 'singing cowboys' Gene Autry and Roy Rogers – but the films that made their fortunes, to say nothing of their writers and directors, are today hardly known except to specialists and 'buffs'. Similarly, the series Western has been mostly ignored by serious criticism. Slotkin (1998: 271–7) devotes just seven of *Gunfighter Nation*'s 850 pages to a consideration of 1930s series Westerns. In his seminal essay on Westerns, Warshow ([1954] 1975b) in the same breath dismisses silents and 'Bs' alike *en masse* as 'nothing that an adult could take seriously' – while confessing to having never seen a single example of either! It seems that the popular conception of the Western as formulaic and simplistic relies upon a sort of folk memory of childhood Saturday matinees or faded television showings of such films.

Stanfield (1998, 2001) argues that the settlement of the frontier (see below) is much less important to 1930s series Westerns than issues around land ownership, regionalism and urbanisation. The critically despised singing Westerns of Gene Autry – most of which featured contemporary, not frontier settings – directly addressed 'the difficulties his audience confronted in making the socioeconomic change from subsistence farming to a culture of consumption, from self-employment to industrial practices and wage dependency, from rural to urban living' (Stanfield, 1998: 114). Leyda's (2002) work on a variant form even further below the critical radar of standard accounts, the 'race' (black audience) Western, has found striking similarities with the mainstream series Western.

Such research, simply by extending the genre's historical and critical purview, changes the context for understanding the Western. In the case of the post-Second World War Western, more research remains to be done on the significant number of routine Westerns still being produced until the mid-1960s. The key task facing genre criticism of the post-1945 period, however, may be less the extension of the canon – as we have seen this is already heavily weighted towards the postwar Western – than critical interrogation of the received understanding of the genre's central preoccupation in this period – the frontier.

THE WEST(ERN) OF HISTORY

Neale points out that the critical focus on the theme of the frontier, largely constructed in terms of the 'desert/garden' opposition derived from John Ford by structuralist critics, not only obscures large portions of the historical record of Western production but has also tended to have difficulty with such important categories of contemporary criticism as gender, sexuality and class. 'It is at least worth asking whether the male-oriented versions of frontier mythology promoted by post-war western theorists are borne out in full by the industry's output, or whether the critical preference has tended to obscure the existence of ... other trends and titles' (Neale, 2000: 142). It is equally important to consider whether, in light of renewed critical interest in the series Western, the Western's apparent preoccupation with the idea of the frontier itself represents a significant shift of generic focus, and what the factors impelling that shift might have been. Whereas Slotkin (1998), for example, argues for the ideological centrality of the frontier myth throughout the twentieth century and indeed before, Engelhardt (1995) proposes that a progressive crisis in the dominant 'victory culture' in the postwar period, attendant on social change and setbacks and confusions in foreign policy, made conventional notions of American identity, such as those vested in the frontier myth, objects of urgent debate.

The institutionalisation of the myth of the frontier as the dominant paradigm for discussing the Hollywood Western owes a good deal to two influential, loosely 'structuralist' studies that adapted Lévi-Strauss's model to identify the Western's basic conceptual materials – its imaginative building-blocks. Jim Kitses (1969) identified a set of 'shifting antinomies' (p. 11) organised around a central opposition of wilderness and civilisation,[6] while Will Wright (1975) outlined four main models of Western narratives and their numerous variant subsets.[7] These and other accounts of the Western in many ways take as their point of departure the Western's imbrication in American history. Nor is this surprising: the Western is, ostensibly at least, the most historically specific and consistent of all film genres. According to Phil Hardy, 'the Western is fixed in history in a relatively straightforward way': specifically, 'the frontier, and, more particularly, the frontier between the Civil War and the turn of the century, forms the backdrop to most Westerns' (Hardy, 1991: x–xi).

Hardy freely acknowledges, as do most similar surveys, the need for generic boundaries flexible enough to accommodate such obvious 'Westerns', albeit displaced in time and/or space, as *Drums Along the Mohawk* (1939, set in Colonial New England), *Coogan's Bluff* (1968, a contemporary urban thriller) and *Westworld* (1973, a science fiction film). Hardy's identification of 'the frontier' as the general organising imaginative and conceptual axis of the Western is also entirely conventional. And like virtually every other writer on the Western, he asserts from the outset that the Western transforms historical material into archetypal myth. Yet there is nonetheless an inherent underlying problem in using 'the frontier' as a straightforward historical category and a means of arguing the historicity of the Western. For, as this section explores, the version of history that in such accounts is 'mythified' by the Western is itself already as much myth as history – and, like so many Westerns, consciously so.

'The frontier' has a deceptively precise and stable ring: but according to its most influential chronicler, historian Frederick Jackson Turner, whose celebrated ([1947] 1986) essay 'The Closing of the American Frontier' defined the terms of Western historiography for over half a century, in reality the frontier was always and by definition mobile, not a clear boundary but an uncertain and shifting prospect alongside, or just ahead, of the leading edge of the white colonial advance across the North American continent. Although white settlement took some three hundred years, from the early seventeenth century to the dawn of the twentieth, to span the continent from the Atlantic to the Pacific Ocean, the generic focus of the modern Western is usually on the decades following the end of the Civil War. These were decades of large-scale industrialisation and population growth during which, with the support of the federal government in Washington and encouraged by enthusiastic boosterism in the Eastern press, the major wave of white colonisation penetrated the vastnesses of the American interior west of the Mississippi. The defining images of this epochal story – the covered wagon; the construction of the transcontinental railroad; the 'claim' staked out in the trackless prairie; the one-street frontier township; the cowboy as the paradigmatic Westerner; above all, the encounter of white settlers with the Native American tribal populations they aimed to displace and the subsequent brutal Indian Wars, the exterminative campaigns of pacification waged by the US Cavalry on the colonists' behalf – in turn became the key motifs of the Western film.

Turner's frontier thesis is worth exploring briefly – not least because recent challenges to the Turnerian account of Western history have had as decisive, if mediated, an impact on the Western as did the intellectual and conceptual hegemony of the original argument. For Turner, the moving frontier had been the defining element of American history. As a source of 'free land', the seemingly inexhaustible Western wilderness allowed American society to grow and develop in unique ways (Turner, [1947] 1986: 259–61). Because of the challenges of pacifying and settling the frontier, the American national character was shaped not by the urban class conflicts that typified the industrialising European economies during the nineteenth century, but by the encounter between civilisation and untamed, sometimes savage nature (p. 3f.). In fact, the frontier acted as a 'safety valve' for potentially explosive class conflicts by allowing marginalised social elements – the poor, newly arrived immigrants, etc. – to start afresh and forge their own destinies while playing their part in the inexorable advance of American civilisation (pp. 263–8). The frontier was thus nothing less than the 'crucible' of American democracy, and its singular and defining aspect.

Even on such a heavily abbreviated account, the power of Turner's thesis is clear. Its historical sweep and the bold, broad brushstrokes with which Turner outlines an entirely novel account of American history certainly captured the public imagination as few other academic theses did, a result that Turner doubtless fully intended when he delivered his original paper at the Columbian Exposition in Chicago in July 1893 (see Peterson, 1994: 743–5). And the influence of the extensively popularised 'Turner thesis' on the fictive West is widespread and profound. Sometimes the debt is explicitly acknowledged, as in the debate concerning the nature of 'progress' conducted by the civic worthies heading to the frontier town of *Dodge City* (1939) on the first westbound train. More generally, the schematisation of the frontier experience in terms of a Turnerian opposition between the values of (White) civilisation and the raw wilderness (typically including the non-White cultures of Native Americans) is readily identifiable in numerous Westerns, and figures consistently as the central preoccupation of the genre's two pre-eminent directors in the sound era, John Ford and Sam Peckinpah.

Although a full exploration is beyond the scope of the present work, a brief look at the genre's treatment of social space reveals the impact of Turner's ideas on Westerns. The most quintessentially 'civilised' of spaces, the city, enjoys a very mixed reputation in Westerns. As Edward Buscombe (1988: 88) notes, a significant proportion of the population of the Old West lived in cities; yet cities as such are offscreen presences, railheads, unreached destinations (such as Junction City, where the train will be held for Senator and Mrs Stoddard at the end of *The Man Who Shot Liberty Valance*), points of pioneer departure or cultural reference – pre-eminently such paradigmatically 'Eastern' cities as Boston, whence hail Doc Holliday and Clementine with their ambivalent baggage of both culture and corruption in *My Darling Clementine* (1946). The inclusion of an actual cityscape in a Western (Caspar in *Heaven's Gate*, or Machine in *Dead Man*, 1995) is a cast-iron guarantee of revisionist intent. Numerous Westerns from *Hell's Hinges* (1916) on have what might be called proto-urban settings, usually 'wide-open', i.e. as yet virtually lawless, townships whose sustainability remains very uncertain, and whose pacification thus provides the basic narrative material of the 'town-taming' Western (for example, *Dodge City* and its several imitators). The 'settled' Tonto and the 'wide-open' Lordsburg, the two towns that bookend the fateful journey in *Stagecoach*, respectively embody snobbery, bigotry and hypocrisy, and violence, anarchy and degradation: the decidedly mixed 'blessings of civilisation', as the film's famous closing line puts it.

Similar ambiguities beset the representation in Westerns of the city's 'other', the wilderness. The Western is, of course, supremely a genre of exteriors. More accurately, it is a genre where definitive experiences and understandings are usually to be found out of doors, preferably in the unconfined spaces of prairie, sierra or desert. Although interior spaces do feature regularly, they usually have the rough, unfinished, provisional quality one would expect of frontier settlements – sometimes literally, as in the church, as yet barely a scaffold outline against the big sky, around which the nascent community of Tombstone gather in dedication of the building and of themselves in one of the most celebrated sequences in any Western (in fact, in all American cinema) in Ford's *My Darling Clementine*. By contrast, the jerry-built, half-finished wreck of a house built by Little Bill, the brutal, amoral sheriff of Big Whisky in *Unforgiven*, points not to an evolving civilisation but to one in civic and moral decline. The crudely functional quality of most Western interiors – saloons, homesteads, cabins – confesses their newness and confirms the need for ongoing decisive action beyond the threshold if their fragile purchase on the wilderness is not to be swept aside. (Refinements of design and elaborate architectural features tend to denote sexual licence – such as the brothel in *The Cheyenne Social Club*, 1970 – moneyed corruption – the palatial ranch house in *The Big Country*, 1958 – or both – Barbara Stanwyck's altogether *outré* mansion in Samuel Fuller's wildly stylised *Forty Guns*, 1957.)

It is not, however, purely in the depiction of these apparently dichotomous spaces, interior and exterior, urban and wilderness, but in the ambivalent relationship between and the values reposed in them, that the Western finds its determining ground. In the famous paired opening and closing shots of *The Searchers*, Ethan Edwards respectively arrives from and retreats back into the desert that is his only real 'home', filmed in both cases from *inside* the warm darkness of a domestic space he is committed to defend yet within which he is a powerfully disruptive, even a destructive, force. And although Ethan's every action bears powerfully on this sheltered familial space – defending, avenging and finally restoring it – the sphere in which he conducts such decisive action, like the man himself, remains fundamentally separate from and outside it. Although he does not cite Turner, Kitses' 'shifting antinomies' reflect classically Turnerian attitudes towards the almost contra-dictory interdependency of wilderness and civilisation. For on the one hand Turner's account is a hymn to progress; hence the taming of the wilderness is a, perhaps *the*, quintessential American triumph. But as the advance of settlement moves the frontier westwards, it also inexorably shrinks it. Turner's paper therefore not only sought to make the case for the frontier as the definitive aspect of the American national experience, but explored the implications of its disappearance. The closing of the frontier[8] – formally pronounced by the 1890 Federal Census three years prior to Turner's presentation in Chicago – paradoxically threatened the very American demo-cracy to which it bore witness by eliminating the force that made America unique. Thus there is an undertow of both nostalgia and anxiety for the future in Turner's survey of an ostensibly triumphant present: contradictory but powerful impulses that the postwar Western in particular would take up and make its own.

The ambivalences and ironies of the 'closing' of the frontier came to dominate the imaginative landscape of the postwar Western. Although Western film-makers have largely ignored the conclusions Turner drew,[9] Westerns have long drawn on the valedictory quality of his account as a source of dramatic tension and elegiac colour. 'Boys,' intones William S. Hart in his final film *Tumbleweeds* (1928), 'it's the last of the West'. Ford's *The Man Who Shot Liberty Valance* deals quite explicitly with the 'closing of the frontier' theme, with the film's protagonist Ransom Stoddard an advocate of statehood and the rule of law and the villainous Valance the hireling of big ranching interests who have profited from the more loosely regulated territorial status. Valance is a psychopathic thug and there is no question where the film's sympathies lie. Yet Valance's actual killer, the honorable frontiersman Tom Doniphon, retreats into the (literal and figurative) shadows and subsequently declines to an alcoholic pauper's death in a way that suggests that the cry – 'Liberty's dead!' – that rings through Shinbone following Valance's murder carries an ironic charge. The film's rich symbolic lexicon makes it clear that the story of Shinbone is a parable of the closing of the frontier and an object lesson in the 'valences' of 'liberty'.

Two other notable Westerns released alongside *Liberty Valance* in 1962, *Lonely Are the Brave* and Peckinpah's *Ride the High Country*, dealt with the same theme. With these three films, the elegiac strain present from the Western's inception emerged as the dominant theme of the decades during which the genre itself experienced its most marked and seemingly terminal decline. The 'end-of-the-line' Western, in which the Western hero is brought face to face with the inescapable fact of his own redundancy, dominated the genre in the 1960s and 1970s. *Butch Cassidy and the Sundance Kid* (1969) meet their doom in a mood of amiable acquiescence rather than bloody despair, and with the consolation of their crystallisation into legend; the doomed heroes of *Death of a Gunfighter* (1969), *Wild Rovers* (1971) or *Tom Horn* (1980) are less fortunate, their ugly, painful deaths merely testifying to the venality of the society that has lost its use for them. *Will Penny* (1967), *Monte Walsh* (1970), several modern-day Westerns including *The Misfits* (1962), *Hud* (1963) and a cycle of early 1970s rodeo films – *J. W. Coop, When the Legends Die, The Honkers* and Peckinpah's *Junior Bonner* (all 1971) – rendered the mythic West's heroic codes bleakly irrelevant to the working Westerner's subsistence-level daily grind. Many of these films seemed to be claiming to strip away the trappings of myth to show the West 'as it really was'. On the other hand, their interest in doing so was clearly motivated by a desire to provide a counter-history (or myth) to the dominant one. This raises questions about the kind of history-making process in which Westerns themselves participate, which the following pages will explore.

THE HISTORY OF WESTERNS

'This isn't the Wild West. I mean, even the Wild West wasn't the Wild West'. John Spartan (Sylvester Stallone), *Demolition Man* (1993)

Recent critiques of the Turner thesis make it very clear that Turner self-consciously rendered his account of frontier history in the simplified, archetypal terms of national myth. Much the same can of course be said about the film Western. Film-makers consistently attest to the rigour of their historical research and the resulting historical 'authenticity' of their productions – indeed there is a sort of generational contest in this, each new wave of Western film-makers aiming to retrieve a 'truer' picture of the 'real West'. But even the first great Western stars of the silent era, Broncho Billy Anderson and (especially) William S. Hart, derived the outward trappings of their screen personae from the elaborate paraphernalia of the Wild West Show cowboy more than his comparatively drab real-world working counterpart (see Lusted, 2003: 90). And the powerful character types they synthesised – notably Hart's 'Good Bad Man' – in their turn established firm representational parameters (and created audience expectations) against which subsequent film-makers were inevitably compelled to define their own versions of the West, even if their stated intention was to return beyond such fictions to a putative historical actuality.

In the wake of modern histories of the West – which have had an undeniable, if usually rather delayed and unpredictably mediated, impact upon the fictional Western (see Worland and Countryman, 1998) – it has become apparent that some of the Western's most central motifs have their origins in the intersection of popular memory, cultural myth and ideological necessity rather than 'real' history. To take one example, the professional gunfighter, a key figure in the postwar Western from *The Gunfighter* (1950) to *The Quick and the Dead* (1995), 'for whom formalized killing was a calling and even an art,' is, as Slotkin (1998: 384) puts it, 'the invention of movies … the reflection of Cold War-era ideas about professionalism and violence and not of the mores of the Old West'. Even guns, or at least handguns, may have been less ubiquitous than Westerns would have us believe: Robert Altman is perhaps on to something in *McCabe and Mrs Miller* (1971) when the sidearm McCabe sports provokes curious/alarmed comment upon his arrival in the mining settlement of Presbyterian Church (it is left deliberately unclear whether McCabe is indeed, as the townsfolk assume, the notorious gunslinger 'Pudgy' McCabe, or indeed whether 'Pudgy' is himself merely another figment of the frontier imagination).

Moreover, the process of rendering history as myth is the explicit focus of a significant number of important postwar Westerns. Historians themselves – especially if one broadens that category to include reporters and dime novelists – feature surprisingly frequently in Westerns, particularly from the 1960s onwards as the genre becomes marked by a growing self-consciousness about its role in fabricating the national self-image. The 112–year-old Jack Crabbe in *Little Big Man* tells his life story to a bemused ethnographer, while sensationalising hacks are a standard feature of most versions of the Billy the Kid story. Perhaps the most famous line of dialogue in any Western (the apocryphal 'a man's gotta do what a man's gotta do' aside) is spoken by one such chronicler towards the end of John Ford's *The Man Who Shot Liberty Valance*. The local newspaper editor in the Western outpost has just listened to hometown celebrity US Senator Ransom Stoddard's startling confession: the heroic reputation on which Stoddard has built a national political career – that many years before in the streets of Shinbone, then a lawless frontier outpost, Stoddard shot down the notorious gunman Liberty Valance – is in fact a lifelong lie. In reality it was local rancher Tom Doniphon, whose pauper's funeral Stoddard has returned to Shinbone to attend, who shot Valance unseen to save the greenhorn Eastern lawyer from certain death. Stoddard wants to set the record straight as a form of restitution – to the dead Doniphon, to his wife Hallie (originally Doniphon's girl) to history, to himself. Yet the newspaper editor refuses to print Stoddard's truthful, but revisionist, account on the grounds that 'This is the West, sir. When the legend becomes fact – print the legend!' – a maxim often cited as a reflexive summary by the genre's most celebrated film-maker on the Western's own ambiguous relationship to history.

In the film's account of how history is written, alternate versions and perspectives are available only through fantasy, a point Ford underlines by employing a self-consciously stilted, almost archaic visual style during Stoddard's flashback, marking the element of self-serving distortion in his account; however, this remains the only account we have. 'History' begins and ends in legend, and that legend is essentially autonomous of either historical fact or any individual retelling of it. So the lesson Ransom Stoddard finally learns as he, like Tom Doniphon in his coffin, is nailed back into the mythical identity which time, circumstance and historical necessity have all forced upon him, is that while this may not be the (Western) history he (or we) want, it remains the history we've got. Hence any naive attempt to 'set the record straight' is doomed by its own idealistic illusion that history exists outside of retellings of it; the ideological overdetermination of some stories prohibits their redemption from within the representational paradigms by which those stories are conveyed. By this pitiless generic logic, not only must the legend, famously, be printed, but the possibility of printing (or filming) anything else – anything more 'truthful' – never really existed.

A similar implication is communicated by the rather majestic final shot of Sergio Leone's *Once Upon a Time in America* (1969), the Spaghetti Western maestro's first American studio picture. As the dust settles on the climactic gunfight to which the entire epic film has been inexorably building in orthodox generic fashion, and the surviving gunfighter, with equal predictability, rides into the sunset, the first train arrives on newly laid rails into the embryonic town of Sweetwater and the frontier life fades before our very eyes. As if to confirm that the railroad and the monopoly capitalism it represents are indeed harbingers of historical time and the simultaneous retreat of the mythic West into legend, the film's title (excluded from the opening credits), etched in classic 'Western' typeface, spirals into the frame and eventually fades away into the dusty plains. Thus *Once* ... purports to provide the prehistory of the Western. But for the spectator, the film's representational paradox is that this prehistory has itself been accessible only in the terms of the Western itself. For while the action of the film may address the Western myth's foundational moment, it can do so only in the genre's own para-digmatic narrative and characterological norms (silent revenger, 'outlaw hero', Bad Man, unscrupulous businessman, whore, etc.). *Once* ... strips bare the Western's claims on historical verisimilitude and pushes its innately ritualised and stylised aspects to near-parodic extremes that evacuate the film of narrative credibility and psychological realism alike, to the point where we become fundamentally aware only of the pre-given structural relations between generic elements. Leone's ludic film at every stage challenges the Western's ability to sustain genuine historical enquiry and develops the object lesson in generic necessity taught Ransom Stoddard in *Liberty Valance* into its central performative contradiction. The not-so-simple truth is that for the spectator there is no access through representation to any putative time 'before' the Western itself – and no spectator of *Once Upon a Time in the West* could doubt it – hence no possibility of direct historical representation. In other words, in the West it has always already been 'Once upon a time'.

Given this ineluctable textuality, it should come as no surprise that the film Western's version of Western history is often only loosely wedded to the historical West recovered by historians. For example, although the story of the settlement of the West is in large part a story of farming and entre-preneurial activity, Schatz (1981: 48) notes that the Western typically pays mere lip service to the agrarian ways of life that it narratively champions: from *Shane* to *Pale Rider* (1986) the virtuous, industrious husbandsman is opposed to the ruthless rancher, prodigal of natural resources and indifferent to communitarian principles, yet 'Hollywood's version of the Old West has as little to do with agriculture – though it has much to do with rural values – as it does with history'. Farmers and small businessmen (as opposed to cattlemen and robber barons) are rarely central figures in Westerns – unless like *Jesse James* (1939) or *The Outlaw Josey Wales* (1976) restlessness or injustice compels them to abandon their homesteads. Exceptions to this rule, such as *Goin' South* (1978) and *The Ballad of Little Jo* (1995) tend also to be generically atypical in other ways.

It is after all not the rich loam of Missouri or Idaho but the red dust of Arizona and the austere peaks of the Rockies that supply the genre's most readily recognisable landscapes. In fact, the postwar Western often discovers a pathos in the conflict of irreconcilable values between the itinerant cowboy or gunfighter and the farming communities he defends and to which he is partly drawn, yet which he can never become part of. Despite little Joey's heartbroken appeals, Shane rides away into the plains whence he arrived, perhaps fatally wounded. As the two surviving members of *The Magnificent Seven* (1960) depart the Mexican village they have saved from marauding bandits (a third has returned to his own peasant roots), it seems to Chris, the Seven's leader, that 'the farmers won. We lost. We always lose' (1930s 'B' Westerns, by contrast, typically ended with the hero romantically paired off and headed directly for the altar, supporting Stanfield's (1998, 2001) argument that the settlement of the frontier is much less important to these films than land ownership, to which since the Regency and Victorian novel comedies of marriage have been intimately linked).

In short, the image of the historical West in the Western is always and already just that – an image, framed in the light of a historical record that is itself anything but innocent and impartial. This of course does not mean that Western history is in any facile sense 'unreal' or 'false'. It does, however, mean that such histories have been from the outset 'overdetermined' cultural productions – that is, subject to multiple and sometimes contradictory causal factors. As Alexandra Keller (2001: 30) observes, 'if westerns had no real relationship to historical discourse, they would hardly have the power they do. But the relationship is far more complex than the genre itself typically suggests'. Janet Walker (2001) points out that Westerns are rooted in history in some fairly obvious yet also fundamental ways. Westerns clearly draw on the documented history of the West for their narrative premises. Individual historical figures like Wyatt Earp, Billy the Kid, Jesse James, George Armstrong Custer, 'Wild Bill' Hickok, 'Calamity Jane' (Marthy Cannery), Geronimo and many others figure centrally or peripherally in many Westerns, while the larger narratives of the Indian Wars, the building of the transcontinental railroad and the Gold Rush supply a number of the basic Western narrative paradigms identified by Wright (1975) and serve as a backdrop to fictitious storylines.

More complexly, however, given that the 'real' history the Western exploits is itself 'fragmented, fuzzy and striated with fantasy constructions' (Walker, 2001: 10), it would be equally naive to insist on any unambiguously factual historical reality (to which we could in any event have no unmediated access, since all history is of necessity constructed through discourse and narrative). The railroad- (and nation-) building epic *The Iron Horse* (1924) claims in its opening titles to be 'accurate and faithful in every recorded particular', and climaxes in a tableau-like restaging of the famous meeting of the Continental and Pacific Railroads at Promontory Point in Utah. However, given that the image Ford recreates here was itself carefully staged by railroad photographer A. J. Russell, the precise nature of the 'history' being rendered is open to question. As the final section of this chapter will discuss, most analyses of Westerns in fact emphasise the importance of the immediate contexts – industrial, social and/or political – of their production, or the Western's internal conversation around its own evolving generic paradigms, rather than focusing on the elements of Western history being recorded, even if those elements, as they frequently do, dramatise real events and personalities.

THE WESTERN IN HISTORY

Sam Peckinpah's Westerns of 1969–73, *The Wild Bunch*, *The Ballad of Cable Hogue* and *Pat Garrett and Billy the Kid* are quintessential examples of the 'end-of-the-line' Western discussed above (p. 66). With *Junior Bonner* as a less tragic modern pendant, in these films Peckinpah explored the West's shrinking horizons and the Westerner's few remaining options in an era when, as the Bunch's leader Pike Bishop (William Holden) memorably observes, 'We've got to think beyond our guns. Them days are closing fast.' Peckinpah's protagonists typically find themselves unable or unwilling to adapt to the new times, but equally unable to hold back the inexorable pace of social change. As Douglas Pye has commented (1996: 18), their 'range of action [is] finally limited in some cases to a choice of how to die' – as at the climaxes of *Ride the High Country* and, above all, the notorious bloodbath in which the Wild Bunch finally immolate themselves (and several score of Mexican soldiers and camp followers). Tellingly, the Bunch make their final stand surrounded by avatars of a technological modernity compared with whose industrial killing practices their own brutality seems merely the violent child's play depicted in the film's viscerally upsetting opening sequence (children torturing insects). These murderous modern monuments include a Prussian military advisor and a Maxim gun, both foretelling the imminent mechanised mass slaughter of the First World War (the film is set in 1913), American entry into which conflict would definitively export the frontier of

American experience away from the Old West and into the wider world. This traumatic transition to modernity is at one level a moment in and of history; at another, this recorded history is also continuous with the historical moment of the film's production, within which one historically contingent consequence of America's own violent modernity was the Vietnam War, whose escalating bloody barbarism Peckinpah explicitly intended *The Wild Bunch*'s unprecedented ferocity to invoke. (On Peckinpah, see Prince, 1999; Dukore 1999; Prince 1998; Seydor 1997.)

Jack Nachbar (2003: 179) writes that 'the subject matter of Westerns has usually been the historical West after 1850, but the real emotional and ideological subject matter has invariably been the issues of the era in which the films were released.' *The Wild Bunch* and other, more explicit 'Vietnam Westerns' of the early 1970s such as *Little Big Man*, *Soldier Blue* and *Ulzana's Raid* (1971) are obvious instances where the Western addresses itself to an immediately topical event outside its ostensible historical frame. In the case of Vietnam, the tangible if impressionistic sense of American foreign policy recapitulating the mythic version of frontier history combined with the outrage at the war some film-makers shared with the antiwar movement to make such revisionist Westerns not only socially and industrially (given the impossibility of making actual Vietnam combat films: see Chapter 4) but also generically necessary (on Vietnam and the Western, see Slotkin, 1998: 520–48, 578–92; Engelhardt, 1995: 234–40). In general, the 'revisionist' Westerns of the late 1960s and 1970s are usually seen as confronting and subverting the genre's traditional affirmative mythologies in the context of Vietnam, the civil rights struggles and the New Left. In various ways, films such as *McCabe and Mrs. Miller*, *The Last Movie* (1971), *Kid Blue* (1973), *The Missouri Breaks* (1975), *Buffalo Bill and the Indians* (1977) and *Heaven's Gate* are motivated at least in part by an anti-Establishment cultural politics that finds expression in transgressing this most 'official' and normative of Hollywood genres. In fact, although the critical interest in the 'movie brat' New Hollywood directors of the 1970s has tended to overemphasise the extent of attitudinal and artistic shifts within the industry in this period, in the Western at least oppositional and revisionist attitudes undoubtedly predominated.

Both because the Western has such a long history and because its own ostensible subject matter is historically circumscribed, the imprint of its various contingent historical contexts has to different degrees and at different times been especially marked. Some of these – such as the wartime mobilisation of series Western heroes to combat Nazis and Japs – are superficial and obvious, while others are deeper rooted. Stanfield's work on the series Western (where in fact the sense of historical period is often weaker) perceives an emphasis on struggles over land ownership related directly to the immediate economic preoccupations of the 'B' Western's primary (mostly rural) audience during the dustbowl years of the Depression. After the war, as several writers have remarked, the growing emphasis on the victimisation of American Indians in Westerns since the 1950s has in most cases less to do with a renewed interest in Indian rights as such than with the civil rights struggles and racial politics of the postwar period, for which 'the Indian' offered a usefully displaced and relatively uncontroversial metaphor (though Neale (1998) rightly warns against simply eliding Indians and Indian history – which after all are concretely present in the pro-Indian Western, whatever its metaphoric intent – with African-Americans).

Westerns in general had been no more (or less) conventionally racist in their limited portrayal of African-Americans than most classic Hollywood films (for instance, the timorous, reluctantly liberated darkies deploring the extremism of anti-slavery crusader John Brown in *Santa Fe Trail*, 1940, direct descendants of Griffith's 'faithful souls' in *Birth of a Nation*, 1915). But unlike other genres, race was already explicitly a core element of the Western, since dramatising the settling of the frontier necessitated depicting relations between white settlers or soldiers and the indigenous Native American population. Issues of miscegenation and interracial conflict were carried over wholesale from the Western's principal narrative sources, from eighteenth-century captivity narratives to dime novels and melodramas, typically focusing on White–Indian relations but with some treatment of Hispanic characters too. While there are exceptions to this general rule of Indians as 'stand-in' victims of persecution and genocide (which might include Ford's *Cheyenne Autumn*, 1964, *Dances With Wolves* (1990), and the modern Westerns *War Party*, 1988, and *Thunderheart*, 1992), even when reconceived as victims of genocidal American imperialism, Native Americans remain constructions of a white social imaginary. 'Pro-Indian' Westerns are almost always narrated from the perspective of a classic Western figure, the white 'man who knows Indians'. This ethnocentric frame remains largely intact from *Broken Arrow* and *Devil's Doorway* through *Tell Them Willie Boy Is Here* (1969) to *Dances With Wolves* and *Geronimo: An American Legend* (1993).

The advance of the US civil rights movement ensured that Black faces gradually started to appear in substantive though still subordinate roles from the early 1960s, with Woody Strode establishing himself as a member of John Ford's repertory company (*Sgt Rutledge*, 1960; *Two Rode Together*, 1961; *Liberty Valance*) to the point where he could function as a symbol of the classic Western for Leone in *Once Upon a Time in the West* and Mario van Peebles in *Posse* (1993). Sidney Poitier directed and starred in the carefully revisionist *Buck and the Preacher* (1971), which features an alliance between former slaves and Indians based in their common victimhood at the hands of the white man. Yet – possibly because of the genre's indelible association with white supremacist attitudes – Black-centred Westerns have remained very rare: notably, both blaxploitation-era hits like *The Legend of Nigger Charley* (1972) and *Posse*, a 'gangsta' Western, distance themselves ideologically from the mainstream tradition of the American Western by adopting the stylistic motifs of the Italian Western, which has a distinctly different political and cultural trajectory (see below).

The role of the Western in constructing models of American masculinity, particularly in its 1950s heyday, has recently been the subject of considerable critical interrogation (see, for instance, Tompkins, 1992; Mitchell, 1996). However, situating this in a determinate historical context (beyond general evocations of 'the 1950s') has proved somewhat harder: Leyda (2002), in attempting to specify the audience (juvenile African-American males) interpellated by black singing Westerns and consequently concretising the particular kinds of male behaviour identified as worth emulating, is notably successful in this regard. In fact, for all the voluminous commentary on the genre, the postwar Western has only rarely received as rigorous a reconstruction and exploration of its historical contexts as, for example, the silent Western in recent years (see above, 'Histories of the Western'; though Slotkin (1998) and Corkin (2000) have related evolving postwar reconceptions of the frontier myth to concurrent ideological debates among elite opinion-formers and policy-makers).

A wholly different, and admittedly speculative, perspective on the Western's decline since the early 1960s might note the simultaneous *rise* to national political prominence of the West and South-West, the Western's traditional geographic heartland. Between 1900 and 1945, the hitherto rather marginal and underpopulated 'Sunbelt' states had sent just one representative (Herbert Hoover) to the White House; since 1945 all but two presidents have hailed either from west of the Mississippi (California, Texas, Nebraska – twice each – and Missouri) or from the former Confederacy (Arkansas, Georgia). One possible outcome of this decisive and much-analysed shift in the political geography of the US is that the West, now a highly visible, influential and (some would say) all-too concrete political and economic force in US life, is less easily overwritten by the traditional mythic terms of the Western. Although such mythic rallying-points as the Alamo remain enormously popular tourist attractions, the West may no longer be the space onto which metropolitan America projects its fantasies of national identity: now increasingly it is the (urbanised, entrepreneurial and polluted) West that itself defines the terms of American culture.

Nonetheless, the Western is not 'dead': the evolutionary model of genre history is disproved by nothing so much as allegedly moribund genres' refusal to give up the ghost. Rather, the Western lives on both as point of cultural reference and a source of narrative and thematic motifs in a wide variety of Hollywood films, including *Star Wars* (1977), *Die Hard* (1986), *Falling Down* (1994) and *Toy Story* (1995), and as a permanent part of Hollywood's generic repertoire available for periodic renewal. The Western has seen at least three major revivals in the twenty-five years since *Heaven's Gate* allegedly killed it off, in 1984–88, a more extensive and successful cycle in 1990–95 centring on the major critical and commercial successes *Dances With Wolves* and *Unforgiven*, and most recently in 2004, with the release of *Open Range*, *The Alamo*, *The Missing* and the European Western *Blackberry* as well as the HBO mini-series *Deadwood* (on the two earlier cycles, see Neale, 2002: 29–34).

BEYOND HOLLYWOOD

So intimately is the Western woven into the imaginative fabric of American life that it is surprising to realise that the genre has been successfully taken up by several other national cinemas at different times. Westerns were successfully produced in Germany, for example, from the silent era through to the outbreak of the Second World War – including several productions in the Nazi era – and again in the 1960s, in many cases drawing on Karl May's popular turn-of-the-century novels (the best-known probably *Der Schatz im Silbersee/ The Treasure in the Silver Sea*, filmed in 1962, and *Old Shatterhand*, filmed in 1964). Koepnick (1995) finds in German Westerns of the 1920s a specific redaction of the ubiquitous Weimar Republic fascination with 'Americanism', using the primitivism of the mythic West to balance and ground the rationalised hyper-modernity with which the US was typically associated. Thus German audiences were enabled to make 'crucial compromises with modernity' (p. 12), compromises that in Nazi-period Westerns predictably tipped over into more unequivocally reactionary attitudes.

By far the best-known as well as the most numerous European Westerns, however, are the Italian 'Spaghetti Westerns' (often, in fact, trans-European co-productions), of which Wagstaff (1992: 246) estimates some 450 were released between 1964 and 1978 (far outnumbering American Westerns in the same period, and comparable as Wagstaff notes to the rate and mode of production of serial Westerns in the 1930s). Discussion of the Spaghetti Western has been heavily distorted by the colossal status of its principal auteur Sergio Leone, whose increasingly ambitious, stately and classical films are, however, as unrepresentative of the disorderly, pop-baroque style of many of his contemporaries as Ford's 'Cavalry Trilogy' is atypical of the 1950s Hollywood Western. The growing critical literature on the Spaghetti Western can be divided into those commentators who see the European Western as a 'critical' (subversive, carnivalesque, sometimes – notably in the films of Sergio Damiano – politically radical) version of the American Western (notably Frayling, 1997), and those – in disciplinary terms more likely to be specialists in Italian cultural studies than in film studies – who locate Italian Westerns in the institutional and cultural contexts of the Italian film industry and popular culture in the 1960s (Wagstaff, 1992; Eleftheriotis, 2004). Landy (2000: 181–204) locates the Italian Western in such performative traditions as the *commedia del'arte* and also explores the direct implication of many films in debates about class and regional (Southern) identity in contemporary Italian politics. Many commentators in both schools note the general absence in the Italian Western of either the empathy or the ethical concerns that had come to typify the Hollywood Western in the 1950s. What is certainly clear is that the sometimes crude but vigorous style of Italian Westerns decisively shifted the tenor of the US genre, dramatically increasing the level of graphic violence (including not only gunplay but often elaborate torture) while diminishing the ethical significance of individual violent acts, and establishing new motific codes for the staging of showdowns and other set pieces. A routine early 1970s US Western like *Lawman* (1971) clearly demonstrates the impact of the Italian style, as do the baroque flourishes and bizarre gamesmanship of a later revivalist Western like *The Quick and the Dead* (1995).

CASE STUDY: *THE OUTLAW JOSEY WALES* (1976)

Clint Eastwood's *The Outlaw Josey Wales* is by no means as aggressively 'revisionist' a genre entry as many of the decade's other notable Westerns, from Arthur Penn's *Little Big Man* and Ralph Nelson's sensationally gruesome *Soldier Blue* in 1970 to Cimino's 1980 epic of range war as class struggle, *Heaven's Gate*. In fact, it may be more instructive to consider *Josey Wales* alongside John Wayne's valedictory Western, *The Shootist*, directed by Don Siegel and released just six weeks after Eastwood's film. Quite unlike most of Wayne's obstinately traditional 1970s Westerns, many directed by Andrew V. McLaglen (e.g. *Big Jake*, *The Train Robbers*, *Cahill United States Marshall*), *The Shootist* is both elegiac and highly reflexive, explicitly inviting the audience to identify the dying gunfighter Wayne plays with Wayne himself (the career of Wayne's character J. B. Books is summarised beneath the credits in a montage of sequences from Wayne's silent and series Westerns) and the 'golden age' of Westerns for which he is the metonymic signifier. The film's deployment of the tropes of the 'end-of-the-line' Western – by 1976, itself a very well-worn generic variation – took on an added poignancy from the common knowledge that Wayne himself was facing death from the same cancer that was eating away J. B. Books's insides.

From *The Outlaw Josey Wales* (1976). Reproduced courtesy Warner Bros/The Kobal Collection.

Like Steve Judd in *Ride the High Country*, the Wild Bunch, and Butch and Sundance – but more purposefully than any of them, and with none of the Bunch's Dionysiac frenzy – Books arranges a final showdown, and with his passing the West itself recedes.

Wayne had been ranked *Variety*'s Number One box-office star from 1950 to 1965. In 1972 Eastwood reached that pinnacle for the first time, during an unbroken twenty-year run in *Variety*'s Top Ten from 1967 to 1987. Eastwood had made his name in the three ironic, near-parodic, heavily stylised and (for the time) ultra-violent Sergio Leone *Dollars* Westerns in the mid-1960s. In their gleeful evacuation of the Western's traditional moral codes – above all, the traditional Western hero's reluctance to resort to lethal force and his ultimate commitment to a cause or code beyond himself – in favour of indiscriminately virtuosic gunplay and nihilistic self-interest, Leone's pop caricatures of the Western radically redrew its ethical and narrative topographies and established Eastwood's brand of cool invulnerability, devoid of any visible inner life, as a new heroic model that only grew in popularity as the idealistic 1960s collapsed into the cynical 1970s. While Wayne himself was amply conscious of his own ossified status as a kind of national landmark by the early 1970s, his invariant character nonetheless retained some human and social dimension, however clichéd (usually, for instance, granted a romantic and/or familial involvement that neither Eastwood's 'Man With No Name' nor his modern urban corollary, 'Dirty' Harry Callahan, ever hinted at). Of Eastwood's previous American Westerns, *Hang 'Em High* (1969), *Two Mules for Sister Sara* (1970) and *Joe Kidd* (1972), had been fairly formulaic affairs that traded heavily on the *Dollars* persona and milieu, while *The Beguiled* (1970) and Eastwood's own *High Plains Drifter* (1972) were both intense, almost hallucinatory psychological allegories with a strong sado-masochistic strain that explored a Gothic strain in the genre far distant from the terrain of Ford or even Mann. In *Josey Wales*, adapted by Phil Kaufman (who was originally assigned to direct the film but was fired by Eastwood one week into shooting) and Sonia Chernus from Forrest Carter's novel *Gone to Texas*, for the first time Eastwood's Western character acquires a set of personal and communal responsibilities and a dimensionality that extends beyond his gunslinging facility and extravagant cynicism.

Josey Wales not only revises and humanises Eastwood's familiar mono-syllabic gunslinger character but self-consciously reconnects Eastwood to the American Western tradition and affirms him as Wayne's rightful successor. *Josey Wales* carefully establishes links, both honorific and critical, to earlier Westerns. The graphic and plentiful violence clearly differentiates *Josey Wales* from classic Westerns – an early scene where Josey turns a Maxim gun on a Union camp, mowing down scores of soldiers, many unarmed, would have been inconceivable pre-Leone for a sympathetic character even in justified anger, as Josey's surely is (he has just seen his comrades murdered by the treacherous Union commander Terrill).

The loose, almost picaresque narrative structure (which recalls both Mann's *Winchester '73* and Eastwood's last film with Leone, *The Good, the Bad and the Ugly*, 1966) allows the film to take in a wide variety of traditional Western scenery and narrative situations, from the thickly forested borderlands where the film begins to the red Texas desert, and from bar-room face-offs to Indian parleys, and to make numerous allusions to previous classic Westerns. The trajectory of Josey's own character, as Sickels (2003) notes, invites the viewer to draw parallels to Ethan Edwards in *The Searchers* (something of a privileged film in the New Hollywood, directly quoted in Martin Scorsese's *Mean Streets*, 1973, and providing the narrative model for Paul Schrader's script for Scorsese's *Taxi Driver* – a film, as we shall see, of particular relevance to *Josey Wales*). Both men are on obsessive quests for vengeance; both unreconciled to the defeat of the Southern Confederacy (Ethan refuses to swear an oath to the Texas Rangers because 'I already took an oath of allegiance'); both are, as it seems, 'doomed to wander forever between the winds', existing as itinerants on the margins of white society. In several ways, however, *Josey Wales* revises and critiques the earlier film.

Whereas Ethan refuses to recognise the parallels – which are obvious to the audience – between himself and the renegade Comanche Scar, at his first meeting with Lone Watie Josey recognises in his story a kindred spirit: 'Seems like we can't trust the white man'. The feisty, attractive and vocal Sioux female character Little Moonlight is a clear revision of the infamously caricatured and objectified 'squaw' 'Look' who attaches herself to Ethan and Marty in *The Searchers*. Although Fletcher identifies Josey as a figure of remorseless vengefulness, in the film Josey is arguably the quarry rather than the pursuer of an obsessive hate-filled ideologue, Terrill. The key difference in Eastwood's and Ford's films, however, is less the superficial updating of racial attitudes (Ethan's pathological racism is of course very much the focus of Ford's film) than the resolutions they offer their respective protagonists. Unlike Ethan Josey is permitted – in fact invited – to re-enter society at the end of the film.

Whereas the end of Ethan's quest, and his ostensibly redemptive gesture in saving rather than killing Debbie, leaves him finally without remaining direction or purpose, Josey's similar revelation of the limits of vengeance comes about in the context of values that have come to replace vengefulness. Josey's final meeting with Fletcher (John Vernon), the former commander of his band of Confederate irregulars, implies an acknowledgement by both men that some wounds, paradoxically, run too deep to be avenged and can only be reconciled. This is where *Josey Wales*'s generic revisionism – and its purpose, which unusually for the period is con- rather than deconstructive – becomes evident. Josey's accretion of a heterogeneous, multi-racial 'family' during his travels enforces on the would-be lone rider an initially unwelcome host of attachments that ultimately persuade him of the impossibility of living outside social relationships (unlike, say, Shane, though perhaps recalling Randolph Scott's similarly encumbered Ben Brigade in the ironically titled *Ride Lonesome*, 1959). By presenting this passage to settlement with little of the nostalgic ambivalence with which John Ford treats similar transitions (for example, in *My Darling Clementine* – nodded to in *Josey Wales*'s barn dance scene at the Crooked River ranch – or *Liberty Valance*), Eastwood undemonstratively transforms archetypal genre patterns. While *Josey Wales* gratifies audience expectations with ample evidence of Josey's prowess at solo gunplay, it also repeatedly shows others coming to Josey's aid as his self-imposed isolation gradually modifies over the course of the film.

This aspect of *Josey Wales* might be seen in generic terms as less the frustration of generic expectations than a refusal to allow genre conventions to determine outcomes as they reflexively do for so many other 1970s Western protagonists. Josey's earlier encounter in Santa Rio with a bounty hunter identifies the crux: Josey tries to talk the man out of starting a fight they both know he will inevitably (given Josey's speed on the draw) lose: 'You know, this isn't necessary, you could just ride on'. The bounty hunter turns and slowly leaves, only to return a few moments later: 'I had to come back', he says, regretfully. Josey nods his understanding; they shoot it out; the bounty hunter is killed. What is at stake here – why the bounty hunter 'had to' come back – certainly includes status, male self-identity and the difficulty of peaceful resolution in a culture grounded in violence, all ideas *Josey Wales* repeatedly engages; but it is perhaps above all the rules of the generic game, a logic that ruthlessly subordinates individual will. (A similarly impersonal generic imperative is at work, as Maltby (1995a: 123–32) notes, in Peckinpah's *Pat Garrett and Billy the Kid*, 1973.) By the end of the film, Josey has successfully changed the generic situation.

This transformation has a social and political context that the film alludes to both in its Civil War setting and in its final dialogue exchange. As part of the two men's tacit agreement to let the dead bury the dead, Fletcher declares his intention to seek Josey in Mexico: should he find him there, he intends to 'tell him the war's over'. By way of reply Josey (looking offscreen) mutters, 'I guess all of us died a little in that damn war'. Audiences in 1975 would doubtless have understood the allusion to America's more recent 'civil war' – the intense social divisions and the crisis of the American political system surrounding the war in Vietnam. *Josey Wales* thus situates itself at a generic intersection of the Western and the emergent genre of the Vietnam veteran film (*Tracks*, 1975; *Rolling Thunder*, 1976; *Taxi Driver*). Unlike both those films and *The Searchers*, however, *Josey Wales* affirms the possibility that the returning veteran need not compulsively act out the traumas of defeat in a society whose own ongoing violence is barely under control, but can move through and past violence into a renewed social contract – one, moreover, where the Western hero's masculinity is not diminished, though it is necessarily changed, by his incorporation into communal and personal relationships.

NOTES

1. Exhibitors were free to splice this image onto either the start or (more usually) the end of the film.
2. Figures of Western releases for the sound era are tabulated in Buscombe (1988: 425–7). For the silent period, see the *AFI Catalog of Motion Picture Produced in the United States: 1893–1910* (1995), *1911–1920* (1988), *1920–1930* (1971).
3. Poague's (2003) account of the marketing of *Stagecoach* cited in Chapter 1 is a good example.
4. '"We didn't want just another Western," [UA President Andy] Albeck agreed. "We wanted an epic, an Academy Award-winning epic"' (Bach, 1985: 217).
5. Note, however, that Gallagher makes the wildly hyperbolic claim that from 1909 to 1915 'there were probably more westerns released *each month* than during the entire decade of the 1930s': this would mean roughly 1,000 westerns a month, or 12,000 a year! I have found no figures to support such a grossly inflated reckoning.

6. Kitses' model is cited sufficiently often to be worth reproducing in part once again
   here:

THE WILDERNESS	*CIVILISATION*
The Individual	*The Community*
freedom	restriction
honour	institutions
self-knowledge	illusion
integrity	compromise
self-interest	social responsibility
solipsism	democracy
Nature	*Culture*

7. Namely, the 'classical plot' (e.g. *Shane*), the 'vengeance variation' (*The Naked Spur*), the
   'transition theme' (*High Noon*) and the 'professional plot' (*The Professionals*, 1966).
8. Defined as a population density of fewer than two persons per square mile.
9. Turner argued that with the loss of the social 'safety valve' of 'free land' American
   society in the twentieth century would finally have to confront the problems of all other
   modern industrial nations, including class antagonisms.

CHAPTER 4

The Musical: Genre and Form

A t the end of Mel Brooks's Western parody *Blazing Saddles* (1973), a sprawling bar-room brawl exceeds the boundaries not only of its diegetic situation (with bodies and furniture flying in standard Western style through windows and doors out into the street) but its generic location: a particularly powerful haymaker sends a cowboy tearing through the wall of the saloon set and – not into the adjoining room in the saloon, but into the next-door soundstage, where an elaborate musical production number somewhat in the regimented Busby Berkeley manner, 'the French Mistake', is being performed. As burly, unshaven cowboys, dudes and saloon girls tumble pell-mell into the gleaming polished proscenium to mingle with and assault the dancers, the stage is literally set for a riotous generic encounter. Brooks's stereotypically epicene dancers, campily fleeing across their never–never-land set from this sudden intrusion from a definitively 'masculine' generic universe and shrilly defending if not their honour then their looks ('Not in the face!' squeals one, faced with a knuckle sandwich; '... thank you!' he gasps as the attacker redirects his punch into his balls), reflect dominant perceptions of the musical as organised around tropes of narcissistic display and artificiality as opposed to the Western's rugged veracity. As ever, the parodic thrust cuts both ways: while the streamlined, pristine musical set bespeaks an 'artifice' in contrast to the rough, workmanlike surfaces of the Western, at the same time the latter's incorporation into the generic space of the musical both undermines the Westerner's monolithic masculinity and also reminds us that their ostensibly more 'historical' milieu is, as a construction of genre, in its way as stylised and out-of-time as that of the musical. In fact, the Western and the musical are two halves of a whole: the cowboy and the song-and-dance man together are strong and universal metonymic signifiers of Hollywood, and Hollywood genre, as a whole.

Ranging in structure from revue to integrated musical drama, in setting from Manhattan to medieval England, and in musical style from light opera to rock, the American musical is remarkably heterogeneous. From another perspective, however, the musical may be regarded as the 'purest' of all film genres. Unlike the Western or the gangster film, the musical seems unencumbered by any ongoing commitments to social realism, historical authenticity or for that matter any suggestion of performative naturalism (though the genre may embrace any or all of these at different times). The musical creates a hermetically enclosed generic world whose conventions and verisimilitudes are purely and peculiarly its own, and whose function is to enable and situate the musical performances that define the form.

Uniquely, the musical is named not for its subject matter (the Western, the war film, etc.) or even its effect upon the spectator (the horror film), but for its mode of performance. 'Music' in the film musical of course usually means singing, accompanied by inventive (not necessarily lush – several memorable musical numbers feature improvised accompaniment on 'found' objects) orchestration and above all dance. Although a great many non-musicals include songs (less often dance), sometimes as interpolated 'turns' but quite often as narratively integrated and even central elements (for example, *Casablanca* (1942) includes several musical performances at Rick's Café Americain; at least two of these, 'As Time Goes By' and the singing of the *Marsellaise* orchestrated by Victor Laszlo, are crucial to the story), dance and song offer the forms of visual pleasure that help define the musical. Much critical discussion of the musical has identified the construction of narrative opportunities for musical numbers as a focal point of the genre; this in turn has promoted analysis of the specific forms of expressivity promoted in the musical, and the ideological positions these open up or foreclose upon. For these reasons, compared to other genres the musical is unusually often treated in terms of its formal mechanisms and attributes. Sometimes – for example in discussion of the musicals created by Busby Berkeley at Warner Bros. in the 1930s – this entails the explicit subordination of the consideration of the specific narrative content of individual films, which may be dismissed as wholly stereotypical and superficial, merely an inert 'carrier' for the musical numbers. Conversely, the 'integrated' musical that renders musical performance an 'organic' extension and direct expression of issues within a character-driven narrative – pre-eminently the films made at MGM in the first decade after the Second World War by the production unit overseen by Arthur Freed – has often been regarded as the most fully achieved form of the genre and has drawn the largest body of critical discussion.

THE CLASSICAL MUSICAL

Self-evidently, the musical is a genre of the sound era: *The Jazz Singer* (1927), the first feature-length 'talkie', was also the first musical feature, and indeed the strong audience appeal of music and song as much as or more than spoken dialogue helped 'sell' sound technology not only to audiences but to sceptical exhibitors faced with the expenses of conversion. By 1930, as Hollywood converted to sound, more than 200 musicals had been released by the major and minor studios (see Altman, 1996: 294–7; Balio, 1993: 211–18). What the new sound technology enabled was the immediacy of direct address to the audience – as in Al Jolson's 'You ain't heard nothin' yet!' in *The Jazz Singer* – that would emerge as one of the genre's distinctive formal markers. Jolson's famous interpellation, like many subsequent examples, was mediated by the presence of a diegetic (on-screen) audience in a live performance setting: this establishes early on the film musical's adoption of live theatrical performance and the direct interaction with the audience as a performative ideal, invoked most clearly in the backstage musical – musicals about the staging of musicals or musical performances – but arguably a persistent structuring presence even in 'integrated' musicals where the performers sing and dance in purely expressive ways 'for' themselves or each other, without the self-conscious invocation of a performance situation. It is worth noting here that live musical accompaniment – including singing – was the norm throughout the silent era, and dancing was a featured attraction in a great many silent films. Unlikely as it may now seem, there were silent adaptations of both popular operettas like *The Merry Widow* (1925) and classical operas like *Carmen* (1915) and *Der Rosenkavalier*. Thus there is a certain historical irony that the vividness and 'immediacy' of the sound-era musical was achieved at the cost of an actual *de*realisation of the audio-visual experience of moving-going that found compensation in what Collins (1988: 270) describes as a 'sense of nostalgia for a direct relationship with the audience' that is a generic constant throughout the classical era.

As already noted, certain kinds of film musical have attracted much more critical discussion than others. Neale (2000: 108) notes the sparsity of critical discussion of the musicals produced at the other majors compared to MGM, let alone the minors. This selectivity extends also to formal variants. The musical comedy-revue, for example – comprising the majority of the early sound musicals between 1927 and 1930–31, revived by Paramount for its series of 1930s 'radio revues' starting with *The Big Broadcast* in 1932, and including patriotic wartime spectacles like *Star Spangled Rhythm* (1942) and *Stage Door Canteen* (1943) – has been largely overlooked by serious criticism (although the recent upsurge of interest in the silent 'cinema of attractions' and its legacy in the classical and post-classical era suggests that a reassessment of these largely non-integrated, 'attraction'-led entertainments may be due[1]). A much longer-lasting and in the 1930s very popular form, the operetta (for example, the films starring the duo of Nelson Eddy[2] and Jeanette MacDonald at MGM such as *Rose Marie*, 1936, *Sweethearts*, 1938, and *Bitter Sweet*, 1940) has also received very little attention as a cinematic form (there is a more extensive literature on the theatrical operetta that includes some discussion of film adaptations), although individual films have been analysed (see, for example, Altman's (1987: 16–22; also in Cohan, 2002: 41–5) analysis of the 'dual-focus' narrative of the MacDonald-Eddy vehicle *New Moon*, 1940; also Turk (1998)). Whereas the lack of interest in the revue may be attributed in part to its 'primitive' serial structure, this is clearly not the case with the operetta – among the most integrated of all forms of the musical. Rather, it may be the perception of the operetta as an ineradicably *bourgeois* form, 'theatrical' in the bad sense, that accounts for its critical disfavour. Not only its stilted romantic narratives but its nostalgic invocation of a pseudo-aristocratic Old World conflicts with the widespread perception of the Hollywood musical – pre-eminently, again, the Gene Kelly MGM series – as a distinctive expression of the (idealised) American national character: optimistic, unaffected, can-do and democratic (see especially Schatz, 1981: 196ff.). In fact, this perception of at least some film operettas was current in the 1930s: *Variety* described the French stage property on which Paramount based its MacDonald-Maurice Chevalier effort *Love Me Tonight* (1932) as 'alien to American ideas' (quoted in Balio, 1993: 214). (Recently, *Evita*, 1996, displays affinities with the operetta tradition.)

As with other classical genres, therefore, the critical canon of the classical musical betrays a significant degree of preferential treatment. Within that canon, for that matter, the distinction between the genre's key formal variants has decisively privileged the integrated musical – in which the musical numbers are woven into the narrative structure, motivated by character psychology and/or plot development and expressive of the emotions, opinions or state of mind of the singer(s) – over the non-integrated – in which numbers simply accumulate serially, and are effectively stand-alone spectacles connected only loosely, if at all, either to each other or to the narrative in which they are embedded. Apart from Busby Berkeley, who is treated as something of a special case, almost all of the most popular as well as the most widely discussed and critically favoured musicals – above all, the Astaire–Rogers series at RKO in the 1930s and the MGM Freed Unit/Kelly–Donen–Minnelli productions – have been integrated musicals. Solomon (1976, quoted in Neale, 2000: 107) states that 'there is no evident reason' for privileging integration in this way; but it is equally plain that the perception of a unified aesthetic totality fits a traditionalist critical agenda quite well. Whatever the reasons, since these structural distinctions have been of such importance in critical studies of the musical, it will be helpful to explore them in a little more detail.

The notion of 'integration' is not quite as straightforward as it might at first appear. Focusing on the Astaire-Rogers musicals, Mueller (1984: 28–9) offers six different possible relationships of musical number to plot, ranging from complete irrelevance, through 'enrichment' (a rather vague term we could also understand in terms of amplification or complement, for example 'Somewhere Over the Rainbow' in *The Wizard of Oz*, 1939), to those that clearly advance the plot. In the latter category he includes both songs like 'Getting to Know You' in *The King and I* (1956), whose lyrical content alerts the characters to new information or insights about one another, and the very different example of musical numbers in the backstage musical whose staging provides the narrative with its (ostensible) object. However, the inclusion of the backstage musical complicates this taxonomy by highlighting the perhaps counter-intuitive ways in which 'integration' here is not simply synonymous, as one might expect, with dramatic 'motivation' – that is, accounting for passages of expressive performance by providing narrative situations where the characters (rather than the performers) can plausibly sing and dance. Typically this is achieved by creating characters who are professional entertainers – which is where the backstage musical comes in, one of the genre's most durable forms from early classics like *42nd Street* (1933) and *Gold Diggers of 1933* (1933) to *Cabaret* (1972), *For the Boys* (1991) and rock musicals like *The Rose* (1979) and *Grace of My Heart* (1996).

The backstage musical is thus arguably the most highly 'motivated' of all forms of the musical: the characters perform only onstage or in rehearsal (or, as in the 'I Only Have Eyes For You' number in *Dames*, 1935, in dreams or their mind's eye) accompanied by diegetic orchestras or bands. However – and leaving aside for the time being the many ways in which Busby Berkeley's backstagers at least play fast and loose with the verisimilitude of their theatrical milieu – some 1930s backstagers also typify the non-integrated musical: that is, the on-stage performances have little or no dramatic relation to the romantic and professional conflicts played out in the backstage, non-musical portions of the film. Even in *42nd Street*, which famously pioneers one of the genre's hoariest clichés – an ingénue plucked from the chorus line sent out to understudy the injured star with the words 'You're going out a youngster – but you've *got* to come back a star!' – the chorus girl's inevitably triumphant performance is played with almost no suggestion of or for that matter interest in her emotional or psychological reaction to the experience during the performance itself. Rather, the visual pleasure of the musical numbers is virtually autonomous of the (usually) mundane progress of the backstage narrative. (A useful contrast here might be the many sequences in rock musicals such as *The Rose* or *The Doors*, 1991, modern variants on the backstage mode, where the performance itself cathartically works through, or alternatively is visibly wrecked by, the emotional, psychological or pharmaceutical crises of the performer-protagonist.) Later backstage musicals offered a much higher degree of integration, either through the inclusion of directly expressive numbers that are part of the protagonist's onstage routine (*A Star Is Born*, 1954; also the 1977 rock musical remake) or by using the musical numbers to offer ironic commentary on the characters' sexual, social or political attitudes (*Cabaret*).

In fact, the distinction of integrated and non-integrated forms is, predictably, not an absolute one. Very few musicals are wholly unintegrated after the fashion of theatrical variety shows: indeed, the backstage musical itself emerged as a response to the declining box-office appeal of the rush of revue-style musicals at the very start of the sound era (for example, *The Hollywood Revue of 1929*, 1929; *Paramount on Parade*, and *King of Jazz*, both 1930). After a brief ensuing lull in musical production *42nd Street* introduced the relatively more integrated form and its stock personae of the driven visionary director or impresario (a fixture up through *All That Jazz*, 1980), the naive ingénue who gets her big break in the circumstances outlined above, the wisecracking, worldly-wise chorus girls and the besotted millionaire who bankrolls the production. Conversely, some or all of the musical numbers in even the most integrated musicals are to some degree 'excessive' in relation to their basic narrative function – inevitably, one might say, given the genre's basic contract with its audience, which is not storytelling as such but delivering memorable songs and/or pyrotechnical dance performances. *An American in Paris* (1951) 'smuggles' many of its musical numbers into the film by presenting them as feats of exuberant improvisation in workaday environments like cafés and city streets, performed for an 'audience' of passersby who participate with casual enthusiasm rather than the regimented high-kicking of the professional chorus line (the film also includes by way of pointed contrast, and as a clear example of performative inauthenticity, a brief excerpt from a stage performance in the grand manner, complete with feather boas and an illuminated staircase – a grandiose version of the famous Astaire/Rogers 'Big White Set'). However, *An American in Paris* also famously concludes with a lengthy rhapsodic ballet sequence with a strongly non-integrative drive (like the comparable climactic sequences in other Freed Unit musicals such as *On the Town*, 1949, and *Singin' in the Rain*, 1952, it essentially recapitulates the main narrative in stylised, archetypal form) whose function is to deliver the postponed, but not denied, pleasures of breathtaking visual display in the form of both virtuosic dancing and elaborate sets. Rubin (1993: 12–13) argues that the history of the musical is 'not so much a relentless, unidirectional drive towards effacing the last stubborn remnants of nonintegration, but a succession of different ways of articulating the tension and interplay between integrative (chiefly narrative) and nonintegrative (chiefly spectacle) elements'.

Thus the apparent opposition of integration and aggregation is in fact an oscillating and interdependent relationship, and in this regard rehearses the larger issue of the dialectical interplay in the 'classical Hollywood style' between narrative – to whose linear, centring imperatives all the elements of Hollywood cinema in the continuity era are, according to Bordwell, Staiger and Thompson's (1985) influential account, ultimately subordinated – and the contrapuntal force of spectacle, conceived as largely static and in narrative terms non-developmental. (This highlights the interesting point that at least at this structural level there are therefore marked affinities between the musical, stereotypically a 'feminine' genre, and the emphatically masculine genre of the contemporary action film: for more on this and a more detailed discussion of the question of narrative and spectacle, see Chapter 10.)

In any case, a third term may have to be added to the integration/non-integration dyad if one is to give an adequate account of the most remarkable variant of the musical to emerge in the 1930s, the cycle of Warner Bros. films directed and/or choreographed by Busby Berkeley. These – strictly speaking, their spectacular musical numbers – have provoked extensive critical discussion for their transformative objectifications of the human (typically female) form – what Fischer ([1976] 1981) calls their 'optical politics' ('Pettin' in the Park' in *Gold Diggers of 1933* features dancers in lingerie and in nude silhouette); their similarities to various European avant-garde cinemas of the period (Arthur Freed remarked on Berkeley's 'instinctive surrealism'); and even their affinities with the 'fascist aesthetics' of Leni Riefenstahl's films of mass ceremonials in Nazi Germany (see Sontag, 1966). Sequences such as the 'Hymn to My Forgotten Man' in *Gold Diggers of 1933*, which introduce narrative and in this case social content (the descent of the First World War veterans into poverty and despair) quite unprepared for by and unrelated to the backstage story, typify Berkeley's non-integrative mode. Equally remarkable, however, is their elastic treatment of diegetic space, which has no ready parallel in any other classical Hollywood form and which might well be characterised as 'disintegrative'. All of the musical numbers in a Berkeley musical ostensibly form part of a theatrical performance, preparations for which constitute the binding backstage narrative. However, in visual style and technique as well as sheer scale Berkeley's numbers explode far beyond the confines of any plausible theatrical show or for that matter auditorium. The stupefying scale and variety of these numbers renders them 'blatantly and audaciously impossible in terms of the theatrical space in which they are supposedly taking place' (Rubin, 1993: 58). Berkeley's approach is typified by his signature ultra-high-angle overhead shots – the 'Berkeley top shot' – where massed ranks of dancers form shifting complex patterns ranging from flowers and abstract shapes to actors' faces (as in *Dames*), his most famous and widely copied device (also the most parodied, for example in *The Producers*, 1968, where a chorus line of goose-stepping SS arrange themselves into a swastika): the camera's vantage point which renders these visionary biomporhic transfigurations visible to the cinema audience would simply be unavailable to any conceivable theatrical audience.

Berkeley's work remained unique; a wholly different, and in the long term more influential, approach was adopted in the series of nine RKO musical romantic comedies starring Fred Astaire and Ginger Rogers (with choreography by Hermès Pan) in the 1930s starting with *Flying Down to Rio* (1933). Whereas Berkeley was notoriously unconcerned about his dancers' abilities, interested rather in achieving an appropriate blend of uniformity and complementary contrast in physique and physiognomy (see Fischer, [1976] 1981: 74), Astaire and Rogers' own performative gifts and the promise of pyrotechnical dancing displays constituted the major appeal of these star vehicles. Even the musical leads amid Berkeley's serried armies of dancers were such pleasant but uninteresting figures as Ruby Keeler and Dick Powell (with the dramatic momentum in the backstage scenes maintained by forceful non-dancing male stars like Warner Baxter in *42nd Street* and James Cagney in *Footlight Parade*, 1933); Astaire and Rogers were at the undisputed centre of their films, featuring in numerous duets (Astaire also has many solo numbers), and even in the larger-scale production numbers the chorus line or background dancers remain anonymous and strictly secondary. This relationship is emphatically symbolised in a famous number in *Top Hat* (1935), perhaps the best-known Astaire-Rogers production, when Astaire transforms his cane during 'Top Hat, White Tie, and Tails' into a tommy-gun with which he mows down his top-hatted 'rivals' in the chorus line, a routine that Edward Gallafent (2000: 35) among others has characterised as an assertion of both 'phallic potency and … (Astaire's) standing as a massively successful professional'.

The Astaire–Rogers musicals decisively shifted the musical away from mass spectacle to individual expressivity and the exploration of the conditions of and constraints on that expressive drive. These would become the key concerns of the classically integrated MGM musicals of the late 1940s and early 1950s, a period that continues to dominate critical discussions of the musical. Since the case study for this chapter looks closely at one such MGM musical, *Singin' in the Rain* (1952), the following section focuses less on textual detail and looks at the relationship of the musical's characteristic forms to ideological structures.

'GOTTA DANCE'

The most obvious formal element that sets the musical apart from the great majority of other American films is its radical departure from the forms of realism that dominate the rest of classic Hollywood practice. As limited (compared to, say, Italian neorealism or British 'kitchen sink' social realism) and stylised as this Hollywood brand of 'realism' certainly is, the musical is nonetheless quite clearly 'unrealistic' in still more marked and fundamental ways. Rubin (1993: 57) suggests that the classic musical may even be defined by its inclusion of 'a significant proportion of musical numbers that are impossible – i.e., persistently contradictory in relation to the realistic discourse of the narrative'. The most obvious and manifold examples of these impossibilities are the ostensibly spontaneous yet often hugely elaborate, flawlessly conceived and executed song-and-dance routines that typify the Hollywood musical, particularly in the classically integrated versions that, as we have seen, are often regarded as defining the form. This quality of impossibility is not determined by the regime of verisimilitude specific to a given narrative: whether a musical is as avowedly and visibly fanciful as *Yolanda and the Thief* (1945) or as social realist as *West Side Story* (1961), the transdiegetic quality of its musical numbers is a constant. Interestingly, it is the integrated musical of which this is truest. For whereas the impossibility of (most) Busby Berkeley numbers consists not in their spontaneous effusion – they are in fact presented as painstakingly rehearsed theatrical performances by professional entertainers – but, as we have seen, in their defiance of principles of spatial and temporal continuity and integrity, the impossibility of the numbers in (most) integrated musicals involves the apparently unconscious, or at any rate unselfconscious, discovery of music and movement by the characters as a perfect externalisation and expression of inner states of mind. In other words, the integrated musical emphasises the *expressive transformation* of the object world at the expense of conventionally understood forms of realism; and its impossibility involves both the ostensibly spontaneous perfection of the expressive form, and the plasticity of a world (the places and people in it) that consents to be taken over for, or actually to participate in, such expressive transformations.

This aspect of the musical has been influentially interpreted by Richard Dyer ([1977] 1981; also in Cohan, 2002) as lending the genre a utopian dimension: this utopianism consists less in the literal fabrication of ideal on-screen worlds, although this may sometimes happen – for example in the magical make-believe realms of *Brigadoon* (1954) or *Xanadu* (1980) – nor even, primarily, in the emphasis on reconciliation and the creation of the romantic couple (most classic Hollywood genres, after all, would be utopian in this sense). Rather, according to Dyer the musical shows us what utopia would

feel like: the reconciliation not simply of individual characters (like the sparring couples serially impersonated by Astaire and Rogers) or even of communities (like the crowds of Parisian children and street vendors who
applaud and flow around, in and out of Jerry's (Gene Kelly) improvisational
dances in *An American in Paris*), but of space, style and expressive form. It is
a quite literally harmonious experience, charged in Dyer's account with
energies of intensity, transparency, abundance and community.

Of course, this utopian dimension in the musical is firmly located within
its own social and historical coordinates, and critics have been quick to note
the clear limits on its transformative aspirations. Dyer himself notes that the
very suggestion that free expressivity is possible in a society actually closely
constrained by social and economic barriers can be seen as an ideological
fantasy, while inasmuch as the musical numbers promote hegemonic values
that confirm, rather than challenge, those of the narrative (romantic and
professional fulfilment and consensual social values) they also promote ideological homogeneity. (More recently, Dyer (2000) has noted that the privilege
of joyous self-expression in the classic musical is policed along racial lines –
it is a privilege enjoyed only by whites, never by performers of colour.)

Nonetheless, even raising the possibility of finding a utopian dimension in
a central Hollywood genre powerfully challenges some abiding assumptions
about 'industrially produced' commercial popular culture. Notably, the Frankfurt School writers Theodor Adorno and Max Horkheimer, in their critique
of the 'culture industry' (Adorno and Horkheimer, [1944] 1972), reserved
particular scorn for popular musical forms like Tin Pan Alley and big-band
jazz, regarding their crudely pentatonic rhythms as regressive and repressive
in equal measure and their lyrics as asinine doggerel. For Adorno (who had
studied with the pioneering atonal composer Arnold Schoenberg before
turning to philosophical aesthetics and political economy), the romantic escapism
of popular music typified the duplicity of mass culture: appearing to promise
freedom from the drudgery of late capitalism, mass-produced popular music
was part of the very structures from which it falsely proposed relief. It was
quintessentially part of the problem, not part of the solution. Adorno would
have greeted with incredulity the critical favour attracted to the integrated
musical in particular, and would have been contemptuous of claims that its
sophisticated interplay of performative expression and dramatic and/or
comedic complexity makes it something like the Wagnerian concept of the
Gesamtkunstwerk – the 'total work of art'. Rather, he would doubtless seize
upon those moments when musical performers, in the preamble to a number,
admit to experiencing almost a physical compulsion to dance – for example,
Astaire's lead-in to 'No Strings' in *Top Hat*, or Kelly's incantatory 'Gotta
Dance!' at the start of the 'Broadway Rhythm' ballet in *Singin' in the Rain* –
as unintended textual confessions of the musical's inherently coercive nature.

From *Singin' in the Rain* (1952). Reproduced courtesy MGM/The Kobal Collection.

   Adorno put what little faith he retained in art's emancipatory capacity in a few avant-garde forms (Schoenberg's music, Beckett's theatre of privation) which retained a massively attenuated utopian aspect – not, like the musical, in their abundance and promises of freedom, promises Adorno regarded as lies, but precisely in their formal difficulty, their denial of easy pleasure or for that matter access to the mass audience. Only by saying 'no' to the universal 'yes' of the culture industry, Adorno argued, could art hold out any image, be it merely a negative one, of a world geared to a different order of human social relations than the one that actually exists. Adorno's commitment to this 'autonomous' art, which is perhaps more justly criticised for its rigidity and generality than, as it has often been, for its elitism, clearly and specifically excludes such mainstream genre forms as the musical.

However, since musicals, as we have seen, operate according to generic verisimilitudes that differ in some fundamental ways from Hollywood's dominant quasi-realist regime of representation, it is at least possible that this formal differentiation affords them a correspondingly greater freedom to explore dimensions of human social experience closed off to more conventional forms. Dyer's construction of the musical as at least potentially an ideologically progressive form opens up the possibility that musicals may have offered a space, however limited, for the articulation of subjectivities otherwise marginalised by classic Hollywood conventions. Given the musical's clear emphasis on the personal and experiential (rather than, say, historical or political) and also – through the centrality of performance – the bodily, it might make sense to see whether there is a greater dimensionality than the Hollywood norm in the genre's treatment of gender and sexuality. Indeed, these have been important areas for contemporary research on the musical.

As previously noted, Fischer ((1976) 1981: 75), in line with Laura Mulvey's (1975) contemporaneous conclusions concerning visual pleasure and gendered spectatorship, argues that Berkeley's mass spectacles effectively reified the female form – 'a vision of female stereotypes in their purest, most distillable form' – and nullified any suggestion of active female agency in the backstage narrative (see also Rabinowitz, 1982; Mellencamp, 1990). More recent writers, influenced by Joan Rivière's theorisation of female masquerade, Judith Butler's work on gender performativity and other queer theorists, have suggested that the camp excess in Berkeley's work may in fact invert these very techniques of objectification, throwing into relief the typically invisible ways in which female identity is constructed through, but not necessarily for, a male spectatorship (see Robertson, [1996] 2002). Similar theoretical positions have worked to reconceive the musical's relationship to masculinity and male sexuality. The traditional class terms in which the contrast of Astaire's urbane *haute bourgeois* elegance with Gene Kelly's muscular blue-collar physicality has been conceived, for example, is reassessed in terms of complementary models of masculinity: Cohan ([1993] 2002: 88) notes Astaire's exploitation of 'the so-called "feminine" tropes of narcissism, exhibitionism, and masquerade', while both he and Dyer ([1986] 2002: 111–12) remark on the contradictions of the more conventionally 'virile' Kelly's construction of his own body as spectacle in *The Pirate* (1948) and other MGM musicals.

Then there is the matter of the politics of the musical text itself. Jane Feuer ([1977] 1981) notes the ways in which the late Astaire and MGM musicals in particular both de- and remystify the act of performance itself through a dialectic of reflexivity that works to promote the illusion of the film musical as a spontaneous, 'live' performance. In many ways, 'art musicals' like those of the Freed Unit perform many of the formal moves associated with the avant-garde and hence with resistant or oppositional art forms (art that articulates a challenge to hegemonic values through its subversion or abandonment of the formal conventions bound up with the maintenance of that hegemony, for example the films of Jean-Luc Godard): the standard narrative device of 'putting on a show' reflexively addresses the text's own production; direct address through the conventional 'fourth wall' is also frequently found in musicals – for example, Gene Kelly's announcement (direct to camera, in sudden tight close-up) that 'the best is yet to come!' as the lead-in to the climactic number in *The Pirate*, and the oscillation between 'ordinary Joe' character and star performer that occurs across the 'impossible' transitions from narrative to number and back again draws our attention to the gap between the musical's idealised world of personal fulfilment and our own more constrained reality.

We will look in more detail at how this works in the analysis of *Singin' in the Rain* below. However, the key paradox Feuer identifies is that, all these reflexive modernist touches notwithstanding, the musical is of course not a radical form – it remained rather for many years securely at the epicentre of Hollywood's profitable enterprise. Critics have therefore addressed themselves less to 'claiming' the musical for a hitherto unsuspected radicalism than to exploring, first, the fissiparous and potentially multivalent qualities of what the Frankfurt School perceived as the mass-culture monolith, and second and conversely, the ways in which unconventional formal devices previously unproblematically associated with radical intent may in fact be domesticated and accommodated to hegemonic systems by context. Thus Feuer notes that while MGM musicals appear to lay bare the mechanisms of their own production as commercial entertainment, at the same time they typically end up reaffirming 'myths' of spontaneity, integration and immediacy. Very similar questions have been considered in relation to music video by Kaplan (1986) and Goodwin (1993), who recognise the extent to which any number of formal devices previously confined to experimental and art film are taken over and exploited without difficulty in the supremely commodified world of the promo. The value of such debates is their recognition of the need for film studies to move away from a formalist essentialism that attributes specific political valences to formal practices outside of their actual contexts of production and consumption.

THE MUSICAL IN POST-CLASSICAL HOLLYWOOD

More than any other genre – even the Western, news of whose demise, as we have seen, has been considerably exaggerated – the fortunes of the classical musical deteriorated dramatically with the waning of the classical Hollywood style and the transformation of the American film industry from the 1950s onwards. While for most historians of the musical the early to mid-1950s marked the musical's creative as well as commercial peak, above all in the Freed Unit musicals at MGM (see above), this vitality did not persist beyond the end of the decade. It was 1957 which saw the effective culmination of the musical careers of both Astaire (*Silk Stockings*, 1957) and Kelly (*It's Always Fair Weather*, 1955, was Kelly's final film as star/choreographer and *Les Girls* his last starring musical role, though he would continue directing musicals and making cameo appearances as a dancer into the 1980s). This is not to say that musicals did not continue to enjoy considerable popularity into the early 1960s. Musicals' scale and spectacle made them a key element in the studios' battle with low-resolution, monochrome television, while their apparently reliable appeal across a wide range of audiences made them an attractive investment in an era characterised by audience fragmentation and justified increasingly large budgets and roadshow (limited run, reserved seating) engagements. Blockbusters like *South Pacific* (1958), *The Music Man* (1962) and *My Fair Lady* (1964) were indeed major successes – as was *West Side Story*, which in addition won several Oscars including Best Picture and Best Director. However, as these examples – all adaptations of Broadway hits – would suggest, Hollywood was increasingly reliant on the 'pre-sold' cachet of stage success for its properties and decreasingly successful in generating popular original musicals itself (on 1960s musicals, see Mordden, 1982).

A much greater problem in the longer run was the growing disjunction of the classical musical's formal and thematic direction and both the world and the industry of which it remained a part. The musical's high-gloss, studio-bound aesthetic was almost diametrically opposed to the low-key, location-shot naturalism favoured by a new generation of feature film directors emerging from television in the early 1960s, such as Sidney Lumet, Martin Ritt and John Frankenheimer. Similarly, the musical's increasing escapism, typified by the trend for exotic, picturesque settings distanced either in time, place or both was at odds with the fashion for contemporary urban subjects – for example *Marty* (1955), *Sweet Smell of Success* (1958), *The Hustler* (1961) – and a greater measure of engagement with difficult social and political realities such as racism, poverty, Cold War tensions and disaffected youth, all of which had started to crystallise as pressing public preoccupations with the dynamic John F. Kennedy's election as President in 1960. *West Side Story*'s transposition of Romeo and Juliet to gang warfare in New York's white and

Hispanic slums, shot partly on location in the Bronx, was an exception that proved difficult to emulate. Thus as the decade wore on the musical became increasingly the province of classical-era directors such as George Cukor (*My Fair Lady*), themselves approaching the end of their careers, and visibly creaky both in form and content.

None of this of course mattered to the studios as long as the musical remained commercially viable, and the enormous success of Disney's part-animated Victorian fantasy *Mary Poppins* (1964) and Fox's *The Sound of Music* (1965) which rapidly overtook *Gone With the Wind* to become the all-time box-office champion, seemed to prove the genre's durable appeal. However, *The Sound of Music* proved not the harbinger of a new era for the classical musical, but its swansong. In the wake of the film's commercial and critical success – *The Sound of Music* emulated *West Side Story*, also directed by Robert Wise, in winning Best Picture and Director Oscars – the major studios plunged into a series of enormously expensive attempts at repeating the trick, including *Doctor Dolittle* (1967), *Thoroughly Modern Millie* (1967), *Star!* (1968), *Goodbye, Mr Chips* (1969), *Song of Norway* (1970), *On a Clear Day You Can See Forever* (1970, directed by Vincente Minnelli) and *Hello, Dolly* (1970, directed by Gene Kelly). All of these were large-scale flops and contributed significantly to the near-ruinous financial situation in which the majors found themselves at the turn of the 1970s. Perhaps the most obvious of these productions' failings in conception and execution was their common assumption – encouraged by *The Sound of Music*'s success – of a now-chimerical family audience, classic Hollywood's default setting, but in the age of *Bonnie and Clyde*, *The Graduate* and *The Dirty Dozen* (all 1967) neither easily reached nor, as it increasingly proved, necessary for a film's profitability. The surprise success of *Easy Rider* (1969) seemed to confirm the commercial viability of the youth market; importantly, moreover, although music and songs featured prominently in both *Easy Rider* and *The Graduate* in the form of a contemporary pop and rock soundtrack, these pointed up thematic and narrative developments in a new way that differed both from the standard 'through-scoring' of the classical Hollywood soundtrack and from the set-piece song-and-dance numbers of the classical musical.

For the younger generation of film-makers emerging from television and film school by the late 1960s – the so-called 'movie brats' – the musical was like the Western, an object both of admiring study and critical enquiry, and they approached both genres in a generally ironic, parodic and satirical spirit. Rare attempts at 'straight' musicals by New Hollywood directors like Francis Ford Coppola (*Finian's Rainbow*, 1967, starring Astaire) and Peter Bogdan-ovich (*At Long Last Love*, 1975, sufficiently disastrous almost to qualify as a 'lost' film) were unqualified failures. Undoubtedly the most important and ambitious New Hollywood 'musical' – though on its original release, in a drastically shortened edit, the film found favour with neither critics nor audiences – was Martin Scorsese's *New York, New York* (1977), of all his films the most intensely intertextual as well as self-referential, and in effect a complex thesis on both the utopian appeal and the ineluctable disenchantment of classic Hollywood forms, enacted through a deconstructive performance of Hollywood's most potently alluring genre. A quintessential example of what Noel Carroll (1982) terms the 'cinema of allusion', *New York, New York* includes numerous references, direct and indirect, to the Technicolor musicals of the genre's postwar peak, including those of Kelly and Minnelli, and closely models its narrative after the somewhat obscure 1947 melodrama *The Man I Love* – although to most audiences its story of the marital and professional conflicts of two musicians will more readily recall the 1954 version of *A Star Is Born* (see Grist, 2000: 167f.). Casting Judy Garland's daughter Liza Minnelli in the lead role of Francine Evans (opposite Robert De Niro as saxophonist Jimmy Doyle) highlights this debt of influence. *New York, New York* subverts the musical's optimistic romantic master narrative by juxtaposing a stylised period narrative, filmed in the saturated colours of the postwar period, with De Niro's improvisational performative style and neurotically contemporary persona. The film's critical take on the musical – which might be summed up as 'the myths don't work' – can be compared to the contemporary revisionist Westerns (discussed in Chapter 2), though without those films' clear political dimension or topicality.

In *New York, New York*, the musical's (literally) harmonious imaginary, quickly established in Jimmy's personal mythology of the 'major chord' – 'when you have the woman you want, the music you want, and enough money to get by' – is exposed as unattainable. Early on in the film, Jimmy watches a sailor and his girl dance alone, silently, illuminated by the lights of a passing elevated train. The couple are a direct and unmistakable allusion to *On the Town*, in whose most famous number – which lends *New York, New York* its title – real Manhattan locations were used as the spectacular backdrop for the three sailors' exuberant, transformative celebration of self. Here, by contrast, as elsewhere in *New York, New York*, we are ostentatiously and anachronistically on a studio set, its theatricality highlighted by the stylised play of moving light and shadow and Jimmy's position, low in the frame with his back to camera but looking down on the dancers as if from the front row of the circle. The formal distanciation of the setting as well as the absence of music – as if the dancers, who move with the precision and grace of their golden age forbears, are moving to a prerecorded score in their own heads – emphasises the artificiality of the classical musical 'number'. At the same time, the vignette (which is wholly narratively redundant) is limpidly beautiful, evocative and oddly melancholy – as the dancers skip away into the darkness around the featureless urban space they have briefly made their stage, they carry with them a yearning desire for the simpler pleasures of the classical musical. That such pleasures are no longer available is, however, confirmed by Jimmy's response, or rather lack of it – annoyed at being excluded from his hotel room so his friend Eddie can try (unsuccessfully) to coax his pick-up into bed, he watches the dancers silently and moves on, showing no emotion or even any particular interest.

Impelled by the conventions of the genre and the attractions of the two stars, we may wish to believe that sax-player Jimmy and singer Francine belong together; they may even for a time believe it themselves. But as the film unforgivingly unfolds the realities of a dysfunctional and abusive relationship we become increasingly aware that it is convention alone that keeps the pair together when they would be – and indeed, once separated, are – far better apart. *New York, New York* climaxes with 'Happy Endings', an extended film-within-the-film-within-the-film 'starring' Francine as a theatre usherette ('Peggy Smith') who dreams of becoming a star. Predictably, a chance encounter propels Peggy to stardom, heartbreak and ultimate redemption – only, in a dizzying *mise-en-abîme*, for her to realise, first, that it has all been a dream, and second, for her dream to actualise itself in the 'reality' of 'Happy Endings'. Shot in the stylised, oneiric mode of Kelly's climactic extended ballets in *On the Town*, *An American in Paris*, and *Singin' in the Rain*, like those sequences 'Happy Endings' (excised from the original release print of *New York, New York*) echoes the narrative in which it is embedded. Unlike them, however, it acts not as a utopian fusion of desire, music and movement but as an ironic commentary on the unsustainability of such desires as well as on the form – the musical – in which such hopes are fostered. The large-scale production numbers that climax the sequence (including Francine/Peggy heading a chorus line of usherettes against a backdrop of giant popcorn cartons) are self-consciously absurd. Moreover, in an echo of the earlier scene by the El, we view the entire sequence through Jimmy's unimpressed eyes. In the film's uneasy gender politics, although Francine is depicted sympathetically, Jimmy is clearly portrayed as both the more dynamic (often violent) and realistic of the couple, and Francine/Peggy's yearning immersion in the seductive fallacies of the silver screen recalls the frequent attribution by mass culture critics of such stereotypically 'female' qualities as passivity and suggestibility to the 'dupes' of the culture industries.[3] When Jimmy dismisses Francine's hit film as '*sappy* endings', she significantly has no answer.

Jimmy, a figure of 'street' realism who rejects the musical's palliative myths, stands in a sense for the 1970s audience, assumed to be intolerant of the classical musical's optimism and romanticism along with its defining stylistic characteristics.[4] Contemporary musicals, as Telotte (2002) notes, have had to find various ways to deal with modern audiences' apparent reluctance to countenance the staple and distinctive gesture of the classical integrated musical, the moment when a character breaks from speech into song. Attempts have periodically been made to revive this traditional form of the live-action musical, with some success in the late 1970s, for example *Grease*, *The Wiz* (both 1978) and *Hair* (1979): perhaps significantly, all nostalgia films that also adopted softened and homogenised forms of rock music in place of Tin Pan Alley standards. Since the 1980s, however, traditional integrated musicals have largely failed to find an audience (*Newsies*, 1992; *I'll Do Anything*; 1994, *Evita*). The few exceptions to this rule have tended to rely heavily on camp and knowing irony (*The Rocky Horror Picture Show*, 1975; *Little Shop of Horrors*, 1986; *Moulin Rouge*, 2001) or *faux-naif* nostalgia (*Everybody Says I Love You*, 1996). The surprise success of *Chicago* (2002) relied on numerous tactical accommodations of contemporary audience preferences, notably establishing heterogeneous discursive spaces – one broadly naturalistic, the other essentially a straightforward recording of the original stage show – for narrative and numbers in which the latter reiterated and ironically expanded on the former. *Chicago* also relies on a technique pioneered in *Flashdance* (1983) and *Footloose* (1984), in that its musical numbers largely (and necessarily, given its principals' strictly limited abilities as crooners and hoofers) deny the audience the traditional genre pleasure of seeing skilled performers undertake complex and technically demanding routines, filmed in long full-figure takes; the film instead relies on MTV-style fast cutting and regimented team dancing in the style pioneered by Paul Abdul as choreographer for Janet Jackson and others in the early 1990s (see Dodds, 2001: 49–56).

Alongside this apparently irreversible decline in its traditional live-action form, however, the classic musical has strikingly re-emerged in the animated feature. Disney, the traditional leader in the field, having diversified into adult features earlier in the decade, successfully relaunched its reinvigorated animation division in 1989 with *The Little Mermaid*, subsequently re-establishing the animated musical as the centrepiece of its annual release schedules and enjoying major hits with *Beauty and the Beast* (1991), *Aladdin* (1992), *The Lion King* (1994) and *The Hunchback of Notre Dame* (1996).

BEYOND HOLLYWOOD

Making music and song is as universal a human impulse as one can imagine, and every national cinema without exception has developed its own forms of musical film. Few of these, however, are well-known to audiences beyond those national borders, and almost every English-language study of non-Hollywood musicals opens with a reference to the near-universal identification of the film musical with its American form, both in the popular imagination and in historical criticism. Furthermore, one problem studies of film musical traditions repeatedly encounter is determining the extent to which the Hollywood musical established standards, generic norms or, for that matter, conventions from which indigenous musicals can consciously distinguish themselves.

Probably the best-known non-Hollywood and non-English language musical form is the Hindi film. With its high levels of output, range of production values from blockbuster to bargain-basement, strong generic traditions (far more rigidly conventionalised and policed, in fact, than any Hollywood genre) and industrialised production system, 'Bollywood' offers numerous points of suggestive comparison with the classic Hollywood musical. One obvious and major difference is that the great majority of Hindi films feature musical (vocal and dance) performances, and to a viewer accustomed to the integrated musical in particular the transitions from serious dramatic content to upbeat and diegetically heterogeneous musical number is bound to seem jarring. In fact, the conventions of musical integration in Hindi cinema are fundamentally different, operating not at the sub-generic level (i.e. the distinction between the Berkeley and Freed musical) but in a trans-generic manner: musical performance is an accepted dramatic convention in a discourse which operates according to different regimes of verisimilitude and concepts of realism than the Hollywood or European model. Thus whereas to a Western viewer the Hindi musical might be conceived as a single if expansive 'musical' genre, in opposition to the social realist cinema of Rhitvak Ghatak or the international art cinema of Satyajit Ray (Binford, 1987), to Hindi audiences powerful generic distinctions operate *within* a set of representational conventions that operate in parallel to the equally conventionalised and invisible 'realist' ground of Western cinema. Pendakur (2003: 119–144) suggests that both the musical (with decreasing reliance on traditional instruments and tonalities) and visual styles of musical performance in contemporary Hindi cinema show the impact of urbanisation and westernisation in Indian society as a whole.

Folkloric traditions, a marked feature of Hindi cinema, also figure in other national musical cinemas and mark a significant point of difference from the Hollywood model. Hopewell (1986: 48) describes the folkloric musical as 'the big genre' in Francoist Spain during the 1950s, while Bergfelder (2000: 81–3) stresses the importance of folk song to the postwar German *Heimatfilm* ('Homeland films'). In both cases, it appears that the inclusion of distinctive native musical traditions in film musicals expressed powerful ideological drives towards the re-establishment of cohesive national identities in societies fractured by major historical traumas.

CASE STUDY: *SINGIN' IN THE RAIN* (1952)

Singin' in the Rain is generally regarded as the apotheosis of the integrated musical: indeed, it has no real rival as the most popular and highly regarded of all musicals, making the BFI's Top Ten in its most recent polls of all-time greatest films (the only musical to do so). Gene Kelly, who starred in and co-directed the film (with Stanley Donen) himself regarded it as his most successful achievement, and more than any other film it embodies the spirit and character of the musicals produced by the Freed Unit at MGM between 1939 and 1959. Not only does *Singin' in the Rain* typify the domesticated modernism that Feuer ([1977] 1981) sees as characterising the Hollywood musical, but with its numerous intertextual glances and allusions, the film amply makes the point that reflexive parody/pastiche as generic functions are by no means limited to the post-classical New Wave of the 1970s, but can smoothly be incorporated into a film that is often seen as a virtual emblem of classic Hollywood. Moreover, as Cuomo (1996) argues, *Singin' in the Rain* extends the musical's characteristic reflexivity into a reflection on the genre as a whole at a key stage in its evolution – one might even say it reflects on genre in general. *Singin' in the Rain* after all tells the story of an actor who is compelled by technological and industrial changes (the conversion to sound) to change his star and generic personae.

Singin' in the Rain may not be a critical modernist text, but it remains clearly a modernist – rather than a postmodern – film: indeed, it illustrates the differences between the two quite clearly. While many of its traits – intertextuality, reflexivity, nostalgia (the film is set in 1928 Hollywood during the conversion to sound) – are confusingly associated with both modernist and postmodern forms, in *Singin' in the Rain* these are all located in relation to a discourse of (re-)integration that marks out an essential difference between the modernist text and the postmodern celebration of untrammelled heterogeneity, difference and fragmentation.

Integration, in fact, may be seen as at once the narrative and thematic focus and the performative mode of *Singin' in the Rain*. In narrative terms, integration is crucial in terms of the illicit disassociation/disintegration of voice and image that occurs when Lina Lamont appropriates as her own the vocal talents Kathy has 'lent' her for *The Dancing Cavalier*. The goal of the narrative thus becomes the reintegration of voice/speech and body (finally achieved through Cosmo's exposure of Lina at the film's premiere). Peter Wollen (1992: 55f.) relates this aspect of the film to Jacques Derrida's thesis of the organising 'logocentrism' of western culture in which speech, its authenticity vouchsafed by the singularity and integrity of the speaking body, is privileged over writing, whose transmissibility and multivalence makes it potentially untrustworthy. It is suggestive in this regard that the film closes with Don and Kathy regarding a billboard advertising their new star vehicle, 'Singin' in the Rain', 'a clinching self-citation' (Stam, 1992: 93) through which, as Steven Cohan (2000: 57) puts it, 'the film and its diegesis mesh ... perfectly'. The unity of the romantic couple is associated with the restoration of Kathy's voice and her belated recognition as a musical star in her own right: this climactic and celebratory accumulation of successful integrations effectively overwhelms our awareness of film's necessary mediation (*as* film) of performance and accomplishes the same nostalgic invocation of immediacy as the backstage musical. Thus *Singin' in the Rain* justifies Feuer's ([1977] 1981: 161) claim that the Freed Unit musicals 'used the backstage format to present sustained reflections upon, and affirmations of, the musical genre itself'. The film promotes a distinction of image and inner reality in the on-going conviction that behind and beneath the mask of the former it remains both possible and ethically vital to encounter the latter. However, this straightforward appearance/reality dialectic is complicated in *Singin' in the Rain* because the reintegration of (personal, private) self and (professional, public) style is accomplished not, as in integrated backstage musicals like *The Band Wagon*, through the representation of live and unmediated (i.e. theatrical) performance but in relation to the 'second-order' reality of film itself.

Don and Kathy's duet 'You Were Meant For Me', set on an empty sound stage, epitomises the film's playful engagement with these multiple contra-dictions. As has been widely noted, the number at once acknowledges and disavows the artifice of the musical: acknowledges it, by establishing Kathy's idealised image as a function of the technology Don arranges around her to produce it – coloured gels, a wind machine, a spotlight – yet disavows it, by excluding these tools of illusion from the frame once the song begins and playing 'straight' the resulting classically idealised image of the romantic couple. In this regard, the number revises and updates for the medium of film what Feuer characterises as the 'let's-put-on-a-show!' myth in the musical, where the artifice of musical performance is registered by making the principal characters professional performers, but cancelled by represent-ing their (successful) performances as originating in their own vigour and native enthusiasm. Musical numbers in the musical promote 'the mode of expression of the musical itself as spontaneous and natural rather than cal-culated and technological' (Feuer, [1977] 1981: 165). (In the case of *Singin' in the Rain*, the visible artifice of 'You Were Meant For Me' contrasts interestingly with the unacknowledged use of similar technologies – in fact, aeroplane engines – to create the draught that billows up Cyd Charisse's scarf in the 'Broadway Rhythm' ballet.) Since film performance by its nature never encounters its audience 'live', Don and Kathy's duet that simultaneously evokes and cancels the technological artifice and mediation of cinema can be seen as staging the return out of artifice to the self and creating an imaginary space, at once inside and outside the diegesis, where perception and reality can be reintegrated.

Elsewhere, integration is foregrounded in, for example, 'Fit as a Fiddle', where the discrepancy between Don's voiceover account of his early career, narrated to the Louella Parsons-like gossip columnist Dora Bailey, and the flashback vignettes we see of Don's and Cosmo's 'real' past – not, as Don maintains, 'dignity, always dignity', high society and the *conservatoire*, but pool halls, the bread line and the hard grind of the burlesque and vaudeville circuits – enact a mismatch of public and private self that must be rectified. (Don's fake bio is quite literally a public affair: Don speaks to Dora over a microphone in front of an audience of fans at the premiere of his latest film with Lina Lamont, *The Royal Rascal*.) Don, like several of Kelly's other characters in his MGM musicals, for example *For Me and My Gal* (1942) and *On the Town*, must retrieve an authentic inner self from underneath a shallow defensive veneer – often associated with a 'slick' urban persona, a carapace to cope with the vicissitudes of big city life – if he is to achieve happiness. Characterising Don as in 'a state of self-division', Cohan (2000: 62) notes how the 'real' biography revealed in 'Fit as a Fiddle' casts him repeatedly as a substitute, literally a 'stand-in'. In such a context, 'Make 'Em Laugh' – which was conceived as a virtually autonomous showcase for Donald O'Connor's gymnastic abilities – proves thematically integrated, as it represents a reconnection of sorts with Don and Cosmo's suppressed performative past. In the narrative, it is Kathy – established in her initial appearances as unaffected and attractively artless compared to the 'fake' Lina Lamont – who provides the means of Don's redemption.

Finally, the film is not only formally but in the most concrete way predicated on the principle of integration, as a 'catalogue musical', that is a vehicle for the recycling of an existing catalogue of song material (in this case, the 1920s songs of Freed and his writing partner Nacio Herb Brown, to which MGM had purchased the rights in 1949) around which a narrative had to be organised. Wollen (1992: 31f.) records that in the case of *Singin' in the Rain* it took Betty Comden and Adolph Green, the screenwriters charged with the task, 'a desperate month and a half at least' to produce a viable structure and scenario.

In one regard alone is *Singin' in the Rain* ostentatiously non-integrative: the extended ballet sequence, 'Broadway Rhythm', that climaxes the film's performative spectacle (although it does not close out the narrative). Indeed, the extraneous (in narrative terms) nature of this sequence is comically remarked by the dialogue exchanges that bracket it, with Don first 'pitching' the concept of a ballet ostensibly to be included in *The Dancing Cavalier* to Monumental Pictures head of production R.F. At the end of the sequence we return to Don, Cosmo and R.F., who responds to Don's proposal with the line, 'I can't quite visualise it. I'll have to see it on film first'. This reflexive gag underlines that the 14–minute ballet we have just witnessed literally has no 'place' in the film's diegetic world of 1928 Hollywood (it also clearly has no conceivable relationship to the costume musical *The Dancing Cavalier*): it exists in a different realm of pure performance and spectacle. Kelly's co-director on *Singin' in the Rain* (and also *On the Town*), Stanley Donen, later criticised Kelly's desire to interpolate heterogeneous ballet sequences into both films as 'interruption(s) to the film's main thrust' (quoted in Wollen, 1992: 59).

Yet there is, as Cohan (2000: 59f.) notes, an irony in *Singin' in the Rain*'s integrative enthusiasm – that Debbie Reynolds, playing Kathy whose dubbed voice Lina Lamont claims as her own, was dubbed by the singing voice of Betty Noyes and by Jean Hagen – who played Lina – for dialogue. Thus the material circumstances of the film's own production give the lie to the seam-less integration – the 'marriage' – that the text seeks so tirelessly to promote. In fact, the introduction of dubbing as both plot device and dominating metaphor (for inauthenticity and splitting) seems almost like the musical's textual confession of the impossibility of its own utopian project, setting loose a rogue, unanchored discursive field whose energies can only be contained by the magical delivery of the clown who pulls aside the curtain.

NOTES

1. On the 'cinema of attractions', see below Chapter 10.
2. Eddy's screen presence is succinctly captured in Mordden's (1982) description of him as a 'singing tree'.
3. Woody Allen's *The Purple Rose of Cairo* (1984) makes similar assumptions about women's susceptibility to the siren song of the silver screen.
4. Note, however, that *New York, New York* suggests that Jimmy (and we) remain in thrall to such mythologies: for the film ends by holding out the prospect – initiated by Jimmy – of the couple's reunion, only for Peggy to refuse, not without regret, the offer. Having so unsparingly demonstrated that these two people are definitively *not* suited to be a couple, the film still plays on and off the audience's yearning (like Peggy/Francine) for such a redemptive conclusion, and exposes it as masochistic and driven only by the genre's powerful narrative conventionality.

CHAPTER 5

The War/Combat Film: Genre and Nation

In a spectacular sequence – one of many – midway through Giovanni Pastrone's silent epic *Cabiria* (Italy, 1914), a powerful Roman fleet lays siege to the fortified city of Syracuse, ally of Rome's nemesis Carthage. The imminent threat rouses Archimedes, a Syracusan scholar, from his esoteric ruminations to invent a radical new weapon to save his city from the invader by harnessing the power of the sun itself. His wildly anachronistic, da Vinci-like invention uses an array of mirror 'petals' around a central lens to focalise a deadly beam of light and heat that incinerates everything in its path. The weapon – particularly in its small prototype – bears a striking resemblance to one of the new high-intensity incandescent lights that were in the early 1910s rapidly transforming the nature and range of lighting effects being achieved on sound stages throughout America and Europe, its 'petals' identical to the movie light's adjustable 'barndoor' shutters. The association is heightened when Archimedes tests his invention on a square of white canvas that could pass for a movie screen; the lethal ray itself looks for all the world like a projector beam. When the death ray is turned on the Roman fleet to devastating effect, as Marcia Landy (2000a: 34) notes, the combination of para-cinematic technology with scenes of battle and terrible carnage underscores cinema's long-standing affinity with the technologies of war.

Warfare has been one of the movies' principal subjects since their infancy. The invention of cinema coincided with a decade of imperialist military conflicts (the 1898 Spanish–American War, the 1899–1902 Boer War, the 1904–5 Russo-Japanese War), and consumer demand to see these events onscreen stimulated the new medium (Bottomore, 2002: 239). Although the technological and representational limitations of early cinema inhibited the immediacy of such depictions, which comprised either staged recreations or scenes filmed well to the rear of the front lines, the elaborately staged battle scene, the larger the scale the better, emerged as a favourite crowd-puller in early feature films – including, of course, Griffith's *Birth of a Nation* (1915). Griffith's masterful synthesis of the developing grammar of narrative film, and his innovative use of the close-up and object-gaze (point-of-view) shot sequences decisively relocated the audience's relationship to screen warfare away from the simple consumption of war-as-spectacle towards narrative participation and empathetic participation in the terrifying experience of modern war. While occasional films such as *Full Metal Jacket* (1987) or *The Thin Red Line* (1998) have rendered battle as a distanced object of spectatorial contemplation, a far more consistent theme of the war film ever since has been the progressive annihilation of the self-preserving distance between the cinema audience and the bloody realities of military conflict, deploying increasingly innovative and high-intensity stylistic and technological strategies, from *All Quiet on the Western Front* (1930) through *A Walk in the Sun* (1945), *Come and See* (USSR, 1984) and *Platoon* (1986), to *Saving Private Ryan* (1997).

It is these combat scenes, playing a central dramatic role, that generically define the war film. A comprehensive historical account of any conflict, or of war as a whole, necessarily includes the home front, supply lines, espionage, diplomacy, government and military general staff, to say nothing of the build-up to and the aftermath of conflict, alongside accounts of battle; and every national cinema of course includes a large number of films dealing with most or all of these subjects, some of them – such as spy films and stories of returning veterans – comprising distinct sub-genres in their own right. Rubenstein (1994: 456) identifies eight major generic variants of the (Hollywood) war film – the Embattled Platoon; the Battle Epic; the Battling Buddies (in which two rivals, for example for the love of the same girl, fight each other as much as the enemy but eventually bury the hatchet, prototypically *What Price Glory?* (1926),[1] later *Flying Fortresses* (1942), *Crash Dive* (1943)); the Strain of Command; the Antiwar Film; the POW Escape; the War Preparedness Film; the Service Comedy-Musical (an extremely elastic category that runs from jovial farces like *Buck Privates* (1941) and morale-boosting musical revues like *Stage Door Canteen* (1943) to fierce later anti-war and anti-military satires like *M*A*S*H* and *Catch-22* (both 1970)). Such a list obviously makes the war film a diverse and expansive category, and for this reason most commentators tend to follow Basinger, who argues that the 'war film' as such 'does not exist in a coherent generic form' (1986: 10) and sets aside war-related strains such as musicals and the POW film to isolate the film of combat, represented primarily by the first four categories. As ever, such distinctions are anything but watertight: combat scenes feature importantly, for example, in both the classic war preparedness films *The Fighting 69th* (1940) and *Sergeant York* (1941).[2] The war/combat film deals distinctly with modern warfare: while historical dramas with military themes, from *The Charge of the Light Brigade* (1936, GB 1968) to *Braveheart* (1995) obviously intersect with the modern war film in their presentation of military tactics and staging of battle scenes, it is the experience of modern, mechanised warfare that gives the genre its distinctive syntax. Notably, too, the conflicts which have provided the most enduring generic variants – the First World War, the Second World War and Vietnam – were all fought by conscript armies, thus lending an important representative quality to the service experience (although more recent films dealing with the modern professionalised military like *Black Hawk Down* and *Behind Enemy Lines* (both 2001) suggest that perhaps the notion of soldier as Everyman is so firmly established that the combat genre can dispense with this).

The operative definition of 'combat' in the war/combat film is from the military analyst's point of view quite narrow and excludes many if not most key areas of modern warfare. The combat film usually focuses not on strategic military planning – indeed the ignorance, cynicism or even contempt of serving troops for the grand strategic designs that have placed them in harm's way is a repeated generic motif – but on the direct experience of battle of the small military unit with clearly defined membership and boundaries (paradigmatically the infantry platoon, gunship or bomber crew). Badsey (2002: 245) observes that these units are 'a very small minority in any real overall war-effort', compared to logistical, planning and supply operations or homeland defence, but their dramatic appeal is precisely the clarity and simplicity of their task: they engage in fighting 'as Homer understood it'. Pierre Sorlin (1994: 359–60) argues that this emphasis on the self-contained unit, creating an 'imaginary war … represented as the sum of heroic actions carried out by handfuls of individuals' so well suited to narrative cinema's dramatic needs, owed something to changing modern military theory in the late nineteenth century in the light of colonial episodes such as the siege of Mafeking or the battle of Rorke's Drift (fictionalised on film in *55 Days at Peking* (1963) and *Zulu* (1964), respectively).

The evolution of the war (or combat) film is marked perhaps more directly than any other by developments in the world beyond the frame. The shift from *The Big Parade* (1925) to *The Sands of Iwo Jima* (1945) and thence to *Platoon* (1986), *Three Kings* (1999) and *Black Hawk Down* obviously cannot simply be explained in terms of internal generic evolution or 'life-cycles'. Changing perceptions of particular wars and of war itself, arising from the cumulative shared cultural experience of different conflicts and their embedded politics, elicit unusually direct effects in the shifting tenor, iconography and generic verisimilitudes of war films. Thus, as we shall see, while First World War and Vietnam combat films tend to emphasise the futility, brutality and suffering of war – in the universal or the particular – Second World War movies are more likely to emphasise 'positive' values of valour, patriotism and purposeful sacrifice. Similarly, different national experiences of conflict and of victory or defeat ensure a remarkable dissimilarity in the generic conventions by which wars are rendered in different national cinemas – sometimes even curtailing direct representation altogether (for instance the 'unavailability' of Second World War combat as a direct topic in postwar German cinema). At the same time, war films exercise their own powerful capacity to structure popular memory and hence to 'rewrite' history. Finally, the war film is also notable for the high degree of interest and sometimes active involvement (or interference) it attracts from national governments and its implication in propaganda efforts. For all of these reasons, while retaining a focus on Hollywood, this chapter will throughout consider and compare variants of the war/combat film across several national cinemas, sampled primarily through their different representations of four major conflicts: the two World Wars, the Korean War and Vietnam.

THE FIRST WORLD WAR

The consequences of the First World War (1914–18) for global cinema were in their way as far-reaching as for world politics and economics. The deformations the war effort inflicted upon the economies of the warring European nations retarded the development of distinctive national cinemas; in Russia, the most extreme case, military collapse, revolution and civil war effectively annihilated the domestic film industry until the mid-1920s. Conversely the American film industry, sustained by its huge internal market and America's late entry (March 1917) into the war, was well placed to take competitive advantage of the situation and emerged from the war enormously strengthened, for the first time clearly the globally dominant industry. The war also made plain film's unprecedented potential as a tool for disseminating information and propaganda, resulting in significant changes to the relationship between governments and national film industries. In the USA, as Ward (1985) argues, although film had only a limited impact upon American audiences during the brief US involvement in hostilities, industry–government collaboration on war bond drives led to former Treasury Secretary William McAdoo's appointment to a senior position at the newly formed United Artists, setting a precedent for what would subsequently become a fairly frequent exchange of personnel between government and Hollywood and a far more favourable attitude in government circles generally for the hitherto unrespectable medium of film. In addition, the Wilson administration's acceptance that the film's industry's economic independence need not be compromised or curtailed for the cinema to be mobilised in the national interest would prove hugely significant for the next war.

While all the warring countries produced highly partisan patriotic wartime dramas and propaganda films, no clear generic template for the representation of the First World War coalesced until later in the silent period, when it formed part of a much larger cultural and political reckoning with the meaning and implications of the war. Notably lacking during the war itself was the later identification of combat scenes as central to making dramatic sense of the war, with spy films, hagiographic biographies of military and political leaders and – especially – sensational melodramas that purported to depict (largely invented and soon discredited) German atrocities on civilian populations in occupied France and the Low Countries all vying to define the war for audiences at home. Perhaps the most lasting consequence of such infamous entries as *The Beast of Berlin* (1918) was the later reluctance of Allied film-makers in the Second World War to inflict such crude, bare-knuckle propaganda upon sceptical audiences (see Dibbets and Hogenkamp, 1995).

Cinematic representations of the 'Great War' in the 1920s and 1930s demonstrate very clearly the close relationship between this genre and contemporary politics. In the Allied countries, the initial jubilation of victory quickly gave way to a negative perception of the war's aftermath that in turn came to colour understandings of the war itself. The best-known expressions of this mood of disillusionment are two large-scale anti-war melodramas, Abel Gance's *J'Accuse* (France 1919), with its uncompromising depiction of the horrors of war following hard on the Armistice itself, and *The Big Parade* (1925), whose hero returns from the trenches minus his illusions, most of his comrades and his leg to find a glib and shallow civilian world that shabbily exploits fighting men's sacrifice for its own self-interested ends.

This contrast between the fierce integrity of the blood brotherhood of combat troops and the callowness or indifference of civilians and, sometimes, military brass became a hallmark of First World War films. Notably, this sympathy was able to cross the lines of former hostilities in the name of a shared humanity, most famously in *All Quiet on the Western Front* (1930), the story of a young German soldier's suffering and death in the trenches. (The revelation of German war crimes and the Holocaust would make the sympathetic treatment of Second World War German soldiers much more difficult, although a clear distinction was often drawn between 'decent' Wehrmacht officers such as those played by Michael Caine in *The Eagle Has Landed* (1976) and James Coburn in *Cross of Iron* (1977) and their convinced Nazi superiors.[3]) It is worth noting incidentally that this widespread elevation of the experience of the trenches into a kind of Calvary or existential crucible, generating privileged insights transcending the trivialities of the home front, was not necessarily associated with pacifism or liberalism: although the Nazis (still an opposition party) and other right-wing German nationalist parties violently denounced *All Quiet ...* and disrupted screenings, the extreme right shared a perception of the war as a transcendent experiential moment that demanded expiation and restitution. The dominant iconography of the First World War that emerged from *All Quiet* ... and its European counterparts – notably *Westfront 1918* (Germany 1931) – is of the trenches, the moonscape of No Man's Land, mud, decay, squalor and (physical and moral) confusion. Chambers (1994) suggests that such 'anti-war' films should be generically distinguished from 'war films'; Kane (1988: 87) on the other hand insists that such films, which operate by complicating or inverting standard generic dualities, 'represent a predictable place on the established genre continuum'. In fact, very few combat films about any war are 'pro-war' in any simple sense: most retain a serious awareness of the suffering and loss war entails even if they wholeheartedly endorse the reasons for fighting (as is the case with the overwhelming majority of US and UK Second World War combat films through the 1960s and in most cases beyond).

The situation was somewhat different in Britain, where despite the influential portrayal of the war during the 1920s by (mostly officer class) veterans through memoirs, novels and above all poetry as 'wholly traumatic and catastrophic', films tended to cleave more closely to official versions (which as recent revisionist histories have suggested may also have in fact more closely reflected the common soldier's experience and understanding of the war: see Burton, 2002). Thus although 'they deplore the carnage of war ... they do not question the necessity of duty' (Landy, 1991: 120). In this sense British portrayals of the Great War did not 'catch up' with other national cinemas until the 1960s, when according to Korte (2001: 121–2) 'a new context of sceptical self-examination' definitively disassociated the image of the First World War from positive notions of patriotic sacrifice and attached it exclusively to suffering and pity. (Korte notes that this is the period when the war poetry of Siegfried Sassoon and Wilfrid Owen became standard school texts.) Burton suggests that it was in fact the institutionalisation of the Second World War as Britain's 'finest hour' that reinforced the cinematic representation of the First World War as, by necessary contrast, brutal carnage at the behest of a corrupt and cynical establishment, for instance in *King and Country* (1964) and more recently *Regeneration* (1997); such early sound-era Great War dramas as *Tell England* (1931) may accordingly prove upon closer inspection less blindly patriotic and affirmative than often believed.

It would be wrong to suggest that every cinematic treatment of the First World War is polemically anti-war in spirit and bleak in tone. Notably, a robust sub-genre depicting the (in strategic terms fairly marginal) air war celebrated the dashing cavalry spirit of the fighter ace (*Wings*, 1927; *The Dawn Patrol*, 1930, remade 1938; more recently *Aces High*, GB 1976). Moreover, in many First World War combat films there is a strong train of (albeit sometimes despairing) romanticism that mitigates the bloodiness of the slaughter:

Journey's End (1931), which like *Tell England* eulogises the tragically honourable British officer class, is perhaps the classic example (see also Kelly, 1997; Burton, 2002). Nonetheless, so firmly was the image of the First World War as futile slaughter lodged in the American public mind by the 1930s that the earlier war presented real problems as a background against which to encourage war preparedness in the years leading up to Pearl Harbor for those studios that were keen to do so – notably Warners, who did manage to produce two of the most important preparedness films, *The Fighting 69th* and the multi-Academy-Award-winning *Sergeant York*, in First World War settings (see Leab, 1995).

THE SECOND WORLD WAR

Uniquely, the generic paradigm of the Second World War combat film was established during the war itself, and has been largely maintained since. Moreover, this generic model subsequently becomes the principal frame of reference for almost all later combat films. Regarding the Hollywood combat film, key factors in this speedy and enduring generic crystallisation, compared to both earlier and later major conflicts, would presumably include the much more extensive (compared to the First World War) conversion of US society to the war effort, the high degree of consensus about the necessity and value of the war (unlike Vietnam) and clarity about its aims and outcomes (unlike Korea). America's four-year participation in the conflict (1941–45) also allowed ample time for the establishment and refinement of a viable generic model (by contrast, post-Vietnam conventional campaigns, with the notable exception of the second Iraq War (2003–), have been completed in weeks or days). Moreover, what is true for Hollywood is true as well for the national cinema of every other major combatant. Also without exception, testifying to the war's political and cultural centrality not only for the war generation themselves but for those who were children during the war and those born in the following decade (in US terms, the 'baby boomers'), national cinemas have periodically returned to the Second World War combat film, updating and revising the classic generic paradigm in the light of both new understandings and perceptions of the war itself – notably, the growing centrality to Second World War historiography of civilian suffering in general and the Holocaust in particular – and the changing contemporary political environment (the two are of course closely linked). For this reason, this section is subdivided into two parts, dealing respectively with Second World War combat films made during the war and those made subsequently.

The Second World War Combat Film 1939–45

The experience of the Second World War highlights the extent to which the war/combat film is implicated in the political needs of its moment of production and subject to wholesale revision. Hollywood was cautious about dealing with war-related, let alone explicitly anti-Nazi themes during the late 1930s, mindful of the still-fragile state of its finances in the lingering Depression, its reliance on lucrative foreign (principally European) markets, and hostility from isolationist elements in Congress. With the outbreak and spread of the European war these markets were progressively closed to Hollywood, until only the UK – in any event Hollywood's most important overseas market – remained (thus confirming the studios in an anti-Nazi, interventionist line). Simultaneously, as Schatz (1998: 92–4) points out, Roosevelt's massive rearmament drive after 1939 both put a definitive end to the Depression and boosted working populations and incomes in those very urban industrial areas where moving-going was strongest – thus ensuring that Hollywood's own rising fortunes were firmly hitched to the war economy. 'Never before or since', he argues, 'have the interests of the nation and the movie industry been so closely aligned, and never has Hollywood's status as a national cinema been so vital ... [with an] effective integration of Hollywood's ideological and commercial imperatives' (p. 89). The production of war-related (though rarely actual combat) themes rose from a bare handful in 1939–40 to some three dozen (still only 6.5 per cent of total output) in the last year of peace, 1941 (see Shain, 1976).

As Thomas Doherty (1993: 85–121) argues, neither of the twin paradigms established for Hollywood representation of the First World War during the 1920s and early 1930s – pacifist despair in the trenches, giddy heroism in the air – were appropriate to the needs of the conflict into which the USA was finally impelled by the attack on Pearl Harbor in December 1941. The group ethos promoted during the conflict would require not only the recasting of existing war film motifs but the subordination of prevalent attitudes and their corresponding narrative templates in Hollywood genres and for that matter in America at large. 'The necessity of personal sacrifice and the value of communitarian purpose were not exactly main currents in American thought ... The cheeky newspaperman, the lonesome cowboy, the private detective, the single-minded inventor, even the will to power of the urban gangster strike chords unsounded by the rewards of group solidarity and communal work' (Doherty, 1993: 105). Thus the theme of 'conversion' emerged as central to the wartime film industry, both as narrative template of war-oriented films and a touchstone for the reorganisation of production processes, as studio operations and established story formulas and star personae were retooled for the war effort.

Building on the lessons of the First World War, the US government maintained an arm's-length relationship to the film industry during the war, liaising and coordinating production of war-related films through the Office of War Information (OWI) but stopping well short of gross propagandising or direct state control in the German or Soviet mode. Indeed, democratic pluralism and diversity, as we shall see, became the defining motif of Hollywood's war effort. The dominant tenor adopted by the combat films produced by the Hollywood studios during the war itself was – contrary to the popular received wisdom of Boy's Own heroics – a hard-bitten, sometimes grim professionalism rather than the showy valour of prewar period military films such as *The Charge of the Light Brigade* (1936). In keeping with government concerns not to raise unrealistic expectations of early victory, the war was presented as a tough, often grimly attritional struggle against fierce, organised and ruthless enemies (in the case of the Japanese, often freighted with negative racial stereotyping). In the first disastrous months after Pearl Harbor, as Allied forces were rolled back across the Pacific Theatre, Hollywood combat films were not guaranteed happy endings: the Embattled Platoon variant found its classic expression at this time in such tales of heroic annihilation as *Wake Island* (1942) and *Bataan* (1943). In any case, with some six million US servicemen and women serving overseas by the war's end, fantasy versions of the war could be quickly discredited. Such factors, combined with the imperatives of historical immediacy – Columbia's *Submarine Raider* (1942) was in cinemas within six months of Pearl Harbor, and such tight turnaround times were not unusual – and the influence of wartime newsreels, lent Hollywood a new degree of realism.

One should not overstate the element of wartime innovation as opposed to traditional industrial adaptation: Schatz for instance notes how not only James Cagney's familiar tough-guy persona was carried over into the war milieu in *The Fighting 69th* but also a reformation/conversion narrative – here, his suppression of his anti-social super-individualism in favour of the team – familiar from his gangster film *Angels With Dirty Faces* (1938) and aided by the same means – a priest played by Pat O'Brien. Yet combat film narratives did show marked differences with the prewar norm. Dana Polan (1986: 112) argues that Hollywood's classical narrative paradigm with its individual protagonist and clearly resolved conflicts underwent a temporary but profound shift to accommodate the war effort, subordinating the individual to the collective (or 'team') and the romantic couple to the gender-specific wartime duties of men and women (see also Ray, 1985). The theme of sublimating personal ambitions and desires into a larger unit becomes commonplace, focusing either on the need for several individuals to pool their differences or on the lone maverick who becomes a team player. Paris (1997) shows how the depiction of the bomber crew in an early Second

World War film like *Air Force* (1943) consciously moves away from the 'lone eagle' heroics that characterised 1930s aviation movies, with their emphasis on fighter aces, towards the prevailing model of democratic 'teamwork' – exemplified in *Air Force* by the transformation of the initially embittered failed pilot Winocki into a 'team player'. As part of the developing pattern, war films showed how the services could reward all skills – and not just the ostensibly more 'glamorous' ones – with a key role in the team: in *Rear Gunner* (1943), pintsize crack-shot backwoodsman Burgess Meredith finds his ideal niche in the tail cockpit of a B-25 bomber crew. Such examples, readily multiplied, support Basinger's argument that the 'hero' of the Second World War movie is a collective one, the combat unit – the infantry platoon or the bomber crew, an ethnically and socially variegated crew whose differences are suppressed, superseded or set aside for the duration of their mission and whose different skills and abilities (and sometimes even weaknesses) complement each other to mould a unit whose value is definitively more than the sum of its constituent parts. (Landy (1991: 162) identifies a similar project in the British combat film: 'War narratives like *The Way Ahead* (1940) are dramas of conversion, but unlike traditional conversion patterns, which focus on a single character, this film focuses on transformations of the group.' In both *Air Force* and *We Dive At Dawn* (GB 1943), the opening credits identify characters by rank or function rather than name.)

Although Kane (1988) notes the general lack of *explicit* ideologising in Second World War combat films, the 'teamwork' model was instantly legible in terms of the prevailing ideology of the 'good war': Wood (1981: 98) describes the bomber crew as 'an ideal democracy in microcosm' who achieve 'a perfect balance ... between individual fulfilment and the responsibility of each member to the whole. The crew enact the values they are fighting for,' a reading wholly supported by contemporary industry publicity and correspondence with the OWI and universally endorsed by commentators. Democratic diversity importantly extends to demography too: the ethnically diverse platoon – emblematically enacted in the roll-call of recognisably 'hyphenated American' names – is of course an abiding genre cliché, and, as Basinger (1986: 55) observes, overtly invokes the 'melting pot'. This interpretation again conforms to industry and government's contemporary relay and forms part of the conventional critical wisdom. Thus Paris (1997: 48) argues that 'from *Gung Ho!* (1942), in which a Marine colonel ... orders his racially mixed unit to "cast out prejudice, racial, religious, and every other kind", to *Pride of the Marines* and *A Walk in the Sun* (both 1945), the combat group has stood as a metaphor for a democratic society.' This democratic inclusiveness, however, has its contradictory dimensions, particularly in relation to race. Not only were mixed racial groups at odds with the realities of military segregation (in *Gung Ho!* and *Bataan* they are accounted for dramatically by the ad hoc nature of these films' combat units, patched together for special missions from the remnants of routed larger forces);[4] Slotkin (2001) argues that the broadening of the US ethnic and racial community enacted in films like these[5] was achievable only through the outward expansion of the 'racial frontier' and the projection of the negative stigma of the racial Other onto the enemy, usually the Japanese.

Street (2002: 93) records that British wartime films were popular and highly regarded in the US. In Samuel Goldwyn's opinion, the war had enabled British cinema finally to discover a distinctive style of its own, 'broader and more international' than Hollywood and expressive of 'the intimate universality of everyday living'. Like its US counterpart, British wartime cinema used depictions of combat not only to record the course of the war but to project the core values of the struggle: whereas US combat films reinforced and extended traditional American democratic principles, however, their British counterparts helped construct a novel collectivist ethos that was defined by its differences from prewar society: 'The ideology of the people's war which emerges from (British) wartime films is one of national unity and social cohesion: class differences have all but disappeared and have been replaced instead by a democratic sense of community and comradeship' (Chapman, 1998: 161; see also Kuhn, 1981). As a naval power, maritime combat features more prominently in British than in US war films, and the enclosed community and enforced intimacy of seagoing warfare lent themselves readily to object lessons about about the new professional alliances emerging from the war effort, challenging and superseding traditional class differences. In the submarine film *We Dive at Dawn*, successful soldiering resolves the confusions and complications of domestic and civilian life. (The British war film has probably been the most thoroughly explored of any national cinema: see also Hurd, 1984; Landy, 1991: 146–66; Chapman, 1998; Murphy, 2000; Paris, 2000.)

Noting the relatively small number of Soviet front-line combat films made during the war – particularly in light of the genre's notable and consistent popularity in the postwar era – Kenez suggests that 'perhaps the struggle was for the Soviet people too serious an affair to be depicted as a series of adventures. Or maybe the directors considered the stability of the home front a greater concern than the behaviour of soldiers under fire' (2001: 176). By contrast, films about partisans were more numerous, more popular and generally regarded as better quality. Parallels to the multi-ethnic combat unit in the Hollywood war film can be found in the stress on multinational and pan-Slavic cooperation against the Nazi threat – an important propaganda line given Nazi attempts to exploit (justified) anti-Bolshevik nationalist resentments among the minority nationalities in the Soviet Union. However, a distinguishing feature of Soviet films such as *She Defends the Motherland*

(USSR 1943), *The Rainbow* (USSR 1944) and *Zoia* (USSR 1944) is their focus on female protagonists whose sex mitigates neither their involvement in the resistance to the Nazis nor indeed the ferocity of their violence (here drawing on Soviet cinematic precedents, for example Pudovkin's *The Mother*, 1926). Another notable difference was the stress in Soviet 'historical' wartime epics on heroic inspirational leader figures such as Kutuzov (with the inevitable and transparent analogy to Stalin). Gillespie (2003: 128–9) finds the Russian war film 'deadly serious, with a more visceral immediacy' than its western counterparts, and notes the much more graphic depiction of extreme and sadistic violence. Unsurprisingly, given that the Soviet film industry was wholly state-owned and controlled, Soviet war films were also often more crudely propagandistic than American or British films, as revealed, for example, by a comparison of the deliberately low-key depiction of submarine warfare in *We Dive at Dawn* with the absurd heroics of *Submarine T-9* (USSR 1943), in which 'a single submarine sinks countless enemy ships, raids a German port and even lands some marines ashore to blow up a strategic bridge, all with the loss of just one man' (Gillespie, 2003: 130).

The wartime films of the defeated Axis powers are rarely seen and hence little known except by specialists. There is, however, a fairly considerable literature on Nazi film generally, including war films, of which probably the best known is the historical epic *Kolberg* (1945), produced under Goebbels' personal supervision (but ironically barely seen by German audiences before the war's end since Allied bombing had closed most German cinemas by the time *Kolberg* premiered in January 1945). Japanese war films are even less well-known in the West: however, according to Freiberg (1996), Japanese combat films of the late 1930s – responding to the mixed fortunes of the 1937 invasion of China – surprised subsequent western viewers (including military analysts) in their bleakness, austerity, relative lack of propagandising and cardboard heroics, and acknowledgement of suffering. Following Pearl Harbor and Japan's initial spectacular successes in southeast Asia, however, a fully mobilised film industry increasingly employed nationalist and military rhetoric hitherto absent from the genre. 'Generally', Freiberg notes, 'wartime films posit the army unit and the nation as an extended family, or surrogate family, to replace the biological family … All personal relationships, including those among real family members, were to be subordinated to national service. Romantic love and even family affection had to be repressed in these films of national unity' (pp. 33–5). (On Japanese combat films see also Manvell, 1974, and Anderson and Richie, 1983).

The Second World War Combat Film since 1945

Broadly speaking, the Second World War combat film was a staple of the principal Allied national cinemas – the USA, the USSR and Britain – until the late 1970s, at which point the genre falls into disuse until the end of the Cold War and a series of large-scale public commemorations of Second World War anniversaries provoke a revival in the 1990s.[6] Kane (1988: 86) identifies 24 Hollywood combat films produced between 1942 and 1945; after this there is a two-year hiatus until production of combat films resumes in 1947, following which at least one Second World War combat film is released each year until 1970. By contrast, in the defeated Axis powers, the combination of defeat, wholesale social and economic reconstruction, rapid incorporation into the western anti-communist alliance and the shameful but largely unaddressed legacy of war crimes made the production of combat films, particularly in (West) Germany or Japan, too problematic and contentious a proposition to generate more than a handful of films until much later. The mythology of resistance in Italy and France offered alternative narrative paradigms for the war, but the nature of partisan warfare sets these in some degree outside the mainstream combat genre tradition.

The divergent British and American experiences of actual warfare post-1945 of course provide essential context for the differences between the directions taken by the combat genre in their respective national cinemas. In both America and Britain, the cessation of hostilities saw a corresponding immediate demobilisation of the film industry, upon the assumption that war-weary audiences favoured a return to either lighter fare or serious dramas more relevant to the new challenges of 'winning the peace' (as in the cycle of postwar social problem films dealing with racial discrimination in the US: *Gentleman's Agreement*, 1947; *Pinky*, 1949). Upon the genre's re-emergence in the late 1940s – coinciding with the renewal of large-scale overseas military operations in Korea (see below) – interesting divergences appear between the US and British models.

British warfare during this period was typified by the series of bloody, protracted and messy campaigns against nationalist insurgents in the shrinking Empire, but these were massively overshadowed by the 1956 Suez Crisis, a disastrous, divisive and humiliating episode which effectively extinguished Britain's ambitions to remain a Great Power on the world stage. Counter-insurgency and postcolonial adventurism alike compared very poorly to still-fresh recollections of wartime experience where military valour allied to moral rectitude and national unity laboured to secure ultimate victory. The ensuing boom in war film production in the 1950s both contributed to and reflected the rapid crystallisation of wartime memory into defining nostalgic national myth. Richards (1997) and Geraghty (2003) identify in British war films of the 1950s a move away from the collectivist tone of the war years towards a renewed focus on the officer class alongside a new emphasis on processes of elite planning and decision-making. *The Cruel Sea* (1953), one of the decade's most successful war films in the UK, eliminates much of the below-decks material in adapting Nicholas Monserrat's best-seller and focuses more narrowly on the captain's sometimes intolerable burden of command. The popular sub-genre of POW-camp escape films such as *The Wooden Horse* and *The Colditz Story* (both 1955), confined to the officer class, emphasise meticulous planning and the role of a 'management class' (the escape committees). Scientists and strategists – 'boffins' in wartime lingo – emerge from the shadows to stand alongside selected cadres of specialist commandos in recreating notably novel, and now declassified, tactics such as midget submarines (*Above Us the Waves*, 1955) and the 'bouncing bomb' (*The Dam Busters*, 1954). (On the postwar and 1950s British war film, see Medhurst, 1984; Pronay, 1988; Rattigan, 1994; Murphy, 2000: 179–239; Geraghty, 2003: 175–95; Chapman, 2000).

Far more than its US counterpart, the British 'war film' is virtually synonymous with the Second World War: colonial and postcolonial conflicts (such as the 1982 Falklands War and British military involvement in Northern Ireland from 1967) have not been depicted on-screen as generic combat situations (see McIlroy, 1998). The British combat film shrivelled alongside other traditional genres during the near-collapse of the domestic film industry in the 1970s; while it would appear to offer suitable material for either of the dominant genres of the 1980s, social realism and the heritage film, combat films of any kind did not feature until the turn of the millennium, and then only in such generically marginal examples as the First World War-set *Regeneration* and *Deathwatch* (2002, a trench warfare-horror hybrid).

The defining US engagement of the immediate postwar period was the 'police action' in Korea (1949–53), in which US forces, leading a UN-sponsored international coalition, confronted the new Communist enemy for the first time in the shape of first the North Korean and subsequently the Red Chinese armies. The absence of any immediate threat to US territory, as well as the anti-Communist hysteria dominating the domestic political landscape throughout the war's duration climaxing in the divisive Red-hunting campaigns of Senator Joe McCarthy, made Korea a difficult war to 'sell' in the inspirational terms of the Second World War – by now firmly established in US national mythology as the 'Good War'. Despite its later reputation as the 'forgotten war', however, at least two dozen war/combat films dealt with Korea, the great majority made between 1952 and 1956. In the absence of a distinctive iconography, Korean combat films like *Retreat, Hell!* (1952) and *Men at War* (1957) tended largely to adopt the established

Second World War platoon model, superficially updated to include new military technologies such as the helicopter and jet plane (e.g. *Sabre Jet*, 1953) and new social realities – notably the racially integrated military. The confusing, attritional nature of the conflict (in which periods of stalemate alternated with enormous campaigns of manoeuvre, while objectives changed hands several times over the course of the war), however, may account for the weary, unillusioned tone that increasingly characterises both Korean *and* Second World War combat films in this period.

Pork Chop Hill (1959), a late Korean War entry – released closer to the start of full-scale US military involvement in Indochina in 1965 than to the end of the Korean conflict itself – includes most of these elements alongside interesting glances at earlier genre traditions. The action takes place during literally the final hours of the conflict, and depicts an infantry battalion charged to retake and hold a North Korean position of minimal strategic value other than as a counter in the negotiations concurrently taking place between the UN/US and Communist commands. Some traditional Second World War elements are updated: the multi-ethnic platoon now includes a Nisei (second generation Japanese-American) junior officer as well as Black soldiers – one of whom is mutinous (it is implied, as a result of his experiences of racist treatment) and has to be persuaded that his country deserves his loyalty. Enemy propaganda – often glancingly featured in the genre in the form of airdropped leaflets or (as in *Bataan*) a radio operator inadvertently tuning into 'Tokyo Rose' – is a major presence in *Pork Chop Hill* via the character of a Chinese Communist broadcasting morale-sapping news to the troops. (So-called 'brainwashing', a novel Korean War fear prominently featured in US media, would supply the premise of *The Manchurian Candidate* (1962), which opens with a Korea combat sequence.) A striking anachronism – remarked upon as such by the protagonists – is a fixed-bayonet 'over the top' assault on the Korean lines: in fact, the cross-cutting between the fighting men, the operational HQ in a shell-beset bunker and the wrangling top brass whose choices about lines on maps are life and death to the men under their command combine with the iconography of trenches (complete with street signs and chicken hutches) and barbed wire to lend the film at times a decidedly First World War ambience.[7]

Given the widespread interest in governing elites disseminated down from American sociology during the 1950s, one might expect a similar pattern in US combat films to the prominent 'boffins' in the British war film. However, this is not obviously the case. Arguably, the fabrication of technocratic military-scientific-governmental alliances in confronting external enemies becomes a major feature of the science fiction films of this decade (see Chapter 8; see also Biskind, 1983), but it is noticeably less prominent in combat films. In fact, second-wave combat films retain the wartime films' focus on the day-to-day experience of ordinary fighting men. If anything, more than ever the infantryman's perspective, which (possibly with Korea in mind) now emerges as clearly the paradigmatic combat experience, is depicted as removed, even bafflingly distant, from the grand strategies of generals and politicians. *Battleground*'s (1949) portrait of 'the battling bastards of Bastogne' shows the platoon poring over week-old copies of *Stars and Stripes* to determine whether they are in France or Belgium. The footslogger's perception of his role in the opaque workings of grand military strategy is a simple one: 'nobody cares'. Here and elsewhere in the period, with the real war won and in the past, morale-raising and overt ideological lessons are superseded by weary resolution and an ever more hard-bitten tone that increasingly verges on outright cynicism: *Battleground*'s reluctant hero explains that his PFC rank stands for 'Praying For Civilian'. The implicit individualism of such attitudes, strongly at odds with the didactic collectivism of the classic Second World War model, emerges strongly post-Korea in the loners played by William Holden in *The Bridge on the River Kwai* (1957) and Steve McQueen in *Hell Is For Heroes* (1962). In *The Dirty Dozen* (1967) and other late 1960s 'dirty group' films, almost any sense of shared endeavour has been jettisoned in favour of a brutally Darwinian landscape in which friend and foe alike are perceived as merely obstacles to the overriding objective of individual survival.

While undergoing these generic shifts, Second World War combat films continued to thrive into the late 1960s in the context of the bipartisan consensus on US strategic objectives and policies: the ideological dogmatism and ruthlessness of these films' Nazis and Japanese could be readily construed as stand-ins for the equally fanatical Communist opponents America confronted in theatres from Havana to Hanoi. As this consensus fractured under the combined strain of military failure and increasingly strident domestic political opposition during the Vietnam War, however – with student protestors decrying GIs as 'babykillers' and comparing US leaders to Nazis – the resulting ideological vacuum appeared not only to put Vietnam itself off limits as a dramatic subject, but to have stripped away the credibility of all and any heroic depictions of US military action. Disaffection with unaccountable authority and disinclination to conceive even the 'Good War' in terms other than individual self-preservation are elements that grow stronger in the coming decades: Neale (1991: 48) identifies *Attack!* (1956), *The Dirty Dozen*, *Play Dirty* (1967) and *Tobruk* (1967) as films in which representatives of command draw up plans and issue orders 'which are both contrary to the interests of the men and (in some cases) … of little or no strategic value'. Rather earlier than the Western and in a more condensed period, the ideological disjunction between genre and its socio-political context results in a heightened revisionism followed by a wholesale generic collapse. Thus, between July 1969 and July 1970 ten US-made Second World War combat films (and one Korean War film, *M*A*S*H* – although the film's anarchic 'Korea' was universally understood as a transparent mask for Vietnam) were released onto US screens, a rate of production in keeping with the rest of the decade. And just as highly traditional Westerns like *Chisum* (1970) and *Big Jake* (1971) were being released alongside revisionist landmarks like *Little Big Man* (1970), some of these combat films, like *The Bridge at Remagen* (1969) and *Mosquito Squadron* (1970), hewed very closely to the traditional model; others (*Too Late the Hero*, 1969); *Kelly's Heroes*, 1970) – in both cases the titular 'heroism' is beyond ironic) pushed the demythifying tendency to an extreme, while still others (*Catch-22*, 1970) were coloured by counter-cultural sensibilities. The poor box office of the massive US–Japanese co-production *Tora! Tora! Tora!* (1970) tarred the combat film with the same brush of expensive failure as the family musical. Thereafter production dwindles to almost nothing: the next twelve months saw just five releases – and then no Second World War combat films of any kind until the block-buster historical recreation *Midway* in 1976 (possibly encouraged by the upsurge of patriotic sentiment attendant on that year's Bicentennial cele-brations).[8] The late 1970s saw a handful of productions, including *Cross of Iron*, the 'critical epic' *A Bridge Too Far* (1977) and Samuel Fuller's magis-terial *The Big Red One* (1980); following the release of *The Deer Hunter* (1977), however, the combat film's centre of historical gravity had shifted decisively to Vietnam (see below). Apart from oddly anachronistic vehicles like *Memphis Belle* (1990, a fictionalised retelling of William Wyler's 1943 documentary of the same name), the Second World War combat film remained in abeyance until its spectacular revival in *Saving Private Ryan* (1998), followed by *The Thin Red Line* and *Enemy at the Gates* (2000, a pan-European co-production about Stalingrad shot in English with British and American stars).

In the other major wartime Allied nation, the Soviet Union, the 'Great Patriotic War' (as the Second World War was officially known) became the focal national cult during Stalin's last years and beyond; numerous wartime re-enactments produced according to rigid Socialist Realist principles glori-fied Soviet military accomplishments and Stalin's personal military genius (most notoriously *The Fall of Berlin*, 1949). Critical attention has focused on the ways in which, starting with the 'thaw' period under Kruschev in the late 1950s and early 1960s, new approaches to this central plank of Soviet ideo-logy became a means of exploring hitherto illicit complexities and alternative perspectives on the Communist experiment in Russia, and ultimately of challenging the validity of the entire system (see Lawton, 1992; Youngblood, 1996, 2001; Gillespie, 2003: 64–79). Collaboration, for example, long a taboo subject in USSR cinema, emerged tentatively during the 'thaw' (e.g. *The*

Fate of a Man, 1959) and with much more force in the 1970s and 1980s, with a growing suggestion of the underlying moral equivalence of Nazi and Stalinist tyranny in *Trial on the Road* (1971, released 1986), *The Ascent* (1976), *Sign of Disaster* (1986) and the shattering *Come and See*. Youngblood sees the latter film as 'a cinematic reflection of the Soviet public's morale near the end of the regime. No one believes in the cause in *Come and See*; no one seems to understand it. All humanity has degenerated, although the Germans are undeniably much worse than others' (Youngblood, 1996: 94).

As the defeated aggressors in the most destructive conflict in world history, further burdened by the revelation of war crimes and crimes against humanity, Germany and Japan, the principal Axis powers, in different ways confronted throughout the postwar period the challenge of what Charles Maier (1991) has called 'the unmasterable past'. This still incomplete process of cultural reckoning in both cases, although to different degrees at different times, entailed processes of abjection, amnesia, denial, guilt and defiance. The perception that Japan and Germany had failed fully to work through their tarnished historical legacies ensured that any representation of Japanese or German combat experiences would be greeted with suspicion and subjected to an unusually high degree of critical scrutiny in the former Allied nations. It is therefore understandable that before the late twentieth century very few combat films of any kind emerged from either country. A conspicuous exception – and a major critical and commercial success – was *Das Boot* (*The Boat*, 1981), which earned a theatrical release as a three-hour film edited down from the original ten-part West German television series. Possibly the perception of the Battle of the Atlantic as a 'clean fight' largely unembarrassed by the atrocities of the Occupation and the Eastern Front (to say nothing of the Holocaust) accounted for its enthusiastic reception as a stirring story of men and the cruel sea. The attempt in *Stalingrad* (1992) to recast the Russian war in similarly unproblematic generic terms was correspondingly less successful. Japanese war films have until very recently focused almost exclusively on the national trauma of atomic devastation at Hiroshima and Nagasaki; the 2001 release of *Merdeka* marked virtually the first point at which the combat experience of Japanese forces was made the central dramatic focus of a major Japanese film.

VIETNAM

The history of the Vietnam combat film is well known: absent, with the notorious exception of John Wayne's *The Green Berets* (1968), from US screens during the conflict itself (US troops were engaged in Vietnam from 1965 to 1973; South Vietnam finally fell to the Communist North in 1975),[9] the

Vietnam combat genre emerged in the late 1970s in several diverse forms, some (*Go Tell the Spartans*, *The Boys in Company C*, both 1978) clearly patterned after the standard Second World War model, others (*The Deer Hunter*, 1977; *Apocalypse Now*, 1979) owing more to the stylistic experiments of the early 1970s 'Hollywood Renaissance'. The Vietnam combat film peaked in the mid-1980s with *Platoon* (1986), *Hamburger Hill* (1987), *84 Charlie Mopic* (1989) and others: these too largely adopted the 'embattled platoon' variant of the Second World War combat film (notably, given the jungle setting, the Pacific campaign version), but combined a familiar generic syntax with novel semantic elements such as napalm, drug abuse, 'fragging', rock music sound-tracks, graphic, visceral violence and a distinctive and memorable jargon ('grunts', 'gooks', 'clicks', 'on point', and so on) to establish a distinctive and – briefly – very popular generic strain (see Adair, 1989; Auster and Quart, 1988).

Both the Vietnam combat film's belatedness and the terms on which it eventually crystallised into a recognisable sub-genre reflect the intense and ongoing politicisation of the war and the fallout from modern America's first experience of defeat (see Klein, 1994). The Vietnam film foregrounded a thematics of male identity formation through combat that drew on the conservative discourses that had developed by the late 1970s for making sense of the war. To some extent, the Vietnam film's focus on masculinity extends a well-established aspect of the combat film generally, which Susan Jeffords characterises as

> first and foremost, a film not simply about men but about the con-struction of the masculine subject, and the combat sequence – or, more generally, scenes of violence in combat films, whether as fighting in battle, torture, prison escapes, or explosions – is the point of excess, not only for the film's narrative, but for masculine subjectivity ... (Jeffords, 1989: 489)

It has often been pointed out that the combat film is one of the few genres in which men are 'allowed' to cry without being diminished. This element of pathos points up the combat film as another melodramatic modality, albeit one in which, unusually, masculine rather than female subjectivity is explicitly thematised.

That issues around the (re-)construction of masculine identity would come to the fore once Vietnam emerged as an acceptable commercial proposition was perhaps inevitable, given the terms on which the US defeat in Indochina had already been culturally conceived. During the conflict itself, US President Lyndon Johnson repeatedly justified his obsessive commitment to the war in terms of competitive phallocentricity – a 'pissing contest' between himself and both North Vietnamese leader Ho Chi Minh and also anti-communist hawks at home (see Dallek, 1998). According to Johnson's successor, Richard Nixon, post-Vietnam the US risked global ridicule as a 'pitiful, helpless giant'. Unsurprisingly, therefore, in this climate of urgent phallic anxiety the principal foreign policy project of the New Right, which took the White House with the election of Ronald Reagan in 1980, became what Susan Jeffords (1989) calls 'the remasculinisation of America'. Vietnam films, both combat and homefront, were highly receptive to this cultural discourse around masculinity: sexual dysfunction as a result of war wounds is the dramatic focus of both *Coming Home* (1978) and *Born on the Fourth of July* (1989), the Vietnam veteran anti-hero of *Rolling Thunder* (1977), a survivor of VC torture, suffers a symbolic emasculation by having his hand forced into a waste disposal unit, and a GI is actually castrated by the NVA in *Dead Presidents* (1995).

Hollywood's mobilisation of these tropes of damaged and/or recovered manhood has been highly ambiguous. The idealised images of Michael, the hero of *The Deer Hunter*, posed on the trail against misty peaks and mountain streams as a model of the American frontiersman, explicitly invoking Natty Bumppo, the eponymous *Deerslayer* in James Fennimore Cooper's celebrated nineteenth-century novel – and thus by extension associating Michael's personal 'one shot' ideology of the clean, 'pure' kill with the long American tradition of 'regeneration through violence' (see Slotkin, 1998) – also provoked comparisons with fascist imagery. However, whether 'one shot' and all it metonymically stands for should be seen as undermined or reaffirmed by its traumatically parodic reworking as Russian roulette in the film's pivotal Vietnam combat and captivity sequence, the film leaves (deliberately?) unclear. Oliver Stone's two Vietnam films of the 1980s, *Platoon* and *Born on the Fourth of July* – the first a 'pure' combat film, the second like *The Deer Hunter* a would-be epic saga whose Vietnam combat episode organises and defines the film's thematic and ideological concerns – explicitly foreground the emerging trope of Vietnam as a mythic landscape across which symbolic narratives of American male selfhood are enacted. While its dominant mode is clearly the Second World War combat film, *Platoon* also disinters some First World War 'lost generation' motifs in its fable of American everyman Chris Taylor's passage to disenchanted manhood and lost innocence (the jungle setting offers opportunities for such heavyhanded Edenic touches as a lurking coiled serpent) via the symbolic intercession of 'good and bad fathers' in the shape of his platoon's two sergeants, the saintly Elias and the demonic Bates. *Born on the Fourth of July* is even more explicitly Oedipal, as idealistic recruit Ron Kovic returns from Vietnam a paraplegic. The film devotes the greater part of its second half to Kovic's reckoning with the loss of his sexual function, an emasculation the film strongly associates – in a replay of 1950s pop-Freudian myths – with his 'castrating' patriotic mother and Kovic/

America's entrapment in an infantile dependency, both sexual and ideological. The film's climax, in which the radicalised Kovic leads fellow veterans in 'taking' the hall at the 1972 Republican National Convention, apparently proposes a commitment to the public and political as a way of breaking free from this complex; however, it is notable that the very last images of the film – which see Kovic, now an honoured activist, taking the platform at the 1976 Democratic Convention – are filmed as a recapitulation of the opening, with applauding expectant faces beaming down at the wheelchair-bound Kovic as before at his childhood self, fulfilling his mother's vision of his destiny which echoes, without obvious irony, on the soundtrack (see Jeffords, 1989: 19).

If Stone's Vietnam films chart an Oedipal trajectory of sorts from dependency towards adulthood, the hugely successful *First Blood* (1982) and *Rambo: First Blood Part II* (1984) fix their eponymous hero, the child-man Vietnam veteran John Rambo, in a regressive spiral. The monosyllabic simplicity of Rambo's understanding of the world – he is wounded by the abandonment of his symbolic 'parents', the nation – betrays an emotional and ideological vulnerability at odds with the hypertrophic masculinity of his pumped-up body, and the key mediating figure in his battle to make sense of the incomprehensible complexities, insincerities and betrayals of the adult world is his former commander and surrogate father, Col Trautmann. At the end of *First Blood*, it is Trautmann to whom the besieged Rambo – whose scapegoating in the film represents an extreme version of widespread cultural myths around the victimisation and rejection of returning Vietnam veterans (see Lembcke, 1998) – explains that 'we [i.e. Vietnam vets] just want our country to love us as much as we love it'. At the start of the sequel, given the opportunity to return to Vietnam on a POW rescue mission, Rambo frames the film's ensuing fantasy rerun of the war as a GI Joe-style fantasy with the childish question 'Do we get to win this time?' *Rambo*'s central premise – that American troops remained, to obscure purpose, captive in Vietnamese camps a decade and more after the war's end, a New Right shibboleth shared by *Uncommon Valor* (1983) and *Missing In Action* (1984) – offers a 'rescue fantasy', analysed by Burgoyne (1994) in terms of a regressive complex operative at various levels. (Among others, these films 'return' to the goal-oriented certainties of *Objective, Burma!* (1945) and its like: *Rambo*'s 'Vietnamese' soldiers are indistinguishable from the Imperial Japanese in Second World War combat films.) It also connects to the Vietnam film's preoccupation with masculinity inasmuch as it offers a contemporary variant of the captivity narratives that featured prominently in American popular culture during the nineteenth century of the Indian wars. In the Vietnam POW myth, however, the traditional object of savage captivity – white women – are substituted by soldiers. The soldiers' recovery (they are usually roused from passive despair to play an active role in their own liberation) represents a parallel restoration of American manhood – particularly since defeat of the Vietnamese enemy (sometimes accompanied by Soviet advisors, in an even more uncannily exact inversion of US involvement in Vietnam from 1960) is typically accomplished in the face of indifference or actual opposition from an incompetent, hypocritical or even outright traitorous governmental bureaucracy.[10]

POST-VIETNAM CONFLICTS

The 'asymmetrical warfare' of post-Vietnam conflicts – with US forces deploying overwhelming manpower and military technology power in lightning campaigns against hopelessly overmatched developing-world opponents in Grenada, Panama, Iraq and Afghanistan – apparently offered few compelling narratives to shift the combat film's dominant paradigm away from the Second World War/Vietnam composite. Certainly, these mismatches have enjoyed little screen time: *Heartbreak Ridge* (1986, Grenada) and *Three Kings* (1999, Iraq) are exceptions. In fact, as perhaps the 2004 remake of *The Manchurian Candidate* suggests (relocated to the first Gulf War of 1991 but, with obvious overtones of the second, substituting for the original's mindbending Communists a ruthless military-corporate entity clearly patterned after Halliburton Inc., former employers of Vice President Dick Cheney), the ramified, opaque and infinitely extensible 'war on terror' declared in the wake of the September 11th attacks will propel film-makers closer to the espionage thriller's shadowy world of surveillance and covert action than the combat film's terrain of pitched battles and firefights. Adaptations of Tom Clancy's bestselling techno-thrillers such as *Patriot Games* (1992) and *Clear and Present Danger* (1994) illustrate the form these spy-combat hybrids might take. 'Humanitarian' interventions, whether successful (Kosovo) or catastrophic (Beirut, Somalia), have proved equally unattractive as combat film subjects, although *Black Hawk Down*, an account of the disastrous Somalia episode that adopted many motifs of the standard 'embattled platoon' type, was released amid the post-September 11th war on Afghanistan and quickly pressed into service as a true story of American heroism in defence of universal freedoms.

CASE STUDY: *SAVING PRIVATE RYAN* (1998)

Upon its release in July 1998, Steven Spielberg's *Saving Private Ryan* was quickly recognised as a self-consciously traditionalist Second World War combat film, thus reviving a strain of the combat film that had been largely

From *Saving Private Ryan* (1998). Reproduced courtesy Dreamworks LLC/The Kobal Collection/David James.

in abeyance since the late 1970s. As noted above, from that point on the Hollywood war/combat film became largely synonymous with the Vietnam film – albeit the latter in numerous ways appropriated and adapted the Second World War paradigm. None of the few clear instances of the form in this period – including as well as the films noted above the somewhat revisionist *A Midnight Clear* (1992), which imported the well-known Great War trope of festive-season fellowship across battle lines[11] into the Second World War 'embattled platoon' genre model – were commercial successes, and it has been suggested that studio executives were unreceptive to what they perceived as an uncommercial subject. *Saving Private Ryan* is, as has also been widely perceived, very much a post-Vietnam (film) Second World War film: both the beach-head sequence (in its unprecedented bloodiness and hyper-realism) and the subsequent rescue mission (in recalling the 'missing in action' Vietnam sub-genre: see above) invoke the Vietnam film. What has been less remarked is that *Saving Private Ryan* not only rehabilitates the Second World War combat model but in so doing undertakes a clear project of generic correction in specific relation to the intervening Vietnam combat film.[12]

Saving Private Ryan is carefully modelled after the classic Second World War platoon film, with its ethnically and regionally diverse company including in time-honoured fashion a Jew, an Italian, a Southern Baptist (a deadeye sniper who prays before shooting), a tough-as-nails NCO and even the inevitable platoon member from Brooklyn. Unlike many Second World War (and even more Vietnam) combat films, however, in *Ryan* it is an officer, Captain Miller (Tom Hanks), who is the dramatic and affective centre of the film. Many wartime combat films, as Basinger (1986: 53–4) notes, kill off the commanding officer early in the narrative – demonstrating, she suggests, in the loss of a symbolic father the inevitable costs of war. (A Second World War film with an officer hero that *Ryan* closely recalls is *Objective, Burma!*, whose combination of quest and 'last stand' narratives *Ryan* also echoes. Errol Flynn's Capt. Nelson in the earlier film is a schoolteacher, a profession shared with Miller in *Ryan*, although Miller is – pointedly – a *history* teacher.) In making a commissioned officer the protagonist – and moreover rendering him as a model commander: tough, sensitive and principled – *Ryan* establishes a positive attitude towards established authority that informs the entire film. The ultimate example of this attitude is the portrayal of Gen. George Marshall as a beneficent and farsighted paternalistic leader (explicitly identified with Lincoln by his quotation from memory of the 'Bixby letter').

The respectful – in Marshall's case worshipful – treatment of authority might be read as an act of generic restitution in relation to the Vietnam films of the 1980s, in which combat officers were typically portrayed as irrelevant or incompetent (Lt Wolfe all but invisible in *Platoon*; Lt Gorman in the Vietnam/SF hybrid *Aliens*, 1986) or downright crazy (Col Kilgore in *Apocalypse Now*). It might also be considered a 'screen memory' (in every sense of the phrase) cancelling out the traumatic history of 'fragging' (infantrymen killing their commanding officers) in Vietnam. (Fussell (1989: 142f.) cites instances of this occurring in the Second World War as well.) However, it also revises the even longer-standing combat film trend noted by Neale (1991: 48; see above) towards a deficit of accountability and duty of care by officers to the men under their command. This is of considerable importance in *Ryan* since the mission Capt. Miller's team are sent on – initially damned by Miller himself as a 'public relations stunt' – would seem to exemplify Neale's category of orders issued that are 'contrary to the interests of the men' or 'of little or no strategic value'. Miller and his men come to believe that finding, and saving, Ryan is an objective of enormous, even inestimable, value. Rather as in *Objective, Burma!*, the surviving GIs realise only at the very end of the film the role their mission has played in the larger strategic plan, the higher humanity of military authority becoming apparent to the diminishing ranks of Miller's platoon as they fight their way towards the rendezvous with Ryan. However, the military wisdom thus justified is if anything even more rarefied than in *Objective, Burma!* as it relates not to a military objective – the invasion of Burma – but to an abstraction, the deeper humanity of American values as exemplified and embodied by Gen. Marshall.

This ties in closely with *Ryan*'s depiction of the Second World War as the 'Good War', an understanding fully in line with that of Stephen Ambrose, the author of several bestselling popular histories of the European war from the perspective of the US infantryman (1993, 1995, 1997) that heavily stressed the unique contribution and heroic, unstinting sacrifice of America's 'Greatest Generation' to the cause of liberty and democracy. Ambrose's approval of *Ryan* was solicited (and secured) by Dreamworks prior to the film's release. (Ambrose was subsequently an adviser to the Spielberg-produced HBO mini-series *Band of Brothers*, 1999.) While challenged by some historians (notably Fussell, 1993 and Zinn, 1995), this remains undoubtedly a dominant mainstream understanding of the war in US culture. The question is why this memory needed to be reaffirmed at this juncture, and how *Ryan* exploits genre to do this.

Three contextual factors defined the terms of *Saving Private Ryan*'s revival of the Second World War combat film. First, a rediscovered confidence in US military prowess following victory in the 1991 Gulf War diminished the appeal of the then-dominant combat genre paradigm, the Vietnam film, with its typical focus on victimhood and disenchantment. At the same time, as Auster (2002) notes, the Gulf War itself was too one-sided (and its final outcome, with US ally-turned-archenemy Saddam Hussein forced out of Kuwait but still in power in Baghdad, too ambiguous) to offer viable generic material as a direct alternative. The 50th anniversary of the end of the Second World War, in particular the commemoration of the D-Day landings, thus felicitously spurred renewed interest in a hard-fought, purposeful war with a clean and clearcut victory. Finally, the war – albeit an aspect of it remote from, and in the main suppressed in, conventional combat films – had retained a strong and disturbing presence in American collective memory with the increasing visibility of the Holocaust as a subject of public education, political debate (for example, on possible parallels with the ongoing ethnic and confessional wars in the Balkans) and cultural production, culminating in 1993 with the opening of the US Holocaust Memorial Museum in Washington, DC and the release of Spielberg's own multi-Academy-Award-winning *Schindler's List* (1993): Holocaust awareness is one of the novel elements in *Saving Private Ryan*'s careful mixture of generic tradition with innovation (see also Chapter 11, section III). Auteurist factors also played a part, with Spielberg's elevation to the status of 'serious' historical film-maker secured by the success of *Schindler's List*. Uniquely among the 'movie brats', as Doherty (1999: 303–4) notes, Spielberg's films had repeatedly invoked the war even prior to *Schindler's List*. Moreover, Spielberg's assiduously cultivated personal mythology stressed the centrality of the war – or an image of the war mediated by film and television – to his creative imagination since his youth.

Ryan unusually frames its combat narrative within an explicitly retro-spective framework: the film opens with an elderly man (revealed as Private Ryan when we return to him in the film's closing moments) stumbling through a vast war cemetery and falling to his knees before one among the thousands of headstones. A slow dolly close into his grief-stricken face then cuts to 'June 6, 1944' and leads directly into *Ryan*'s most celebrated passage, the astonishing 25–minute sequence at the Omaha beach-head. This framing of the war as a past event both remembered (by the veteran) and com-memorated (by his family – wife, children and grandchildren – tagging along behind him) is generically atypical: while many combat films both during and after the war opened or ended with title cards recalling to the audience the actuality of the events dramatised in the ensuing film and dedicating the film to the memory of those who laid down their own lives, *Ryan*'s eulogistic opening is more typical of nostalgic heritage films like *Lawrence of Arabia* (1962) – one of Spielberg's most admired films – or *Chariots of Fire* (1981), both of which unfold as (unmotivated) flashbacks from memorial services for the protagonist.

At the same time, Ryan's 'memory' is both uniquely his own and clearly collective – thus, in a sense, generic: for not only is his recollection situated physically in a space of public commemoration, with other veterans and their families glimpsed among the graves and thus generalised, but the 'flashback' which ensues *is not Ryan's own*. Ryan, as we learn in due course, parachuted behind enemy lines with the 101st Airborne Division: thus the landing at Omaha, and indeed everything that follows until the point at which Miller's platoon of Rangers meet up with Ryan's decimated company in the cornfield, is known to Ryan himself only second-hand at best (and then only if we imagine he either heard the story from Miller in an elided offscreen exchange prior to taking on the Panzers, or elicited it from the sole survivor Upham after the battle). Yet the hyper-real quality of the beach-head sequence at least allows us no room to accept it as anything but 'reality' experienced at first hand – indeed, traumatically so. In some ways, the landing sequence stands outside genre conventions, a traumatic assault on the spectator that cannot be readily accommodated to any expectational matrix and simply has to be experienced – 'survived' – by the audience as by Miller and his platoon, with whom an intense identification is thus sutured. While this might be con-sidered another instance of Spielberg's 'fantasy of witnessing', discussed by Weissman (1995) in relation to *Schindler's List*, equally various devices in the film – including the presence of the elderly Ryan's camera-clicking grandson, the almost subliminal re-enactment of Robert Capa's famous war photo-graphs amid the frenzy of the landing, and the inclusion of the bookish outsider Pvt Upham in the platoon as a more ambiguous version of the reporter familiar from *Objective, Burma!*, *The Story of G.I. Joe* (1945) and other combat films (see Badsey, 2002) – hint at the mediated, collective and (re-) constructed nature of this history/memory. I would not suggest that the explicitly generic terms of Ryan's remembrance (a suitably ambiguous term that denotes both personal memory and collective acts of tribute) suggest, like Ransom Stoddard's unreliable memories in *The Man who Shot Liberty Valance* (discussed in Chapter 2), the invidious inescapability of myth: rather, *Ryan*'s explicitly generic aspects may in fact serve to advertise the representative quality of the story and its trans-personal dimension – an important element given the film's generically atypical emphasis on individual rescue.

NOTES

1. This strain was sometimes known as 'Quirt-Flagg' after the sparring protagonists of *What Price Glory?*
2. *Sergeant York*'s publicity pack included an authorised statement from the real-life First World War hero whose story it dramatised advertising the film's timeliness (see Shindler, 1979: 43).
3. A distinction largely erased by recent research and the controversial 1995 exhibition of Wehrmacht war crimes in Hamburg.
4. US armed forces were desegregated by Truman's presidential order in 1948.
5. *Bataan*'s original screenplay included a Native American character.
6. Russian war film production continues throughout the period of glasnost and perestroika in the 1980s until the dissolution of the USSR in 1991: see below.
7. *Pork Chop Hill* was directed by Lewis Milestone, who also directed *All Quiet on the Western Front* as well as the major Second World War combat films *A Walk in the Sun* and *The Halls of Montezuma* (1951).
8. For a comprehensive annotated listing of all combat films released onto the US market between 1941 and 1980, see Basinger (1986: 281–335).
9. Benjamin Storr (1997) has explored parallels between the traumatic and controversial experiences of the Vietnam War in the USA and the Algerian War in France. The absence of direct images of the conflict itself is notable, as is the sense of an 'absence' surrounding the war despite some three dozen French films since 1962 dealing directly with the conflict (almost wholly through homefront or veteran experiences). By the same token, Lawton (1992: 167) and others have compared late Soviet-era and post-1991 films about the war in Afghanistan (widely characterised in the western media throughout the 1980s as 'the Soviet Vietnam' and itself invaded in a surreal juxtaposition by the Vietnam veteran/redeemer John Rambo in *Rambo III*, 1988) in their emphasis on the confusion of physically and psychically maimed veterans with the Vietnam veteran film.
10. See also the discussion of 1980s action film in Chapter 10.
11. For a compelling account of the legendary 'Christmas truce' on the Western Front in 1914 (also invoked on film in this period in Paul McCartney's lavish video promo for the single 'Pipes of Peace', 1983), see Ecksteins (1989: 109–14).
12. Krin Gabbard (2001) sees *Saving Private Ryan* as a rebuttal of the Vietnam era, rendering war once again an object of 'fascination and reverence' in the service of a renewed patriotic militarism. I agree with this reading and would add that it has been amply borne out by subsequent events. However, Gabbard does not work his critique of *Ryan* through an analysis of the film as a genre text.

CHAPTER 6

The Gangster Film: Genre and Society

L os Angeles, 1994. Professional hitmen Vincent Vega and Jules Winfield, returning from another successful assignment, have to deal with an unexpected problem: engaged in an animated discussion of chance and fate, Vincent unintentionally proves a point by accidentally discharging his pistol and killing their associate Marvin – more exactly, he splatters his brains copiously over the back seat and windows of their Lincoln Continental. Understandably apprehensive of the unwelcome attention their sanguinary state might draw should they continue cruising the LA freeway, Jules arranges an emergency pitstop at his friend Jimmie's place. The cool welcome Jimmie gives them has nothing to do with any moral revulsion or even physical squeamishness about murder and bloodshed, and everything to do with his apprehensions at how his wife – a night-shift nurse, entirely innocent of Jimmy's underworld connections – will respond upon her imminent return: 'If she comes home and sees a bunch of gangsters doing a bunch of gangster shit, she's going to flip'.

In this celebrated (or notorious) sequence from his breakthrough hit *Pulp Fiction* (1994), Quentin Tarantino's characteristically memorable summation of his (deliberately) two-dimensional criminals and their milieu as 'gangster shit' reveals a good deal about the place the gangster genre occupies in contemporary Hollywood film. In the first place, we are referred to an instantly recognisable and moreover highly stylised and codified world. We, Jules and Jimmie's wife all know 'gangster shit' when we see it. This familiarity is accentuated, flattened out comic-book style, and pushed to a parodic extreme by Tarantino, recasting the gangster's traditional interest in self-expression through personal cool and sartorial style as an ironic mod uniformity: Vincent and Marcellus inherit from the crew in Tarantino's debut film *Reservoir Dogs* (1991) a parodic underworld 'uniform' of black suits, white shirts and skinny black ties, in homage to the early 1960s style of the contract killers played by

Lee Marvin and Clu Galager in *The Killers* (1964), among others. This retro intertextual styling immediately announces these gangsters' distance from 'real' crime and their imbrication in an elaborate, hermetic world of their own (it also makes the Hawaiian beach gear in which they begin and end the film still more richly incongruous) (see Bruzzi, 1997: 67–94).

Tarantino's version of gangsterdom may be by some distance the most highly stylised and reflexive in contemporary US cinema, but the invocation of a codified, self-consciously ritualised fictive universe is common to many other films of the 1990s and 2000s. In *Things to Do in Denver When You're Dead* (1995), the sharp suit and slick moves of doomed gangster Jimmy 'the Saint' instantly out him as a gangster to the society girl he dreams of romancing. Michael Mann's gangster films push to a hermetic extreme a 'professionalising' tendency built into the genre from its emergence in the early 1930s, excluding the ordinary public almost entirely from their elaborate cops-and-robbers (and killers) arabesques: in *Thief* (1981), *Heat* (1995) and *Collateral* (2004), theft and murder are largely impersonal affairs in which individual interaction is simply a means to work through obscure principles and opaque codes; wealth is not the object of crime as a means to personal enrichment but a virtually abstract entity that provides a notional stake for the essential contest between pursuer and quarry. In many ways the knowing, stagy tenor in which such narratives unfold recalls the Italian 'Spaghetti Westerns' of the 1960s and early 1970s – it is no coincidence that Sergio Leone is a major influence on, and is frequently alluded to by, both Tarantino (particularly in *Kill Bill, Vol. 1*, 2003) and other contemporary gangster *auteurs* such as John Woo (notably *A Better Tomorrow*, Hong Kong 1988).

Contemporary gangster films often make the audience's assumed familiarity with gangster film codes and conventions a source of knowing humour, such as Marlon Brando's impersonation of his own famous Godfather character – a kind of 'Corleone drag' – in *The Freshman* (1990), or similar comic turns by actors with established Mob personae such as Joe Pesci (*My Cousin Vinny*, 1992) and James Caan (*Honeymoon in Vegas*, 1992; *Mickey Blue Eyes*, 1999). Although the comic stylisation in the successful HBO TV series *The Sopranos* (1998–) is less broad, the series still takes as a given the post-classical gangster's inevitable refraction through the archaeology of the genre; reflexivity and intertextuality here are less stylistic flourishes than naturalised facts of Mob life, as Tony Soprano and his suburban crew constantly invoke – albeit they reliably fail to live up to – the heroic models of their screen favourites, above all the *Godfather* trilogy (1972, 1974, 1991). In fact, *The Sopranos*' central conceit – that a contemporary organised crime boss is liable to find the challenges of modern American suburban life as taxing, and harder to resolve, than the traditional Mafia business of murder and extortion – is comprehensible and enjoyable largely because the audience are assumed to be familiar with the generic norms and how *The Sopranos* plays with them (see Creeber, 2002; Nochimson, 2003–4).

OUR GANGSTERS, OURSELVES: CRIME, AMERICA AND MODERNITY

As these examples help demonstrate, the gangster has become a highly visible figure in contemporary cinema. Indeed, while recent decades have seen Hollywood's other classical genre protagonists (the cowboy, the song-and-dance man, the private eye) suffer a fairly steady decline, the gangster has gone from strength to strength. Since *The Godfather* launched a major generic revival in the early 1970s, the genre's popularity has grown, to the point where the gangster can fairly claim to stand alongside the Western hero as a globally recognisable American cultural emblem (albeit a much more ambivalent and controversial one). As Neale (2000: 77f.) notes, the film gangster like the Western hero has often been discussed in socially symptomatic terms; in fact, the gangster is frequently received as the Westerner's urban mirror image, enacting the conflicts and complexities of an emergent urban modern imaginary as the cowboy enacts those of a residual agrarian myth.[1] Like the Westerner, the gangster and his values have been embedded in a fairly stable thematic and iconographic universe established and consolidated through decades of reiteration and revision, and a certain masculine style and the elaboration of a code of behaviour through acts of decisive violence are central concerns in both genres. A number of writers draw parallels between the two genres: McCarty (1993: xii) describes the gangster film as 'the modern continuation of the Western – a story the Western had grown too old to tell.' Direct narrative translations from one genre to the other, however, though not unknown, are infrequent – *The Oklahoma Kid* (1939) is a straightforward transposition of the Warners gangster model to the frontier, complete with Cagney and Bogart, during a transitional period for both genres; *Last Man Standing* (1996) relocates *A Fistful of Dollars* (1964; itself a Western remake of Akira Kurosawa's samurai film *Yojimbo*, Japan 1962) to a Depression-era gangster milieu. The rarity of these generic exchanges may point to some more fundamental divergences.

In the first place, during the classical Hollywood period the gangster featured far less frequently *as protagonist* than the cowboy or gunfighter. The sensational success of the first wave of sound-era gangster films in the early 1930s fired a (largely synthetic) moral panic that has been widely covered by genre historians (see Rosow, 1978: 156–71; Maltby, 1995b; Munby, 1999: 93–110) and whose outcome was the announcement in 1935 by the Production Code Administration of a moratorium on Hollywood gangster film production.

In fact, the gangster cycle may have run its commercial course by 1935, and since the Production Code – an enforceable reality from 1934 – was going to make the sympathetic or even balanced depiction of any kind of professional criminal very difficult if not impossible, the studios may have felt the sacrifice of the gangster film well worth the public relations benefits it secured. The upshot in any event was that after 1935 gangsters became heavies – antagonists to such 'official' heroes as police detectives, FBI agents and T-Men (Treasury Agents), or the balefully anti-social presence that ensured that an 'outlaw hero' like the private eye, however often at odds with official law enforcement, nonetheless remained visibly on the side of the angels (see Ray, 1985: 59–66). Often enough, the same actors who had risen to stardom in the first wave of gangster films, like James Cagney and Edward G. Robinson, now represented the forces of law and order (frequently with fairly minimal retooling of their screen personae). As early as 1939, the traditional racketeering, bootlegging mobster had already become something of a nostalgic figure: Cagney laments in *The Roaring Twenties* (1939) that 'all the A-1 guys are gone or in Alcatraz ... all that's left are soda jerks and jitterbugs'. Films focusing once again not on heroic gangbusters and under-cover agents but on the career criminal himself and his organisation became possible only with the gradual relaxation of the Code during the 1950s and its final abolition in 1966. *The Godfather* – by no means the only Mafia chronicle of the late 1960s and early 1970s, though by far the most successful – combined a careful sense of prior genre history with a new emphasis on the intricate, hermetic inner world of the Mafia, and its scale and seriousness as well as its huge popularity established new and durable parameters for the genre.

Westerns and gangster films share a defining ambivalence with which they engage the values of settled civilisation. However, where the Western typically offers the spectator a subject position *outside* community from which to measure its gains and losses, the gangster's story unfolds for better or worse wholly within the domain of a highly developed and above all urban culture. In fact, just as the Western works through issues around the closing of the historical frontier, the gangster genre answers to the metropolitan experience of rapid, large-scale urbanisation. Both distil material history into a set of narrative paradigms, character types and typical settings that reshape historical experience into meaningful aesthetic form. The gangster is the man of the city as the cowboy is the man of the frontier.

In terms of genre history, the same endemic critical selectivity we have already seen at work upon the Western and musical canons has in this case ensured that the received version of the 'classic' gangster film and its iconic protagonist in the most influential and widely-read accounts has been derived from an extraordinarily small number of films. According to Schatz (1981: 86–95) 'the narrative formula seemed to spring from nowhere in the early

1930s', when effectively just three films make up 'possibly the briefest classic period of any Hollywood genre'. These films – *The Public Enemy* (1930), *Little Caesar* (1931) and *Scarface* (1932), the first two at Warner Bros., the last independently produced by Howard Hughes – have hugely over-shadowed both their predecessors in the silent and very early sound eras and all but a few later gangster films until the gangster revival launched by *The Godfather*. Hardy (1998: 304–12) directly contradicts Schatz's account of the genre's origins, stating that 'the genre did not spring to life fully formed', but while extending the gangster film's prehistory back into the late silent period and *Underworld* (1927, scripted by Ben Hecht, who also wrote the screenplay for *Scarface*, also cited, though not discussed, by Schatz), he too takes the canonical 1930s trio as generically definitive. Shadoian (2003: 32–61) declares that 'the flurry of early thirties gangster films laid down the bases for future developments', but discusses only *Little Caesar* and *The Public Enemy* and otherwise refers in his section on 'the Golden Age' of the 1930s only to *Scarface* and one other 1930s gangster film, the comedy *The Little Giant* (1933), which is cited in passing to exemplify the ways in which (exactly twelve months after the release of *Scarface*, 'the ultimate expression of the genre's early phase'[2]) the Hollywood gangster had become 'a domesticated creature … an anachronism … the stuff of legend more than fact' (p. 31). However, Rosow (1978: 120–210) lists at least nine other directly contemporaneous gangster films of the late 1920s and early 1930s.

In fact, Hardy, Schatz and even Shadoian do all make reference to one very much earlier film about urban criminal gangs, D. W. Griffith's *The Musketeers of Pig Alley* (1912), but none of them explore either the intervening two decades or the possible relationship between the (early/late) silent-era gangster and his more celebrated successors. Shadoian's view that after Griffith the gangster film 'struggled in unfertilised soil through to the end of the twenties' (p. 29) seems to be the majority opinion. However, Grieveson (2005 forthcoming) discusses a range of more than thirty silent gangster films dating back as early as 1906, of which *Regeneration* (1915) – described by its director Raoul Walsh as 'the first full-length gangster picture ever made' – is perhaps the best-known. While some of these films, such as the series of films in the mid-1910s on white slave rings (notably *Traffic in Souls*, 1913) and another, slightly later series about Chinatown and 'Tong' gangs, seem remote from the concerns of later gangster films, others have quite clear connections: for example, the films dealing with the Italian 'Black Hand' (in *The Godfather, Part II*, the predatory Don Fanucci, the young Vito Corleone's first 'hit', is identified as a member of the Black Hand).[3] This genre archaeology is of more than narrowly academic interest since it bears directly not only on the standard accounts of genre conventions but also on the ways in which the gangster film has most often been historically located.

Numerous studies of the genre, including the three cited above, take it as axiomatic that the seminal gangster films are directly contemporary with the phenomenon they depict. The banner newspaper headlines screaming of mob warfare that spiral dizzily out of the screen, an instant genre cliché (nostalgically invoked in *The Godfather*'s 'mattresses' montage), are taken as metonymic of the gangster film's own determined topicality. Organised crime had of course rocketed, and hence come to national prominence, during America's extraordinary and wholly unsuccessful experiment with Prohibition from 1919 to 1933 (although as Ruth (1996: 45) points out, both as criminological fact and as a public figure the gangster 'predated his bootlegger incarnation'). The unremarkable desire to have a drink set millions of otherwise law-abiding citizens on the wrong side of the law; quenching their thirsts required the establishment of regional networks of illegal production, distribution and sale of alcohol, an immensely profitable if risky business that won huge fortunes and in a few cases – most notably Chicago's Al Capone, the original 'Scarface' – nationwide notoriety, aided and abetted by a sensation-hungry press.

As clearly relevant as Prohibition-era gangsters were to the 1930s gangster cycle, however – Rosow (1978: 201–10) incidentally identifies not *Little Caesar* but *The Doorway to Hell* (1930) as the first film based on Al Capone and a strong influence on the better-known later films – if the gangster is truly to be identified with the Prohibition-era mobster one might ask why such evidently topical and compelling material only found its way onto movie screens very shortly before the Volsted Act was repealed in 1933. Schatz (1981: 85) and others argue that the gangster film had to await the coming of sound (in 1927) for the soundtrack of gangland – 'gunshots, screams, screeching tires' and also a specific style of fast-paced, hard-boiled dialogue – to bring the gangster and his urban milieu fully to life.[4] However, what Grieveson and other scholars of early cinema's relationship to urban modernity demonstrate is that throughout the silent era – in US political terms roughly congruent with the Progressive period – there was a well-established discourse that comprehended crime and vice in America's burgeoning metropolises (above all New York and Chicago) in terms of social hygiene and reform (see Grieveson, 1997, 2005 forthcoming; Gunning, 1997), and that the silent-era gangster was more likely to be conceived in these terms than in the quasi-Nietzschean mode often identified with the 1930s film gangster (Rosow, 1978: 67 also notes that gangster films first appeared 'in the context of Progressive documentary realism'). In other words, the silent gangster film used a different, rather than simply an inadequate, 'language' to articulate the experience of urban modernity.

The emphasis on social environmental factors in the production of criminality, and the associated conviction in the efficacy of reform, meant that one of the dominant themes of silent-era gangster films was the concept of personal redemption from a life of crime (such conversion narratives also dominated the Victorian and early-twentieth century stage melodramas that provided early film-makers with many of their dramaturgic models). The striking absence of any suggestion of remorse or efforts at restitution from the protagonists of the early 1930s films who – with the possible and limited exception of Tom Powers in *The Public Enemy* – go wholly unrepentant to their violent ends is often cited as a decisive break and an indication of the classic gangster's breakout into modernity from the residual Victorianism of the silent era. In fact, the reintroduction of such moralistic motifs into later 1930s gangster films, both pre-moratorium (*Manhattan Melodrama*, 1934, whose gangster protagonist Blackie (Clark Gable) virtually lobbies his best friend the DA to send him to the chair) and after (*Dead End*, 1936, with its slum setting and strong elements of social critique, and *Angels With Dirty Faces*, 1938, whose gangster anti-hero (Cagney) feigns cowardly breakdown on his way to the gas chamber to save the next generation of street kids from wanting to emulate him) is often cited as evidence of their generic inauthenticity and the gangster film's general decline after *Scarface*. However, if the 1930–32 classics are not regarded as the gangster film's originary moment but located in a longer generic history, it is if anything the repentance theme that starts to look like the mainstream generic tradition and the titanic *Scarface*-style individualist the exception.

Given for example that the genre has influentially been read as an allegory of both the allure and the potentially catastrophic consequences of untrammelled individualism, it may be no accident that the gangster film thrives in the early years of the Depression, in the immediate aftershock of the Wall Street Crash of October 1929. The traumatic collapse of the 1920s boom – fuelled by wild stock-market speculation rather than industrial expansion – not only undermined the triumphal capitalism of the Coolidge and Hoover eras, but called into the question the very premises of the American social and economic system. In the years before more positive, pro-social models of responding to the crisis emerged under Roosevelt's New Deal, the screen gangster violently articulated the disturbing possibility that the quintessentially American values encapsulated in the 'Horatio Alger myth' – the poor boy who makes good through his own determination, hard work, dedication to achieving his goals and so forth – might actually prove destructive, both to himself and to the wider society, if left uncurbed. The gangster shares the Alger myth's attractive qualities of vitality, vigour and determination; but he also exposes their dark underbelly: recklessness, selfishness, sadism and an ultimately self-defeating spiral of violent self-assertion. Thus the gangster film typically stands in an at least implicitly critical relationship to the society it depicts. In Robert Warshow's ([1948] 1975a) influential argument, to the

(American) audience the gangster is an exemplary and admonitory figure of fatally overreaching ambition, yet one who also bespeaks some uneasy truths about American capitalism. This critical dimension to the gangster film may be qualified by the perception that the gangster's typical narrative trajectory – from obscurity to wealth and power, only to end in inevitable downfall and defeat – is constructed to underpin a simplistic moral that 'crime does not pay'. As Munby points out, however, the intense controversy culminating in the Hays' Office 'moratorium' implies at the very least that such a message, even if intended, was not wholly or satisfactorily transparent to contemporary Establishment viewers of 1930s gangster films. On the contrary, elite opinion in this period was persistently exercised at the prospect that the glamorous portrayal of Mob life in these films – notwithstanding the gangster's inevitable bloody doom – would attract impressionable urban youths towards a life of crime rather than deter them from it (see also Springhall, 1998).

Munby and other commentators also suggest, however, that elite deprecation of the gangster film was in fact less a reflection of real anxiety about these films' role in encouraging an upsurge in violent racketeering than a focal point for a deeper nativist hostility to the growing visibility and political and economic power of new ethnic groups in the early twentieth-century United States, directed at Catholics in general and Italian-Americans in particular. The Depression-era gangsters might thus serve as cautionary fables not only of individualism rampant, heedless of social constraints, but also of the dangers of ethnic particularism versus assimilation. Portraying Italian- (as in *Little Caesar* and *Scarface*) or Irish- (as in *The Public Enemy*) Americans as gangsters might seem to serve such xenophobic ideologies rather well. (The scenes of public outrage at gangland excesses in *Scarface* – interpolated just prior to release over director Howard Hawks's protests and without his cooperation – include a reference to the gangsters as 'not even citizens!' suggesting that one part of the gangster film's agenda is to render criminal violence 'unAmerican'.) Unsurprisingly, prominent Italian-Americans like New York Mayor Fiorella La Guardia quickly denounced such characters as Rico (in *Little Caesar*) as defamatory. (Vigorous protests accompanied the production and release of *The Godfather*, and have themselves become the object of satire in *The Sopranos*.)

On the other hand, by implying that American society, far from welcoming the 'huddled [immigrant] masses' into the mainstream culture, relegated ethnic minorities to the economic margins where asocial activities offered in effect the only escape route from poverty and social exclusion, the gangster film could be read as a corrosive critique of hegemonic American values. And, endowed with so much more vigour, wit and charisma than the ossified forces of established authority (criminal or legal) he opposes and overcomes, the gangster provides a powerful – and a transgressive – figure of identification for the ethnic, urban constituency he represents.

Alongside ethnicity, as an urban form dealing with responses to deprivation in a highly materialistic culture the gangster film also inevitably sheds light on a greater unmentionable, not only in Hollywood but in American society generally: class. While the 'official' American ideology – including the Turnerian myth of the frontier – stigmatised class societies and class struggle as 'Old World' evils that had been purged from the idealised American commonwealth, the growth of labour unions and such political movements as Populism meant that class conflict was in fact at its most intense in American society in the years immediately before and after the First World War. Lulled by the briefly shared prosperity of the 1920s, the onset of the Depression saw the spectre of class conflict return with a vengeance (see Parrish, 1992: 405–21). As with ethnicity, the gangster ambivalently enacts some of the brutal realities of class in modern America, both exposing and falling victim to the exigencies of class struggle. In fact, the gangster might be seen as an exemplary subject of ideological misrecognition: Tony Camonte in *Scarface* mistakes the advertising slogan 'the world is yours' as a personal message and sets out to act upon it. Established at the outset of the narrative as belonging to a lower professional and social order than his boss or patron, the gangster devotes his ferocious energies not to assaulting or overturning this social and economic hierarchy, but to triumphing within it by a more ruthless exploitation of its values than anyone else. Far from being disaffected or alienated from the system, the gangster displays an extreme degree of investment in it. As Edward Mitchell (1976) argues, he wholeheartedly adopts the logic of the key elements of early twentieth-century American ideology that underpinned the existing distribution of resources – a secularised Puritanism (whose concept of the 'elect' could be adapted to underpin the notion of a heroic 'man of destiny', fated to triumph where others fail) and Social Darwinism (where the neutral processes of natural selection were recast as 'the survival of the fittest' and used to justify the vicious dog-eat-dog contest of laissez-faire capitalism). The gangster's progress up the professional ladder is accompanied by the traditional trappings of self-improvement – not only fine clothes, fast cars and the woman of his dreams, but a self-conscious cultivation of taste (Tony Camonte attends a performance of Somerset Maugham's *Rain*, 'a serious show'; Bugs Raymond (Edward G. Robinson) in the gangster comedy *The Little Giant* studies Plato and acquires abstract modern art). Yet his gutter origins ultimately betray him, both to the audience and to his peers: Poppy finds Tony's apartment 'gaudy', the Corleones endures WASP jibes at their 'guinea charm' and 'silk suits'; Noodles in *Once Upon a Time in America* finally accepts his lost love's Deborah's insight that 'he'll always be a two-bit punk'. In fact, it is the gangster's deracination that finally dooms him: his investment in ascending the ladder of class compels him to adopt an alien identity and attenuates the powerful energies of self-assertion that have taken him this far.

A Marxist reading of the genre would stress this notion of self-alienation as an ineradicable function of capitalism, and might point to the corruption of the family, a repeated motif in gangster films since the 1930s, as a key marker. According to Marx and his collaborator Friedrich Engels, the cultural privileging of the 'Holy Family' under bourgeois society is a characteristic ideological ruse – diverting the worker's valid aspirations towards self-realisation in a politically harmless direction (which is also economically necessary to replenish the workforce) while offering him a petty tyranny of his own (over his wife and children) to assuage the misery of his own class oppression. The family unit thus becomes a grim parodic miniature of the unjust and twisted power relations that typify bourgeois capitalism as a whole. However, this implies that the inherently unstable contradictions of class society – and their potential for catastrophic implosion – might also be encountered in the family. From such a perspective, the gangster's characteristic obsession with preserving 'his' family, which nonetheless leads ineluctably to its destruction, becomes enormously revealing. In *Scarface*, Tony Camonte's incestuous bond with his sister Cesca, which drives him to murder her husband, becomes a lover's pact that sees them die side by side in a hail of police bullets. Michael Corleone insists throughout *The Godfather, Part II* that his criminal enterprises, like his father's, are all intended for 'the good of the family'; but as his power crests his family is progressively decimated, and he is himself either directly responsible for, or implicated in, the deaths of his brother-in-law, his brother and his daughter (and his unborn child, aborted by his wife Kay in revulsion against the 'evil' Michael has wrought). His uncomprehending mother reassures him that 'you can never lose your family', but Michael realises that 'times have changed'. Michael's blind pursuit of power, ostensibly in the name of the family, unleashes uncontainable forces that must ultimately destroy it, perfectly encapsulating the Marxist insight that the 'protected' familial realm cannot finally be protected from the atomising forces of the very capitalism that claims to preserve it. In *Force of Evil* (1947) Mob lawyer Joe Morse's involvement with ruthless racketeer Tucker leads indirectly but inexorably to his brother Leo's murder; *The Godfather, Part II* ends with Michael himself ordering the murder of his brother Fredo.

The centrality of the family to the gangster seems at first glance paradoxical: for if anything the gangster is identified with the catastrophic apotheosis of the overweening, even imperial self. The gangster film is in fact the only major genre to be named after its protagonist. Yet as the very word implies, the gangster's apparently hypertrophic individualism is itself only skin–deep and ultimately vulnerable: unlike the Westerner the gangster – an *organised* criminal – is heavily reliant on others not only for his power but for his identity. For all that his story apparently enacts wild self-assertion and radical self-fashioning, from another perspective it becomes apparent that the gangster's selfhood is really constructed through the group. *Goodfellas* (1989) opens with the bald statement in voiceover: 'All my life I always wanted to be a gangster', but the remainder of the film works through with brutal thoroughness the mutually contradictory thrust of the desire on the one hand to belong, and by belonging to confirm an apparently secure selfhood (knowing what one wants and acting to achieve it) versus on the other the inherent logic of violence that will inevitably end up making victims of the gang's own members and reducing the gangster himself to a state of paranoid uncertainty.[5]

Warshow's sense of the gangster as throwing into relief the values of mainstream America is captured in the gangster's ambivalent relationship to his 'family' (the gang *or* his actual blood relations), which may express the profoundly ambiguous place of community in a society that supremely valorises the individual at the expense of the collective. Typically, the gang itself is both indispensable and a burden, even a threat, to the gangster: he needs the support of his soldiers, and it is by his ascent from the ranks that his self-assertion is measured; yet the gangster knows only too well how dangerous it is to rely on any ties, even those of blood. Not only the outright treachery, but the simple unreliability of one's associates is a repeated trope of the genre: Fredo Corleone's weakness and resentment make him an unwitting accomplice to an attempt on his brother Michael's life in *The Godfather Part II* (in the first *Godfather* it is Fredo who is driving his father, and who fails to draw his own gun, when the Don is shot down in the street); Carlito spends most of *Carlito's Way* (1993) trying, and failing, to extricate himself from the toils of his attorney Dave Kleinfeld's greed and recklessness. The gangster film implicitly ironises its subject inasmuch as it stresses the self-sufficient individual the gangster desires to be and insists he is, yet – precisely because he is a *gangster* – he can never become.

This performative contradiction of radical autonomy and dependency can also be read in psychoanalytic terms: the gangster's riotous self-assertion, whether expressed through the violence he inflicts on others or through his characteristic ostentatious displays of wealth and power (clothes, cars, guns, women), literally embodies Lacan's notion of the 'gaze of the Other'. The gangster conceives of himself as self-authored/authorised, in thrall to no one – in fact, as classically in Tony Camonte's ruthless rise to power in *Scarface*, being in the power of, or reliant on, others is intolerable to him. Yet as Lacan's account of the subject's constitution through entry into the Symbolic order (paradigmatically language, but by extension all of the social structures through which the individual is socialised) makes clear, individuality is a function of relationality: identity is confirmed only by its constitution in the regard of an Other. Refusal to register the role of others/the Other in limning the subject's selfhood is at best regressive infantile fantasy, at worst psychotic. Elements of both tendencies are present in the classic 1930s gangsters; as the genre takes on *noir* shadings in the postwar period, in the mother-fixated sociopath Cody Jarrett (James Cagney) in *White Heat* (1949), both are wholly uncontained and violently acted out.

In this section we have touched on several themes that have structured gangster films since the silent era, including individualism and the 'American Dream', selfhood and subjectivity, masculinity, urbanism, the family, class and ethnicity. All of these were very much 'live' categories in the cultural discourses of pre-Second World War America. Following the 1935 moratorium, the gangster was displaced by the pro-social 'official' hero – the police detective, Treasury or FBI agent – in the later 1930s and by the early 1940s had become a nostalgic figure. During the war years even gangsters (on-screen at least) placed their patriotic duty before their private gain (see Young, 2000). Throughout the 1950s, in such films as *The Big Heat* (1953), *The Big Combo* and *The Phenix City Story* (both 1955) gangsters featured as increasingly impersonal antagonists – quasi-corporate crime syndicates that, like the pods in *Invasion of the Body Snatchers* (1955), mirrored contemporary anxieties about both Communism and the domestic culture of conformity – to 'official' heroes whose own motives and methods became increasingly questionable. Mason (2002: 97–119) sees the films of this period as preoccupied with conspiracy and the systemic failures of 'straight' society to protect and enable masculine individuality, consequently provoking that individuality to take on ever more stressful and 'illegitimate' forms.

Other major genres suffered far more from Old Hollywood's terminal crisis than the gangster film, which was neither ideologically central to the outgoing system (like the Western) nor directly implicated economically in its collapse (like the failed musicals of the late 1960s). The Production Code's abolition in 1966 and its replacement in 1968 by a national ratings system also meant that the remaining inhibitions on content – massively attenuated by the mid-1960s, but still with some force to the extent that exhibitors were attached to the Code Seal of Approval – were no longer a problem. The remainder of this chapter will look in more detail at the ways that since the return of the gangster as protagonist in *Bonnie and Clyde* (1967) and *The Godfather*, the thematic preoccupations of the 1930s gangster cycle have been renewed, reviewed and extended, in a period marked in the gangster film as in other traditional genres by an intense self-consciousness concerning generic traditions and the uses of genre revisionism.

THE GANGSTER REVIVAL

The Godfather – whose success was a major factor driving Hollywood's early 1970s nostalgia boom – established an enduring popularity for the 'retro' gangster film, often lavishly mounted prestige vehicles, sometimes on an epic scale, dramatising the halcyon years of the pre-Second World War Mob: examples include, in addition to *Godfathers II* and *III*, *Lepke* (1975), *Lucky Lady* (1976), *F*I*S*T* (1978), *Once Upon a Time in America*, *The Untouchables* (1987), *Miller's Crossing* (1990), *Billy Bathgate* (1991), *Bugsy* (1992) and *The Road to Perdition* (2001). Grandiose thematic pretensions, generally aspiring to statements about the (lost) American Dream, alongside the self-conscious rendering of the gangster as a quintessential American figure, are notable features inherited by many of these films from Coppola's saga (which opens with the line 'I believe in America' – spoken symbolically enough by an undertaker), as is a Stygian visual register aping Gordon Willis's atmospheric photography for the first two films and intended to communicate the murky moral universe inhabited by the characters. Most retro Mob films focus on the trials of leadership and several advertise the parallels between the objectives and the methods of organised crime and those of 'legitimate' corporate business. This marks a subtle yet clear ideological shift in the presentation of the generic material. In post-classical Hollywood the gangster becomes less of an exceptional and cautionary figure, and increasingly representative of the frustration and disillusion that have terminally corroded the promise of America. Exploitative, ruthless organised crime itself is represented – most famously in *The Godfather* – as not a caricature but simply the unmasked truth of 'straight' contemporary American society, in all its relentless dehumanisation. Rumours about Mafia implication in the assassination of President Kennedy in 1963 had gained wide circulation by the start of the 1970s, and with ongoing revelations about criminality at the highest political levels, culminating in 1973 with former White House Counsel John Dean's dramatic refusal to reassure the Watergate enquiry that the Nixon White House's 'dirty tricks' would stop even at murder, the gangster film seemed all too apposite a vehicle for allegorising power relations in contemporary America.

Several post-classical gangster films, including *The Godfather, Part II*, *Bugsy* and *Things to Do in Denver When You're Dead*, re- (and dis)locate the gangster away from his natural dense urban milieu into the Western wilderness, ironically observing the incongruities that result; 'old-school' veterans such as Frankie Pentangeli in *Godfather II* and Joe Hess, the narrator of *Things to Do in Denver*, nostalgically figure the lost verities of the gangster's urban origins and invoke integrated ethnic communities dissipated by suburban dispersal. With the virtual absence of any visible or effective structures of law enforcement in many of these films, the identificatory conflictual locus reorients itself around the clash between an 'old-school' criminal – characterised by loyalty to crew, (some) regard for human life and rugged individualism – and an impersonal, quasi-corporate criminal organisation. The anti-heroic version of the American Dream embodied by the classic individualist gangster seems to dissipate alongside the decline of its 'official' counterpart in mainstream society; thus the old-style gangster becomes a nostalgically heroicised figure standing in opposition to a machine-like bureaucracy whose ruthlessness is intensified, rather than diminished, by its depersonalisation. This sub-genre is foreshadowed in both some prewar gangster films like *The Roaring Twenties* and *High Sierra* (1941) – compare Carlito Brigante's (Al Pacino) characterisation of the contemporary scene where 'there ain't no rackets ... just a bunch of cowboys ripping each other off' with Eddie Bartlett's swipe at 'soda jerks and jitterbugs' in *The Roaring Twenties*, quoted above – and postwar *noir* gangster films like *Force of Evil* and *The Gangster* (1949). However, its paradigmatic film is *Point Blank* (1967), whose dream-like narrative sees the betrayed Walker, in single-minded pursuit of the loot stolen from him, frustrated and suspended – 'on hold' – in an endless series of stonewalling referrals to higher authority. The obsessive simplicity of Walker's quest for 'his' money is repeatedly characterised by the 'suits' he has to deal with as a relic of an older, obsolete way of doing business. *Point Blank* is narrated as a series of stylised vignettes whose frequently unplaceable, dream-like quality opens the possibility that the entire film is the dying Walker's *Pincher Martin*-like fantasy of revenge as he bleeds out on the floor of Alcatraz, and links the film strongly to the oneiric strain in *film noir* (see Chapter 9). More prosaic accounts of mavericks outwitting sclerotic corporate crime in the same period include *Charley Varrick* ('the last of the independents') and *The Outfit* (both 1973).

Alongside mythic and nostalgia narratives, another strand in the post-classical gangster film has been a series of films focusing not on titanic kingpins but on lower-level gangsters: 'wiseguys', 'soldiers' and day-to-day villains who aspire not to the Presidency but to more modest degrees of comfort and status. In this mode, Martin Scorsese's *Mean Streets* (1973), a portrayal of a group of Italian-American petty hoods critically lauded but little seen on its original release, has proved enormously influential. Scorsese's own distinctive style, refined in *Goodfellas* and *Casino* (1995), combines an intense naturalism of setting and performance with a highly demonstrative and intensely aestheticised visual style, resulting in an almost hallucinatory and yet also hyper-real penetration of his characters and their milieu. *Atlantic City* (1981), *State of Grace* (1990), *Donnie Brasco* (1997) as well as *The Sopranos* and the comedies *Mad Dog and Glory* (1989) and *The Whole Nine Yards* (2000) wholly or in part explored terrain opened up by *Mean Streets* (itself strongly influenced by Pasolini's *Accatone*, 1960), though lacking Scorsese's kinetic, visionary style.

The focus on urban small-timers in some cases – such as *Donnie Brasco* – imparts to the mainstream urban gangster film some of the fatalism traditionally associated with its rural variant. Films relating the exploits of Depression-era outlaws from *Machine Gun Kelly* (1958) to *Bloody Mama* (1971) and *Thieves Like Us* (1974) emphasise the roots of their protagonists' turn to crime in dispossession, deracination and despair, and offer fewer corrective alternative models (the priest, the crusading journalist) than their urban counterparts. The most famous rural gangster film, *Bonnie and Clyde* (1967), identifies its highly glamorised couple explicitly with Dustbowl victims of economic banditry – at one point, Clyde hands his gun to an unhoused farmer (and his Black farmworker) to take cathartic potshots at their former smallholding, now foreclosed on by the bank – as well as more loosely with the youth counterculture then adopting a more militant stance in relation to the straight Establishment. While both rural and urban gangsters are typically doomed, rural gangsters seem to enjoy few of the glamorous fruits – the penthouse apartments, sleek automobiles and designer clothes – of their urban colleagues: their pickings are slimmer, their lives more fugitive and itinerant. The rural gang closely resembles a family horde like the James Gang or the Daltons and is correspondingly small-scale, lacking the hierarchical, crypto-corporate aspect of the urban crime Syndicate. Whereas the urban gangster film has usually, as we have seen, been constructed in mythic polarity to the Western, there are strong links between the rural gangster film, some film versions of the Jesse James and Billy the Kid myths (notably *Billy the Kid*, 1930, *Pat Garrett and Billy the Kid*, 1973, and *Jesse James*, 1939), and the outlaw tradition that Eric Hobsbawm terms 'social banditry'. Another traditional syntactic feature of the Western to migrate to the contemporary gangster film is the dream of escaping 'across the border', which features in *Carlito's Way* and the Tarantino-scripted *True Romance* (1994): these films play off the established post-*Godfather* concept of organised crime as the image of a universally oppressive and destructive social reality and suggest that whereas for the classic gangster fantasies of self-advancement and fulfilment were sustainable and even (however briefly) realisable within society, these are today only achievable in an imaginary 'elsewhere'.

The most obvious innovation in the gangster film in recent years is the incorporation of the African-American experience into the classic ethnic gangster paradigm, with films like *Boyz N the Hood* (1990) and *Dead Presidents* (1995) faithfully translating classic models like *Dead End* and *The Roaring Twenties* to the modern urban ghetto. Other films, however – notably *Menace II Society* (1993) – evince a nihilistic despair at odds with all but the most dyspeptically revisionist New Hollywood white gangster films. As Munby (1999: 225–6) and Mason (2002: 154–7) argue, these differences can be attributed to the irrelevance of the mythology of the American Dream to Black Americans – upon whose exclusion from the possibility of 'Americanisation' and *embourgeoisement* the Dream is in fact partly predicated. A controversy virtually identical to that surrounding the 1930s gangster cycle erupted around the African-American themed gangster ('gangsta') films of the early 1990s, with both White elite opinion-formers and Black religious and political leaders inveighing virtually unanimously against the high body-counts and apparent glorification of inner-city drug lords in such films as *New Jack City* (1991) and *Menace II Society*. Both box-office returns and accounts of audience response in African-American neighbourhoods, by contrast, suggested that some Black audiences found in the larger-than-life protagonists figures of these films precisely the kind of militant empowerment their critics so feared (see Munby, 1999: 225f.).

BEYOND HOLLYWOOD

Most national cinemas – other than those, such as the Soviet-era Eastern Bloc, for whom domestic crime was an ideological impossibility – have produced their indigenous variants of the gangster genre, with particularly strong indigenous gangster traditions in Britain and France. Few, however, have used the figure of the gangster himself in the culturally and socially paradigmatic manner of his American incarnation. A notable exception to this rule is Harold Shand (Bob Hoskins), the London gangland boss in *The Long Good Friday* (GB 1980), whose plans to internationalise his operations by a link-up to the US Mafia and to diversify into property development are depicted as a cautionary Thatcherite fable. Harold's plans are ironically undone by the return of a political and colonial repressed, the Troubles in Northern Ireland; Swain (1998: 2) argues that Harold's 'railings against an unseen and unknown enemy (which turns out to be the IRA) are suggestive of a generic as well as political anxiety,' and the film indeed suggests that Harold's aspirations to leave his roots behind (he lives on a boat) and become a player on the global gangster stage are doomed by his (and Britain's) bloody unfinished business at home.

Whereas the American screen gangster takes paradigmatic shape early on in the genre's history, the British gangster mutates through several guises, from the postwar 'spiv' cycle, including *They Made Me a Fugitive*, *Brighton Rock* (both GB 1947), *It Always Rains on Sundays* and *The Noose* (both GB 1948: see Murphy, 1989: 146–67) through Stanley Baker's Americanised crime boss in *The Criminal* (GB 1960). However, arguably it is only with the emergence of the Kray Brothers as mythic gangland archetypes that the British gangster film acquires its defining semantic element, the 'Firm'. British gangster films of the early 1970s such as *Villain* and *Get Carter* (both GB 1971) as well as *Performance* (GB 1970) clearly invoke the Kray myth, which becomes an increasingly nostalgic informing presence in later gangster films including *The Long Good Friday*, *The Hit* (1984), *Gangster No.1* and *Sexy Beast* (both GB 2000), as well as the US-made *The Limey* (2001). (Several of these, as Steve Chibnall (2001: 281–91) notes, adopt revenge motifs from Jacobean tragedy.) The late 1990s saw a cycle of semi-comic gangster films (including *Lock, Stock, and Two Smoking Barrels*, GB 1998, and *Snatch*, GB 2000) whose casual violence and macho posturings have been connected by Chibnall with the concomitant rise of 'lad culture' in the UK (see also Murphy and Chibnall, 1999).

Bruzzi (1995: 26) compares the American and French genres in terms of the gangster's personal style, arguing that whereas classic American gangster films are characterised by frenetic action and fast talking, their French counterparts are quiet and exaggeratedly slow, and despite their generic similarities, 'the French and American films have always diverged on the level of tone. Though the gangster film may come more naturally to Americans, the French do it with more style.'

In non-western cinemas, Keiko McDonald (1992) explores the long-running popularity of the Japanese *Yakuza* film since the 1930s as an example of a genre, like the Western, that over its long lifespan directly reflects changing Japanese social consciousness. Perry Farrell's *The Harder They Come* (Jamaica, 1972), set in the slums of Kingston, renovates tropes from both the urban (*Regeneration, Little Caesar*) and the rural (*Bonnie and Clyde*) US gangster film and demonstrates how the phenomenon of 'uneven development' permits categories originating in Depression America to translate themselves readily into the terms of other cultures undergoing comparable socio-economic upheaval.

CASE STUDY: *ONCE UPON A TIME IN AMERICA* (1984)

Like many epics, the plot of Sergio Leone's four-hour *Once Upon a Time in America* is a long-breathed but simple melody, essentially a plain story of betrayal and loss, dishonour among thieves. In the years after the First World War, Prohibition transforms four petty teenage hoodlums from New York's Jewish Lower East Side into wealthy through still small-time gangsters. Max, the leader of the gang, ambitious beyond his parochial comrades and restless at their self-imposed limitations, embroils the gang with a more powerful Mob outfit and finally proposes a wildly ambitious and almost certainly

From *Once Upon a Time in America* (1984). Reproduced courtesy Ladd Company/Warner Bros/The Kobal Collection.

suicidal heist. Begged by Max's mistress to save her lover from himself, his fellow gang member and best friend Noodles agrees to rat out the gang on their last bootlegging run together so they can share a cooling-off period in the can. But Noodles misses the job, and in the police ambush resulting from his tip-off Max and his two other friends are gunned down – Max's body roasted to an unrecognisable cinder in the firefight. Noodles escapes the

Syndicate killers out for his blood and escapes New York – but not before discovering that someone, sometime, has stolen the gang's accumulated loot, stashed since their first teen exploits in a left-luggage locker at Grand Central station, and to which, as the sole survivor, Noodles is now entitled. Dazed, alone and tormented by guilt for the death of his friends, Noodles buys a one-way ticket to 'anyplace. First bus.' Thirty-five years pass: it's now 1968 and the aged Noodles receives a mysterious summons back to the city. Returning to the transformed streets of his youth, he eventually discovers that all those many years ago Max had double-crossed him, manipulating Noodles and the others, feigning his own death and stealing the gang's money to purchase for himself a new life as Secretary Bailey, a powerful political player. Noodles is innocent of the burden of guilt he has carried for decades. 'Bailey' – who has also married Noodles's childhood sweetheart, Deborah, whom Noodles had long ago alienated by a self-destructively brutal act of sexual violation – now faces exposure by an impending Congressional hearing, and confronting Noodles at his opulent Long Island mansion he invites his old friend to take his long-overdue revenge. But Noodles refuses, preferring to cling to his memories of a 'great friendship' that 'went bad' long ago. Noodles walks away into the night; looking back, he sees Max/Bailey at the gates of his estate. A garbage truck passes between them: when it grinds by, Max/Bailey has disappeared. Has he ended his life by throwing himself into the chopper? Or have the gangland interests threatened by his imminent exposure assassinated him? As a passing carload of revellers dressed in the flapper fashions of the 'Roaring' 1920s recalls for us Noodles's gangster heyday, the film ends on a note of deep ambiguity.

The most ambitious of a series of period gangster films made in the wake of the enormous success of the first two *Godfather* films, *Once ...* self-consciously embraces Coppola's vision of organised crime as less a revelatory mirror image of the American dream (the classic model) than a simple, direct and logical extension of American values into a realm where their violence and corruption are made manifest. As Fran Mason puts it, like *The Godfather, Once ...*

> extend[s] the metaphor of the 'double-cross' to the level of American society which is revealed to be a culture of betrayal and complicity ... where a depersonalised and hostile sociality cannot be transcended, but ultimately extends its ruthless logic. (Mason, 2002: 143)

The film's bootlegging and union racketeering milieu exploits similar material to *Lucky Lady* and *F*I*S*T*, two routine and unsuccessful earlier entries in the Mob nostalgia cycle. However, the film's formal complexities – which have some similarities to *The Godfather, Part II*, and like that film encompass at once the gangster's myth of origins, the alienated present-day reality of corporate crime and an ironic relationship between the two – advertise its ambitions to comment both on its parent genre and, through the gangster film's generic tropes, on American life. Leone's straightforward plot unfolds as an intricate skein of memories, with Noodles's story unfolded in a series of fragmentary interlinking flashbacks and flash-forwards with no clearly established narrative 'present tense' (the opening sequence, combining carefully observed period detail, jarring violence and a growing sense of temporal and spatial distortion – with two flashbacks-within-flashbacks and the disorienting soundtrack punctuation of an amplified, diegetically unplaced telephone – establishes the film's stylistic tenor). The end of the film returns full circle to its beginning, with a final flashback after Max/Bailey's mysterious disappearance outside his mansion to Noodles in 1933, taking refuge from what he believes to be his blood guilt in a Chinatown opium den. The last image is a freeze-frame of Noodles grinning broadly in stoned reverie at something or someone we cannot see.

The opium-den frame invites a reading of the narrative as unfolding largely in Noodles's head: the teenage scenes in the Jewish ghetto his memories, the 1968 sequence his fantasy of a story in which he turns out to be not traitor but victim, not a rat but a patsy. The slightly 'off' tenor of several of Noodles's encounters with figures from his past in this time-frame lends the sequence as a whole an oneiric quality that supports such a reading. In fact, *Once ...* shares this basic ambiguity around the exact phenomenological register of its narrative with some other major post-classical gangster films, notably *Point Blank*, and in rather different ways *The Godfather, Part II* and *Carlito's Way*. All of these films advertise their generic revisionism by employing complex time schemes that fragment their narratives and render them reveries of their protagonists, as often as not at the moment of (real or symbolic) death. Such devices both underscore the generically predetermined downfall of the protagonist, and confirm his story, presented with all the overdetermined and streamlined logic of a dream, as a fable of the fate of individual hope and ambition in fallen corporate America.

Once ... in effect combines *Point Blank*'s radical modernist ambiguity with *The Godfather, Part II*'s critique of corporate gangsterism/capitalism. In fact, the film's insistent and fetishistic accumulation of period detail across not one but three separate periods (1922, 1933, 1968) recalls not only the *Godfather* but Michael Cimino's maniacally authentic recreation of the frontier West in *Heaven's Gate* (1980), like *Once ...* a large-scale, lengthy and expensive revisionist entry in a classic genre that failed to find an audience and was substantially recut for subsequent release. However, whereas *Heaven's Gate* seems to be unaware of the kinds of textual and generic cruxes entailed in the project of historical recovery through genre (see Chapter 2,

'The History of Westerns'), *Once* ... appears reflexively to acknowledge its own periodisation as precisely a function of style and of genre. Amid the elaborate recreations, certain jarring anomalies stand out, notably in the 1968 sequence: a TV news bulletin that looks nothing like TV news footage; Deborah's strangely unaged face when Noodles meets her again, thirty-five years older. These devices not only sustain the reading of the film as Noodles's opium dream, but may be taken as textual parapraxes (Freudian slips), confessions of the inescapably manufactured nature of *any* cinematic past. When Noodles, on his return to Manhattan, hires a car, the wall of the rental office is hung with 'period' photographs of the island – 'framing' the frozen, reified memory of the past as commodity (the scene is scored to a muzak arrangement of Lennon-McCartney's 'Yesterday'). This in turn invites comparison with another New York image glimpsed earlier in the same 1968 sequence: the wall in Grand Central that in 1933 bore a mural advertising Coney Island in the style of Thomas Hart Benton – crowds of archetypal New Yorkers teeming towards stylised rollercoasters, in turn recalling the milling throngs in the film's Lower East Side sequences – this has been replaced in 1968 by an abstracted rendition of the midtown skyline enveloped in New York's corporate urban logo, the Big Apple. *People* are wholly absent from the image, and in many ways this is a film about the loss of not only a future but a past as well – one in which we have almost as much invested as Noodles, but which is as much a fabrication as his own.

Leone is significantly less invested in the mythic grandeur of his protagonists than Coppola. Only Max aspires to truly grand criminal schemes, and only in his stolen second life as Bailey does he in fact become involved with the political circles, grand schemes and ultimately (and terminally) Congressional hearings with which Michael Corleone's Cuban enterprise involves him: and in the film this is only hearsay and TV footage, not centre stage. As mobsters, Noodles's gang's horizons are confined to the (considerable) rewards to be gained from rum-running; Noodles himself is conceived as a nobody, albeit a complex one: his romanticism vitiated by (in fact, indissociable from) his brutality, and unable or unwilling to see beyond his illusions about Max (and Deborah), he remains an outsider and a definitive small-timer. As the plot summary above indicates, in what is ostensibly 'his' story, Noodles is most frequently a bystander, too confused, undirected and distracted ever to match up to the Promethean gangster model of Cagney, Muni or for that matter Brando or Pacino (De Niro of course played the young Vito Corleone in *Godfather II*). The film's meandering plot unfolds at a meditative, even funereal pace with few generic set-piece highlights apart from the shoot-out in the down factory and the drive-by shooting, which Shadoian (2003; 286) suggests is included as a consciously nostalgic throwback to the 'good old days'. In their place *Once* ... provides only a series of unredeeming, exploitative and apparently undirected capers, from the opening (frustrated) 'roll' of the drunk to the jewel heist (with its sidebar rape) and the callous maternity ward swap. What Leone's decentred narrative and simulacrum of the gangster (film) past suggests, however, is 'the old days' themselves were never more than fantasy projections, the desire to defeat the alienations and disempowerments of capitalism through violent means that, as Max understands but Noodles refuses to, could only ever replicate, never challenge, that system.

NOTES

1. The concept of 'residual' and 'emergent' ideologies is from Raymond Williams ([1973] 1980: 40–2).
2. *Scarface* was released on 9 April 1932; *The Little Giant* premiered on 14 April 1933.
3. *Gangs of New York* (2003), loosely based on Herbert Asbury's (1927) popular history of the same title, returns to an even earlier (Civil War) period of New York gang warfare.
4. '[*Alibi*] has the speed and the sinister staccato sound quality of a machine gun' (*Screenland* reviewer, quoted in Rosow, 1978: 133).
5. *Goodfellas* encapsulates this double bind in a montage that choreographs an endless series of gang slayings – motivated not by betrayal but the *fear* of betrayal – to the plangent play-out of Eric Clapton's 'Layla', one of rock's most urgent statements of desire.

Part 2
Transitional Fantasies

The two genres discussed in this section both have roots – in the case of the horror film, deep roots – in the classical studio era. Yet in important ways they also look ahead to the post-classical period, a period of reduced levels of film production and correspondingly weakened genre identities. As fantasy genres, both horror and science fiction depart in significant ways from the prevailing canons of representation in the classical Hollywood style, whether one takes that mode to be a form of realism (not the chimerical 'classic realism') or, as I have suggested, of melodrama. Horror and science fiction also share an identity as unrespectable genres for an undiscriminating juvenile audience (or an audience that has its mind on other things), with strong roots in exploitation cinema, that have only fairly recently emerged as attractive genres for large-scale production at major studios. Finally, both genres have attracted significant critical attention in recent years, and in each case theories of postmodernism and – which is not always the same thing – currents in postmodern theory have played an important part in reconceiving the genre for audiences and film-makers alike. This critical interest is, I argue, related to the relative weakness in both cases of traditional semantic/syntactic matrices of generic identity, lending them a protean aspect that is well suited to exploiting marketplace currents and trends. That horror and SF take their core generic material from the body and technology, respectively, both engines of contemporary critical enquiry and popular cultural debate, has confirmed their relevance.

CHAPTER 7

The Horror Film

The experience of limits, and the transgression of limits, is central to the horror film: the boundaries of sanity and madness, of the conscious and unconscious minds, of the external surfaces of the body and the flesh and organs within, pre-eminently the boundaries of life and death. Yet merely to speak of 'boundaries' or even the transgression of boundaries without registering the very specific affective charge with which the horror genre enacts those moves would be largely to ignore its most distinctive aspects. As the name suggests, while on the one hand horror insistently pierces and penetrates the vessel of bodily and representational propriety, at the same time it registers that move as profoundly, even elementally transgressive, in a flood of visceral, disturbing and often violent imagery (though violence is not a given, being mostly absent from many ghost stories from *The Innocents*, 1962, and *The Haunting*, 1964, to *The Sixth Sense*, 1999, and *The Others*, 2001). Death, and of course undeath and death-in-life, are omnipresent in horror, usually personified as fearful forces to be shunned and/or destroyed, but occasionally as states capable of generating transcendent insight (as in *Hellraiser*, GB 1987).

Horror films dramatise the eruption of violence, often (but not invariably, and much less in recent decades) supernatural and always irrational, into normative social and/or domestic contexts, often with an undercurrent – at times a good deal more than that – of phobic sexual panic. The agent of horrific violence – the 'monster' – is often seen as embodying and/or enabling the expression of repressed desire(s). One of the most obvious examples is Dracula, who animates intense sexual desire in the (typically bourgeois, demure) women he seduces/assaults while at the same time enacting male ambivalence towards female sexuality in blurring lines between seduction and rape, sex and violence. With the progressive slackening of censorship this sexual dimension has become increasingly explicit. In *Nosferatu* (Germany 1922), the vampire

Orlok's grotesque, rodent-like appearance and his visual association with vermin (rats, spiders) mitigates the explicitly sexual aspects of the character in Bram Stoker's original novel of 1893. Dracula's increasingly suave incarnations by Bela Lugosi, Christopher Lee and Frank Langella (1930, GB 1958 (US title *Horror of Dracula*), 1979) progressively blur the dividing line between violation and seduction. The 'underground' *Blood for Dracula* (1974) specifies Dracula's need for the blood of virgins. In *Bram Stoker's Dracula* (1992), the vampire's first assault on Lucy Westenra is associated with her own unsatisfied sexual appetites (when first seen she is paging through a pornographically illustrated edition of *The Arabian Knights* and musing about 'unspeakable acts of desperate passion'), and Dracula, apparating as a man-wolf, couples with her in the gazebo.

In ideological terms, horror is ambivalent: on the one hand, it unmasks latent unspeakable desires in (white, patriarchal, bourgeois) society and shows the inadequacy and hypocrisy of the culture that demands such repression (although the graphic violence is restrained by later standards, this is a particularly strong strain in the British Hammer horror films of the late 1950s and 1960s). On the other, it identifies its protagonist(s) and through them the audience with a project of re-suppression, containment and restoration of the *status quo ante* through the violent elimination of deviance and disturbance – the destruction of the 'monster'.

The status of horror as a critical object has undergone a marked transformation in recent years (it is noteworthy that neither horror nor SF merits a chapter in Schatz's *Hollywood Genres*, perhaps the most 'classically'-oriented work on film genre, but they are extensively discussed in the successor volume, which focuses on the transition from classical (or 'Old') to post-classical ('New') Hollywood (Schatz, 1983). Indeed as Jancovich (2002: 1) notes, the horror film has superseded the Western as the genre that is most written about by genre critics. This says something about not only the enhanced status of the genre but also about the changing priorities of genre criticism. For if, as was suggested in Chapter 1, early film work on film genre prioritised the project of defining secure and stable generic boundaries and establishing a defined corpus of films in each category, more recent work has tended rather to emphasise the porosity and leaky borders of genres; mindful that in any case that the work of definition, if regarded as anything more than a provisional project of practical utility rather than absolute value, is doomed to Quixotic failure, contemporary criticism is minded to embrace and explore textual diversity and contradiction.

Such qualities are themselves central to the kinds of theoretical paradigms that have come to dominate what Feury and Mansfield (1997) call the 'new humanities' since the late 1980s – deconstruction, queer theory, post-Freudian analyses of subjectivity influenced by Michel Foucault and Gilles Deleuze, and a renovated, multi-perspectival historicism. Horror, as a notoriously difficult genre to define satisfactorily – that seems itself to take on the polymorphic, elusive properties of so many horror-film monsters – is well adapted to these altered critical states. Not only embracing as narrative and thematic content contemporary criticism's concerns with race, gender, sexual identity, the body and the self – sometimes in ways that seem quite explicitly informed by contemporary theoretical positions (notably in the films of David Cronenberg and in such independent productions as *Suture*, 1993) – horror today, like science fiction and the action film, revels in the carnivalesque subversion and reversal of generic proprieties and expectations. Compared to horror's trickster moves, the efforts of traditional genres like the Western and the musical to come to terms with the demands of the post-classical context can seem sclerotic and predictable. Finally, horror remains an attractive critical proposition precisely because of its enduring unrespectability: horror has never wholly shed the 'disreputable' flavour noted by Robin Wood (1979: 73), nor its pleasurable *frisson* of the illicit or at least impolite. Horror films in general remain sensational, gory and relatively cheap, and are promoted in ways that discourage 'serious' critical attention. The seriality and repetition to which horror properties are prone (*Halloween*, five instalments since 1978; *Friday the 13th*, nine since 1980; *Nightmare on Elm Street*, seven from 1984 to 1994, plus the parodic franchise 'face-off' *Freddy vs. Jason*, 2003; even the knowing postmodern pastiches *Scream*, 1996, *Scary Movie* and *I Know What You Did Last Summer*, 1997, generating their own part-parodic but seriously profitable franchises) also render horror 'generic' in the old, pejorative sense of the term. Whereas, as Hawkins (2000: 66) observes, previous critical generations were minded to remove horror films deemed worthy of critical attention (usually such European films as *Les Yeux Sans Visage/Eyes Without a Face*, France 1959, *Peeping Tom*, GB 1960, and *Repulsion*, GB 1965) to a different, non-generic frame of critical reference – 'a critical site in which the film's affective [i.e., its sensational and horrific] properties tend to be divorced from its "artistic" and "poetic" ones' – contemporary criticism's highly developed trash aesthetic is eager to explore the cultural purchase of indelibly generic, even exploitative material and to take very seriously not only its sociological, psychological and ideological formations but its formal and thematic dimensions too.

PLACING HORROR

Like other genres, the prehistory and early history of the horror film is dealt with rather sketchily in the critical literature. There is a significant gap between the most ambitious contemporary theoretical constructions of the genre, which largely focus on postwar and in some cases even more recent films, and historical accounts, usually directed at a broader readership, such as Clarens (1968), Gifford (1973), Kendrick (1991) and Skal (1993). The latter pay much greater, sometimes fondly antiquarian attention to the trick films of Georges Méliès (see also Chapter 8), British and American silent films such as the first adaptations of *Frankenstein* (1910) and *Dr Jekyll and Mr Hyde* (filmed several times in the silent era from 1908, the most celebrated version featuring John Barrymore in 1920), and the films of Lon Chaney and Tod Browning at MGM and Universal in the 1920s, as well as the influence of late nineteenth- and early twentieth-century theatrical traditions, notably the gore-laden Grands Guignols spectaculars in Paris (see Hand and Wilson, 2002) and the popular and long-running stage adaptations of *Jekyll*, *Frankenstein* and *Dracula* in London and New York, the last of which was the direct source for the first film in the Universal horror cycle, Browning's *Dracula* (1930), and provided that film's star, Bela Lugosi.

It is useful to note the influence of the domestic stage given the importance assigned in many overviews of the genre to European cinema, notably the German Expressionist films produced between 1919 and 1923, as a defining moment in the crystallisation of the horror film as a genre and a decisive influence on the American form. The argument for Expressionism's direct stylistic influence on horror, as later with *film noir* (see Chapter 9), can easily be overstated: American directors and cameramen did not need the example of *Caligari* or *Nosferatu* to teach them about the dramatic impact of shadow-play, silhouettes and 'low-key' lighting. Such techniques were widely used by both British and American directors and cameramen prior to the First World War and usually to convey a sinister atmosphere, albeit more associated with scenes of crime and melodramatic skulduggery than outright horror. Domesticated Expressionist touches are, however, visible in the first 1930s Universal horror cycle, for instance in the canted, vertiginous sets of *Bride of Frankenstein* (1935) or the sepulchral shadows in the opening sequence of *The Mummy* (1933): this influence owed something to example and something also to the direct participation of some key Weimar film-makers, including among numerous others Edgar G. Ulmer, a former collaborator of F. W. Murnau and Robert Siodmak whose American films included the hallucinatory Universal horror film *The Black Cat* (1935), and Karl Freund, cinematographer on the Expressionist films *Der Januskopf* (an unlicensed adaptation of *Dr Jekyll*) and *The Golem* (both 1920) and for Universal *Dracula*, *The Murders in the Rue Morgue* (1932) and (as director) *The Mummy*. Expressionism's enduring influence, however, perhaps lay in the establishment less of a specific stylistic model than of the principle of a generic vocabulary that expressed extreme psychological states and deformations of reality through the integration of performance, stylised set design and *mise-en-scène*, and above all in its delineation of a narrative terrain that systematically threatened conventional waking rationality with oneiric super-natural terrors.

If Expressionism points towards the classic horror film, with a heavy reliance on sinister, atmospheric *mise-en-scène* and contained visual distortion to create a sense of threat and disturbance, the other internationally celebrated European cinema of the 1920s, Soviet Montage, contains important pointers to the more graphically confrontational aesthetic of contemporary horror. For example, despite his emphatic lack of interest in the inner workings of the human mind – motivated by the conviction that human subjecthood was generated out of and through material circumstances and characterised by productive labour and interaction with the material world rather than internal psychic processes – Eisenstein employed 'shock' effects as a central part of his dialectical montage experiments. Indeed, at the climax of the famous Odessa Steps sequence of *The Battleship Potemkin* (1925), a Cossack officer slashes his sabre directly and repeatedly at the lens: a reverse shot of his elderly female victim, her eyeball sliced open, demonstrates both the overt specular aggression and gruesome violence associated with the contemporary, post-*Psycho* horror film.

The first major horror film cycle, the 1930s and 1940s Universal produc-tions, mostly seem to modern eyes rather calm affairs by comparison with later horror films. (In fact, as Balio (1993) notes, there were two Universal cycles: the first inaugurated by *Dracula*, including the career-defining performances of Universal's series horror stars Lugosi and Boris Karloff and running through until *Bride of Frankenstein*, 1935; the second following on the hugely successful re-release of *Dracula* and *Frankenstein* as a double bill in 1938 and running through the more action- and humour-oriented sequels and 'monster meet-ups' of the 1940s – starting with *Frankenstein Meets the Wolf Man*, 1946 – to the Abbot and Costello horror burlesques of the late 1940s and early 1950s.) Although James Whale in particular employed an occasionally baroque visual style and at key moments something like 'shock' editing – for example, the first appearances of Frankenstein's Monster and of the Bride – for the most part the fantastic, uncanny and transgressive thrust of the narrative material was held in check by a restrained *mise-en-scène* that emphasised atmosphere and the sideshow appeal of make-up effects over graphic horror. The Universal horror film in which contemporary theory, with its investment in marginality, has taken the greatest interest is the notorious (and unseen for many years between its initial release and the 1960s) *Freaks* (1933: see Herzogenrath, 2002).

A different approach, even more reliant on atmospheric *mise-en-scène* but largely abjuring special effects for intense psychological protraiture, was adopted by the 'B' feature production unit headed by Val Lewton at RKO in the mid-1940s. The films of this unit, including *Cat People* (1942), *I Walked With a Zombie* (1943) and *The Seventh Victim* (1945), have long been highly praised both for their 'restraint' (a term which suggests that these are horror films for people who don't usually like horror films, and was in any case partly predicated on their budgetary ceiling of $150,000) and also for their unusual focus on female subjectivity. In some ways, precisely in their avoidance of prewar generic monster clichés and their relocation of (often 'Old World') supernatural threats to contemporary American urban locations (the most celebrated scene in *Cat People* – replayed to lesser effect in the 1982 remake – features a woman stalked by an unseen creature lurking in the shadows around a basement swimming pool), the RKO films bring the viewer into unsettling proximity with the limits of this rational, 'civilised' world's ability to tame and contain the irrational. Although critical praise of the 'power of suggestion' often betrays an unease with horror's more anarchic and carnivalesque aspects, the success of the low-budget, effects-free chiller *The Blair Witch Project* (1999) testifies to the enduring power of this approach (as, in a very different way, does the indistinct, uncanny, half-glimpsed terror of *Vampyr*, Sweden 1932).

Sequels notwithstanding, the Universal cycle had run its creative course well before the end of the Second World War; after the revelations of Dresden, Auschwitz and Hiroshima, the Gothic terrors of Dracula, Franken- stein and the Wolfman may in any event have seemed too quaint to retain much of a *frisson* for audiences. The cycle's studio-bound, dehistoricised Ruritanian milieu was also at odds with the shift towards location filming and greater topicality in postwar cinema. During the 1950s, the debatable generic status of not only the 'creature features' (discussed in more detail in Chapter 8) but many other science fiction/horror hybrids before and since points up the difficulty genre historians and theorists have always had in distinguishing between the two genres. Inasmuch as horror and science fiction (SF) audiences were largely perceived by producers as identical, especially in the 1950s – hence exploitation directors such as Roger Corman as well as studio directors like Jack Arnold (*It Came From Outer Space*, 1953; *The Creature from the Black Lagoon*, 1954) switched between (what might be externally classified as) SF and horror without any evident prior sense of generic differentiation – Wells (2000: 7) is probably right in arguing that 'there is no great benefit in seeking to disentangle these generic perspectives' and that we should instead address our attention to 'the distinctive elements of any one text within a particular historical moment'. All the same, some evident points of distinction may help illuminate important aspects of both genres.

While in itself a distinction between SF and horror drawn on the basis of 'science' versus 'magic' would be quite inadequate, if one accepts the criterion of scientific explanation not as an *outcome* to be assessed (i.e. with reference to contemporary scientific understanding), but rather as a form of *rhetoric* and a *mode of presentation*, it may prove more useful. In the SF universe, that is, the appearance of aliens, monsters and other destructive or malevolent forces is not only depicted as explicable according to the scientific understanding diegetically available (which may or may not map onto our own), but moreover is narratively subject to such analysis, explanation and – more often than not – systematic response. By way of example, although the Monster in *Frankenstein* (1931) is manifestly a creation of misguided/perverted science – stitched together from corpses, animated by electricity, his violence accountable by the erroneous insertion of a 'criminal brain' – the film does not present him as a scientific problem but as a terrifying monstrosity, both pathetic and malign. On the contrary, *Frankenstein*'s narrative arc, spiralling up through intensifying chaos and panic, could hardly be more different from the progress *through* and *past* panic towards a scientific/military solution that characterises innumerable SF alien invasion and monster movies from *The Thing* (1951) to *Independence Day* (1996). Violence, to be sure, may play a ubiquitous role in defeating the intruder and restoring 'normality', but the violence of the SF film is far more likely to be ostensibly rational and considered, that of the horror film, ritualised and reactive (the pogrom-like revenge of the villagers with their flaming torches).

These opposed generic rhetorics, of clarification and the occult, are reflected too in the different visual registers of horror and SF. SF from the 1950s and 1960s in particular generally employs an unobtrusive visual style, which might be seen as affecting a quasi-scientific neutrality appropriate to the solutions that will eventually be found to the threats at hand. This contrasts starkly with the highly stylised and often floridly Expressionistic *mise-se-scène* of classic horror. As Vivien Sobchack (1987: 29–30) usefully suggests, horror and SF are also distinguished by the latter's tendency to lend its threats a public and collective aspect, whereas horror – as the recent dominance of psychoanalytic interpretative paradigms suggests – explores realms both intimate and – in all senses of the term – occult. The claustrophobically constricted spaces of horror magnify and condense profound and phobic impulses regarding the body, the self and sexuality. In the 1970s, however, in SF-horror as elsewhere, such stylistic generic markers become increasingly unreliable.

Horror's status within the film industry has changed significantly in the post-classical period, although not always in immediately obvious ways. Clearly, horror is no longer quite so marginal in industry terms as it mostly was from the end of the Universal 'Golden Age' in the early 1940s until the late 1960s. The massively magnified commercial importance of the college and high-school audience as well as the explosion – intensified since the advent of the Internet established fan cultures with a global and instantaneous reach –

in the popularity, visibility and hence market potential of 'cult' (usually SF and horror) film, television and comic books, have ensured that these former 'pulp' (or worse) genres are now taken very seriously by studios and film-makers. Moreover, new genres such as the serial killer film have spliced more mainstream forms like the police procedural thriller with horror tropes and themes to bring ghastly generic material before a far wider audience than horror's traditional inner-city and juvenile demographic – even, in the case of *The Silence of the Lambs* (1991), earning the ultimate seal of establishment approval, an Oscar for Best Picture (on the generically ambiguous place of *Silence of the Lambs*, see Jancovich, [2001] 2002).

Still, horror has not fully crossed over to the mainstream to the degree of its sister genre science fiction. Whereas since *Star Wars* SF blockbusters (as discussed in the next chapter) have regularly commanded vast budgets, top stars and directors, are often the central 'tentpoles' of annual release schedules, and reliably feature in lists of top box-office attractions, this is rarely the case with horror. Horror budgets remain relatively low, and major 'above-the-line' talent is only infrequently attached to out-and-out horror projects. The more clearly generic the material, the truer this is: thus while understated ghost stories like *The Sixth Sense* are perceived as relatively 'classy', especially if they have a period setting (like *The Others*) and can attract major stars such as Bruce Willis and Nicole Kidman, a slasher film like *Scream*, a traditional shocker like *Ghost Ship* (2003) or a remake like *Dawn of the Dead* (2003) will typically feature a cast of lesser-known actors, sometimes with a 'name' (Drew Barrymore in *Scream*, for example) in a featured or cameo role. Despite the breakthrough success of William Friedkin's *The Exorcist* (1973), few leading directors in the last thirty years have under-taken out-and-out horror films (*The Shining* (Stanley Kubrick, 1980) and *Bram Stoker's Dracula* (Francis Ford Coppola, 1992) being obvious exceptions).

Although they operate at a lower level of visibility than the major summer blockbusters, horror films nonetheless typify the contemporary Hollywood preference for, in industry parlance, 'marketability' – the technique of opening a film in as many venues as possible simultaneously, with a barrage of high-impact print and spot TV advertising – over 'playability' (a film's ability to expand its audience week-on-week through favourable critical reception and word-of-mouth: see Lewis, 2003: 63–70). Horror films usually 'open wide' in hundreds of screens on the same weekend, perform strongly enough in their first week to rise to the top, or near the top, of the weekly box-office list, but then drop off sharply in subsequent weeks to disappear from theatres after a relatively short release. In fact, horror's most lasting contribution to contemporary Hollywood may have been as a paradigm for marketing and promotion in the post-classical era. As Kevin Heffernan's recent research (2000, 2004) has revealed, the techniques identified above as typical of Hollywood's marketing techniques for its most prestigious and expensive projects – wide opening accompanied by saturation TV, radio and print advertising to clearly defined audience demographics – were pioneered in the 1960s on a smaller (regional and citywide) basis by independent and exploitation distributors marketing low-budget horror films, principally to black inner-city audiences. Heffernan's work adjusts standard accounts that single out *Jaws* (and the role of MCA President Lew Wasserman) as innovating such practices, and valuably helps concretise the well-known general narrative of Hollywood's increasing adoption of both genres, narratives and publicity techniques from the drive-in and exploitation markets from the 1950s onwards, as part of its ongoing efforts to retrieve shrinking audiences. During the 1950s, the 'creature feature' cycle – which was dominated by major studio releases – and the short-lived 3–D boom were clear early indicators of this trend.

MAKING MONSTERS

A concept that binds together much cinematic horror is the idea of the 'monstrous'. Monstrosity is not a self-evident category: monsters are created, not born. Furthermore, as several writers have noted, *monster* has its etymological roots in the Latin *monstrare*, 'to show': thus the monster exists to de-*monstrate*, to teach an object (social) lesson of some kind. The visual trope – indissociably one of the genre's semantic constants– of the tight 'choker' close-up on the screaming (usually female) face, giving the spectator ample opportunity to reflect on the terror and horror expressed therein, could be seen as a textual marker of this educative process, an instruction in horror (what we find horrific). In some horror films, the process of 'monstering' – of rendering someone or something an object of fear and revulsion – itself becomes part of the narrative: in different ways films like *Freaks*, *Quatermass and the Pit* (GB 1968), Cronenberg's *The Fly* (1986), *Edward Scissorhands* (1990) and even *Frankenstein* invite their audience to reflect on the psycho-social dynamics of monstrosity. The 1931 version of *Dr Jekyll and Mr Hyde* emphasises Jekyll's 'monstrous' alter-ego as a manifestation of repressed sexual desires that are in themselves perfectly 'normal', but rendered hyperbolic and destructive by their systematic frustration in a rigid social order predicated on denial. Such films might be seen as taking their cue from Franz Kafka's famous parable *Metamorphosis*, whose protagonist Gregor Samsa's sudden transformation into a giant insect and the revulsion and rejection this transformation provokes in his family and friends allegorises bourgeois conformity, hostility to and fear of difference, and social isolation.

Far more horror films, however, appear simply to exploit the 'monster reflex', positioning their audiences so as to share the hatred, terror and aggression justifiably directed against the monsters they depict. Indeed, the misguided sympathy for, or attempts to reason with, the monster on the part of ivory-tower scientists or well-intentioned liberals, usually ending in the cautionary death of the do-gooders, is a familiar genre motif. Robin Wood (1986: 70ff.) identifies this affective charge in horror as at once a graphic enactment of and a reaction to 'surplus repression', the structures of denial and oppression peculiar to 'patriarchal capitalism' (which go beyond the basic repressions necessary, on Freud's account, to the socialisation of the individual). Surplus repression relies crucially on the construction of a terrifying and hateful Other whose embodiment of the forces suppressed by patriarchy – energies centred, for Wood, on sexuality, gender, race and class – reinforce the perception of those desires as monstrous.

Wood, however, goes on to argue that just as repression in the individual, on Freud's account, is liable to generate a 'return of the repressed' in the domain of the unconscious through dreams, fantasies and in some cases neurotic or hysterical symptoms, so too surplus repression in the social meets with a displaced and distorted rejoinder in the transgressive energies of 'low' cultural forms like the horror film.[1] Horror film monsters are rarely wholly unsympathetic, Wood argues (drawing the majority of his examples from the classic Universal and Expressionist horror cycles), and at some level they are acting out our own unacknowledged desires: thus horror films offer 'fulfillment of our nightmare wish to smash the norms that oppress us and which our moral conditioning teaches us to revere' (Wood, 1986: 80). The doubling motifs that abound in the genre are a textual 'symptom' of this ambivalence, revealing the deeper affinity of the pro-social hero and the anti-social monster. (Wood notes that in *Son of Frankenstein* (1939), the eponymous new Baron complains that everyone thinks 'Frankenstein' is the name of the monster his father 'merely' created; similarly, Hardy (1985: 107) points out the ways in which Frankenstein's creations in the Hammer cycle are mirror images reflecting back the Baron's own 'moral flaws and emotional atrophy'.) Thus horror is an unstable and unreliable ally to dominant ideology, at once serving its purposes and articulating the desire to destroy it.

One way of classifying horror's many monsters is provided by Andrew Tudor's (1989) historical study of the genre, which maps out the nature of the threats in different periods across a schematic grid whose key categories are external/internal and supernatural/secular. In prewar horror, threats mostly originated from outside (the individual or the community) and were more likely to be supernatural in origin. The postwar decade, the heyday of atomic mutations and alien invasion, also stressed external threats but shifted decisively towards the secular. External threats could usually be effectively dispatched, given the right knowledge and technology (arcane lore, silver bullets or, in the case of mutations and aliens, the combined scientific-military might of the modern nation-state). For Tudor and others, *Psycho* along with the later *Night of the Living Dead* (1968) mark the transition from the ontological and practical security of externalised horror to the much more uncertain and radically destabilising threats that originate within. That traditional Gothic horror has recently been incorporated into the mainstream action blockbuster (*The Mummy*, 1999; *Van Helsing*, 2004), largely shorn of its horrific elements, may suggest that the genre's focus has shifted away from such 'external' threats towards the less well-defined ground of individual psychology and the paranormal rather than the supernatural.

HORROR SINCE *PSYCHO*

Modern horror films are much more likely to centre on threats originating from inside both the individual psyche (psychopathic killers) and – because even isolated individuals live in necessary relationship of some kind to a larger human community – our own social institutions (above all the family), that are pathological rather than supernatural. 'Monsters' such as Norman Bates and his successors are all the more terrifying because they are not marked, or are less obviously so, by the visible indications of difference – physical deformities, vast size, otherworldly appearance – of their comfortingly unmistakable forebears; they retain the transgressive mutability of earlier shape-shifting monsters such as the Wolf Man, but these symptoms of difference and deviance are now internalised. Clover (1992: 24) identifies *Psycho*'s 'sexualisation of motive and action' as a feature that clearly distinguishes the film from previous horror films. Of course, *Psycho* is also (in)famous for massively intensifying the degree of graphic violence horror films were willing to inflict on their characters and vicariously upon their audiences (notwithstanding that Norman's knife is never seen to penetrate Marion Crane's flesh). *Psycho*'s manipulation of audience sympathies towards characters (first Marion, then Norman, then the investigator Arbogast) only to wrench them violently away is also widely credited with opening a new field in the play of sadism and the gaze in popular cinema (echoed in the subplot involving Detective Kinderman in *The Exorcist*). Maltby (1995: 218–20) credits *Psycho* with the end of 'secure space' in Hollywood film, both literally and figuratively: audiences after *Psycho* could no longer confidently rely on narrative, generic and representational conventions to 'protect' the integrity of their viewing experience, any more than they could be assured that a violent attack would still be prepared for – as had hitherto been the convention – through cutaways to sinister figures shambling across misty marshes, etc.

Hitchcock's decision to make an inexpensive black-and-white thriller using members of the production team from his eponymous television series broke with his then-reputation, established during the 1950s, as a master of the lavish action-suspense film (pre-eminently *North by Northwest*, 1959) and the resulting film undoubtedly shocked and repulsed a proportion of both his mass audience and his critical admirers (see Kapsis 1992: 56–64). However, his successful appropriation of such exploitation-circuit marketing gimmicks as refusing entry to latecomers (a standby of the celebrated exploitation producer William Castle) and more importantly his adaptation, extension and intensification of lurid and grotesque narrative material more than justified the experiment and revealed the enormous market beyond Hollywood's traditional, but increasingly chimerical, 'family' audience for this previously untouchable generic material. Saunders (2000: 75) describes *Psycho* as 'an act of permission for film-makers in the genre to further expose [*sic*] the illusory securities and limited rationales of contemporary life to reveal the chaos which underpins modern existence and constantly threatens to ensure its collapse'.

As Tudor's careful tabulations make clear, however, the generic shift that occurs with *Psycho* is a shift in emphasis, not an overnight generic trans-formation. While various cheaply produced imitations of *Psycho* (and of the previous season's hit psychological thriller-horror hybrid *Les Diaboliques*, France 1959) quickly flooded the market (*Homicidal*, 1963; *Dementia 13*, 1964; etc.), the older, more restrained and comfortingly distanced – in place, time and nature of threat – Romantic Gothic mode persisted throughout the 1960s, notably in Roger Corman's cycle of Poe adaptations (*House of Usher*, 1960; *The Pit and the Pendulum*, 1961; *Tomb of Ligeia*, 1965; etc.) and the British Hammer horror series; so too such low-key ghost stories as *The Innocents* and *The Haunting*. Hitchcock himself developed two aspects of *Psycho* – the relentless assault of the shower scene and the idea of the inexplicability of violence – further in *The Birds* (1963). Although *The Birds* seems to return to the 'external threat' model (and looks forwards to such 1970s 'eco-horror' films as *Frogs*, 1972, *Piranha*, 1977, *Prophecy*, 1979, and even *Jaws*), strong hints in the film suggest that the birds' sudden attack is in some way related to the characters' familial dysfunction and emotional repression.

But it was arguably not until two films of the 1968 season, the exploitation film *Night of the Living Dead* and the major studio release *Rosemary's Baby*, that any horror films repeated *Psycho*'s enormous impact. Both films share *Psycho*'s key generic innovation, the refusal to allow the audience a stable or secure final position. *Psycho*'s refusal to allow its threat to be recuperated by the all-too-neat psychoanalytic categories of the penultimate scene was indelibly etched in the superimposition of Mother's mummified face over

Norman's in the fade-out. *Night* ..., whose horror is more explicitly socially grounded, uses its principal metaphors of zombies and cannibalism to portray US culture in the era of the Detroit and Chicago riots and the Vietnam War as both mindlessly conformist and endemically violent, and rams the point home by having its (Black) hero shot by his supposed 'rescuers', and his body thrown onto an Auschwitz-like pyre at the end of the film. *Night* ... evacuated conventional categories like heroism and good and evil of any relevance to the horror film. *Rosemary's Baby* looked inwards to open up an even more phobic field – the body itself.

BREAKING BOUNDARIES

In her powerful reading of the sub-genre of 'body horror', Barbara Creed (1986, 1993) invokes the notion of 'abjection' explicated in Julia Kristeva's *Powers of Horror* (1982). Emerging in the mid-1970s in films such as *The Exorcist* (1973) and *Alien* (1979), body-horror blended traditional supernatural (demoniacal possession) and threat (alien monsters) motifs with a quite new emphasis on explicit bodily violation suffused with imagery of parturition and monstrous sexuality. In *The Exorcist*, a pubescent girl masturbates with a crucifix and spews green vomit onto the faces of the priests ministering to her. *Carrie* (1976), another adolescent girl, unleashes terrifying telekinetic powers against her schoolmates in a film whose first scene sees her viciously mocked for the onset of her first period. In *Shivers* (Canada 1975), a sexually transmitted parasite produces rampant sexual anarchy. Most infamous of all is the monstrous parody of birth in *Alien* as the embryo creature bursts out of John Hurt's stomach. Creed understands the powerful effect of revulsion operative in these films in terms of Kristeva's analysis of taboo and defilement in (western) societies, a realm of the excluded or 'abject' the construction of which is fundamental to the establishment and maintenance of social norms: for it is through acts of primal prohibition that a discrete sense of the self is effected.

Analysing the feelings of revulsion and disgust elicited by bodily secretions such as faeces, urine, mucus, semen, menstrual blood, etc., Kristeva notes that these 'abject' substances share a quality of extrusion: having once been part of our bodies, they are ejected into the world where they exist, intolerably, as both part of ourselves and as objects outside ourselves, as us and not-us. Ultimately, they recall to us that point at which we will all inevitably become strangers to ourselves, and at which our corporeal persistence will offer no reassurance of our continued existence as subjects – our own death, after which the decaying shell of our bodies remain but 'we' are no longer present. This indicates the source of the powerful affect in body-horror films where, in Kelly Hurley's (1995: 203) words, we find 'the human body defamiliarised, rendered other'. Thus conceived, the larger relevance of the abject to horror, the genre that above all concerns itself with death, decay and – in its supernatural versions at least – the persistence of life after or beyond death, is readily apparent.

Kristeva notes that this revulsion is learned rather than instinctive (animals and infants do not share it) and names the process that results in it 'abjection'. Three points of her complex argument are relevant to horror. Firstly, as noted, the original focus of abjection is those substances and processes that are properly *of* our bodies but become detached *from* it – thus alienating us from our sense of ourselves as coherent, integrated beings. Second, the establishment of a sense of the abject is a key boundary-making device: it sorts out what is clean and what filthy, hence (by social and ideological extension) what is right and proper and what evil and loathsome. That is, the constitution of the realm of the abject plays a crucial role in setting the terms of the normative and desirable: only through a sense of limits and exclusion does the latter become available. But the process of abjection – akin to acts of primary repression in a traditional Freudian schema – is never complete or secure, and the abject reappears in a variety of displaced forms, all sharing a similar aspect as 'what disturbs identity, system, order. What does not respect borders, positions, rules' (Kristeva, 1982: 5).

Employing a different theoretical vocabulary, the work of the radical anthropologist Mary Douglas, Noel Carroll (1990: 33) comes to somewhat similar conclusions about the issue of boundaries. 'Horrific monsters', he notes, 'often involve the mixture of what is normally distinct ... The rate of recurrence with which the biologies of monsters are vaporous or gelatinous attests to the applicability of the notion of formlessness to horrific impurity' (Carroll cites the vagueness of the descriptions of infernal creatures in the horror fiction of H. P. Lovecraft).

> That monster X is categorically interstitial [using Mary Douglas's terms] causes a sense of impurity in us without our necessarily being aware of precisely what causes that sense ... In addition, the emphasis Douglas places on categorical schemes in the analysis of impurity indicates a way for us to account for the recurrent description of our impure monsters as 'un-natural'. They are un-natural relative to a culture's schema of nature. They do not fit the scheme; they violate it. (Carroll, 1990: 34)

Like much psychoanalytic theory, Kristeva's account of abjection has been attacked as universalising – i.e. insufficiently attentive to historical and cultural differences and contexts. However, there is no real reason why abjection cannot have an evident socio-political dimension, one moreover that is immediately relevant to the horror film. Even if the processes of abjection are, as Kristeva insists, universal, its objects are necessarily contingent. In our flight from the intolerable fact of mortality, it is possible to trace a process whereby those aspects we loathe and fear in ourselves – as our body's traitorous confessions of its own limitations – are projected onto specific Others who then take on a murderous quality, as if they were somehow responsible for the death that inevitably awaits us.

Creed's essay suggests the importance of feminism as a context for the films she discusses – construing the 'monstrous-feminine' as a manifestation of male phobic rage against the empowerment of women (as has also frequently been noted, the eruption of the Devil in *The Exorcist* into Washington, DC, in the era of Watergate and Vietnam is not without obvious satiric application). It is certainly possible to extend the application of abjection beyond this time-frame to a broader engagement with the horror film's dynamics of profanation.

QUEER HORROR

As suggestive as Creed's exploration of the abject has been, she still in the end finds horror to be a genre that articulates phobic fantasies of maternal monstrosity with the ultimate aim of recontaining female energies in socially acceptable forms. In this regard, her critique reflects the difficulties experienced by much feminist criticism in recovering a positive dimension from a genre that seems so consistently to trade in the victimisation – the terrorisation and increasingly graphic physical violation – of women. This tendency has been particularly marked in the stalker/slasher films that emerged as belated after-echoes of *Psycho* in the late 1970s. One marked stylistic device of these films was their deployment of a point-of-view camera that seemed frequently to put the audience in the position of the killer stalking his victims and to encourage vicarious identification with the murderous gaze. For Williams (1983: 61), the female spectator of a horror film is 'asked to bear witness to her own powerlessness in the face of rape, mutilation and murder'.

More recently, however, writing about horror from the perspective of queer theory has focused attention on the ways in which the horror film's textual instability and focus on the 'category error' of the monster can be seen as articulating positions whose challenge to conventional dualities of gender, race and especially sexuality are ultimately not recontained by the monster's final destruction. In some cases, indeed, victorious 'normality' triumphs precisely by taking on itself some of the 'deviant' properties of the monster. As pro-social as this move may be in narrative terms – that is, it is aimed at eliminating the monster – it produces not a reversal but a transvaluation of the normative categories that Wood and Creed understand the horror film finally to reinforce. Thus identities are not resecured and the original (imaginary) integrity of the subject remains in process. This has little to do with the narrative incorporation of gay, lesbian or bisexual characters into traditional Gothic horror subjects, for example the homoerotic elements in *Interview With the Vampire* (1994) or the lesbian vampires of *The Hunger* (1989) (see Benshoff, 1997; lesbian vampires have a long cinematic history dating back at least to *Dracula's Daughter*, 1936, and objectified in entirely conventional 'girl-on-girl' pornographic fashion in Hammer's early 1970s cycle starting with *The Vampire Lovers*, 1970: see Weiss, 1992[2]).

A relatively early example of a modern horror text that resists final reincorporation (literally) is the 1982 remake of the classic 1950s SF monster movie *The Thing*. The 1982 version replaces the confident if watchful Cold War tenor of the earlier film's famous conclusion – 'Keep Watching the Skies' – with a much grimmer ending in which the two surviving cast members wait amid the smouldering embers of their Arctic research camp for inevitable death. What makes the ending notable though is not only its bleakness but also its indeterminacy: the film's extraterrestrial is a shape-shifter, able almost instantly to mimic the physical appearance of any organism it attacks. Although the Thing appears to have been destroyed in the climactic conflagration that has destroyed the base, neither the two surviving scientists nor the audience can be absolutely sure that one or other of them is not an imposter, and the film ends having refused to resolve the question.

The Thing focuses narrative attention on the question of identity and 'passing' in its all-male group and seemed to reflect anxieties provoked by the novel threat of the 'gay plague' AIDS in the early 1980s (in a key scene, the group members test each other's blood for alien contaminants). The film's threat originates in a definitive 'elsewhere' (outer space) but penetrates American male bodies in ways that render individuals strange and terrifying. *The Thing* also relies heavily on prosthetic effects to image the monstrous transformations and transgressions. Such effects (as Neale (1990) notes, the object of reflexive commentary in *The Thing* when a character responds to a particularly spectacular/grotesque effects *tour de force* with the words 'you've got to be fucking kidding!') not only render the hidden interior spaces of the body graphically visible but, by inviting the spectator to register their visceral artifice, stress the constructed nature of apparent biological or bodily givens. The most infamous instances of this probably remain the embryo alien's eruption from Kane's stomach in *Alien* and the oozing video slot/aperture in James Wood's stomach in *Videodrome* (1984). Tania Modleski (1988: 289) finds such imagery 'very far from the realm of what is traditionally called "pleasure" and much nearer to so-called *jouissance*, discussions of which privilege terms like "gaps", "wounds", "fissures", "cleavages", and so forth.'

Although relatively few horror films have explicitly explored this rapturous violation – one exception might be *Hellraiser*, with its Bataille-like confluence of pain, mutilation and pleasure – this gives rise to the notion of horror as a 'critical genre' whose subversion of identities extends beyond the transformed or violated body to the text itself: Modleski goes on to argue that

> [the] contemporary horror film thus comes very close to being the 'other film' that Thierry Kuntzel says the classic narrative film must always work to conceal [i.e. because of open-endedness, lack of identifiable characters, nihilistic qualities]: 'a film in which ... the configuration of events contained in the formal matrix would not form a progressive order, in which the spectator/subject would never be reassured ...' (Modleski, [1986] 2000: 291)

Judith Halberstam (1995: 155) similarly asserts that 'the horror film makes visible the marks of suture that classic realism attempts to cover up.' However, Halberstam and other queer theorists differ from Modleski and other earlier feminist writers on horror in their attitude towards horror's textual politics. Queer theory emphasises the disturbances and carnivalesque reversals inflicted upon normative ('straight') identity concepts by the fundamentally unstable nature of categories of sexuality and gender (and in a growing number of queer theory formations also of race, disability and even class), and the rampant semiotic proliferation that is encountered at the borders of such over-determined socio-sexual categories. So whereas Modleski still questioned the political progressivity of horror's oppositional stance inasmuch as it exploited male fear of, hence relied on violence towards, women, Halberstam sees the postmodern splatter film (*The Texas Chainsaw Massacre*, 1974; *The Texas Chainsaw Massacre 2*, 1986) as moving beyond the demonising binarism of the classic monster movie towards a riotous 'posthumanism' where 'orderly' categories of gender in particular are not only not reaffirmed but exploded. Thus whereas 'monster-making ... is a suspect activity because it relies upon and shores up conventional humanist binaries',

> the genders that emerge triumphant at the conclusion of a splatter film are literally posthuman, they punish the limits of the body and they mark identities as always stitched, sutured, bloody at the seams, and completely beyond the limits and the reaches of an impotent humanism. (Halberstam, 1995: 143–4)

The endless procession of sequels that typifies the contemporary horror genre might itself be seen as 'queering' traditional notions of narrative closure and resolution: however apparently fatal and final the end inflicted on Jason,

Freddy or Michael, the audience is well aware that this is merely a formal marker of the film's ending that in no real sense genuinely 'ends' the story.

BEYOND HOLLYWOOD

Horror films, like the musical, are found in every national cinema. Probably best-known outside Hollywood are the British horror films produced by Hammer. Hammer revived and updated the classic Universal Gothic series – Dracula, Frankenstein, the Mummy – along with a variety of home-grown monsters in a series of mostly period films from the late 1950s until the mid-1970s. Hammer horror is often approached in terms of its scrutiny of class relationships (with the middle-class specialist – Van Helsing , for example – like the 'boffins' in British war films of the same era, using his technical expertise to triumph over the combined forces of medieval superstition and an outmoded aristocracy: see Hutchings, 1993). These categories might not have been so relevant in the US, where Landy (2000b: 69) suggests that Hammer horror was able to capitalise on anxieties about authority gone awry and beleaguered masculinity and femininity. Street (2002: 162) adds that 'the cycle's international popularity implies that these gender issues were equally relevant to other [i.e. non-GB] societies.'

The horror film has also flourished in continental European cinemas, with perhaps the best-known traditions those of Italy and Spain. Italian horror in particular received international attention as an *auteur* cinema in the 1960s through the *giallo* tradition in the films of Mario Bava (*The Mask of the Devil*, 1960; *Black Sunday*, 1960), Ricardo Freda (*The Terror of Dr Hitchcock*, 1962) and in the 1970s Dario Argento (*Suspiria*, 1976; *Inferno*, 1980), all of which won critical praise for their bravura visual style and their refunctioning of art-cinema motifs in unexpected genre contexts (see Jenks, 1992). Outside Europe, the Japanese horror film, often with a strong basis in folkloric and native theatrical traditions (*Onibaba* and the anthology film *Kwaidan*, both 1964) has been one of the most notable: recently, such Japanese SF/horror hybrids as *Tetsuo: The Iron Man* (1990) and its sequel *Tetsuo II: Body Hammer* (1991) have contributed to the 'body-horror' sub-genre, while a new wave of turn-of-the-millennium East Asian horror films, principally from Japan (including *Ringu*, 1998; *Battle Royale*, 2000; *Audition*, 2000; *Dark Water*, 2002; and *The Grudge*, 2003) and South Korea have achieved cult and crossover success in US and worldwide markets (see McRoy, 2005).

The expansion of fan culture, as well as horror's arguably universal preoccupations, has led to both the increasing visibility of non-European genre films in the US and UK, a greater – though still limited – penetration of English-speaking markets by non-Anglophone horror films, and importantly the employment on Hollywood horror films of genre film-makers like Guillermo del Toro (director of the widely distributed Mexican horror films *Cronos*, 1993, and *The Devil's Backbone*, 2001, as well as *Mimic*, 1997, and the action-vampire sequel *Blade II*, 2002). (On the internationalisation of horror, see Schneider, 2002.)

CASE STUDY: *RINGU* (HIDEO NAKATA, JAPAN 1998)/ *THE RING* (GORE VERBINSKI, 2003)

Hideo Nakata's *Ringu* – which quickly spawned two follow-up films, *Ringu 2* (1999) and the prequel *Ringu 0* (2000) – is perhaps the most celebrated of the new wave of East Asian horror films to be released in the late 1990s in Western Europe and the US, securing sizeable cult followings. *Ringu* was quickly remade both in a low-budget South Korean version (*The Ring Virus*, 1999) and in the US by Dreamworks as *The Ring*, released in October 2002. The American remake is largely faithful to the Japanese original and indeed includes several shots patterned directly after Nakata's film.[3] The plot involves a mysterious video whose viewers are condemned to certain death exactly one week after watching the tape for the first time. The faces of the victims are frozen masks of indescribable terror, and their hearts seem quite literally to have stopped from sheer fright. A journalist (Reiko in *Ringu*/ Rachel in *The Ring*) following the trail of what she originally believes to be an urban myth, having watched the video finds herself the victim of the curse. Her increasingly frantic search for the truth behind the video in the hope that this will lift the curse, intensified when first her ex-husband (Kyuji/ Noah) and then their son (Yoichi/Aidan) see the curse video, makes up the main body of the narrative. The curse is revealed to have its roots in the strange and tragic story of a child, Sadaka/Samara, born decades previously into an island community with extraordinary but destructive telepathic powers. It is the vengeful spirit of this girl, thrown into a well and left to starve to death by her own father after her mother committed suicide, that has sent the curse video into the world. The film falls into an established category in Japanese horror, the *kaidan* or 'avenging spirit' film (see McRoy, 2005), typically as here focusing on a wronged, usually female entity returning in spectral form to avenge herself upon those who harmed her in life. Sadaka/Samara's appearance, her face cloaked behind a mask of long black hair apart from a single basilisk eye, is iconographically conventional in this tradition. (It has been suggested that the ongoing popularity of this motif in contemporary Japan reflects anxious and/or phobic negotiations in the masculine imaginary of the changing role of women in Japanese society.)

The central device of the curse video illustrates well the horror film's

From *The Ring* (2002). Reproduced courtesy of Dreamworks LLC/The Kobal Collection/
Merrick Morton.

capacity to update its semantic elements while retaining its characteristic generic syntax. The device of the videotape substitutes for the traditional face-to-face imprecation an impersonal medium where the identity of the victim is irrelevant (although Reiko's response to the curse may be seen as in classic horror-film style a challenge she rises to meet). The origin of the tape is left deliberately obscure, as is the precise means whereby (as opposed to why) it comes to be in the inn over the well. In the context of a medium in which sequels and series are *de rigeur* – and a film that would in due course generate two sequels of its own – there is at least the suggestion of an ironic reflexive dimension in the idea of a videotape which demands to be exactly copied and passed on in an endless chain.

Both *Ringu* and *The Ring* confront a perennial problem for the horror film – the visual communication of the otherworldly and the infernal – that has become especially vexed as the traditional 'external' (in Tudor's classification) terrors (Frankenstein's monster, the Wolf Man, Godzilla) have for modern audiences lost much of their capacity to frighten. Jacques Tourneur was compelled by his distributor to add several shots of a fire-breathing giant demon into his otherwise visually restrained satanic thriller *Night of the Demon* (1957), a move generally held to have damaged a well-regarded film. Alongside the decline – or at least the shift into a less horrific affective register – of old-style monsters, however, the post-*Psycho* horror film faces a transformed context of reception where audiences anticipate and require intensified 'shock' value, usually measured in ever more graphic simulations of violence and bodily violation. Films aiming to revitalise horror's traditional supernatural terrain thus perform a difficult balancing act between the 'tasteful' atmospherics of *The Sixth Sense* and its imitators on the one hand and the full-on pandemonium of the splatter film on the other. The attempt in the SF-horror hybrid *Event Horizon* (GB 1997) to convey the experience of a parallel universe of absolute evil into which the eponymous spaceship has slipped illustrates the problem. The transition into the hell-realm is imaged for the viewer by the ship's video log, which shifts from recording routine tasks to fragmentary and fleetingly glimpsed images of violence and madness accompanied by a soundtrack of shrieks, mad laughter and sonic distortion. While this achieves a modestly satisfying visceral frisson in a crowded theatre, as an encounter with a wholly Other order of being its horror-comic images (the ship's captain holding a denucleated eyeball in the palm of each hand and so on) leaves quite a bit to be desired.

The key textual and narrative mediator of the uncanny in *Ringu* and *The Ring* is the curse video, seen entirely or in part several times in both films: this is our bridge to the discourse of the Other in the film, Sadaka's demonic psychic effusions. *Ringu* attempts to communicate a sense of the uncanny without resorting to standard generic shock techniques while also not giving away the secret of Sadaka's story, which unfolds over the course of the film through Reiko's investigations. Quite clearly, if the video is risible or simply uninteresting a great deal of the element of threat instantly leeches away. *Ringu* accordingly takes great care in manufacturing a series of oneiric images that present a sufficiently cognitive rather than merely interpretative challenge to the spectator to be unsettling beyond their manifest content (that is, we are sufficiently unsure about what we are seeing as to challenge our simple demand of what it might *mean*). The video contains just six separate elements – seven if one counts Sadaka's mirrored reflection separately from her mother's – none of them readily generically placeable or indeed placeable in any other way (of all the images, that of the stumbling, contorted people – victims, as we later learn, of Sadaka's telekinetic outburst – is the most disturbing in terms of its content). The video is extremely low-definition and none of the (static) shots have any sense of being 'composed'. The intensely disturbing effects of the sequence are traceable to the inexplicable and incomprehensible nature of its images rather than their superficial horrific content.

The Ring's curse video is significantly longer than *Ringu*'s and although it repeats key images from the Japanese version – the mirrors, the view of the sky from inside the well, the exterior shot of the well – it adds a number of others, several of which are generic 'horror' images: an electrode unspooling from an open mouth, a giant centipede snaking away from underneath a table, a finger impaled on a nail, severed fingers in a box. The images are considerably clearer than in *Ringu*, more strikingly composed and on at least one occasion – Anna's suicide – the camera Steadicams in towards its subject. *The Ring*'s video lacks the key discursive elements of the video in *Ringu* – the word 'eruption' pulsing across the screen, and the ideogram 'Sada' glimpsed in the close-up of Sadako's eyeball – substituting some technological detective work by Rachel who, by manipulating the tracking on the frame of the image of the dead horses, is able to identify the location depicted in the video, her first real breakthrough in her researches. Indeed, several of the curse video's images prove to be straight indexical traces, Samara's memories that provide direct pointers for Rachel to track down and confirm the location of Samara's family.

Rather strikingly, *The Ring* introduces a reflexive anticipation of the audience's rejection of, or indifference to, this much more elaborate sequence of images in Noah's dismissive description of the tape as 'very student film'. (By contrast, Kyuji seems uneasy and unsettled by his first viewing of the tape.) This gesture of disavowal also highlights the different gender politics of the two films, with Noah a significantly more sceptical, 'realist' ('I'm sure it's much scarier when you're alone', he adds) presence than Kyuji, whose investigative partnership with Rachel is motivated by his own externally verifiable evidence (the tell-tale distorted photographs that identify him as a victim of the curse) rather than in direct response to her expressed fear. This reflects a generally more empirical attitude in *The Ring* that shifts the story away from *Ringu*'s roots in folk myth towards the established generic vernacular in contemporary American popular culture for rendering the paranormal (*The X-Files*, etc.). The increased dramatic prominence of Samara's family compared to *Ringu* reflects these different priorities, as does the wholesale suppression of the folkloric element – Sadaka as the child of a sea-god or demon. *The Ring* also introduces two set-piece scenes, the uncanny panic of the horse aboard the ferry and the scene in which Samara's father electrocutes himself in the bathtub. Neither of these have any direct parallel in Nakata's film and appear to have been introduced to give an eventful boost to the narrative of Rachel's quest and meet audience expectations of disturbing and violent plot incidents. *The Ring* also establishes a direct parallel between Samara and Aidan by reassigning telepathic abilities from Kyuji in *Ringu* to Aidan – again accommodating the source material to US generic conventions by echoing *The Sixth Sense*'s trend-setting portrayal of a child with paranormal powers.

The Ring employs a more generically placeable visual style than *Ringu*, using both shock cuts, fast dollies and tracks, and the prosthetic/make-up effects the Japanese version abjures (for instance, the very fast track into the first victim's face as she – presumably – sees Samara offscreen, the last frames of which substitute a horrific make-up effect for the actress' screaming face, the swap masked by the speed of the camera movement). Whereas Reiko is called to Kyuji's apartment by the police, Rachel discovers Noah's dead body herself in a scene that is constructed as a horrific *coup de théâtre*, with a tense build-up to the reveal of Noah's corpse, posed tableau-like atop a dais (this is unexplained as when last seen Noah was scrambling along the floor, but recalls for example Hannibal Lecter's spectacular body-compositions in *The Silence of the Lambs*), his face grotesquely transformed into the 'terror mask' of Samara's victims.

Perhaps the most notable difference between the two films, however, involves the ending. *Ringu* fades out on a high-angle shot of Reiko's car speeding up the motorway: we know she is taking her son Yoichi to show her father the curse video, determined to sacrifice the old man rather than her only child. The film thus ends on a bleak note: there is no escaping the curse, merely the inevitable transmission of the contagion. While *The Ring* reproduces the twist of the copy, at the of the film Rachel makes no answer when Aidan asks her who she intends to show the video to: the specific sense of desperation and cruelty at the end of *Ringu* is considerably mitigated, while also pointing up the different, more atomised, sense of family and community in *The Ring*'s suburban US mileu.

NOTES

1. Its 'lowness' is key to its transgressivity – as apparent detritus, the subversive charge of horror so to speak creeps in beneath the radar of ideological censorship.
2. For an interesting reading of the 'yuppie nightmare' film *Single White Female* (1992) as a lesbian vampire film, see Creed (1995).
3. For a shot-by-shot comparison of the two films, see the fan site at http://www.mandiapple.com/snowblood/ringcompare.htm.

CHAPTER 8

The Science Fiction Film

S cience fiction (SF) is a dominant presence in contemporary Hollywood. *Star Wars* (1977) established a commercially potent alliance between SF and a new breed of action blockbusters (see Chapter 10): of the 100 all-time box office leaders (adjusted for inflation) eighteen are SF films (or, as some SF purists might prefer, action films that derive their narrative content and some or most of their thematic preoccupations from SF's traditional concerns), all released since 1977. SF films number thirteen of the twenty-seven annual top-grossing films between 1977 and 2003, and no fewer than twenty-seven of the top 100 (unadjusted) highest grossers in the same period.[1] Year in, year out, the principal releases onto the lucrative summer market from the major US studios – the blockbuster 'tentpole' films around which a year's schedule is organised, and which can make or break a balance sheet and the careers of studio executives – are dominated by effects-laden SF spectaculars, preferably entries into reliably super-profitable series 'franchises' such as the *Matrix* (1999, 2002, 2003), *Terminator* (1984, 1991, 2003), *Alien* (1979, 1986, 1990, 1997, 2004), or pre-eminently *Star Wars* (1977, 1980, 1984, 1999, 2002) series. Classic comic books like *Spiderman* (2002, 2004) and *X-Men* (2000, 2003), which all centre on classic SF motifs (genetic mutations, radiation poisoning, mind control, etc.) and which from the studios' point of view are attractively 'pre-sold' (i.e. have widespread 'brand' recognition and a dedicated audience in their original medium), have also established strong film series.[2] Intensively marketed and subject to elaborate publicity strategies that build anticipation for months (in the case of *Star Wars*, years) prior to release, such films address themselves to a global spectatorship as crucial media 'events' (though still relying heavily on their appeal to the juvenile, principally male audience that has traditionally provided SF's core constituency).[3] Hyper-modern almost by definition, SF is well-placed to appropriate cutting-edge styles not only in world cinema (for example, Japanese *manga* and *anime* film) but in music, fashion and product design – and in turn to reformat these as 'must-have' elements in co-ordinated global cross-media marketing and merchandising strategies centred on the film (the Ray-Ban sunglasses and Nokia mobile phones prominently featured in the first *Matrix* are a good example).

It was not always thus. SF has risen to industrial pre-eminence both as a function of and a driving force in the rise of the 'New Hollywood', the transformation of the American film industry since the 1970s, in ways that could not easily have been anticipated prior to the mid-1970s. Before *Star Wars* and *Close Encounters of the Third Kind* (1977), whose combined box-office impact transformed prevailing prior assumptions about SF's limited audience appeal, the genre had generally occupied a decidedly secondary position in Hollywood's hierarchy of genres. SF's current ascendancy has gone hand-in-hand with an explosion in the visual effects industry – grown since *Star Wars* into a billion-dollar business in its own right (with Lucasfilm's own Industrial Light and Magic subsidiary still pre-eminent) – but cannot simply be accounted for in terms of the capacity to deliver ever more astonishing and seamless visions of the future and transformations of the present. In fact, the development of a mass audience with an apparently inexhaustible appetite for these technological wonders, which contemporary SF cinema both exploits and carefully nurtures, itself needs to be socially, historically and culturally contextualised.

It would seem that SF's abiding concern as a genre with the – usually threatening – consequences of technological change on human society and identity is particularly well placed to address the concerns and anxieties of a culture in which advanced technology is more central, in rapidly and endlessly mutating forms, than ever before. Any social history of the last fifty years would stress the multifarious ways in which – from the unleashing of the fearsome destructive power of nuclear weaponry, to the introduction of the contraceptive pill in the early 1960s with its far-reaching implications for women's sexual independence, to the ongoing digital revolution starting in the late 1980s – rapid technological change has accompanied and in many cases intensified the often dizzying pace of social and cultural change. As a genre whose speculative futuristic orientation has often combined with a long tradition of both fantasy and social allegory, SF seems far better suited than either nostalgic genres like Westerns or musicals, or intensely topical genres like the war or the social problem film, to mediate these changes and their possible meanings, in narrative forms that are illuminating, challenging, entertaining, yet in most cases not inescapably didactic or directly implicated in ephemeral political debates.

SF's public dimension (noted by Sobchack, 1987) adds to this critical currency. Most clearly typified by the spectacular sequences of urban panic and destruction – or indeed of eerie post-apocalyptic abandonment – where the surging of terror-stricken mobs and/or the downfall of recognised landmarks like the Washington Monument, Golden Gate Bridge or Statue of Liberty via alien attack, natural cataclysm or nuclear war (*Earth vs. the Flying Saucers*, 1956; *The Core*, 2003; and *Planet of the Apes*, 1967, respectively) signify the destruction of human civilisation itself, SF emphasises the transpersonal. Even the isolated scientific crank or obsessive, wilfully probing 'those things man must leave alone', embodies a larger crisis of scientific trustworthiness and accountability. Whereas horror films circle obsessively inwards to a Gothic interior realm of individual dementia and dysfunctionality, SF's unguessable abysses of interstellar space or desert wasteland by contrast minimise and ironise petty human concerns on a cosmic scale. Numerous SF films – especially those with epic pretensions – express this *vanitas* theme with climactic long or extreme high-angle shots, representing nobody's point of view (unless it be God Himself), which dwarf the figure of the human protagonist against a backdrop of implacable nature and/or absolute devastation: *The World, the Flesh, and the Devil* (1959), *Planet of the Apes, THX 1138* (1970), *The Omega Man* (1971). Sometimes humanity is effaced altogether, as in the shot sequences that conclude the nuclear Armageddon fantasies *On the Beach* (1959), *Dr Strangelove* (1963) and *Beneath the Planet of the Apes* (1970).

SF's pressing currency in film history and cultural studies is equally clear. As we shall see, SF has a good claim to be considered the first distinctively post-classical Hollywood genre, and as such occupies an important place in industry history. Moreover, both literary and cinematic SF have become focal points for debates in contemporary cultural theory, and a tally of the kinds of characteristics of contemporary SF cited above helps explain why. Institutionally implicated in shifting practices of global film distribution and marketing; placed at the cutting edge of changes in representational practice such as digitisation that challenge traditional assumptions about the ontology of the photographic image (notably its indexical, or reality-produced and reproducing nature); porous and hybrid across boundaries of genre and national cinema alike; centrally focused on questions of technological change and their impact on human identities; and sceptical about the continuing validity of traditional assumptions about the stability and fixity of human nature: these key attributes of SF film also comprise a virtual checklist of the hallmarks of postmodernism (see Bertens, 1995). SF can thus be regarded both as a quintessentially postmodern genre (if such a concept is not a contradiction in terms) and as an important vehicle for the dissemination of ideas in and about postmodernism to a wide audience.

The degree of generalisation in such comments should certainly invite a healthy degree of scepticism. In particular, given the notoriously elusive location of material history in much postmodern criticism and theory, it may be useful to test and justify these claims through a historical consideration of the American science fiction film.

A GALAXY FAR, FAR AWAY: SF FILM TO 1977

American SF film before *Star Wars* may be divided into three distinct phases: horror themes and juvenilia mark the genre's indistinct beginnings pre-Second World War, sensational pulp narratives and Cold War allegories of interplanetary conflict and atomic mutation dominate the 1950s, while dark dystopic visions predominate in the late 1960s and 1970s. As broad-brush as such periodisations inevitably are, it is perhaps more important to recognise from the outset that these are as ever not really evolutionary stages: each responds as much or more to its immediate industrial and cultural context than to prior stages of generic development, and elements of all three are clearly visible in the post-1977 SF film, true to postmodern form less synthesised into a new and integrated form than jostling in an energetic *bricolage* of periods, styles and ideologies. It is also worth noting, however, that if this capacity to incorporate a wide variety of elements is to be regarded as one of SF's 'postmodern' attributes, this tendency is marked even in the genre's earliest period. Compared to 'strong' classical genres like the Western or the gangster film, SF's generic boundaries are exceptionally porous, particularly as has been widely noted and discussed at the boundary with the horror film. As King and Krzywinska (2001: 57) point out, SF's lack of a consistent iconography means that definitional efforts need to rely more on syntactic propositions than on the relatively concrete semantic dimension. This has posed notorious difficulties of generic definition, again frequently commented on in the critical literature, but for our purposes it may be more useful to note that this relatively amorphous and heterogeneous aspect has lent the genre the flexibility and adaptability that has served it so well in recent decades. SF has been and continues to be a recombinant genre.

This mutability means that prior to the Second World War SF film lacks any clear paradigmatic expression (this is absolutely not the case with literary SF). In fact, as already suggested, science fiction was barely a classical Hollywood genre at all. Most accounts agree that what would later crystallise as SF themes were mostly incorporated into the horror film's Gothic imaginary, for example radioactivity (*The Invisible Ray*, 1936) and miniaturisation (*The Devil Doll*, 1936; *Dr Cyclops*, 1940). The theme of technology, by which the genre will subsequently be defined (see below), is typically tackled in this 1930s 'SF Gothic' through the catastrophic experiments of the 'mad' (usually, in fact, obsessive, monomaniacal, ruthless and wholly unconstrained by moral or ethical scruples) doctor or scientist: for example, *The Invisible Man* (1933), *Island of Lost Souls* (1933), *Mad Love* (1935) and of course *Frankenstein* (1931) and its sequels. Including the Frankenstein myth, one of the foundational paradigms of the horror genre, in a discussion of SF simply emphasises once again the particular porosity of this generic boundary. However, at least two important differences between the 'SF Gothic' 'mad doctors' and the nuclear and genetic scientists of postwar SF might be noted: firstly, the 1930s characters are much more often desocialised, conducting their operations from isolated, distinctly Gothic locations – identifiably versions of the horror film's 'terrible place' – like medieval castles, tropical islands or isolated mansions, rather than military or civilian research centres or hospitals that will later predominate. Secondly, in keeping with this ambience their techniques are less likely to be rendered as futuristic than as surgical or even alchemical. 'This isn't science ... it's more like *black magic*!' protests a horrified Henry Frankenstein when confronted with Dr Pretorius's jarred homunculi in *Bride of Frankenstein* (1935), but the distinction is an extremely fine one in this period. In contemporaneous large-scale European SF films such as *Aelita, Queen of Mars* (USSR 1924), *Metropolis* (Germany 1927) and *Things To Come* (GB 1936) this anachronistic confluence of advanced technologies and pre-modern impulses and rituals, projected onto imagined future societies, propels an enquiry into the nature and social implications of industrial technology and the 'machine age'; however – even though American cities like New York and Chicago and innovative American labour practices like Fordism and Taylorism were the explicit inspirations for these fantasies and allegories – 1930s Hollywood SF seems largely uninterested in such speculative questions, apart from the much more light-hearted *Just Imagine!* (1930)[4] (see Telotte, 2001: 77–90).

The other principal form taken by SF in American cinema before the 1950s was the low-budget 'space opera' serial, the best-remembered of which are *Flash Gordon* (1936, remade in high-camp style in 1980) and *Buck Rogers* (1939). Aimed firmly at juvenile audiences, the serials drew their narrative form from the popular pre-First World War American and European serials (*The Perils of Pauline*, 1914, or *Judex*, France 1916) and arguably looked back even further to cinema's infancy in their reliance on simple modelwork and photographic effects to Méliès's celebrated 'trick films' during cinema's first decade. Unlike 1930s SF Gothic, the serials' tales of interplanetary warfare, time travel and alien civilisations – which drew heavily on both contemporary comic strips and the hugely influential pulp SF magazines – were clearly SF, and their iconography of rocket ships, robots and death rays supplied imagery for numerous later SF films. However, as Telotte (2001: 73) observes, the serials 'offer little hint of the sort of explorations that the best of the pulps and the more ambitious science fiction novels to follow would stake out:

concerns with artificial life, the ethics of scientific experimentation, the designing of society'. Perhaps this explains the widespread feeling among 'serious' SF writers and consumers that despite the SF boom in the wake of *Star Wars*, the conscious and influential invocation of the spirit of the serials by George Lucas gave a poor reflection of the genre's more significant concerns (see Singer and Lastinger, 1998).

SF emerged for the first time as a really significant Hollywood genre at the start of the 1950s, with a dramatic increase in production of SF films by the majors as well as independents and exploitation producers, now including 'A' productions as well as lower-end films. It is not at all the case that, as the received image of Styrofoam bug-eyed monsters and scantily-clad green-skinned space goddesses would suggest, science fiction was exclusively a 'B' film and exploitation genre throughout the 1950s and 1960s. It is on the other hand true that the genre had a fairly low profile at least in the pro-duction schedules of the major studios. The famous 'creature feature' (typically featuring anomalous atomically mutated, or atomically resuscitated, human, or insect monstrosities) and alien-invasion cycles of this era – usually read as articulating in a variety of ways Cold War anxieties and preoccupations – were in purely numerical terms indeed dominated by low- (often micro-) budget features aimed at the teen exploitation market from independent production houses such as the incongruously grandly-named American International Pictures (AIP). The titles and reputations of some of these and their makers – such as AIP's Roger Corman (*It Conquered the World*, 1956, *Teenage Caveman*, 1958, amid countless others) and the inimitable Edward D. Wood, Jr (*Plan 9 From Outer Space*, 1958) – have become fondly remem-bered tokens of a more innocent film-making age, and themselves the occa-sional object of ironic but loving homage/pastiche from New Hollywood fan-directors like Joe Dante (*Explorers*, 1985; *Matinee*, 1988) and Tim Burton (*Ed Wood*, 1994; *Mars Attacks!*, 1996). Yet in their own time, a measure of SF's distance from the centre of the 1950s Hollywood universe was the absence of a single top-ten-ranked star – aside from the burlesque duo Abbot and Costello – from any science fiction themed film in any year of the decade until Gregory Peck's noble submarine commander confronted nuclear doom in *On the Beach*.

Although some SF films of this era enjoyed sizeable budgets, these were devoted primarily to realising spectacular futuristic or alien technologies – an enduringly central generic element – on a scale and with a conviction that their Poverty Row peers could not approach (for example, in the space paintings of Chesley Bonestell, featured in *Destination Moon*, 1950, and *The War of the Worlds*, 1952, and the desolate landscapes of the planet Metaluna in *This Island Earth*, 1955). With some important exceptions like *The Day the Earth Stood Still* (1951) and *Forbidden Planet* (1956), the scripts, casts and performances of even the more expensive vehicles remained rooted firmly in SF's pulp and comic-book heritage, giving rise to what Michelle Pierson (2002: 109) aptly characterises as 'that peculiarly science fictional Hollywood phenomenon, a B-picture film with a below-the-line budget of well over a million dollars'. Good examples are the pioneering George Pal-produced Technicolor effects spectaculars of the early 1950s (*Destination Moon*, *When Worlds Collide*, 1951, and *The War of the Worlds*, the last two produced at Paramount). Vivien Sobchack (1987: 143–5), however, suggests that the often-lamented flatness and lack of directorial signature that afflicts much 1950s SF may operate as a means of naturalising (by understating) fantastic narrative content. The stolid framing, four-square blocking, even high-key lighting and lockjaw acting in 1950s SF bespeaks a confidence in the ultimate transparency and explicability of the physical world mirrored in the technocratic alliance of science and military that typically brings the films of the decade to a satisfactory, if fiery, conclusion.

The launchpad for the new directions explored by 1970s film SF was Stanley Kubrick's landmark *2001: A Space Odyssey* (1968), which not only set a new benchmark for special effects under the supervision of Douglas Trumbull (later to oversee the effects for *Close Encounters*), but in its depiction of a dehumanised, banalised human culture dominated by technology reacquainted American cinema audiences with the idea of SF as a vehicle for social commentary and satire. Many subsequent 1970s SF films focused on dystopic future societies, although Kubrick's characteristic glacial detachment – which received a further airing in *A Clockwork Orange* (1971) – remained uniquely his own. Rather, it was the successful synthesis of vaguely anti-Establishment political satire, fast-paced action and tub-thumping moralising in *Planet of the Apes* (1967) that set the tone for numerous 1970s SF films including, as well as the *Apes* saga itself (four sequels between 1970 and 1974), tales of deep-space alienation such as *Silent Running* (1971) and *Dark Star* (1974) and numerous versions of quasi-Orwellian future tyrannies.

Pre-*Star Wars*, 1970s SF thus manifests clear continuities with the critical trend in many other New Hollywood films of that decade. As what might be termed a 'subaltern genre', less clearly and thoroughly invested in classic Hollywood's (which is to say, mainstream American) ideological imaginary than major genres such as the Western or the musical, and with a less continuous and clear-cut generic identity, SF's critical charge was less prone to find expression through genre revisionism aimed at exposing and subverting generic conventions and assumptions. In keeping with the temper of the times, however, early 1970s SF films were firmly dystopian in their outlook, and were frequently prepared to carry this through to an appropriately bleak narrative conclusion. The narrative arc spanning the five *Planet of the Apes* films portrayed a millennial time loop across which inter-species warfare – transparently allegorising interracial conflict in contemporary America, particularly in *Conquest of the Planet of the Apes* (1973) – cycles inescapably backwards and forwards to global annihilation. (As Greene (1998) notes, the monolithic presence in the first two films of Charlton Heston, a martyred exemplar of white male pathos in other films of this period including the post-apocalyptic *The Omega Man*, complicates the *Apes'* films' racial politics.) The alien-invasion narratives of the 1950s, with their inescapable Cold War overtones, were largely abandoned: the themes of state surveillance, thought control, media manipulation and the struggle to retrieve individual identity, developed in films such as *THX 1138*, *Punishment Park* (1971), *Soylent Green* (1973), *Rollerball* (1975), *Logan's Run* (1976), the remake of *Invasion of the Body Snatchers* (1978) and *Escape From New York* (1979), drew much less on phobic imaginings of the Communist enemy and more on current revelations about the nature of the American national security state in the wake of Vietnam, Watergate and revelations of illicit counter-intelligence programmes up to and including assassinations of opponents of US policy both domestic and foreign.

These films shared a vision of oppressive power as largely depersonalised, even anonymous, its workings confusingly dispersed across a variety of agencies, with the conspiracy-themed crime, political and espionage thrillers that coalesced into a distinct sub-genre during the same period in such films as *Point Blank* (1967), *The Parallax View* (1973), *The Conversation* (1974) and *Three Days of the Condor* (1975). As ever, patterns of generic 'evolution' on closer inspection prove strongly inter- and intra-generic. (It is notable that advanced technology – particularly related to surveillance and intelligence 'processing' – plays a key role in conspiracy thrillers.) Together, SF and conspiracy films helped popularise a version of the 1960s New Left critique of the corporate state – a critique strongly influenced by 1950s sociology, whose critique of consumer culture and corporate conformity in its turn informs some 1950s SF films like the original *Body Snatchers* (1955). (Science fiction's emergence as a favoured vehicle for disseminating New Left attitudes into the broader American culture itself doubtless owed something to the popularity in 1960s countercultural circles of classic SF novels such as Arthur C. Clarke's cosmic evolutionary fable *Childhood's End* (1953) and Robert Heinlein's *Stranger in a Strange Land* (1961)).

Undoubtedly, the enhanced production values and greater sophistication of 1970s SF paved the way for the genre's subsequent expansion, broadening its audience and starting to lift the drive-in/exploitation stigma. Nevertheless, in some key regards early 1970s SF was very different from the SF boom at the decade's end. Its typically sardonic, satiric tone as well as a general preference for future-Earth rather than outer-space settings signalled clear intent to offer commentary on contemporary society. By obvious contrast,

1980s SF's actual instantiation in that decade's febrile culture wars was often veiled behind a surface preoccupation with star voyagers and technological hardware. SF in the 1950s, moreover, was in certain ways clearly the seedbed for the genre's modern Hollywood hegemony: the fond recollection of pulp serials and monster movies at Saturday matinees – followed by the assiduous recreation of favourite genre films in backyards and local parks, and ingenious approximations of special effects techniques – are familiar tropes of the biographies of key New Hollywood players and technophiles like George Lucas, Steven Spielberg and James Cameron. Their successful translation of adolescent generic tastes into creative (and immensely profitable and powerful) adulthood has enabled them to revisit such juvenile pleasures, albeit on an incomparably more lavish and sophisticated scale. The early 1980s saw big-budget remakes of several classic 1950s SF films including *The Thing* (1951, 1981), *Invaders From Mars* (1953, 1986) and *The Blob* (1958, 1988). However – and notwithstanding the heavy symbolism of the little boy fishing in the heavens in the logo for DreamWorks (the studio Spielberg co-founded in 1994) – the alchemy that has transformed such simple if geeky pleasures into solid platinum global brands owes less to following one's star than to a complex and unpredictable synergy of economic, cultural and industrial factors.

THE CULTURAL POLITICS OF SF IN THE 1980S

The general narrative of the New Hollywood's emergence out of the collapse of the classical studio system is by now an oft-told tale, as is the consolidation of a newly corporatised, vertically integrated and increasingly global media business during the 1980s after a period of relative instability and creative experimentation during the 1970s (see Biskind, 1998; King, 2002; Prince, 2000). Science fiction proved unexpectedly crucial in this thoroughgoing industrial transformation because it was able to pull together key elements in the emergent corporate strategies of the new media conglomerates. Out of the unprecedented success of *Jaws* in 1975 and *Star Wars* two years later a new industrial orthodoxy quickly crystallised, centring a radically slimmed-down yearly production schedule on a handful of high-, and soon ultra-high-budget action-oriented summer blockbusters targeted above all at that season's key market, teens and young adults. The willingness, revealed by analysis of *Star Wars*'s dumbfounding success, of high-school and college-age males in particular to view their favourite genre films numerous times over the course of a summer season, and their intense, sometimes ferocious loyalty to favoured movie 'brands', has given this audience a crucial say in setting the cultural and generic profile of contemporary Hollywood cinema. SF's enduring and historic popularity with this demographic (paid cross-generational tongue-in-cheek homage in *Back to the Future* (1985) and *Galaxy Quest* (2001) among others) consolidates its strategic position. (SF fan cultures are analysed in Tulloch and Jenkins, 1995; Penley, 1997; Pierson, 2002). SF, moreover, offers an obvious showcase for spectacular state-of-the-art technologies of visual, sound and above all special-effects design, the key attractions that provide a summer release with crucial market leverage. The genre is well-suited to the construction of simplified, action-oriented narratives with accordingly enhanced worldwide audience appeal, potential for the facile generation of profitable sequels (often, as with the two *Jurassic Park* sequels (1997, 1999), virtual reprises), and ready adaptability into profitable tributary media such as computer games and rides at studio-owned amusement parks (see King, 2000b). Finally, SF is reliably replete with eye-catching artefacts (monsters, spaceships, light sabres, 'technical manuals', etc.) ideal for merchandising across the ancillary markets whose immensely lucrative potential *Star Wars* revealed, in a variety of formats from action figures and comic books to cereal boxes and duvet covers. These industrial conditions governing SF's renewed visibility and prestige have played a significant role in determining the particular sub-generic strains favoured by contemporary Hollywood – in the initial aftermath of *Star Wars* at least promoting a return to deep-space fantasies modelled after the 1930s 'space operas'.

This revival of an earlier era when American SF film abjured *Metropolis*-style social speculation caught the political tide, with Ronald Reagan's election to the White House in 1980 on a platform of conservative populism and homely patriotic platitudes encouraging a wilful disengagement from the late-1970s 'malaise' of social and political complexities in favour of the appealing simplicities of a fantasy past. For many commentators, trends in early 1980s SF confirmed this regressive tendency: not only the hardware-heavy, PG-rated space sagas that aimed to capitalise on the *Star Wars* boom – including the second and third *Star Wars* instalments themselves and *The Black Hole* (1979), *Battle Beyond the Stars* (1980) and *Battlestar Galactica* (1980) – but a new wave of alien visitation films, many featuring beneficent extra-terrestrials in clear rejoinder to the pitiless city-razing invaders of the 1950s (the very un-benevolent alien horror in the remake of *The Thing* proved unpopular with audiences, as did *Outland* (1982), an SF remake of *High Noon* with clear affinities to the 1970s dystopic/conspiracy mode).

At first glance, the reconception of alien visitors in positive terms in films such as *Close Encounters of the Third Kind* and *E.T.* (1982) seemed to imply a more liberal, less Manichean view of the universe than Reagan's simplistic perception of the Soviet Union as (in terms drawn directly from *Star Wars*, life mimicking art) 'an evil empire'. Yet, just as the New Right's foreign policy posturing was arguably directed primarily at a domestic constituency, the politics of the 1980s ET films gestured less to the geopolitical realities of the renewed Cold War (directly engaged as they were in the decade's new action films: see Chapter 10) and more to the fierce *Kulturkampf* waged on the home front. Aliens were often depicted as galactic innocents abroad, all too human in their vulnerability to the violence and corruption of human civilisation. Thus these ostensibly optimistic alien encounters were under-pinned by a desire for other-worldly redemption from the disenchanted present. In fact, the close alliances forged against established (adult) authority between childlike aliens and human children (or childlike adults) in *Close Encounters*, *E.T.*, *Starman* (1984) and *Flight of the Navigator* (1986) seemed to propose the wholesale rejection of the intractable difficulties of contemporary familial and professional life in favour of a numinous enchantment strongly identified with pre-adult perspectives. (*Cocoon* (1985) and **batteries not included* (1987) used extra-terrestrials to valorise 'innocence' at the opposite end of the age spectrum, allying the literally unworldly attributes of the ETs with those of sentimentally imagined senior citizens.) In the era of Reagan, the pursuit of enchantment in these 'regressive texts' was anything but apolitical; on the contrary, it was consistent with the anti-rational appeal long associated with reactionary political tendencies (see Benjamin, [1936] 1970). Their distinctive contribution was to stake out a terrain of *cultural* politics for 1980s SF – the politics of private life, of family, gender and sexuality – that marked a clear break with the public policy preoccupations of their imme-diate precursors in the late 1960s and 1970s (see also Ryan and Kellner, 1988: 258–65; Sobchack, 1987b). More recently, the cosmic family romance of *Contact* (1997) explores some of the same thematic territory.

In considering the enormous success of *Alien*, which in many ways seems to contradict Reagan-era trends, this cultural-political dimension is crucial. *Alien*'s voracious and repulsive predator is clearly the diametrical opposite of cuddly ET, while the film's nameless but evidently mendacious and exploit-ative 'Company' extends the anti-corporate critique of earlier 1970s films like *Soylent Green*. However, the aspect of *Alien* that has been most powerfully addressed in the extensive critical discussion of the film – including two theoretical interventions of major importance for both SF (and horror) criti-cism and gender theory (Creed, 1986, 1993; Springer, 1996) – is its phobic vision of female sexuality and reproduction. As discussed in the previous chapter, Creed adapts Kristeva's theory of abjection to argue that *Alien* (and other 'body-horror' films of the 1970s and early 1980s such as *The Exorcist*, 1973) creates a vision of the 'monstrous-feminine' (citing as well as the film's manifold perverse images of parturition – most infamously the embryo alien that grotesquely 'births' through John Hurt's chest – and the ramified hostility to the maternal expressed, for example, through 'Mother', the duplicitous onboard computer that secretly does the bidding of the nefarious Company). As Bukatman (1993: 262) observes, '*Alien* presents the return of the repressed – the body – to the space of the science fiction film'. At a time when the rise of the New Right put women's reproductive rights back into political play, while also stigmatising autonomous female sexuality and (a seemingly economic issue powerfully roped into the culture wars through the image of the unruly female body of colour) mythical 'welfare mothers', *Alien*'s repulsive images of the female body seemed geared to endorse a powerful disciplinary response.[5] *Videodrome* (1984) and *The Fly* (1986) used similarly visceral 'body-horror' imagery in SF contexts to explore anxieties around sexuality, identity and infection – the latter making very clear allegorical reference to AIDS, stigmatised in the mid-1980s as a 'gay plague'.

In fact, while *Star Wars* is historically of huge significance in establishing SF as a major production category in Hollywood, *Alien* is in many ways the more generically significant film. While like other SF films of the period it translates the public and political concerns of the 1970s into the new cultural terrain of the 1980s, it is nonetheless plugged into the historical mainstream of SF film in ways that the child-alien films of the 1980s are not, in particular through the clear implication that the alien, whose body combines organic and machine-like elements, is effectively if unknowingly allied with the equally inhuman and lethal power of the Company, whose representatives in the film, significantly, are cybernetic: Mother, the ship's computer, and the android science officer Ash. For the unfolding, but usually anxious if not outright hostile, relationship to technology has been SF's closest approximation of a consistent semantic core. It is this relationship to which we will now turn.

SF, TECHNOLOGY AND (POST)MODERNITY

In so far as its preoccupations reflect widely shared experiences of modernity itself, the concerns of science fiction are – unlike, say, the high degree of cultural specificity in the Western – potentially universal ones. Indeed, the audience to whom SF's concerns speak directly has only broadened as the forms and practices of industrial and post-industrial society, formerly concentrated in the First World, have extended themselves inexorably to the rest of the world. Thus, although this chapter has so far considered SF film principally in light of the unfolding institutional context of post-classical Hollywood, it is equally helpful to situate those same shifts in the US film industry, and SF's prominent place in that process, in the context of the much larger – indeed, global – experience for which SF has also been regarded as a key expressive form: the Hydra-headed concept of 'postmodernism'.

On the one hand, SF both directly depicts and thematises the economic and cultural transformations held to typify the onset of postmodernity, in particular the ever-expanding reach and exploding economic importance of new electronic and digital information technologies and the concomitant fragmentation and decline of traditional industries and the communities organised around them. Typically these are rendered in SF in lurid comic-book and video-game images of urban entropy, for example *Judge Dredd* (1995) or *Robocop* (1987). (The landscapes Sobchack (1987a) identifies as characteristic of SF in the 1950s – deserts, beaches, wastelands – have been largely displaced by these decaying cityscapes.) On the other hand, SF's move in from the cultural margins and its appropriation of the industrial prestige traditionally reserved for more 'respectable' forms (the social problem film, the biopic) itself encapsulates the collapse of long-standing oppositions between 'high' and 'low' cultural forms. The contemporary blockbuster SF film, conceived as merely the leading edge of a cross-media promotional blitz across a wide range of ancillary markets spanning several months from pre-release promotions to subsequent cable and terrestrial TV 'premieres' and DVD release (with 'added features'), exemplifies the commodification that has (according to Fredric Jameson (1991) and many others) entirely colonised the cultural space hitherto preserved, however insecurely, for the aesthetic. The growing reliance on 'pre-sold' properties – themselves mainly drawn from the same junk-culture universe of old TV shows and comic books – captures the sense of a constant cannibalistic recycling of an exhausted set of tropes and paradigms to an ever-lower common denominator. And a pro-fusion of knowingly reflexive gestures – a toy Godzilla, representing that summer's rival SF blockbuster, crushed by an asteroid shower at the start of *Armageddon* (1998); a pan across racks of merchandise at the Jurassic Park gift shop, identical down to the logo on the coffee mugs and T-shirts to the promotional materials for the film in which they feature; a brief cutaway of a panicked Japanese businessman fleeing the T-Rex terrorising downtown Santa Cruz in *The Lost World: Jurassic Park II*, a reference back to the fleeing hordes in numberless Toho atomic monster movies of the 1960s – also support Jameson's famous contention that the critical edge of modernist parody has been blunted into the blankly imitative pastiche of the post-modern text (Jameson, 1990: 16–19).

At the formal level, the increasing generic hybridity of SF films (alongside most other major genres) produces the same bewildering *bricolage* of periods, places and styles famously experienced by Deckard, the hero of *Blade Runner* (1982), a film that a number of powerful readings, especially Giuliana Bruno's influential essay (1987), have rendered something of a touchstone for postmodernism in SF and film generally. Deckard walks down (or rather, hovers above) the mean streets of 2019 Los Angeles, a twenty-first-century city steeped in the rain-soaked neon tones of 1940s *noir*, an American conurbation whose streets are a cross between Weimar Berlin and contemporary Osaka or Tokyo, an Earth city whose most affectingly 'human' denizens are the android Replicants, fugitives from the off-world mining colonies they have been constructed to service.

Drawing on theorists such as Jean Baudrillard, Telotte (1995: 233) identifies the 'near fixation on the artificial, technologized body – the robot, cyborg, android' in *Blade Runner* and other SF films of the 1980s and early 1990s (including the first two *Terminators*, *Robocop* and *Making Mr Right*, 1988) as a negotiation of the extreme anxieties induced by human-created technologies that increasingly threaten not only to exceed human understanding or control, but somehow to dilute or even supersede human identity itself. That Deckard in *Blade Runner* may himself be, it is strongly suggested, a replicant whose laconic, Philip Marlowe-esque doggedness and integrity have therefore all been *programmed* into him confirms the point. Elsewhere, Telotte argues that SF since the mid-1980s has decisively reoriented itself around issues of technology – specifically, machine intelligence, androids and their like, and virtual/computer-generated realities – and relates this to the embracing chronotype of postmodernism (Telotte, 2001: 108–20). The ongoing exploration of these themes in *A.I.: Artificial Intelligence* (2002) would seem to bear out his claim.

Androids have certainly provided contemporary SF with a rich vein of thematic material, as the rather complex progressive exploration of the figure of the cyborg in the *Alien* series suggests. The ruthless and treacherous android Ash in the first film is followed in the first sequel, *Aliens*, by the trustworthy and brave Bishop (who expresses a preference for the term 'synthetic person' over 'android'). While *Alien3* does not feature a new android character, the now-terminated Bishop's original human programmer – a dutiful tool of the murderous Company, hence ironically far less humane than his lookalike creation – appears towards to the end of the film to try to exploit series heroine Ellen Ripley's hard-won trust in his creation. Finally, *Alien: Resurrection* (1997) features both a young female android – who taps into Ripley's powerful maternal instinct, established in *Aliens* – and revives Ripley herself as a cyborg-like clone whose blood combines both human and alien DNA.

It is actually rather questionable whether, as has been claimed, this ambivalent technocentrism is really specific to contemporary SF, let alone a manifestation of 'postmodern' forces in Hollywood or the USA. In fact, examples spanning the history of SF film tend to suggest that if anything the genre's elusive semantic core – or the closest thing to it – consists in its enduring focus through serial visions of possible futures on the transformative, sometimes invasive, impact of advanced technology. As early (in terms of genre history) as 1927, *Metropolis* reflects the ambivalent fascination widespread in Weimar Germany and indeed elsewhere in interwar Europe with the technologies of the 'machine age', including the assembly line, the automobile, the telescreen and most famously the robot. The film's sleekly Deco-styled female android and the destructive energies she/it unleashes image perfectly the film's anxiety that modern scientific wizardry – quite literally: the robot's animation is depicted as part science, part Kabbalistic ritual – has outpaced its inventors' capacity to manage or even comprehend it, a note repeatedly struck in SF film ever since. Moreover, as a comparison of *Metropolis* with such celebrated contemporaneous documentary films about the transformation of the experience of labour in the modern industrial city like *Man With a Movie Camera* (USSR, 1929) or *Berlin, Symphony of a Great City* (Germany, 1927) reveals, preoccupations allegedly peculiar to postmodernism such as the cinema's implication in a circulatory system of 'pure' information, and even the notion of the cyborg, extended at this time into avant-garde intellectual circles well beyond the generic matrix of SF: according to Brodnax (2001: 90), *Berlin*'s director Walter Ruttmann 'proposed to merge the body with the cinematic apparatus in order to indice the birth of an adequate, cybernetic person.'

Such examples perhaps confirm that SF can focus and refine in stylised allegorical form concerns widely at issue in the culture. However, they also indicate that SF's relevance to theories of postmodernism may consist less in a specific postmodern turn on the genre's part than in the increasing imbrication of its abiding thematic concerns with those of the larger society whose present has started to match SF's past images of its possible future. One might claim that SF's generic boundaries are necessarily and increasingly porous: for of all genres, SF is the most directly responsive to the massive transformations that advanced technology has effected, and continues to effect, upon our world. As the paraphernalia and jargon of SF, from space travel to virtual reality, from *Star Trek*-style 'communicators' (mobile phones) to Orwellian 'telescreens' (CCTV and webcams) grow ever more inescapably part of our daily life, so SF's thematic preoccupations come to seem less and less the outlandish and juvenile fantasies they struck previous generations: this is, as Sobchack (1988: 237) puts it, 'the very "science fictionalisation" of American culture.' Just as Moon landings, the furthest lunge of quasi-scientific fantasy in the early decades of the twentieth century (*A Trip to the Moon*, 1903; *The Woman in the Moon*, 1927), have become rarely recalled historical fact, other SF tropes like artificial intelligence are the rapidly advancing frontiers of both contemporary computer science and, in response, of philosophy, ethics and even theology.

Few things of course date so rapidly as past visions of a future which has now become our own present or indeed past (in a digital age, the rotary

counters on the shuttle flightdeck in *2001* inevitably jar). A few science
fiction films have foregrounded this odd temporal double exposure: Marty
McFly's many anachronistic double-takes in *Back to the Future* include an
exposure to the visions of 1950s SF – stumbling out of his time-travelling
DeLorean upon first arriving in 1955, his crash helmet and protective suit
transform him in the horrified eyes of a hick family into the alien spaceman
of Junior's comic book. *Mars Attacks!* is a lovingly assembled homage/
parody of 1950s alien-invasion that revels in the period futurism of Bakelite
and the theremin.[6] An isolated spark of originality in *Terminator 3: Rise of the
Machines* (2003) finds John Connor – future leader of the human resistance
movement against the cyborg empire – trapped not in the expected gleaming
twenty-first-century mainframe, but in a mothballed Cold War-vintage
control room complete with state-of-the-art consoles and transistors straight
out of the original *Star Trek* series or *Countdown* (1969). In a film series
whose entries recycle a single plot with minimal variation, this vignette might
be seen as a confession of the cyclical and circular nature not only of the
Terminator franchise but of the genre as a whole.

In any case – given that it is generally accepted that SF's ostensibly
predictive aspect more often masks social allegory or critique – these fallible
future prognostications, which in fact lend a considerable retrospective charm
to past SF, tend instead to highlight SF's enduring focus through such serial
visions of possible futures on the transformative, sometimes invasive, impact
of advanced technology. What qualifies as 'advanced' obviously changes with
the passing of time, but the unfolding relationship to technology has been an
issue of growing fascination and concern in developed societies since at least
the late nineteenth century (usually regarded as the birthdate of modern
science fiction in the novels of Jules Verne and H. G. Wells, even though the
term itself was not in general usage before the 1920s (see James, 1994)) and
has supplied the protean genre of SF with its closest approximation to a
consistent semantic core.

Alien visitants or invaders, for example, by definition possess technologies
more advanced than earthlings (and are often characterised by 'machine-like'
lack of emotion: recently, for example, in *Independence Day*, 1996). Stories
about computers (e.g. *Colossus: The Forbin Project*, 1971; *WarGames*, 1984;
The Lawnmower Man, 1992; *The Matrix*) or androids (*Metropolis*; *Robocop*;
The Terminator; *Eve of Destruction*, 1990) centre on humanoid machines that
mimic and/or threaten human behaviour. Visions of humanity's future reliably
image societies structured and shaped by technology in fundamental ways –
even if, as in post-nuclear-holocaust fantasies from *Five* (1951) onwards, the
effect of that technology has been to bomb subsequent human cultures back
to the Stone Age (literally, in *Teenage Caveman*). Following the lead of
Aldous Huxley's 1932 novel *Brave New World*, future technologised societies

are usually depicted as having in some ways surrendered important human freedoms, even when this subject is tackled satirically (as in *Demolition Man*, 1993). More specifically, SF has concerned itself with the increasing mediation of human experience by technology at all levels, from the public and intersubjective – obvious examples include atomic warfare and space travel – to the psychological and emotional (thus inventions that enable the recording and projection of individual dreams, memories and fantasies figure in *Quatermass and the Pit*, GB 1968, *Brainstorm*, 1983, and *The Lawnmower Man*), and with the threat this poses to the integrity of the human sensorium.

While not every single SF film foregrounds technology, at some level most SF works through technological motifs. *Invasion of the Body Snatchers*, for example, seems on the face of it not to involve technology at all: the alien 'pods' that are taking over the small Californian community of Santa Mira, whatever they are, possess none of the fearsome war-making hardware of other 1950s invasion fantasies (*War of the Worlds*, *Invaders From Mars*; even the 'intellectual carrot' in *The Thing*, though he spends most of the film stomping around murderously and without great obvious forethought, has arrived by interstellar craft); and the process of pod 'possession' is subtle, seemingly organic and quite mysterious – no cumbersome brainwashing apparatus or drugs apparently needed. Even so, the leeching of human emotions and imaginative life the pods bring about – 'love, desire, ambition, faith: without them life is so simple' – resonates strongly with popular notions of the emotionless, implacable machine (and this holds true whether one sees the film as an allegory of 'machine-like' Communism (see Biskind, 1983) or of postwar America increasingly subject to domination by actuarial computation and the new culture of the nascent corporate American techno-cracy (see Jancovich, 1996).[7]

As many commentators have noted, SF's prevailing mood – perhaps surprisingly or even paradoxically, given the historical importance in the genre of technical advances in visual effects, which since the early 1980s have relied in ever greater measure on computer technologies – has most often been technosceptic if not outright technophobic. Perhaps the ultimate symbol in SF film of the fatal *hubris* of technological wizardry is the literally towering achievement of the extinct Krell in *Forbidden Planet*: circuits and generators banked miles deep, tools of an unguessable intelligence. As usual, the Krell's story reveals the necessary limits on technical mastery, given the frailty of the flesh: their drive to liberate themselves altogether from reliance on crudely physical instrumentality unleashed 'monsters from the id', an unreconciled primitive psychic residue that, once tapped into the boundless powers of Krell technology, acquired annihilating powers the Krell were powerless to defeat. However paradoxically, SF frequently appeals to pre- or trans-technological means as a solution to narrative crisis.

Most famously, in *Star Wars* Luke Skywalker must learn to 'trust the Force': only by turning off his sophisticated targeting mechanism and channelling the mystical animistic power that in the film's mythology binds together the living fabric of the universe can Luke destroy the Death Star, an artificial planet that symbolises the death-dealing nature of technology allied to pure will-to-power, unconfined by morality or compassion. The entire code of the Jedi Knights is founded on this conviction of the fundamental inadequacy of mere technological mastery (echoing similar oppositions in Arthurian legend, one of the many sources of Lucas's syncretic mythology): the Jedi's chosen weapon, the light sabre, is itself (as an excited Thermian observes of the matter transporter in the delightful *Star Trek* parody *Galaxy Quest*) 'more art than science' (see Ryan and Kellner, 1988: 245–54; also in Kuhn, 1990: 58–65).

In general, this surprising technophobia is placed in the service of a larger humanistic ideology, where the unchecked growth and/or misuse of a definitively inhuman, or even anti-human, technology becomes the inspiration for a return to 'real' human qualities – if, that is, it isn't already too late. The famous 1950s cycle of atomically mutated monstrous insects – as Jancovich (1996: 27) points out, carefully selected from those parts of the animal kingdom least susceptible to the sort of anthropomorphisations that had rendered earlier monsters like *King Kong* (1933) and his descendants so oddly sympathetic – compels us to reflect back upon the human qualities they lack yet that are so urgently needed to combat them. Sometimes the screen function seems very overt indeed, as in the amorphous *Blob*, whose very lack of any distinguishing features makes it an irresistible symbol of half-shaped fears. Technology is a contextual rather than an explicit force in the creature features; but the *Terminator* and *Matrix* films, centred on the struggle against genocidal machine tyrannies, have similar stark messages on the need to place reliance in basic and indelibly human qualities like love, community, valour and self-belief. The persistence of this humanistic, and if anything premodern, ideologeme[8] suggests that, just as the hardware that in past SF signified an unguessably technic futurity now seems quaintly antiquated, similarly some at least of the more enthusiastic and uncritical prognostications of SF film's postmodern prospects in the early 1990s, such as the final chapter of Landon's *The Aesthetics of Ambivalence* (1992), have dated as quaintly as the Futurist and Constructivist machinist manifestos of the 1910s and 1920s.

It seems clear enough, in any case, that SF's recombinant aspect endows the genre with continuing vitality and validity entering the twenty-first century and taking on board new developments in technology, such as genetic engineering (explored in *Gattaca*, 1997, and *Code 146*, 2004). One mark of this continuing energy may be the way in which traditional SF devices have recently started to be incorporated as narrative premises for films whose principal concerns are quite distant from SF: for example, surveillance and artificial societies (*The Truman Show*, 1998), rejuvenation (*Vanilla Sky*, 2002, previously addressed in *Seconds*, 1966), and memory alteration (*Eternal Sunshine of the Spotless Mind*, 2003).

BEYOND HOLLYWOOD

Science fiction has not been an equally popular genre in all national cinemas, largely it would seem for practical reasons. As devoted as literary SF has frequently been to exploring the philosophical implications of the fantastic, narrative cinema is better suited to realising its potentially spectacular material dimensions. With some conspicuous but isolated auteurist European exceptions – Alain Tanner's *Jonas Who Will Be 25 in the Year 2000* (Switzerland 1976) and *Light Years Away* (GB/France 1981), Godard's *Alphaville* (France 1965) and *Weekend* (France 1967), and Nicolas Roeg's *The Man Who Fell to Earth* (GB 1976) – SF cinema has subordinated ideas to images. Thus filmic SF tends to lay a heavy emphasis on the visualisation of futuristic technologies – computers, spaceships, future civilisations and so forth. This in turn inevitably favours Hollywood as by far the best-resourced and technically proficient global cinema, particularly after *2001: A Space Odyssey* set new standards for special effects: it is surely no accident that large-scale SF films with a socially speculative dimension such as Fritz Lang's *Metropolis* and *The Woman in the Moon* were produced when Germany's UFA studios were (with significant US investment) the largest and best-capitalised in the world after Hollywood. (Much more recently, the multinational European production *The Fifth Element* (1997), suggests that the integrated EU economy may in time again support a film industry capable of challenging Hollywood's near-monopoly on large-budget genre production.)

This is not to say that SF films have not been produced outside the US, sometimes very successfully. I. Q. Hunter (1999) argues for the distinctiveness and specificity of British SF film: however, his own review admits that rather than setting new trends in its own right British SF tends to follow the American lead, for example in the alien-invasion cycle of the 1950s and the post-*Alien* 'body-horror' films of the 1980s (British examples of the latter include *Inseminoid*, GB 1980, and *Lifeforce*, GB 1985), and inflecting these in distinct directions – for instance, focusing in the 1950s less on the threat of Communism than disturbances in postwar consensus (see also Landy, 1991: 395ff.). Moreover, the dominant (and cheaper) Gothic tradition means that British SF is always likely to fall back on horror motifs and modes.

Despite the abundance of science fiction and utopian literature in both pre- and post-revolutionary Russia, Telotte (1997: 34) finds that 'as in the case of the more thoroughly industrialised nations, Soviet science fiction

finds only a weak reflection' in film. The fascination with an eagerly anticipated (proletarian) technologised future that coursed through early Soviet
society found expression in two films. Lev Kuleshov's *The Death Ray*
(USSR 1925) condensed the popular adventure serials of the time (rather as
his *Mr West*, USSR 1923, had aped the style of the silent comedy), and *Aelita,
Queen of Mars* (USSR 1924) was notable as much for its Constructivist décor
as its propagandistic narrative (see Telotte, 1999: 37–46). The state-run
Soviet film industry was obviously sufficiently resourced to compete with
Hollywood, and some epic productions included *Road to the Stars* (USSR
1954), *Planet of Storms* (USSR 1962), whose manned Venus expedition
coincided with the real Soviet (unmanned) Venus landing mission,[9] and *The
Andromeda Nebula* (USSR 1968); but the Cold War ensured that few mainstream Russian SF films secured a western release. (Several Russian SF
films, however, purchased cheaply by Roger Corman in the mid-1960s, were
subsequently cannibalised to provide material for AIP productions including
Voyage to the Prehistoric Planet (1965), and *Queen of Blood* (1966).) Two that
did were Andrei Tarkovsky's *Solaris* (USSR 1972) and *Stalker* (USSR 1979),
but these are in essence SF variations on Tarkovsky's preoccupations elsewhere. As Gillespie (2003: 173) observes of *Solaris*, '(O)uter space is simply
the backdrop to a philosophical reflection on man's relationship with the
earth, his home and his family … although ostensibly a sci-fi rumination on
the impact of scientific discovery on human life, *Solaris* is, in fact, an anti-
science film, asserting the superiority of art and poetry.' The troubled
scientist Snout declares in the film that 'we don't need other worlds, we need
a mirror, man needs man'.

Japanese cinema of course made a major contribution to the genre with
Gojira/ Godzilla (Japan 1955) and his innumerable monstrous rivals, but even
here the film-makers at Toho Studios were in large measure elaborating (and
enlarging) a concept previously unveiled in the US in *The Beast from 20,000
Fathoms* (1953). The impact of Japanese animated films – or *anime* – from the
mid-1980s may be more profound: in particular, the phantasmagoric encounters with transformative technologies in *Akira* (Japan 1988) and *Ghost in
the Shell* (Japan 1995), while themselves clearly influenced by *Blade Runner*,
have manifestly influenced both the narratives and the *mecha* 'look' of the
Matrix films, among others (see Telotte, 2001: 112–16; Newitz, 1995).

CASE STUDY: *THE MATRIX* (1999)

In 1878 Eadweard Muybridge (*né* Edward Muggeridge), an Englishman working in San Francisco, arranged a series of still cameras along a track to record
the movement of a cantering horse, part of a set of motion-study experiments

funded in part by the ex-governor of California, Leland Stanford. He projected the results by slotting photographic plates into large revolving discs in a device called (typically of the elaborate nomenclature of the late Victorian period) the Zoopraxiscope: the result, in which images were projected in a rapid sequence, gave an illusion of movement to the spectator for the display's brief duration. Muybridge's work is among the most famous contributions to the prehistory of cinema: his eerily evocative side-on images of horses, other animals, men and women, shot against neutral backgrounds, are widely reproduced in histories of film and have been invoked by film-makers as different as Peter Greenaway, George Lucas – and Andy and Larry Wachowski, writer-directors of *The Matrix*.

In 1998 American visual effects company Manex organised an array of 120 still cameras in a looping pattern around Keanu Reeves and other performers for blockbuster action producer Joel Silver's latest project, *The Matrix*. Developing a technique known as 'time-slice' originated by British film-maker Tim McMillan in the early 1980s, Manex produced a stunning effect labelled (typically of the canny marketing of turn-of-the-millennium Hollywood) 'bullet time'. As Ricketts (2000: 185–6) explains, each shot had been pre-visualised in a computer model to determine the precise positions, aiming and shutter intervals of the cameras in the array. Laser positioning ensured that the computer model was followed to the most minute degree. A circular green-screen around the cameras would enable the images of the actors subsequently to be isolated and composited into new backgrounds. As Reeves performed, each camera took its single photograph, all 120 cameras shooting in sequence in one second or less. When the resulting 120 frames were projected at the standard cinematic speed of 24 frames per second, the resulting sequence 'stretched' one second of action into a five-second shot with the camera apparently circling around a 'frozen' central image. Further computer manipulation enabled the duration of the sequence to be extended to 10 seconds by interpolating one new digitally generated frame for each 'actual' frame, and the finalised footage was then composited into new, again computer-generated, cityscape backgrounds. The resulting sequences were among the most widely-discussed and celebrated effects of the decade, seeming perfectly to illustrate the film's crypto-philosophical insights on the phantasmic and manipulable nature of what we (mis)take for 'reality'.

There is an odd symmetry between the two efforts to capture, isolate, dissect and finally to restore motion, both applying state-of-the-art, indeed cutting-edge (a phrase that didn't exist in 1878) technology to the solution of problems within the field of movement. Widely enough spaced in time, they are an aeon apart in not only their levels of technical sophistication but their objectives and their motives. One is part of cinema's prehistory, motivated in the first instance by disinterested scientific curiosity (though see Williams,

1999: 37–43); the other is a function of the contemporary commercial cinema's most elaborate and technically ambitious ventures and the imperative to deliver a commercial smash. Whereas Muybridge was an individual artisan funded by a scientifically-minded philanthropist, Manex is a well-capitalised specialist business in a billion-dollar sector of a multi-billion-dollar industry, working for one of its most commercially-minded and successful producers. More fundamentally perhaps, whereas Muybridge used photographic technology to penetrate the mysteries of natural motion, 'bullet time' distorts and recreates motion in a digital environment in physically impossible ways. Finally, Muybridge was limited to an inexact and time-limited reproduction of motion by the absence of adequate means for recording and projecting images (notably of a flexible celluloid photographic emulsion which could pass rapidly enough and for long enough through an intermittent mechanism to record more than mere snatches of movement). Manex of course are able to expand, change and radically alter movements that are not recorded on a physical surface at all but rather digitally.

The echoes of Muybridge make *The Matrix* a film whose reflections on reality and perception extend beyond the basic and immediate questions of sensory and cognitive experience with which Neo is traumatically confronted, to take in our media/ted constructions of the real. Thus *The Matrix* highlights, although in an unusual way, the reflexivity that shadows much SF film. With its ubiquitous screens, monitors and A/V presentations (like the guides to the Death Star presented in slideshow fashion in *Star Wars* and in improved holographic form in *Return of the Jedi* (1984), or the pioneering CGI (computer-generated imagery) Genesis sequence in *Star Trek II: The Wrath of Khan* (1982)), SF maintains a running implicit commentary on its own means of representation. In *Brainstorm* (1983), the intensified sensorium accessed in the film through a breakthrough technology that records the mind's unconscious and fantasy images was conveyed in premiere engagements by swapping the standard 35 mm-gauge frame for an enlarged higher-definition 70 mm widescreen image for the 'point of view' shots in the fantasy sequences. Several films, from *Tron* (1982) to *The Lawnmower Man* (1992), made pioneering use of CGI to convey the simulacral environment of virtual-reality realms. Such reflexive touches make SF in a sense the flipside to the musical, which according to Feuer is characterised by its repeated inscription of its own textual processes rendered not as artifice but as spontaneity (see Chapter 4): by contrast SF film, and contemporary ('postmodern') SF film in particular, often invites its spectator to register the role technology plays in our possible future, and also in how those futures are rendered.

The Matrix actually lacks many images of audio-visual technology: the rebels' experiences and 'movements' while jacked into the Matrix are monitored through their somatic traces – heart rate, brain waves and so on –

and the computer world itself cannot be 'seen' except as the hallucinatory endless streaming of code. This ties in to the film's counterposing of tangible flesh-and-blood 'reality' to mediated 'unreality': with the additional twist, of course, that the 'unreal' world of the Matrix is largely undifferentiable from our, the audience's, own reality (though somewhat richer in *noir*-ish spaces – alleyways, photogenically derelict buildings and the S/M thrash club where Neo first follows the white rabbit to meet Trinity – and shot universally through green filters to lend the whole a tell-tale green-screen ambience).

In its ambivalent technophobia, *The Matrix* seems to be quite thoroughly in what we have previously identified as the generic mainstream of SF film. The film's narrative premise – the rise of a machine tyranny – is of course very similar to that of the *Terminator* series, and *The Matrix* also similarly blurs a distinction between inert high technology (such as spaceships and guns), which can be put to effective and spectacular use in the film's main action sequences, and the self-conscious and hence proactive technologies of artificial intelligence. The film's apparent complexities mask a basically simple opposition between a 'real' that once established remains unquestioned and ontologically unproblematic, and an 'unreality' whose principal confusion is that it resembles the viewer's own extra-textual reality, that is late twentieth-century Earth (for no very good reason established in the text: wouldn't the machines have been better advised to fashion a pre-industrial or at least pre-digital imaginary where human subjects would lack the necessary knowledge to challenge or even conceive the Matrix?). As Lavery (2001) has noted, this is a considerably less labyrinthine structure than that of David Cronenberg's *eXistenZ* (1999), a contemporaneous film whose virtual reality computer game reveals at least four narrative 'frames' nesting, Chinese box fashion, inside one another, with no guarantee that the final and presumably outermost frame is in fact 'the real', rather than the film's own abitrary foreclosure of what is in effect an unguessable *mise en abîme*. Arguably, *The Matrix* is also less challenging than *Total Recall* (1990), where the audience is left uncertain whether Arnold Schwarzenegger's world-saving heroics are simply the unfolding of a VR scenario he has paid to experience. Neo's heroics in *The Matrix* are never ambiguous in this way (although in the incomprehensible first sequel *The Matrix Reloaded* (2003), it is suggested that Neo, like the Oracle, is simply a recurring 'bug' in the Matrix base code that loops endlessly in a series of failed rebellions against its programmers). Thus *The Matrix* appears to bear out Scott Bukatman's (1993: 17; quoted in Wood 2004: 119) claim that even in postmodern SF, 'the utopian promise of the science fiction film – the superiority of the human – may be battered and beleaguered, but it is still there, fighting for validation.'

However, the relationship may not be quite as straightforward as it first appears. In her discussion of the film, Wood (2004: 120) cites Samuel

Delaney's notion of 'paraspaces' – juxtaposed alternative worlds which supply an ongoing commentary on one another. The concept of 'paraspace' allows the film's two 'realities' – our own late-twentieth-century location that is derealised by the narrative, and the diegetic reality that is wholly manufactured – each to call into question the claims and assumptions of the other. That Neo takes a pill – associated through the Alice in Wonderland imagery with LSD, famously hymned in The Jefferson Airplane's 'White Rabbit' – to access the 'real world' identifies his journey both with 1960s-style spiritual awakening through hallucinogens, and with a pharmacological flight from social reality into a hermetic interior realm. Furthermore, the powerful fantasy construction that Neo's revealed messianic identity buys into – the proverbial ordinary man rendered superhero – may act reflexively upon the audience's wish-fulfilment fantasy constructions. On the one hand, we want the freedom fighters to smash the Matrix and triumph over alienating technology: given the Matrix's simulacrum of our own world, this jacks into powerful anxieties and desires about the degree of disempowerment and estrangement in the modern world. At the same time, in the film's own terms 'victory' for the rebels means dematerialising that world (visually, our own) into the numinous streams of base code which Neo perceives as a digital epiphany when he vanquishes Agent Smith. Finally, as Wood points out, the binary polarities of *The Matrix*'s rendering of the alternatives – 'real' slavery/ freedom fighting versus 'false' material comfort, with no third term permitted or possible – themselves bear the characteristic schematic neatness of a fantasy construction (they also link the film back to the typical dualistic constructions of melodrama).

There is a rather obvious irony in that the 'real' in *The Matrix* – the stygian subterranean spaces negotiated by the *Nebuchadnezzar*, as well as the hives or coils in which the 'coppertop' humans are stacked so their massed brainpower can provide the machines with the energy they need to survive – is necessarily constructed on-screen almost entirely through computer-generated imagery, while the Matrix as the 'false' world the 'coppertops' (as they think) inhabit is shot on location in contemporary North America. The distant echoes of Muybridge may invoke a time when film could aspire to a heroically scientific status, an objective tool for the deeper penetration and understanding of the natural world, but ironically situating that memory within a contemporary cinematics that is generically and institutionally oriented not towards capturing the secrets of nature, but instilling and rendering fantasies and illusions.

NOTES

1. This does not include another seven entries in the closely related – and in terms of its core audience and marketing strategies, largely indistinguishable – fantasy-adventure genre from the Indiana Jones, Harry Potter and *Lord of the Rings* series.
2. Of course, this fan base can also pose problems by voicing dissatisfaction at perceived failings or transgressions in the screen adaptation. Probably the best-known and most organised of these fan communities are the *Star Trek* fans, or 'Trekkers', but with the massive boost from the advent of the World Wide Web to fans' ability to network, exchange views and organise, other such factions have employed the pressure tactics pioneered by Trekkers. On SF audiences, see Tulloch and Jenkins (1995).
3. This audience is, however, by no means homogeneous: for instance, as Peter Krämer (2004) demonstrates, there are clear differences between the *Star Wars*, *Jurassic Park* and other series addressed centrally to children (often including a child protagonist as a point of identification), and R-rated properties like the *Matrix* and *Alien* series, which highlight 'adult' content like graphic violence and (much more rarely) sexuality and in which a degree of thematic complexity or intellectual pretension is itself a key part of the brand identity.
4. Such speculations, as Corn (1986) and others show, certainly formed part of the discourse of both American modernism and literary American SF in this period. On *Metropolis*, see also below.
5. *Aliens* relies less on visceral birth imagery but if anything centres even more clearly on motherhood, bifurcating the maternal into the 'good' Ripley and the 'bad' Alien Queen.
6. Invented by Leon Theremin in 1919–20, the theremin used radio frequencies which when interrupted by the hands of the 'player' transmitted tonalities that could be modulated from melodic music (Theremin's own intention for his instrument) to unearthly wails – the latter featured prominently in the soundtracks composed for *The Day the Earth Stood Still*, *The Thing* and *It Came From Outer Space* (1953) by Bernard Herrman, Dmitri Tiomkin and Henry Mancini, respectively. On the theremin and 1950s SF, see Wierzbicki (2002). (Hannibal Lecter incidentally plays a theremin in Thomas Harris's novel *Hannibal* (1999: 453).)
7. Note that the pods are dispersed nationwide via the nascent freeway network, a powerful symbol of the atomising forces at work in postwar America to erode traditional communities.
8. The term is Fredric Jameson's (1981) adaptation of the Lévi-Straussian notion of the 'mytheme'.
9. The Soviet *Venera* programme of unmanned missions to Venus ran between 1967 and 1984. *Venera* 9 transmitted the first photographs from the planet's surface in 1975, thirteen years after the US spacecraft Mariner 2 first orbited the planet.

Part 3
Post-Classical Genres

The genres discussed in this final section are all 'post-classical' in one or more senses: they emerge historically once the decline of the studio system is underway (using the *Paramount* decision as a historical marker); they come to industrial prominence in new configurations in the post-classical period; and/or they are simply uncanonical as genres either in terms of classic Hollywood (Holocaust film), in American commercial cinema as a whole (documentary), or in mainstream narrative cinema generally (pornography). The first two chapters deal with genres, *film noir* and the action blockbuster, that have in different ways become central to the critical enterprise of academic film studies and to contemporary Hollywood economics, respectively. The final chapter addresses – in considerably less detail – genres that in different ways seem to me to pose challenges to and complicate (productively) the enterprise of genre theory and criticism itself. Because the entries in this final chapter are brief, they are necessarily more general and also more speculative than the lengthier discussions of individual genres elsewhere in this book. They are very much intended as introductory comments for further study and discussion.

CHAPTER 9

Film noir

High-school students in the UK undertaking an 'A' level (diploma) course in Media Studies frequently undertake a module on film genre. A typical assignment for their final assessment is to create 'publicity' materials – which, depending on the school's resources may be confined to print media (posters, DVD covers, etc.) or may extend to filmed 'trailers' – for a (non-existent) film in an assigned genre. The most commonly attempted genres are the horror film and *film noir*. There are obvious reasons why such an exercise would favour genres that rely more on mood than on material re-sources and are relatively unconstrained by time or place (hence can be shot in students' houses, local parks, garages, etc.). Clearly such factors will discourage attempts to mimic war films, science fiction films or Westerns (though equally clearly the case might be different in a high school in, say, Wyoming). Given such exigencies, student presentations predictably pay greater attention to iconographic and stylistic conventions than narrative, let alone thematic, elements: thus much effort is put into manufacturing 'moody' lighting and including such generic prerequisites as guns, cigarettes, rain-drenched streets (preferably reflecting neon signage), ceiling fans and seductively threatening 'femmes fatales'. Such economic considerations con-tributed significantly to *noir*'s memorable visual style, and students some-times achieve a strikingly plausible *noir* pastiche. Nonetheless, it is striking that *film noir* should be presented quite so routinely as a mainstream film genre – given that at least until relatively recently the genre had no existence at all *as a genre* beyond film criticism.

This vignette indicates the extent of *noir*'s dissemination into contem-porary popular culture. In fact, *noir* is arguably as instantly recognised and influential in contemporary media culture as was the Western for the post-Second World War generation, liberally quoted, pastiched and parodied from television advertising to graphic novels. Yet this example also illustrates the ways in which *noir* has become reified – detached from the historical and cultural contexts that originally inspired it into a set of formal moves and stylistic motifs largely divorced of meaningful content. Enquiry of the students who are producing these teasing simulacra (textbook examples of Jean Baudrillard's notion of the perfect imitation with no original) reveals that while sometimes they will have seen part or all of *Double Indemnity* (1944), often their knowledge of *noir* is confined to viewings of recent neo-*noirs* such as the Coen brothers' *Blood Simple* (1984) or John Dahl's *The Last Seduction* (1994). These films are knowingly allusive, richly intertextual; yet increasingly the fictive and social universe of the late 1940s and 1950s they invoke, which charges their own fabric with meaning, is constructed only through and out of these allusive gestures themselves.

A second, very different example is even more suggestive of *noir*'s potent, ramified presence in contemporary culture. David Thomson's cult 1984 novel *Suspects* is at once a meditation on the place of the movies in the American imagination and a playful genealogy of *film noir*. *Suspects* comprises a series of encyclopedia-like entries on a host of characters from key *noir* films like Swede Larsson (from *The Killers*, 1946) and Jeff Markham/Bailey (from *Out of the Past*, 1947) that extend their stories beyond – before and after – their screen appearances, allowing them to mingle with (frequently to father, couple with, or murder) their descendants in neo-*noirs* such as *China-town* (1974), *American Gigolo* (1980) and *Body Heat* (1981). It comes as a shock to find that that at the dark heart of this dense web of narrative and textual intrigue lies, of all films, Frank Capra's *It's a Wonderful Life* (1946), a film that repeated television showings have in the half-century since its original (coolly received) release rendered a Christmas perennial and one of the definitive filmic representations of mythic small-town America. However, the annual celebration of family, community and the little man to which Capra's film has become consecrated ignores the distinctively *noir* shadings of ambivalence if not outright despair that actually colour its picture of George Bailey's 'wonderful life' in Bedford Falls.

As Robert Ray (1985: 179–215) points out, *It's a Wonderful Life*'s exemplary tale of George's ingenuously pivotal intervention in the lives around him can be seen as less an affirmation of core American values than a salutary reminder of how slender and fortuitous is the thread which separates that Norman Rockwell vision of soda parlour and friendly beat cop from its *noir* Other, the infernal Pottersville – a quintessential Dark City – of the nightmare vision George receives at the hands of his guardian angel Clarence. Moreover, the film's near-hysterical insistence on the individual citizen's integrity as the pivot of historical change and progress, and the allied depiction of George's albatross, the Bailey Building and Loan (an emblem of middle-class financial probity since ironised by the spectacular collapse of the

US savings and loan industry in the late 1980s) as the crucial bulwark between the depredations of unbridled capitalism personified by the nefarious banker Potter and the proletarianising urban jungle of George's vision, places *It's a Wonderful Life* firmly in the *noir* tradition. Although his story does not turn, like most classic *noir*, on the melodramatic cliché of a criminal act and/or illicit sexual desire, the fragility and desperation of George Bailey's balancing act – an ordinary, decent man trying to make sense of a nightmare from which he is struggling to awaken – is mirrored in numerous *noir* protagonists of the postwar era such as Professor Warmley and Chris Cross (both played by Edward G. Robinson) in *The Woman in the Window* (1944) and *Scarlet Street* (1945), Frank Bigelow (Edmond O'Brien) in *D.O.A.* (1950) or Jim Vanning (Aldo Ray) in *Nightfall* (1957). Equally, the *noir* elements in George Bailey's nightmare – urban blight and alienation, anonymity and the omnipresent threat of violence – also creep into the edges of other late 1940s films that are clearly not themselves *noir* but which, like Capra's film, are also preoccupied with male identity in a changing and unstable world, such as the social problem film *The Best Years of Our Lives* (1946).

In a transgressive and poignant postscript to *Suspects*, Thomson rewrites George and Mary Bailey's family romance as the core of *noir*'s palsied vision of American life, and simultaneously locates *noir* at the centre of the postwar American experience: *Out of the Past*'s tragic Jeff Bailey is revealed as Harry Bailey, last seen as George's Second World War fighter ace brother; the Baileys are in fact the parents of two key avatars of post-Watergate, post-Vietnam neo-*noir*, Harry Moseby and Travis Bickle (protagonists of *Night Moves*, 1975, and *Taxi Driver*, 1976, respectively); in a final Borgesian reversal, Thomson indicates that the whole fantastic landscape of *Suspects* is fashioned by the disappointed, disorientated imagination of George Bailey himself as he travels the backroads and the late-night motel television screens of a twilit America, seeking from the fragments of a disappointed life and a broken mythology the missing pieces of a jigsaw that, like Susan Alexander Kane in another near-*noir*, *Citizen Kane* (1940), he is doomed never to finish.

Thus George Bailey proves doubly exemplary of the larger *noir* imaginary, not only enacting a tragic *noir* saga in his own story and that of his extended family, but also an inveterate watcher of old films who constructs from those films a meaning – however bleak – for an atomised and disoriented life. *Suspects* seems to work through an insight about *film noir* shared not only by its many critical commentators but more recently by two generations of cine-literate film-makers: that this group of mostly low- to-medium-budget crime melodramas, the majority produced between the end of the Second World War and Eisenhower's inauguration as President in 1953, and comprising only a small proportion of Hollywood's total output in that period, nonetheless provides a key to unlocking the apparently monolithic edifice of

Hollywood's confident American imaginary. *Noir* is the buried seam of doubt, neurosis and transgressive desire along which that monument can be split open. Mike Davis (1991: 38) characterises *noir* as 'a transformational grammar' working to invert the – in any case false – categories of late capitalism, American-style. For Paula Rabinowitz (2003), *noir* is 'America's pulp modernism'. For such large, even grandiose claims to be sustainable, *film noir* would perhaps need to be considered in the first instance a mood or even an attitude rather than a genre, a paranoid and hostile sensibility that extends out from its historic core to pollute the superficially brighter visions of more mainstream films, before it finally emerged as a durable and clearly defined generic presence in the disenchanted 1970s.

Unlike the Western or other prominent genres like the musical, the genre's thriving existence *as* a contemporary genre owes much less to industrial than it does to critical practice. Originally a term applied by French critics to a (contested) group of wartime and postwar Hollywood thrillers and melo-dramas, *noir* illustrates the active role that academic film criticism can sometimes play within the industry's own relay, given the now-established passage into professional film-making via university film programmes with a theoretical and historical component. Its central place in contemporary film studies clearly owes much to *noir*'s particular concerns and content: the sense of a genre (or mode, or style, or mood, or tone, or tendency, or even world-view – all of these terms and more have been used to characterise *noir*, often to signal its historical and institutional differences from more classical genres) operating in some sense from the margins of Hollywood (and America), with the potential for critique and even subversion of norms such a position implies, continues to intrigue academic critics who are themselves both fascin-ated by and deeply ambivalent about the ideological positions promulgated by mainstream Hollywood cinema (on this 'fascination', see Harris, 2003).

CLASSIC *NOIR*: ORIGINS, INFLUENCES, (IN-)DEFINITIONS

Towards the end of the Second World War and immediately thereafter, US reviewers were well aware of a tendency in current crime thrillers towards bleakness and cynicism and an apparent preoccupation with psychological disturbance. However, as is fairly well known, the term *film noir* itself was not a category used by either American film-makers, reviewers or film-goers at any stage during the 1940s or early 1950s.[1] The crystallisation of the memorable and durable concept of *noir* was the contribution of French *cinéastes* and was itself the result of a confluence of several factors. During the Occupation (1940–44), the French market, like every other in Axis-dominated Europe, was closed to American film exports. Following the

Liberation, the rush of Hollywood releases onto French screens clustered alongside new releases such as *Double Indemnity* and *Laura* (both 1944) several older films including *The Maltese Falcon* (1941) and *This Gun For Hire* (1942), accentuating what struck French critics as a new 'dark' tendency in Hollywood, in striking opposition to the traditional optimism of US cinema. The nocturnal settings, Expressionistic lighting schemes and staging, complex, sometimes cynical and anti-heroic characters, and tortuous, often downbeat narratives of criminal intrigue, deception and violence featured – though by no means consistently or uniformly – in these films starkly differentiated them from the standard Hollywood register of high-key optimism. First baptised *film noir* in 1946 by Nino Frank – who was applying for the first time to American films an existing critical designation in prewar French film culture – this 'dark cinema' commended itself to French intellectuals for other reasons too. As Naremore (1998: 17ff.) shows, these films' preoccupation with the transgressive power of sexual desire resonated with the concerns of surrealism, still an important force in postwar intellectual circles (interestingly, *noir*'s sometimes dreamlike labyrinthine narratives and anti-realist visual style appear to have been less striking), while *noir* protagonists' lonely quest for self-realisation in a hostile and fundamentally meaningless universe were also key ingredients in existentialism, the hot philosophical trend on the Left Bank in the immediate postwar years. Angst and pessimism, the hallmarks of this new tendency, struck answering chords in a France prostrated – Gaullist mythology notwithstanding – by the humiliations of defeat and occupation, and even its pulp origins and distinctively American vernacular, hitherto deprecated by French intellectuals, now seemed a fresh and authentic New World rejoinder to an exhausted and morally and ideologically bankrupt European culture. Finally, French viewers could recognise many of *noir*'s character types – notably the vulnerable male and the sexually aware, morally ambiguous city woman – from the 'Poetic Realist' films of the 1930s. Such films as *Le Jour Se Lève* (1938) are more meditative and fatalistic than most American *noirs*, but can be seen as important mediators for *noir*'s postwar reception in French film circles. (*Le Jour Se Lève* was remade as a Hollywood *noir*, *The Long Night* (1947), while Jean Renoir's *La Chienne* (1931), was the original for *Scarlet Street*.) (On the film and cultural contexts of *noir*'s French reception, see Vincendeau, 1992; Vernet, 1993: 4–6.)

The twenty-two Hollywood pictures identified as *noir* in Borde and Chaumeton's influential *Panorama du Film Noir Américain*, published in 1955 (1983) (rising from just seven in the initial postwar essays) included more spy and intrigue films (*Journey Into Fear*, 1943; *The Mask of Dimitrios*, 1944; *Notorious*, 1946) and private-eye mysteries (*The Maltese Falcon, Murder, My Sweet*, 1944; *The Big Sleep*, 1945; *Lady in the Lake*, 1946; *Out of the Past*) than the studies of criminal desire that would later become synonymous with the form. (Such 'canonical' *noirs* as *Double Indemnity*, *Laura*, *The Postman Always Rings Twice* (1946), and *Night and the City* (1950), were all relegated to a satellite category of 'criminal psychology'.) This perhaps suggests that for French viewers the association of *noir* with the tradition of the 'hardboiled' pulp[2] thriller – a bleak French version of which the series published by Gallimard under the brand of *série noire* lent *noir* its original usage – was stronger than the elements of psychological distortion and libidinal energy that for many later writers would define the style. Certainly, much of *noir*'s most characteristic narrative material, as well as the distinctive style of *noir* dialogue – brusque, cynical and aphoristic – is derived from the 'hard-boiled' writers of the 1920s and 1930s, the best known of whom are the pioneering private-eye novelists Dashiell Hammett and Raymond Chandler, and their grimmer, more carnal and sometimes hysterical contemporaries James M. Cain and Cornell Woolrich. Novels and stories by all of these writers were adapted into *noir* films during the 1940s and early 1950s, while Chandler adapted Cain's *Double Indemnity* for Billy Wilder.

However, the private eye, perhaps the best-known 'hard-boiled' type, rather complicates the effort to locate *noir* firmly in either style or ideology. To many, Humphrey Bogart is the definitive screen gumshoe and his two roles as private detectives in adaptations of classic 'hard-boiled' thrillers are canonical, even definitive *noir*: *The Big Sleep* makes most lists of classic *noir*, while *The Maltese Falcon* is sometimes cited as the progenitor of the entire cycle. Yet while both films involve complex (in the case of *The Big Sleep*, infamously and bewilderingly so) criminal conspiracies in variously sleazy and down-at-heel urban settings, *The Maltese Falcon* at least lacks most of the stylistic disorientations usually associated with *noir*: on the contrary, bar a tendency towards low-angle shots that distort his characters' (notably Gutman) physiognomy, Huston's compositions are mostly balanced and his scenes evenly lit. *The Big Sleep* is by contrast replete with shadowy interiors and sinister night-time settings; but a still more notable divergence from the presumptive *noir* standard is the effect communicated by Bogart's performances in both films. This effect is overwhelmingly one of *control*: although Sam Spade and Philip Marlowe, respectively, are frequently endangered and sometimes deceived, Bogart's classically hard-boiled, virile persona here rarely displays the confusion or vulnerability exhibited by the private-eye protagonists of, for example, *Murder, My Sweet* or *Out of the Past* (or for that matter by Bogart's own performance as the screenwriter Dix Steele in the strongly *noir* *In A Lonely Place* (1950)). Yet such fallibility and weakness – particularly in relation to an insecure masculinity – has again been cited as a defining *noir* attribute (see Krutnik, 1991).

Gangsters feature strongly as antagonists in the private-eye films, and *noir* clearly takes over the subject of organised crime and criminal conspiracy from the gangster cycle of the early 1930s. However, where the classic gangster was a career criminal, typified by his virile individualistic energy and ruthless ambition (see Chapter 5), *noir* protagonists are usually smaller-time, are more likely to be drawn into crime by simple greed or sexual desire, external pressure or simple error than by ambition, and are typically far more passive and easily defeated than Tom Powers or Tony Camonte – more likely to go out with a whimper than a bang.

Alongside these native influences, *noir* displayed more perhaps plainly than any previous American cinema the impact of prewar European art film – albeit in a much modified and inevitably Americanised form. While the influence of such trends as German Expressionism can be seen in many studio films of the 1920s and 1930s – for example, John Ford's *The Informer* (1935) – *noir* seemed to put these influences to work in something like a systematic way. Both 1920s Expressionist film and, as already noted, French Poetic Realism of the 1930s bear clear affinities with the later American form. As already discussed in relation to 1930s Universal horror, American directors and cameramen had a well-established native tradition to draw on in using night-time settings, shadow-play and the like to depict sinister or criminal milieus – and these elements are in any case much less ubiquitous in classic *noir* than their adoption as a stylistic fetish appropriation by contemporary music video and advertising would suggest. (For a sceptical discussion of the thesis of Expressionist influence, see Vernet, 1993: 7–12.) Perhaps as influential as Expressionism on *noir* was its immediate successor in Weimar cinema, the *Neue Sachlichkeit* ('New Objectivity') and its preferred genre, the street film, also bequeathed *noir* its characteristic milieu: the night-time city. A film like *The Street* (Germany 1922), stylistically a transitional film between Expressionist excess and the more neutral style of the New Objectivity, clearly prefigures such classic *noirs* as *Scarlet Street* in its tale of a civil servant who impulsively breaks away from stifling bourgeois domesticity for the allure of the city by night – only to find himself ensnared in a nightmarish web of vice and even murder (see Petro, 1993). In one striking vignette early in his prowl, the civil servant is taken aback by the apparently rebuking gaze of a giant pair of eyes (an optician's sign) – at one level obviously a literalisation of his guilty conscience, but also flagging the theme of surveillance that would become so prominent in *noir*. Ginette Vincendeau (1992: 53–4) meanwhile suggests that the portrayals of Paris in French Poetic realist films of the 1930s bridge the abstract, studio-created Expressionist city with the still stylised but – especially with Hollywood's return to urban location filming in the late 1940s (see Saunders, 2001: 226ff.) – increasingly concrete city of *noir*. Edward Dimendberg (1997, 2004) has identified the increasingly decrepit, even entropic depictions of the city as *noir* moves from the 1940s into the 1950s with the phenomenon of postwar suburban flight from the teeming, densely populated traditional inner cities. This finds an objective cinematic correlative in the shift from New York to Los Angeles and from the vertical skyscraper city – whose soaring structures had inspired the titanic dreams of prewar gangsters like Tony Camonte in *Scarface* (1932) – to the dispersed extra-urban sprawl of tract homes and freeways across which the drifters and chancers of films like *Detour* (1945) and *Kiss Me Deadly* (1955) find, or lose, their way. LA's association with the Hollywood 'dream factory' also allows ample scope for sardonic reflections on the promise and the reality of the American Dream.

The image of the nocturnal metropolis as a labyrinth with the sexually available and aggressive women at its centre is key to many American *noir* films. Prototypical femmes fatales had first appeared on-screen in Europe before the First World War, impersonated by such 'vamps' as Asta Nielsen, but aggressively, even destructively sexual women were another notable feature of Weimar cinema, most famously Lulu (Louise Brooks) in *Pandora's Box* (Germany 1928). Lulu's voracious sexuality is instinctual rather than conniving, but in his first American film, *Sunrise* (1927), F. W. Murnau presented not only a phantasmagoric nocturnal city, but in the character of 'The Woman from the City', a high-heeled seductress who entices a simple countryman with lurid fantasies of urban high living and almost manages to persuade him to murder his innocent wife, a clear precursor to the celebrated 'spider women' played by, amid others, Barbara Stanwyck (*Double Indemnity*, *The Strange Love of Martha Ivers*, 1946), Claire Trevor (*Farewell My Lovely*, 1944; *Deadlier Than the Male*, 1947), Rita Hayworth (*Gilda*, 1946; *The Lady From Shanghai*, 1948) and Lizabeth Scott (*Dead Reckoning*, 1947; *The Pitfall*, 1948).

If this brief summary indicates some of the widely ranging references and sources on which *noir* drew in fabricating its distinctive style, it still leaves the question of what the factors were that crystallised these diverse elements into the *noir* style in late-1940s Hollywood. A common answer is that *noir* reflects the pervasive anxieties besetting American culture in the immediate postwar period. This interpretation typically invokes such factors as the economic upheavals inevitably involved in the conversion from a war to a peacetime economy, including labour unrest (as workers agitated for pay rises postponed for several years in the interests of the war effort) and job losses. One particularly vexed issue relates to gender conflict in the workplace. The new-found (though limited) economic freedom enjoyed by women mobilised into the industrial workforce during the war provoked some anxiety if not outright hostility in their returned boyfriends and husbands – ill-feeling returned in kind when women were laid off, as frequently occurred, to make room for returning male workers. It has been argued that the manifold negative portrayals of predatory women who aspire to or actually achieve (usually though illicit means and at the expense of men) a degree of financial and sexual independence can be seen as a phobic projection of male fear of and hostility towards female autonomy. *Mildred Pierce* (1945), the story of a wife who leaves her indolent husband and becomes a successful businesswoman, only for her mismanagement of her domestic life to lead to tragedy, has been read as a cautionary allegory of women in the wartime workplace (although the war is never mentioned in the film, adapted from a 1941 James M. Cain novel): the final shot, in which a chastened Mildred, reunited with her husband, passes by a pair of charwomen on their knees scrubbing the floors of the forbidding, gloomy police headquarters, may be seen as a symbolic relegation of women back to their socially 'appropriate' roles (see Cook, 1978: 79–80).[3]

However, Thomas (1992) has suggested that what is at centrally stake in *noir* is less women's place than men's: in particular, the conflicting masculine identities at play in the immediate postwar era, when the martial male subjecthood offered by the war – which promoted a violent, homosocial masculinity underpinned by the ubiquitous threat of sudden death – faced accommodation to the conflicting demands of peacetime – domesticity, docility and social conformity. In such a reading, not only the famous femmes fatales but the 'good' women with whom they are often doubled (Phyllis Dietrichson's daughter Lola in *Double Indemnity*, for example, or Ann Miller in *Out of the Past*) are projections of deep-seated male ambivalences and anxieties. This account can be usefully extended by reference to debates in postwar media about the 'maladjusted' male – desocialised and rendered incapable of adjusting to domesticity and productive work by the traumatic violence he had both suffered and inflicted during the war. Murderous veterans featured in *The Blue Dahlia* (1946) and *Crossfire* (1947) (though softened in the former under pressure from the armed services and the Breen Office: see Naremore, 1998: 107–14).

As the immediate postwar period segued into the conformist 1950s, the flipside to the unstable, hypertrophically masculine veteran emerged in the shape of parallel anxieties about emasculation generated by the rise of the corporate culture and the salaried office worker as the pre-eminent forces in the postwar economy. Widely-read popular sociological works suggested that traditional (male) American individualism and entrepreneurship were being transformed into conformism and passivity by the new conditions of white-collar work. Impersonal crime 'syndicates' – also a feature of gangster films in the 1950s – threatening the freedoms of the individual figure prominently in numerous *noirs*: *Force of Evil* and *The Big Heat* feature particularly vivid depictions of corrupt quasi-corporate criminal enterprises, in the former explicitly counterposed to a more humane, 'small business'-style racket.

Vernet suggests that the prototypical *noir* protagonist can be identified with the petty-bourgeois small businessman, anxious at the perceived threats to his (imagined) self-sufficiency and class status in the increasingly corporatised world. This interpretation tallies well with not only such venal and/or desperate middleman protagonists as Walter Neff in *Double Indemnity* (an insurance salesman) or Frank Bigelow in *DOA* (a certified accountant) but also *It's a Wonderful Life*'s George Bailey. It is also possible to situate the private eye – for many viewers, an archetypal *noir* protagonist – in this class perspective, as a self-made man whose role is to expose the corruptions of a decadent ruling elite (such as the Sternwood family in *The Big Sleep*), to reign in the excesses of overmighty 'combines' and in so doing to reassert the value of a suitably humanised capitalism. (This self-conception and its delusions seems explicitly to inform Roman Polanski's revisionist portrayal of the private eye in *Chinatown*, 1974: see below.) However, it runs somewhat counter to the perception of *noir* as a genre that pays unusual attention to working-class experience, often with conscious political motivations. Brian Neve (1992: 145–70) notes the involvement in *noir* production of numerous members of the 1940s Hollywood Left – including such later victims of the blacklist as directors Edward Dmytryk, Abraham Polonsky (*Force of Evil*) and Jules Dassin (*The Naked City*, 1948), writer-director Robert Rossen (*Body and Soul*, 1947) and producer Adrian Scott (*Farewell My Lovely, Crossfire*) – and emphasises the prominence of class, illicit power and authoritarian power structures in many *noirs* (see also Andersen, 1985).

The critical emphasis on pathologies of masculinity helps illuminate *noir*'s much-commented oneiric (dream-like) aspects, exemplified not only by its sometimes surreal visual distortions and spatial disorientations but its looping, often confused narratives, its grotesque apparitions of violence and desire, and the prevalence of uncanny doubling. If these are dreams, however, they are clearly dreamed by men, as a pivotal scene early in *Scarlet Street* illustrates. The nondescript bank clerk Chris Cross is making his way home from a dinner where he has been honoured for his years of selfless service to the bank with the time-honoured gold watch. After enviously watching their employer J. J. Hogarth leave with his young mistress, Chris and his colleague Charlie share an umbrella to the bus stop, exchanging wistful banalities about youthful 'dreams' that 'never pan out'. Left alone, Chris wanders through the deserted night-time streets of Greenwich Village, eventually seeking directions from a policeman as 'these streets get all turned around down here'. The Village's established associations with social and sexual deviance, emblematically figured in the Manhattan street plan's abdication of the gridlines above 14th Street, set it apart spatially and experientially from Chris's drab workaday reality (a motif revived by Martin Scorsese's 'yuppie nightmare' neo-*noir After Hours*, 1985): it is a labyrinth of desire. As the older part of the city, the Village may also be associated with a wishful regression on Chris's part to a time when he could still realise the 'dreams' of his youth. What happens next seems, for Chris, literally to fulfil those dreams. Happening upon what he takes to be a robbery or sexual assault – a young girl in a transparent plastic mac being beaten by a young man – Chris runs heroically to her 'rescue', brandishing his umbrella – the symbol of his middle-class, middle-aged propriety transformed into a phallic weapon. Although Chris barely touches him, the girl's assailant miraculously falls unconscious to the ground. Chris uncoils from his protective crouch to find himself the 'saviour' of a beautiful young woman.

This entire scene is strikingly staged by Fritz Lang with an eerie distanciation: throughout the 'fight', the only sound on the soundtrack is the noise of a passing subway train, which crests to a deafening roar as Chris vanquishes his opponent. Framed initially against the surrounding cityscape in extreme long-shot, the girl (Kitty) and her attacker (Johnny) struggle soundlessly and as if in slow motion. Chris's absurdly easy victory seems to reflect what he *wants* to happen more than any imaginable reality (his subsequent wilful and self-destructive refusal to recognise either the 'beautiful young girl' Kitty's real nature – she is a prostitute – or her utter contempt for him confirms this fantasy element).

The diagnosis of US society in the late 1940s as anxious and angst-ridden also cites developments in foreign and national security policy: the uncertainties attendant upon America's unprecedented and clearly ongoing involvement in European and world affairs at the war's end, a decisive shift away from traditional US exceptionalism and isolationism; the revelation of the dreadful power of the atomic bomb, used against the Japanese at Hiroshima and Nagasaki; the swift transformation of the USSR from wartime ally to Cold War antagonist, armed after 1949 with its own Bomb; and in 1949 the renewal of large-scale US combat operations abroad in the Korean War. Domestic politics were dominated by the hysterical pursuit of (largely imaginary) Communist subversion, with public paranoia skilfully exploited and intensified by demagogues such as Joseph McCarthy and the young Richard Nixon, leading to significant curbs on civil liberties, a huge expansion of the internal security apparatus and hundreds if not thousands of people driven from their livelihoods, imprisoned and even, in the case of the alleged atomic spies Ethel and Julius Rosenberg, executed. In the early 1950s, *noirs* began to engage with the panic about infiltration and subversion, either through metaphor and allegory (*Panic in the Streets*, 1950) or directly (*The Woman on Pier 13*, 1949; *Pickup on South Street*, 1952). The apocalyptic late *noir Kiss Me Deadly* (1955) perhaps conjoins the various gender and political paranoias of the period better than any other film.

These critical approaches often throw a great deal of light on the textual politics of both individual *noirs* and the cycle as a whole. However, industrial factors as always played a crucial role too. The reduced production schedules of the majors in the wake of the 1947 *Paramount* decision (that declared the vertical integration of production, distribution and exhibition an illegal monopoly practice and compelled the studios' parent corporations to sell off their theatre chains), with a shift towards fewer, prestige productions, opened up greater opportunities for both independent producers and existing minor studios to produce cost-effective genre films to meet the gaps in the market. The generally small-scale atmospheric *noir* thriller was well suited to tight budgets, while some independents at least saw the competitive advantage in tackling riskier (more topical or violent) material than the majors. Although both were short-lived enterprises, the independent Diana Productions – which brought together veteran independent producer Walter Wanger, his wife actress Joan Bennett and director Fritz Lang – and the left-liberal venture Enterprise Productions made major contributions to the *noir* cycle with Lang's *Scarlet Street* and *The Secret Beyond the Door* (1948) for Diana, and Enterprise's *Body and Soul* and *Force of Evil* (see Spicer, 2002: 34–5).

What none of this energetic critical activity has delivered is any consensus on the definition or extent of *noir* production in postwar Hollywood. There are certainly a number of films that virtually everyone agrees belong in any putative *noir* canon, among them (in chronological order) *Murder, My Sweet, Double Indemnity, The Woman in the Window, Scarlet Street, The Postman Always Rings Twice, Gilda, The Killers, Crossfire, Force of Evil, Out of the Past, Detour, Night and the City*, and two late, highly self-conscious entries: *Kiss Me Deadly* and *Touch of Evil* (1958).[4] Set against these, however, are a much larger number of films whose *noir* status is subject to debate: costume films like *Rebecca* (1940), *Gaslight* (1944) and even *Dr Jekyll and Mr Hyde* (1941) – all included by Borde and Chaumeton ([1955] 1983) but more obviously in the Gothic tradition, as is another problematic candidate, *The Spiral Staircase* (1945) – or gangster and police films like *White Heat* (1949) and *The Big Heat* (1952).

However the canon is drawn up, there could be no pretence that such films comprised anything like a plurality, let alone a majority of Hollywood production even in the immediate postwar years when the *noir* tendency was said to be at its strongest (a point made at the time by Leslie Asheim in the course of an exchange with producer John Houseman in the *Hollywood Quarterly* about the merits of the postwar wave of 'tough' thrillers[5]). Depending on whose reckoning one prefers – and both the timeline of *noir* production and the criteria for inclusion vary enormously from one critic to another – the total number of *noirs* could be as few as twenty-two or as many as 300. Even the higher figure, however, as Steve Neale (2000: 156) points out, represents under 5 per cent of total Hollywood production during this period. On the other hand, Andrew Spicer's (2002: 27–8) comparative tabulation of *noir* figures suggests that in its peak year (1950), *noirs* comprised at least 8 per cent and possibly as much as 15 per cent of Hollywood releases. But *noir*'s perceived significance has never been estimated in crudely quantitative terms. In fact, viewed as a 'tell-tale' genre – a form, that is, that was able to speak unpalatable truths about and to American society of a kind typically excluded from Hollywood product – or in other words as a kind of return of the socio-cultural repressed, *noir* would of necessity be a minority genre. After all, oppositionism and subversion – both impulses with which *noir* has sometimes been credited – are virtually by definition minority, even marginal, concerns. (One might add that throughout its critical history, the *frisson* of marginality and deviance has been vicariously enjoyed by *noir*'s defenders and commentators.)

As *noir* has moved from a *cinéaste* preoccupation to wider critical acceptance and popular visibility, the critical debates around the dimensions and even the existence of *noir* have only intensified. Neale (1999: 188) maintains that '*noir* is as a critical category and as a canon of films both logically and chronologically incoherent' (see also Neale, 2000: 173). However, while most writers accept the difficulties of codifying or containing *noir* many perhaps regard this unfixable quality as an integral part of *noir*'s nature and forming a central element in its transgressive charge. *Noir*'s textual and generic instabilities, like those of horror, commend it to the attentions of postmodern cultural theory.

The concept of *film noir* would in due course be translated back, first to American critics, subsequently to film-makers,[6] and eventually popularised for a mass audience. *Noir* entered the film-critical lexicon as part of the wider upsurge in film culture through 'serious' criticism in small journals, film societies and college film appreciation courses that provided the seedbed for the emergence of the New Hollywood 'film generation' (or 'Movie Brats'). Classics of the *noir* canon were staples both of late-night television and of the urban repertory houses that in a pre-home video age supplied young cinephiles with a grasp of film history and evolution. And French film culture, perceived as significantly more sophisticated and advanced than the homegrown variety, offered both influential critical models such as auteurism and, in the critics-turned-film-makers of the *Nouvelle Vague*, a model of how a critically informed practice could appropriate, rework and revitalise the ossified conventions of American commercial movie-making. It is noteworthy that one of the most influential, and still much anthologised, early American essays on *film noir* was written by Paul Schrader ((1972) 1995), then a freelance film critic but soon to become a significant New Hollywood player and subsequently writer and/or director of a loose 'trilogy' of strongly *noir*-influenced urban dramas (*Taxi Driver*; *American Gigolo*, 1980; *Light Sleeper*, 1991).

NEO-*NOIR*: PARODY AND PASTICHE

Noir's rediscovery coincided with the professional emergence of a generation of American directors and writers who came to prominence in the wake of Hollywood's crisis of confidence and direction in the late 1960s. These writers and directors were armed with a highly developed sense both of Hollywood film history and, particularly in the light of the 1960s European New Waves' experiments with narrative film form, a sense of how national cinema traditions could be revitalised through critical appropriation. *Noir* provided an apt model for such experiments. As constrained as the formal, let alone political radicalism of the 'Hollywood Renaissance' was by the caution and conservatism of an emphatically commercial industry, numerous films produced at major studios between 1967 and 1977 abandoned the well-lit high road of classic Hollywood for the seductive, subversive shadow-world of *noir*.

While some 1970s 'neo-*noirs*', as the cycle became known, like *The King of Marvin Gardens* (1972) echoed the defeatist strain of classic *noir* represented by *Out of the Past*, *In a Lonely Place* or *He Ran All the Way* (1951) – and arguably the form's most characteristic mode – a much larger number adopted the private-eye variant, as this seemed to allow more room for revisionist manoeuvring. The implicit intertexts for such films as *The Long Goodbye* (1973), *Chinatown* and *Night Moves* were Bogart's star vehicles *The Maltese Falcon* and *The Big Sleep*. Sometimes this intertextuality was not only evident but explicit: *Chinatown*'s monochrome opening credits mimic those of *The Maltese Falcon*; in *Night Moves*, cuckolded private eye Harry Moseby is tauntingly invited by his wife's lover to 'take a swing, just like Sam Spade would'; confronted with hostile cops in *The Long Goodbye*, Elliot Gould's Marlowe cracks relexively wise: 'Isn't this where I say "what's this all about?" and you say "We'll ask the questions"?' (One should be careful though not to overstate the novelty of such reflexive touches: facing down gangster Eddie Mars at the climax of *The Big Sleep*, Bogart's Marlowe demands: 'Whaddya want me to do, Eddie? Count to three like they do in the movies?')

The subversive purpose of this festival of generic allusion might be summarised as exposing the private eye, often as we have noted the exception to *noir*'s rule of masculine crisis, to the rigours of that generic paradigm. *Chinatown*, as has been often pointed out, ruthlessly exposes the limitations of its would-be street-smart private eye hero, Jake Gittes (Jack Nicholson), by repeatedly placing him at a disadvantage in situations where Bogart's Marlowe would have smartly triumphed: a ribald joke embarrasses him in front of a client; his nose is sliced open by a diminutive psychopath (contrast Bogart's effortless disarming of the hapless gunsel Wilmer in *The Maltese Falcon*), forcing him to wear an enormous bandage for much of the film (a joke too at the expense of Gittes's carefully-modelled Hollywood-style 'star' persona); in the course of his investigations a crippled farmer beats him senseless with his crutch; and so on. Above all, Gittes mistakes the intrigue into which he stumbles for a conventional, if far-reaching, story of civic corruption, and his employer/lover Evelyn Cross (Faye Dunaway) for a classic femme fatale: when in fact she is the victim of her own perverse and unscrupulous father, whose incestuous fathering of a daughter upon Evelyn signifies titanic desires that are transgressive far beyond Gittes's horizons – asked what he wants, Cross simply replies 'the future, Mr Gittes. The future.'

While the tortuous narrative of *Night Moves* – involving a promiscuous teenage runaway, the fringes of the movie industry, sexual exploitation and a complex antiques-smuggling ring – is closer to traditional *noir* territory, Harry Moseby (Gene Hackman) is equally rudderless – a metaphor devastatingly literalised in the film's final high-angle image of the wounded Harry helplessly circling around in a boat ironically named *Point of View*. Harry is passive-aggressive, easily manipulated, and the dead ends of his investigation in the film parallel the frustrations and disappointments of his personal life. As an adaptation of Raymond Chandler's final (and most self-consciously literary) novel, Robert Altman's *The Long Goodbye* is of all the 1970s private-eye films the most securely located in *noir*'s traditional narrative territory. However, Altman's Philip Marlowe (whom he conceived as 'a loser', also the judgement passed on Marlowe by his treacherous friend Terry Lennox) is even less the classical model than Gittes or Moseby. In fact, Marlowe is firmly located as a man wholly out of touch with the world around him – a patsy even to his cat. Altman substitutes for Marlowe's world-weary yet savvy narrative voice in the novel a rambling running commentary mumbled by Gould throughout the film in a *sotto voce* monotone, typically concluding with the careless coda 'S'okay with me ...' – worlds apart from Marlowe's fierce moral and ethical implication in the sleazy world he explores without inhabiting (but directly anticipating 'It Don't Worry Me', the know-nothing anthem of Altman's most celebrated film, *Nashville*, 1976).

The timeliness of *noir*'s revival was underlined by the renovation of the 'maladjusted veteran' theme from the post-Second World War cycle to take in the yet more dangerously desocialised casualties of the far more controversial and brutal war in Vietnam. As well as *Heroes* (1975) and *Taxi Driver*, a late and criminally undervalued entry in the 1970s neo-*noir* cycle, *Cutter's Way* (1980), developed traditional *noir* themes of the abuse of power in an emotional moonscape shadowed by the Vietnam War, of which Cutter is a mutilated, embittered veteran.

Spicer (2002: 148) argues that 1970s *noir* was mostly uninterested in reviewing the classic femme fatale in light of the women's movement. Certainly, male subjectivity remains the central focus of most of these films, with the strong strain of white male pathos previously noted in some contemporaneous SF films (see Chapter 8) finding expression in a flurry of castration imagery – Gittes's slashed nose, the bullet in Harry Moseby's thigh (and the cane used by his wife's crippled lover), Cutter's amputated limbs. Moreover, in general these films steer clear of the compulsive sexuality portrayed in the 1940s James M. Cain adaptations. Yet they do revisit the figure of the manipulative, sexually desirable woman, and subvert this generic type to the same deconstructive logic as her male partners. As already noted, Evelyn Mulwray in *Chinatown* – all haute couture and razor-slash rubied mouth – appears an archetypal scheming woman, and for much of the film both Gittes and we expect that she will turn out to be implicated in the murder of her husband. The revelation that Evelyn is a victim, not a villain, comes too late to save either her or, probably, her teenage daughter from the logic of a world in which corrupt power holds absolute sway: 'Forget it, Jake, it's … *Chinatown*', as the film's famous last line has it. The adulterous and devious Eileen Wade in *The Long Goodbye* matches the traditional model more closely, but the film's most indelible image is of another brutalised innocent, the teenage girlfriend of brutal mobster Marty Augustine (played by director Mark Rydell) whom he smashes in the face with a bottle simply to prove to Marlowe that he is ruthless enough to get what he wants. The teen nymphet Delly in *Night Moves* again initially appears a modern version of the drug-addicted nymphomaniac Carmen Sternwood in *The Big Sleep* (who at the end of the film is destined for punitive institutionalisation: Marlowe muses that 'maybe they can cure her') but she too dies tragically and futilely. In the same film, Paula (Jennifer Warren), with whom Harry Moseby briefly shares a bed and (it seems) some moments of mutual tenderness in a film where such things are at a premium, turns out another fake in a film full of fakery (she makes love to Harry simply to distract him while her smuggling ring retrieves a sunken consignment), but her duplicity is treated by the film simply as another index of Harry's impotence: her death at the end of the film is horrific, not remotely gratifying.

A strong emphasis on sexuality is one of the main factors distinguishing the second wave of neo-*noirs* inaugurated in 1981 by *Body Heat* and the remake of *The Postman Always Rings Twice*, accompanied by a shift away from the revisionist private-eye/conspiracy model back towards crime-of-passion narratives. A number of these films use the far greater sexual explicitness of the post-Code era to emphasise the helplessness of their male protagonists faced with the sexual allure of their vastly more intelligent femmes fatales. Films such as *The Last Seduction*, *The Hot Spot* (1990), *Basic Instinct* (1991) and *Body of Evidence* (1993) keep their gender politics carefully ambiguous, balancing the incipient misogyny of the 'phallic woman' fantasy against narratives that asserted women's power and satirised the culpable gullibility

of the hapless and often self-regarding and unlikeable men who get involved
with them. (For a discussion of *The Last Seduction* as a narrative constructed
around a 'female subject', see Bruzzi, 1997: 127–32; see also Stables, 1999).
Black Widow (1987) sidelined men almost entirely, reframing the *noir*
doppelganger narrative as a story of desire and pursuit between two women,
a female murderer and a federal agent. This exploration of the allure of
forbidden sexuality has been extended in the flourishing genre of the 'erotic
thriller', usually made for cable or released straight-to-video, whose unique
industrial position both relocates *noir* tropes to the borders of soft pornography and provides a rare context in contemporary Hollywood (or possibly
'off-Hollywood') film-making that most closely resembles the low-budget
'programmer' production of the late classical period (on the erotic thriller,
see Williams, 1993, 2005; Eberwein, 1998).

One genuinely novel development in the 1990s has been the exploration of
noir territory by black film-makers like Carl Franklin (*One False Move*, 1992;
Devil in a Blue Dress, 1995) and Bill Duke (*A Rage in Harlem*, 1991; *Deep
Cover*, 1992) – a genuinely transgressive move not only inasmuch as Black
Americans were as largely invisible in classic *noir* as in all other Hollywood
genres, but because *noir* itself traded both explicitly – in the descriptions in
Chandler and other *noir* writers of their heroes' 'dark passage' into the
'Negro' quarters of LA and other cities – and implicitly – in the dominant
associative trope of *noir*/'blackness' itself – in a racialised discourse.

If the 1970s neo-*noirs* in general, to apply Fredric Jameson's (1991: 16–19)
famous distinction, inclined to modernist parody – the pointed satirical revision
and inversion of genre conventions such as the heroic and capable private eye
– the 1980s and 1990s versions tended towards pastiche – defined by Jameson
as 'blank parody', the painstaking renovation of tropes and styles without any
critical perspective.[7] An extreme example of this is Wim Wenders' formalist
rehearsal of *noir* tropes in the hyper-reflexive *Hammett* (1983). Narrative
structures of spiralling complexity, recalling but significantly intensifying classic
noir patterns – in the most extreme examples, such as *The Usual Suspects*
(1995) and *Memento* (2001), to the point of radical narrative indeterminacy –
replaced the allegorical conspiratorial ramifications of 1970s modernist *noir*.

As Leighton Grist (1992: 285) observes, 'what is vital is not so much the
continuation of *film noir*, as the perspective of its reworking: whether its
conventions present and analyse social tensions, or just exists as a collection
of generic signifiers'. Certainly, no one can doubt that *noir* has become an
essential frame of stylistic and thematic reference for contemporary visual
(not just film) culture. The impact of *Blade Runner* (1982) and 'tech *noir*' (see
Chapter 8) have ensured that *noir*'s distinctive vision of urban entropy and
anomie has become the default setting for depictions of the dystopic near
future in SF films as different as *The Matrix* (1998) and *Star Wars Episode*

II: Attack of the Clones (2002). It is perhaps appropriate that as contested and non-identitarian a form as *noir* should have been adopted as one of polymorphous postmodern culture's preferred self-representations.

BEYOND HOLLYWOOD

Film noir's polyvalence, 'phantom' generic identity and international influences make it unsurprising that other national cinemas have adopted *noir* modes and motifs, although its fatalism and perversity may appear less radical in cinemas less geared to high-key optimism than classic Hollywood. In addition to the prewar proto-*noir* European trends – Expressionism, New Objectivity and Poetic Realism – noted above, *noir* traditions have been especially strong in France and in Britain, while Jordan and Morgan-Tamosounas (1998: 86–105) discuss the importance of Spanish *cine negro* from the 1950s to the present day, where its influence can be seen in such films as *Live Flesh* (1998). They argue that *cine negro* found a particular purchase during the transition to democracy after Franco's death in 1975, a period whose revelations about the Spanish state apparatus meant that 'the corruption and cynicism at the centre of classic American *noir* movies found a resounding echo in contemporary Spain' (p. 89).

Spicer (2002: 175–203) explores the tradition of British *noir*, arguing strongly for a tradition of crime melodramas that, like their American counterparts (and, although in different ways, like Hammer horror) strongly challenge the middle-class verities and complacencies of mainstream British cinema. While Spicer's *noir* canon is somewhat diffuse, taking in alongside contemporary thrillers with evident *noir* attributes like *Odd Man Out* (1947), *They Made Me A Fugitive* (1947), *The Third Man* (1949), *Hell Is a City* (1960) and *Get Carter* (1971) – but strangely not *Brighton Rock* (1948) – a large number of period films. *Gaslight* (1940), *Pink String and Sealing Wax* (1945) and even *Oliver Twist* (1948) seem to belong, but *Great Expectations* (1946) and *Kind Hearts and Coronets* (1948) seem in both stylistic and narrative terms remote from *noir*. A problem here may be the importance of the English Gothic tradition combined with (before Hammer's breakthrough in the mid-1950s) the lack of a clearly established cinematic Gothic. However, Spicer is able to trace an important lineage for such contemporary British neo-*noirs* as *Dance With a Stranger* (1985) and *Mona Lisa* (1986) and more recently *Shallow Grave* (1995) and *Croupier* (1999). Of these, one might note that the 1980s films seem to partake of the Thatcher years' intense politicisation and address themselves clearly to British class, racial and gender pathologies, whereas the 1990s films are in properly postmodern fashion rather more socially decontextualised.

Austin (1996: 109–11) discusses *Poussière d'Ange* (1987) as a contemporary French *film noir*; Buss (1994) meanwhile identifies 101 French *noirs*, preponderantly from the post-*Nouvelle Vague* period, but like Spicer some of his inclusions are curious: alongside such obvious *noir* candidates as *Rififi*, *Bob le Flambeur* (both 1955), *Lift to the Scaffold* (1957) and the later *La Balance* and the flashy *Diva* (both 1981) are listed Godard's *Weekend* (1967) and Robert Bresson's *L'Argent* (1983). Another of Buss's selections, Robert Bresson's *Pickpocket* (1959), provided the model for Paul Schrader's neo-*noir* *American Gigolo* (there are also strong echoes of Bresson in *Taxi Driver*). Examples such as this and the adaptations of Patricia Highsmith's Ripley novels produced in the US (*The Talented Mr Ripley*, 2000; *Ripley's Game*, 2003), France (*Plein Soleil*, 1959) and West Germany (*The American Friend*, 1977) are strong testimony to *noir*'s international appeal as a mode for exploring themes of exploitation, violence and transgressive desire.

CASE STUDY: *OUT OF THE PAST* (JACQUES TOURNEUR, 1947)

Robert Ottoson (1981: 132) speaks for many in declaring *Out of the Past* (UK title: *Build My Gallows High*) 'quite simply the *ne plus ultra* of forties *film noir*'. The film's convoluted plot of criminal intrigue, murder, fatal attraction and betrayal; its dense visuals, periodic narrative confusion, flashbacks and voiceover narration; its iconographically apt private-eye protagonist Jeff Markham/Bailey (Robert Mitchum) – complete with belted trench coat, soft-brimmed hat and permanently lit cigarette (Grist, 1992: 206) – and quint-essential femme fatale Kathie Moffat (Jane Greer) – cool, sexually confident, manipulative, untrustworthy and murderous; its melancholy, fatalistic tone of doomed nostalgia and downbeat, ambiguous ending – all comprise, as Tom Flinn (1973: 38) puts it, 'a veritable motherlode of *noir* themes and stylisations'. *Out of the Past*'s institutional and production contexts are also archetypal *noir*. The film adapts a number of the economical but effective stylistic elements (particularly a structured alternation of high-key and low-key lighting to reinforce character and thematic relations) previously refined by director Jacques Tourneur in the well-regarded horror films he made for RKO's 'B' production unit headed by Val Lewton earlier in the 1940s (*Cat People*, 1942; *The Seventh Victim*, 1943). Tourneur also inherited cinemato-grapher Nicholas Musuraca from the Lewton features: a specialist in 'mood lighting' (Spicer, 2002: 17), Musuraca made a major contribution to the *noir* cycle, his other *noirs* including *The Spiral Staircase* (1945), *The Locket* (1946), *The Woman on Pier 13* (1950), *Clash by Night* (1952) and *The Blue Gardenia* (1953). The screenplay was adapted from his own novel by Daniel Mainwaring

From *Out of the Past/Build My Gallows High* (1947). Reproduced courtesy of RKO/The Kobal Collection.

(writing as Geoffrey Homes), later to write the *noir*-ish gangster films *The Big Steal* (1949) and *The Phenix City Story* (1955), with contributions from, among others, James M. Cain.[8] Of the film's principal cast members, Mitchum (*The Locket, Crossfire, Pursued*, 1947 – a Freudian *noir* Western – and *Macao*, 1952) is particularly strongly identified with 1940s *noir*. As Maltby ([1984] 1992: 52) sums up, 'whatever *film noir* is, *Out of the Past* is undoubtedly *film noir*'.

As a private-eye film, *Out of the Past* is firmly located in one of the narrative paradigms most closely identified with the *noir* world. However, *Out of the Past* goes some way to reconfigure the private-eye narrative away from its classically 'hard-boiled' versions (such as *The Big Sleep*) towards *noir*'s more typically disoriented, self-destructive vision of masculinity. For Krutnik (1991: 112), *Out of the Past* undertakes 'a remarkable problematising of the Spade-type private-eye hero' and the narrative never finally or fully resecures Jeff's masculine identity in the patriarchal order he destabilises through his illicit relationship with Kathie. Whereas Bogart's impersonation of Spade and Marlowe enacts alpha-male dominance, Mitchum's Jeff Markham is characterised by a wilful passivity: having tracked Kathie down to Acapulco in his assignment to retrieve Whit's purloined $40,000, Jeff surrenders both his professional responsibilities and his individual will in a mood that Grist (1992: 207) aptly characterises as 'ardent abandonment' (of scruples and of self), silencing Kathie's protestations of innocence with the memorable line 'Baby, I don't care'. After the couple flee to San Francisco, Jeff's voiceover of his debased condition obsessively insists on his careless abjection: 'I opened an office … Cheap little rathole which suited the work I did. Shabby jobs for whatever hire. It was the bottom of the barrel, and I scraped it. But I didn't care. I had her.'

Despite the emphatic last sentence, however, Kathie, is an elusive signifier who will not be 'had', or possessed (unlike Jeff, who will be 'had' in the other sense of the term – duped, conned); her narrative function, like so many *noir* women, is to illustrate the fugitive, fantasy nature of desire itself. Moreover, and characteristically for male *noir* protagonists, Jeff's own morality, though shaky, is more resilient than he professes: when he finally discovers that Kathie has actually stolen Whit's money, he is disenchanted and repelled. Jeff suffers the *noir* male's repeated double bind: affecting a cynical, world-weary familiarity with the ways of the world, he nonetheless remains prey to insistent romantic fantasy constructions whose inevitable disenchantment leaves him disempowered and directionless. The narrational and sexual dis-empowerment of the masculine ideal represented by the 'hard-boiled' private eye in *Out of the Past* confirms that the variously inept, inadequate and/or impotent 'private dicks' of 1970s *noir* are less examples of aggressive genre revisionism in the fashion of contemporaneous Westerns, musicals and war films than intensifications of *noir*'s existing tendencies to paranoia and male pathos. As Maltby ([1984] 1992: 67) observes, postwar *noir* is distinctive in its refusal of a place for 'the separate heroic figure, the embodiment of the American individualist heroic tradition', either reintegrating its 'maladjusted' protagonists into normal society (*The Big Clock*, 1948) or, as in *Out of the Past*, compelling a fatal expiation of past guilt.

In the later San Francisco scenes as Jeff undertakes his second assignment for Whit (he accepts the job as an act of restitution only to find that Whit intends to frame him for a murder), the fantasy aspect of the narrative is made clear as the film slips into the characteristic *noir* oneiricism discussed above. This sequence, involving a fairly impenetrable intrigue and intro-ducing important characters quite late in the film, unfolds in an elliptical, dislocated and fragmentary way, posing difficulties of basic legibility – of space, of motivation and of identity – that centre on the striking visual confusion of Kathie with Meta Carson (Rhonda Fleming), the film's secondary and super-numary femme fatale. The blurring of identities, sudden melodramatic reversals and spatial dislocation of this sequence can be read as textual stresses answering to Jeff's own intensifying inner conflicts and confusions at this point in the narrative.

Meta provides a 'negative' double of Kathie mirrored by her 'positive' female counterpart in the film, Jeff's Bridgeport girlfriend Ann (Virginia Huston), emphasising the film's tendency towards a symbolic schematism in its narrative arrangements: Ann is identified with the small-town mountain community of Bridgeport, initially at least a daylight/'high-key' world of tradi-tional relationships and solid, if mundane, decency (tracked down by Whit's underling Joe Stefanos, Jeff lectures him on the values of traditional American entrepreneurship: 'We call it making a living. You may have heard of it some-where') contrasted to the various low-key, urban or foreign milieus associated with Kathie and Whit and with dishonest or at least undeserved wealth.

Such schematism seems to reinforce simplistic oppositions of city and country, sex and marriage, the 'good' self (in Bridgeport, Jeff renames himself Jeff Bailey) and the 'bad'; however, it can also can be read as drawing attention to the fantasy, or mythic, nature of such dichotomies and the cultural logics that subtend them. The more effort the narrative puts into holding apart the valorised and the vitiated discursive and actantive realms, the more they insist on collapsing back into one another. The narrational stress of the San Francisco scenes confesses this ideological tension in one way; the gradual but growing penetration of Jeff Markham's low-key *noir* urban world into the high-key small-town one of 'Jeff Bailey' is another (as in the night-time dialogue between Jeff and Ann towards the end of the film). We should note, moreover, as Oliver and Trigo (2003: 224f.) suggest, that Ann is not quite the one-dimensional homebody that in many ways the film's narrative schema seeks to render her: her readiness not only to go against her family's wishes and ditch her long-time hometown suitor for Jeff but to abandon Bridgeport altogether and go off with Jeff indicate that the idealised small-town world is perhaps no more satisfactory for the 'good girl' than for the 'femme fatale'. Early in the film, Jeff confesses to Ann that he has been 'a lot of places': 'Which one did you like the best?' she asks him, to which Jeff replies, 'This one right here'. 'Bet you say that to all the places',

Ann responds. Ann's playful fusion of the places and the women in Jeff's life not only reveals her to be more knowing than her homespun image would imply, but points up the ways in which fantasy relations and oppositions structure Jeff's experience of the social and the sexual alike: the overdetermined opposition of the small-town ideal and the urban jungle mirrors that of Kathie and Ann as good and bad objects in Jeff's psychic economy.

This exchange makes the end of the film all the more poignant. With Jeff and Kathie dead, Ann faces an implicit choice between staying – which means, in effect, quashing the curiosity and desire for change that her attraction to Jeff bespoke – or leaving Bridgeport altogether, this time alone. Jeff's mute assistant confirms to her that Jeff was leaving town with Kathie – a 'good lie' that frees her from Jeff's memory and enables her to return to her long-time suitor Jim. Thus the film ends with Jeff's posthumously successful recontainment of energies of female autonomy: having volunteered to enter Jeff's *noir* world, Ann is restored to a stable location – the daylight 'good girl' – within the dichotomous masculine fantasy structures her self-awareness had briefly threatened to puncture. Indeed, in a sense Jeff goes knowingly to his death precisely to secure this outcome. It is interesting therefore to consider whether in a sense it is Ann, rather than Kathie, who is the film's femme fatale: her 'threat' consisting precisely in her *not* consenting (unlike Kathie or Meta) to be constructed purely on and in the terms of *noir* fantasy – until, that is, Jeff's final reassertion of patriarchal authority, far more successful in death than he had been in life (the last image of the film is Jeff Bailey's name atop his garage).

NOTES

1. See the contemporary reviews and essays collected in Silver and Ursini (1996).
2. So called because the magazines that specialised in hard-boiled material – notably *Black Mask* – were published on cheap wood-pulp paper.
3. Linda Williams (1988), however, cautions against too facile an identification of Mildred and the cleaners, stressing that their different class positions entail equally different forms of patriarchal subjection.
4. Note, however, that Borde and Chaumeton's (1955) list excludes *Scarlet Street* – though not, oddly, its companion film *The Woman in the Window – Force of Evil* and *Detour*.
5. The exchange is quoted and discussed in Maltby ([1984] 1992: 56–8).
6. Although Silver and Ursini (1996) cite a photograph of Robert Aldrich on the set of *Kiss Me Deadly* holding a copy of Borde and Chaumeton's ([1955], 1983) *Panorama du Film Noir Américain*.
7. Note, however, that Jameson cites *Chinatown*, which he classifies as a 'nostalgia film', as an example of pastiche.
8. For more details of the film's production history, see Grist (1992: 203) and Schwager (1991).

CHAPTER 10

The Action Blockbuster

Of all the genres discussed in this book, the action film/action blockbuster is at once the most contemporary, the most visibly relevant to present-day Hollywood film-making, and also the least discussed and least well-defined. Until the publication of a recent anthology (Tasker, 2004), relatively little has been written about action film as a genre: the notable exceptions, the studies by Tasker (1993) and Jeffords (1994), focus specifically on constructions of masculinity in the high-octane male action films of the 1980s and early 1990s. The contemporary blockbuster has become a scholarly focus even more recently, notably in Wyatt (1994), King (2000a), Hall (2002) and Stringer (2003). Whereas Tasker and Jeffords focus on the ultra-violent, usually R-rated vehicles for pumped-up stars such as Arnold Schwarzenegger, Sylvester Stallone, Jean-Claude van Damme and their like, the emphasis in the blockbuster studies is much more on institutional context and the aesthetics of spectacle in special effects-driven, large-scale SF and fantasy films from *Star Wars* to *The Lord of the Rings*.

It may seem therefore that there is a basic incoherence in the idea of the 'action blockbuster'. It is certainly the case that neither of the two terms involved is as straightforward as other genre concepts used in this book. One difficulty in defining the blockbuster is that while most critics identify excessive scale (including cost and length) as a generic marker, others include consumption – that is, runaway success at the box office – as itself a sufficient cause for blockbuster status. In some ways, a form like the action blockbuster pushes genre study to its limits, requiring it to integrate several diverse critical approaches (film-historical, economic/institutional and aesthetic/ ideological) in the very process of constituting, defining and historicising a generic field. This already daunting task is made yet more difficult by the rampant generic hybridity of contemporary Hollywood in general and the action blockbuster, as the paradigmatic contemporary Hollywood genre, in particular. *Starship Troopers* (1998), for example, combines the teen film, the war/combat film, elements of the Western and the SF monster movie, while satirising all three.

Nonetheless, in simple iconographic terms the action blockbuster does have some reliable constants, most of which relate to the spectacular action sequences that are an immutable feature of the genre. Sky-high orange fireballs; vehicles and bodies pitching, often in slow motion, through plate-glass windows; characters diving and rolling across wrecked interiors, either under the impact of rapidly fired bullets or to escape from them; automatic pistols and large-calibre portable weaponry like grenade launchers; death-defying stunts: these are all immediately recognisable attributes of the action blockbuster.

The structure of the action blockbuster punctuates intense linear momentum – plot events drive the picture forward, usually excluding the narrative space available for explorations of character psychology or relationships or reducing these elements to a series of terse exchanges – with spectacular passages of action, often prominently featuring special effects and/or stunt work that radically exceed the needs of the narrative situation that gives rise to them. Car chases – which in strict narrative terms often deliver very little – typify this structure.[1] Thus rather than the 'well-made' complex plot of the traditional thriller, the central narrative premise of an action film may come to seem little more than a thin spine from which dangle essentially disconnected large-scale action episodes. A lack of interest in genuine complexity may hardly be novel in Hollywood action and thriller cinema, but whereas, for example, Hitchcock used his famous 'MacGuffins' as a means to not only trademark 'Hitchcockian' set-piece sequences, but the exploration of emotional and psychological relationships of dependency and manipulation, the contemporary action blockbuster seems largely uninterested in any plot element except as a narrative ruse through which to deliver explosions, chases and gunfights, the bigger the better. The blockbuster typically opens with a large-scale action sequence of the type that might have climaxed a classic Hollywood film: thus whereas *Foreign Correspondent* (1940) concludes with a plane crash, *Face/Off* (1997) opens with a high-intensity chase sequence involving a jet, numerous police cars and a helicopter, at the end of which the jet ploughs through the usual plate-glass curtain wall into a hanger.

Identifying the generic syntax of the action blockbuster is more difficult. Geoff King (2000a) has argued that frontier motifs are a submerged presence in action films; 1990s action films often centred on confusions of identity and the self, which featured in *Face/Off*, *Total Recall* (1991), *Eraser* (1996) and *The Long Kiss Goodnight* (1997) among others. But the bottom line of most action blockbusters is the decisive (usually violent) action taken against overwhelming odds by a 'maverick' individual, most often unsupported by or even in conflict with establishment authority, to restore order threatened by a large-scale threat. The action hero, who may be paired with a more law-abiding or convention-respecting 'buddy' – the *Lethal Weapon* series (from 1988) is the obvious example – is thus a version of the classic 'outlaw hero' as discussed by Robert Ray (1985: 59–66). Opposition to authority, whether arising out of principle (*Con Air*, 1997), wrongful conviction (*Minority Report*, 2002), betrayal (*Rambo: First Blood Part II*, 1985; *Gladiator*, 2000) or simply personal style (*Independence Day*, 1996; *Armageddon*, 1998) ensures that the action hero is denied recourse to the (dramatically uninteresting) procedures of the justice system and must fall back on inner resources: whereas these are often – as with John Rambo and John McClane (in the *Die Hard* series, 1988, 1990, 1995) – simply a given, at other times the hero's discovery of these capacities for violent action constitutes his narrative 'arc': for example the initially desk-bound characters played by Nicolas Cage and John Cusack in *The Rock* and *Con Air*.

Some commentators have discerned a degree of estrangement in the hyperbolic visual style of contemporary action cinema and particularly in action sequences' distortion of normative temporality and spatiality – through the use of slow motion and multiple camera angles (effects that owe a great deal to the pioneering action sequences of Sam Peckinpah in *The Wild Bunch*) – and the fetishistic attention both to the kinds of hardware that conventionally signify wealth and (male) status (powerboats, sports cars, etc.) and to their literal dematerialisation (being spectacularly torched or blown apart). The knowing humour and wilful excessiveness, whether in deploying ultra-violence or in prodigality of consumption, that typify the work of such fashionable action directors as Paul Veerhoeven, Quentin Tarantino and John Woo, would tend to support such claims. However, it is equally clear that most action films seem less interested in activating their spectators in quasi-Brechtian fashion than in exploiting the unparalleled technical resources of contemporary Hollywood simply to overwhelm any capacity for disengagement by the violent sensory assault of kinetic visuals and multitracked sound effects and music.

The emergence of the contemporary action blockbuster as (in financial terms at least) Hollywood's dominant genre since the mid-1980s is accountable in terms of the New Hollywood's own transformation into a global centre of conglomerate media activity. In fact, one could argue that the millennial (1990s and 2000s) action film is generically characterised by its own repeated enactment at every level, from narrative to distribution and marketing, of the same imperatives of relentless market domination that typify modern corporate Hollywood. Contemporary action spectaculars ruthlessly colonise traditional genres such as the historical epic (*Braveheart*, 1995; *Gladiator*; *Troy*, 2004) and most often science fiction, and casually subordinate such classically crucial elements as narrative and character to literally show-stopping special-effects- and stunt-driven action sequences. These action sequences comprise the action film's principal selling-point and feature centrally in the saturation marketing campaigns that attend these films' release, and they typically employ a 'high-gloss' visual style, drawing heavily on advertising and music video, involving a markedly accelerated cutting rate (compared to Hollywood films of the 1970s and before: see Bordwell, 2002) that intensifies the already kinetic experience of the action-laden story. Traditionally secondary (or in any case back-room) areas of film production such as star 'branding', the dominance of the 'high concept' and the aggressive marketing of aspects of film-making technology (e.g. CGI) are given a new prominence. These combine with a heightened public awareness of production costs and box-office returns to create a genre whose film/spectator interface is no longer confined to the textual level but enters the public realm – carefully husbanded through the multiple arms of vertically integrated media conglomerates – as cross-media 'events'.

Dominating and integrating all of these is the central 'high concept', in defining which term reference is usually made to the producer partnership of Don Simpson (d. 1994) and Jerry Bruckheimer, whose series of enormously successful action vehicles from the mid-1980s onwards (*Beverly Hills Cop*, 1984; *Top Gun*, 1986; *The Rock*, 1996; *Armageddon*, 1998; etc.) consolidated the elements listed above in a glossy package topped by a high-profile male star (Tom Cruise, Eddie Murphy, Bruce Willis) in an easily summarised plot formula ('A streetwise black Detroit cop in Hollywood', 'a hotshot fighter ace learning lessons in love and in combat') (see Wyatt, 1994). (Robert Altman's Hollywood-on-Hollywood satire *The Player* (1988) guys the high concept with increasingly baroque and absurd pitches: '*Pretty Woman* meets *Out of Africa*'.)

Yet as ultra-modern – even postmodern – as in so many ways the action blockbuster obviously is, it also manifests abiding continuities with and through the history of Hollywood genre. In its combination of visual spectacle, sensational episodic storylines, performative and presentational excess, and starkly simplified, personalised narratives, the action blockbuster is umbilically linked to the foundational melodramatic tradition of Hollywood film. Although this chapter will focus on the institutional contexts, textual politics and issues of spectatorship informing critical reception of the action film and the blockbuster, in many ways the genre can best be understood as the emphatic restoration to industrial pre-eminence of the originary mode of the American cinema – it is in fact most profitable to regard it as 'action melodrama', a form that synthesises both the blood-and-thunder and the domestic/pathetic melodramatic traditions.

IN YOUR FACE: THE RISE OF A POST-CLASSICAL GENRE

Most accounts of the New Hollywood identify the period 1975–77 as a watershed in the transition from the New Wave-ish 'Hollywood Renaissance' period to the popcorn era of the 1980s and since (see, for instance, Schatz, 1993; King, 2002). But neither the action film nor the blockbuster materialised out of *Jaws*' deep blue sea in 1975 or *Star Wars*' intergalactic space in 1977. In fact, the term 'action blockbuster' pulls together a well-established genre – the action-adventure film – with deep roots in classic Hollywood back to the silent era, with a mode of production – the blockbuster – most strongly associated with the changing economics of the post-classical period. A third term that often triangulates this pairing, 'spectacle', relates simultaneously to the action blockbuster's properties of visual display, how these affect audiences' consumption of the moving image (a subject of considerable controversy, particularly in relation to narrative and characterisation), and finally the cultural construction of the blockbuster film as a 'spectacular', or in industry parlance an 'event', through marketing and media. This section will trace how these separate strands have come together into the contemporary action blockbuster.

Action and action-adventure

In one sense, of course, every motion picture is an 'action' film. More to the point, a great many classic Hollywood genres – notably the war film, the gangster film and the Western – include and are in some measure defined by scenes of violent action. Thus the contemporary usage of the term 'action film' to describe films such as *Saving Private Ryan* (1997), *Face/Off* and *Starship Troopers*, all of which could be and are equally well located within these more traditional generic traditions, confirms the category is an expansive one. This expansiveness in turn might reflect the increasingly mutable nature of genre identities in contemporary Hollywood.

A loosely defined category of 'action-adventure' has existed in Hollywood since the silent era. Neale (2000: 55) notes that the term was applied by contemporary reviewers to a 1927 Douglas Fairbanks vehicle, *The Gaucho*, and Fairbanks's star persona – courageous, earnest, light-hearted and supremely athletic – established a romantic heroic style taken up by later action stars such as Errol Flynn and Burt Lancaster. During the classical period, the action-adventure genre incorporated swashbucklers, sea-going and lubberly (Fairbanks' *The Black Pirate*, 1927; *The Adventures of Robin Hood*, 1935; *Horatio Hornblower, R.N.*, 1951), jungle-quest and safari adventures (*King Solomon's Mines*, 1951; *Hatari!*, 1962), Foreign Legion yarns and other examples of what John Eisele (2002) has recently called 'the Hollywood Eastern' (*The Lost Patrol*, 1934; *Beau Geste*, 1939), and Hitchcockian thrillers of espionage and international intrigue (*Foreign Correspondent*, 1940; *North by Northwest*, 1959). The popularity of long-running characters like Edgar Rice Burroughs's jungle aristocrat Tarzan (impersonated by several actors in at least 40 features and serials from 1918 to the late 1960s) indicates the genre's strong appeal to a juvenile male audience. As such examples indicate, action-adventure often involved a significant displacement from contemporary American life, into exotic, far-flung locales like colonial Africa or the 'mysterious Orient' and/or the historical past (the picturesque Revolutionary and Napoleonic eras were especially favoured), with a strong scenic emphasis. Taves (1993) points out that this touristic quality necessarily implicates the genre in recognisably imperialist tropes, albeit in some ways qualified by the emphasis on freedom-fighting and the restitution of injustices (for example in the numerous versions of the Zorro story). Action-adventure films tended to flaunt high production values, were likely candidates in due course for colour and widescreen treatment, and usually featured attractive, robust stars in relatively light-hearted romantic and/or quest narratives.[2] *Star Wars*' debt to classic swashbucklers (as when Luke vaults across the fathomless core unit in the Death Star clasping Princess Leia in his arms) is obvious. Emphatically a family genre, the action-adventure film has really never gone out of fashion, although alongside other traditional large-scale genres it suffered from Hollywood's temporary shift of attention in the early 1970s towards smaller-scale, more character-centred contemporary dramas. Between 1970 and 1975 only *The Three Musketeers* (1973) could be clearly identified as an action-adventure in the traditional sense. However, the same season, 1975–76 – perhaps significantly the year after the end of the Vietnam War – that saw the emergence of the new style of action blockbuster with *Jaws* also saw something of a revival in the traditional exotic/historical adventure film with such large-scale productions as *The Man Who Would Be King* and *The Wind and the Lion* (both 1975).

Blockbusters

The blockbuster – massively spectacular productions conceived and marketed on the grandest possible scale – has featured importantly in American, and world, film history for even longer than the action-adventure film. D. W. Griffith's epochal Civil War melodrama *Birth of a Nation* (1915), whose release according to standard histories of film marks both the culminating moment of cinema's formative decades and the crystallisation of what would become the classical Hollywood style, was not only the longest, largest and most expensive American film to date; it was also the dearest to see (with

ticket prices for its premiere engagement fixed at the unheard-of sum of $1)
and the most profitable, with domestic box-office revenues estimated at $3
million. Subsequently, physical scale, stars, cost and length would all mark
out the blockbuster. Griffith himself was responding to the enormous success
on the US market of recent antiquarian Italian epics such as *Cabiria* (1913)
and *Quo Vadis?* (1914) and effectively 'Americanising' the mode after his own
previous film in the Italian style, *Judith of Bethulia* (1914) (see Bowser, 1990).
With his next production, *Intolerance* (1917), Griffith aimed even higher,
recreating Biblical Babylon on a scale of stupefying lavishness; however,
Intolerance's ambitious attempt to explore an abstract concept in a set of
interlinked scenarios spanning centuries proved far less popular with audiences
than *Birth of a Nation*'s simple (and reactionary) family saga. A nascent
Hollywood derived twin lessons from Griffith's experiences: that the blockbuster's massive earnings potential was matched by colossal risks; and that to
minimise those risks as far as possible simplicity of conception, familiarity of
subject matter and emphasising action over reflection were a more promising
recipe than philosophical speculation to appeal to a diverse mass public.
Thus the failure of *Intolerance* confirmed that the preferred mode of subsequent blockbusters would be, and continues to be, melodramatic.

Prior to the Second World War, in fact, ultra-high-budget spectacle films
– known as 'superspecials' – featured only intermittently on the major studios'
production schedules, which were mainly geared to offset risk through mass-
producing a diverse slate of releases to all market sectors in a steady stream
year-round, rather than emphasising one production at the expense of all the
others; the best-known prewar 'superspecial', the hugely successful *Gone
With the Wind* (1939), was produced independently by David O. Selznick,
and was one of only three pictures released by Selznick International Pictures
that year.[3]

As Neale (2003: 48–50) outlines, it was the film industry's changing
postwar fortunes that propelled large-scale productions back to the fore, as
the majors radically reshaped their operations in the early 1950s in the face
of shrinking audiences and the loss of their exhibition arms. In an era when
occasional, rather than routine, moving-going was becoming the norm, high-
profile one-of-a-kind 'specials' seemed a good way to draw this increasingly
selective public into theatres. Average budgets increased markedly during the
1950s as blockbusters took on increasing importance, both in defining a
studio's public profile and in its annual accounts. This period accordingly
saw the return of the proverbial 'cast of thousands' in remakes of silent-era
Biblical and Roman epics such as *The Ten Commandments* (1956), *Quo Vadis?*
(1951) and *Ben-Hur* (1959) alongside newly minted peplum behemoths like
The Robe (1953) and *Cleopatra* (1963) and globe-trotting costume capers like
Around the World in Eighty Days (1959), their spectacular aspects further

enhanced by colour and the new widescreen formats (see below). True to Hollywood traditions, postwar blockbusters relied heavily not merely on scale – crowds of milling extras and enormous sets – but on their deployment in dynamic action sequences involving daring stunt work: among the most celebrated were the chariot race at the Circus Maximus in *Ben-Hur* and the enormous battle scenes in *Spartacus* (1960). Blockbusters showcased the leading male action stars of the time, such as Victor Mature (*Samson and Delilah*, 1949; *Demetrius and the Gladiators*, 1954), Charlton Heston (*The Ten Commandments, Ben-Hur, El Cid*, 1961) and Kirk Douglas (*The Vikings*, 1959; *Spartacus*). Visual and photographic effects also sometimes played a part, notably in the parting of the Red Sea in *The Ten Commandments*. Yet in general these films were stylistically quite unlike today's breathlessly kinetic action spectacles. On the contrary, their grandiose physical scale tended to lend narrative and staging a ponderous quality while dialogue in search of classical *gravitas* too often came out sounding leaden and stilted – qualities that in its own time also clearly separated the epic blockbuster from the faster-moving, quicker-witted action-adventure film. Some of these difficulties were related to the problem of satisfactorily integrating narrative and spectacle, discussed below.

An important bridge to the contemporary action blockbuster was the disaster cycle of the early 1970s, particularly Irwin Allen's big-budget productions *The Poseidon Adventure* (1971), *Earthquake* (1974) and *The Towering Inferno* (1975, jointly financed by Warner Bros. and Universal, then a highly unusual move[4] that would become more common in the 1990s era of the $100+ million picture, for example *Titanic*, 1997). Clearly, aspects of these films – for instance, the emphasis on costly visual effects, large-scale action sequences, simple narrative premises and novel technologies like Sensurround (used for *Earthquake* and *Rollercoaster*, 1976) – foreshadow aspects of the contemporary blockbuster. However, their general stylistic conservatism, including a reliance on all-star casts studded with Old Hollywood faces (Ava Gardner, Shelley Winters, Fred Astaire, William Holden) rooted them recognisably in the old-style blockbuster culture of the 1950s and early 1960s.

Thus the successful alloying of the action-adventure film and the blockbuster was by no means predictable. And in fact, neither *Jaws* nor *Star Wars*, the two enormously successful films usually credited with transforming New Hollywood aesthetics and economics, in themselves typified the action blockbuster that would achieve such unprecedented industrial centrality in Hollywood in the 1980s and since. Rather, the most important elements from each – elements themselves artfully synthesised and refined from current trends – would subsequently be distilled into the new action blockbuster.

Jaws, as has often been noted, bears affinities to the disaster film as well as other mid-1970s genres such as the conspiracy film (in its portrayal of the attempts of Amity's petty bourgeois elite to suppress news of the rogue shark in their own economic interests), while also foreshadowing the later stalk-and-slash horror pictures. More character-centred than most of its successors, *Jaws* built up a relentless momentum in its second half that would be much imitated. *Jaws'* prescience consisted above all in its iconically effective marketing campaign masterminded by MCA president Lew Wasserman – the famous poster image of the gigantic phallic shark nosing its way towards the naked female swimmer; pioneering high-impact TV spot ads; the avalanche of pre-publicity centring on the film's troubled production and the travails of its principal special effect, the mechanical shark 'Bruce'; its 'wide' opening (i.e. simultaneously in several hundred theatres nationwide rather than in selected prestige theatres on the East and West coasts) and summer release; its runaway success – quickly becoming the highest-grossing film of all time to date – transforming a traditionally minor season into the fulcrum of Hollywood's fiscal year (see Gomery, 2003: 72–6).

Jaws at least was recognisably a blockbuster production, based on a best-selling novel, its eventual negative cost substantially exceeding its already considerable budget. *Star Wars*, by contrast, although it too overran its original budget (largely because of R&D costs associated with its innovative special effects techniques), was not an especially expensive film; it was also a considerably darker horse and initially regarded with confusion and little optimism by its distributor Twentieth Century-Fox. Compared to *Jaws*, *Star Wars* represents a much more decisive stylistic break with mainstream 1970s Hollywood. Not only did it revive a genre – the action space fantasy – barely seen since the Flash Gordon and Buck Rogers serials of the 1930s; as Peter Krämer (2004) notes, George Lucas targeted his film firmly at a juvenile (adolescent and younger) audience, at this stage an almost invisible market sector barely catered to by Disney's low-budget live-action family comedies and ignored by the studios, who since the success of *The Graduate*, *Bonnie and Clyde* (both 1967) and *Easy Rider* (1969) had assiduously been courting the college-age audience. Both the film's box-office returns and even more the vast new profit centres carved out by the associated merchandising bonanza confirmed the logic of Lucas's strategy. Formally, *Star Wars* was also distinctive and hugely influential, departing – much more decisively than *Jaws* – from the more relaxed approach to plotting and characterisation that had typified the 'Hollywood Renaissance'. *Star Wars* is ruthlessly focused on delivering a specific and new kind of moving-going experience that combines the visual splendours of the old-style blockbuster (and its imperial themes) with the fleet-footed rough-and-tumble of the action-adventure film. Yet a historical perspective on genre film reveals that the novelty of all this can easily be overstated. Emphatically simplistic in its approach to character and morality (which is by no means to say wholly uninterested in them, especially the latter), episodic, thrilling and spectacular, *Star Wars* in fact drilled down past the superficial realism of classic Hollywood's prevailing regimes of verisimilitude to retrieve something like a distilled essence of Hollywood's foundational melodramatic mode.

TRADITIONS OF SPECTACLE

Where *Star Wars* could indeed be credited with an innovative generic synthesis was in its inauguration of a new regime of visual pleasure in which action *is* spectacle and vice versa. The novelty of this action-spectacle alliance arises from the ways it conjoins narrative and spectacle. Spectacular elements have often been understood as tending to narrative redundancy or even interfering with narrative integration, interrupting the flow of the story by encouraging spectators to contemplate the technical achievement of a spectacular sequence – scenery, production design, special effects and the like – at the expense of empathetic involvement in the characters and the unfolding plot. The clumsiness of 1950s epics has been cited as an example of the way that the need to give maximum exposure to spectacular production values is at odds with the creation of a compelling narrative, as longer shot lengths resulted both from the visual density of the panoramic images and (at least in the early years of widescreen processes) uncertainty over the correct handling of the horizontally extended frame. Moreover, whereas the best-known accounts of classical Hollywood cinema stress the centrality of narrative, spectacle as a stylistic dominant is associated with the pre-classical cinema.

The post-classical action/spectacle cinema has been interpreted in some quarters as a return of sorts to the 'cinema of attractions', in Tom Gunning's influential conception the organising principles of what used to be called 'primitive' (now more usually 'early') cinema. In a series of essays, Gunning (1990, 1995) identifies in early (pre-1915) silent cinema an organisational principle radically different from the linear, character-centred narratives that came to predominate with the advent of the feature film. Early cinema relied rather, Gunning argues, on an 'aesthetic of astonishment'. Films of this period did not solicit audiences' empathetic identification with psychologically motivated and developed characters, nor their immersion in a complex plot animated by the interactions of these characters as well as enigmas and dramatic plot reversals. Instead, early films engaged audiences by inviting them to marvel at visual spectacle. Initially, the miracle of filmic movement itself drew large audiences: many early films consist 'merely' of documentary scenes of modern (especially urban) life that allowed spectators to review their own environments in unprecedented ways. The ways cinema addressed its spectators at this stage could be compared to carnival 'attractions' or vaudeville 'turns', and prior to the development of purpose-built cinemas in fixed locations films were often viewed as touring exhibitions in portable auditoriums, sometimes even actually as part of travelling fairs; short films themselves might comprise merely one element, or 'turn', in a variety bill alternating with stage acts and musical numbers. Although the silent cinema moved towards more extended and complex narratives to retain its audience once the new medium's novelty faded, the principle of the marvellous remained central, and early narratives remained highly reliant on spectacle, whether understood as scenic effects, exciting action sequences or increasingly elaborate special effects sequences like the eruption of Mount Etna at the opening of *Cabiria*.

The hugely influential account by Bordwell, Staiger and Thompson (1985) asserts that the spectacular effects of early cinema, with their tendency to overwhelm or stall the unfolding story, and the ensuing distanciation of the audience, were suppressed in the classical style in favour of linear narratives centred on psychologically motivated, goal-oriented characters. As we have seen, however, the dominance of narrative was bound up with film industry structures and economics, and the postwar need to recapture shrinking audiences and – not least – to challenge the impact of television led to a heavy investment in technologies that could promise the cinema spectator a sensory experience distinct from, and in aesthetic terms at least enormously superior to, monochrome low-definition early TV. The large-scale conversion to colour, the introduction of widescreen processes and stereophonic sound, as well as shorter-lived fads like stereoscopic 3-D, all served to emphasise the visual spectacle of cinema-going. The ultra-widescreen process Cinerama, whose non-narrative spectacle film *This Is Cinerama!* ran for two years in a specially converted theatre in Times Square, in particular seemed in many ways a throwback to early cinema's 'aesthetic of astonishment' (see Belton, 1992).

In fact, narrative and spectacle have always existed in a two-way relationship. As much as classical Hollywood narratives focus on compelling central characters through whom narrative incident is focalised, ample space still exists for the narrative to pause and take in, for instance, large-scale tableaux that aim to impress the spectator by advertising the opulence and scale of the production. A good example is the burning of Atlanta sequence in *Gone With the Wind*, which on the one hand excites because of the perilous situation of the central characters, but on the other amazes the spectator with the sheer scale of the destruction in rich (and in 1940 still novel) Technicolor. The elaborate preparation for the sequence was publicised by the film's producer David Selznick and heavily covered in the press, with the result that the burning of Atlanta became one of the film's principal 'attractions' (featuring prominently in the poster art), anticipating today's media attention to innovative special effects techniques like CGI (*Terminator 2: Judgment Day*,

1991; *Jurassic Park*, 1993) or *The Matrix*'s (1999) 'bullet time'. Conversely, even very early cinema was not devoid of narrative interest; it simply presented very basic (by comparison with classical narratives) narrative material in uncomplicated ways. Cinerama certainly departed radically from classical practices, but the 1950s historical epics – although we have already noted their difficulties in successfully integrating narrative and spectacle – deployed spectacle in more conventional ways. The question of spectacle is closely related to that of visual pleasure and stylistic 'excess' generally, and as we have seen such 'excessive' elements form an important part of the appeal of genres such as the musical – whose alternation of 'straight' dramatic passages with spectacular 'numbers' offers one paradigm for the blockbuster's alternation of scenes of familial or romantic intimacy with large-scale action sequences – and of course melodrama, the action film's dominant mode.

Perhaps all the same *Star Wars* (1977) does mark an evolutionary turning-point for the Hollywood film, away from the more reflective mood of the earlier 1970s (which in any event by the end of the decade was giving way to large-scale, ultra-high-budget 'auteur blockbusters' like *New York, New York* (1977), *Apocalypse Now* (1979), *1941* (1979), and *Heaven's Gate* (1980), all with a notably spectacular dimension) towards action-driven 'popcorn movies'. However, the extent to which this shift involved a transformation of classical narrative style, even a reversion to a kind of 'cinema of attractions', is much more contentious. A favourite reference point in this debate is *Star Wars*' famous opening shot – the vast, seemingly endless bulk of the massive Imperial cruiser grinding overhead into the starfield, its oppressive weight bearing on the audience, diminishing us and crushing us back into our seats. In narrative terms, this shot quite effectively emblematises the brutal, authoritarian tyranny of the Galactic Empire. Yet audiences in the main appear not to have responded to the cruiser's oppressive occupation of the frame with fear or horror; rather, the sheer scale of the image appears to have elicited a widespread sense of exhilarated awe – the first New Hollywood example of the 'wow factor' that would become such an important and frequently mobilised aspect of the development of the blockbuster (more recently a central element of such mega-hits as *Titanic* (1997) and *The Lord of the Rings* (2001–3)).

This 'wow' response – often seen as a 'dumbed-down' version of the diminution and liminality of the self expressed in Romantic theories of the Sublime – has led to charges that the blockbuster encourages the spectator to relinquish the adult capacity for critical discrimination in favour of an undiscriminating rapture. The director most strongly associated with this rapturous regression is Steven Spielberg, some of whose films – notably *Close Encounters of the Third Kind* (1977) – valorise a pre-adolescent fixation on 'wonderment' at the expense of such inessential and unwelcome complications of adult life as parenthood, sexual love, professional work, etc. A much-discussed sequence early in *Jurassic Park* (1993) when the dinosaurs are for the first time revealed in all their CGI wonder to both characters and audience seems to offer the viewer a virtual primer on the 'correct' way to look at such marvels. The dinosaurs' initial appearance is bracketed by a montage of close-ups of the various characters gawping in astonishment, but quite clearly not all looks are equally validated by the film: the unaffected reactions of Alan Grant and Ellie Sattler, the central couple, in which initial shock is transformed into amazed delight, is contrasted to the frankly avaricious gaze of the shady lawyer Gennaro ('we are going to make so much money!'). The cynical yet likeable theoretical mathematician Ian Malcolm is a more complex proposition, yet the transformation of his initial hostility ('the crazy fools ... they actually did it!') into pleasure, as a reluctant grin creeps across his face, can be seen as a redemptive triumph of innocent awe over world-weary over-sophistication: unlike the greedy lawyer, who will in short order become the dysfunctional theme park's first fatality, Malcolm will survive the forthcoming ordeal. Finally there is John Hammond, the genially entrepreneurial sire of the whole venture, whose ringing delivery of the line 'Welcome ... to *Jurassic Park!*' – addressed ostensibly to the other characters, but delivered frontally, direct to camera and thus effectively to the audience – segues into the film's first 'money shot', a large-scale extreme long-shot scenic tableau of herds of dinosaurs teeming across the island, held for several seconds to allow the spectator's eyes to scan the image (this shot drew spontaneous applause from audiences at the film's premiere engagements).

A scene such as this would seem to support the charge that the contemporary blockbuster privileges spectacle over narrative. Quite clearly, the self-conscious 'presentational' mode ('Welcome to Jurassic Park!'), the length of the sequence in general and the prolongation of the climactic special-effects shot in particular, and the redundant emphasis on the gaping amazement of all the characters, one by one, is excessive to simple narrative purpose; indeed, it effectively suspends narrative progress, albeit only briefly, in order to emphasise the spectacular visual effects (in the novel, the visitors' realisation of the nature of Hammond's project is triggered in a much more understated way). Clearly, too, the sequence is constructed this way as so to speak a textual acknowledgement that a large part of *Jurassic Park*'s 'draw' is precisely the ground-breaking combination of animatronics and then-novel CGI technology to create convincingly photorealistic (or, in Pierson's (2002) more precise usage, photosimulative) dinosaurs. Permitting or actually encouraging spectatorial scrutiny of these visual effects – for instance, by setting them 'on display' in a prolonged unbroken shot, as here – asserts the film-makers' confidence in the illusionistic viability of their creations (thus marking a significant development in CGI's mimetic utility). Something much more complex than the usual 'suspension of disbelief' is going on here: rather, a consciously *disbelieving* spectator is invited to assess, dispassionately, the technical achievement and measure it against both their expectations and against criteria of 'lifelikeness'. *Jurassic Park* asks us, in short, if we can see the join and if we cannot asks us to celebrate the artistry involved. Having Hammond 'present' Jurassic Park/*Jurassic Park* does not elide the difference between the diegetic and the computerised and pro-filmic recreation of dinosaurs (through recombinant DNA and the combined efforts of Industrial Light and Magic and Stan Winston, respectively), it advertises it.

However, it does not follow from the presence of such sequences centred on spectacular display – and other examples are not hard to find – that narrative has been simply displaced by spectacle in contemporary block-busters. On the contrary, as Geoff King (2000a, 2000b) has argued, narrative remains not merely a 'carrier' for spectacle but integral to its signification. *Jurassic Park* has been frequently cited as a film with only a nugatory interest in narrative and characterisation; and certainly, few audience members were drawn to theatres by the compelling dramatic interest of Alan Grant's conversion to liking kids. Yet following the scene discussed above, the remaining major effects scenes are all fully integrated into a thrilling and suspenseful narrative. Even if the human characters are stereotypical and one-dimensional and it is the CGI dinosaurs we 'really' want to see, the dinosaurs themselves – especially, of course, the villainous velociraptors – are narrativised and rendered dynamic by their violent interaction with the humans. Indeed, it might be argued that the inhumanity of the film's antagonists partly compensates for, even if it doesn't excuse, the thinness of the characterisations – given a straight choice between humans and reptiles we have no difficulty deciding who to root for (with the exception of the sleazy computer hacker Nedry). In a sense, this starkest possible – species-based – oppositional structure might be seen as a kind of *reductio ad absurdum* of melodrama's habitually polar narrative and moral schemas. There is in fact no such thing as 'pure' spectacle outside of the world of IMAX films at museums and amusement parks (and possibly not even there: see King, 2000b). Claims that contemporary action blockbusters have 'dispensed with' narrative usually reveal themselves as judgements on the *kinds* and *quality* of narrative sophistication and satisfaction offered by such films – that is, on their perceived inadequacy.

ACTION MELODRAMA

In the wake of *Jaws* and *Star Wars*, the 1980s action film diverged into two distinct strains, each clearly stamped in the melodramatic mode. The first looked to the blood-and-thunder tradition of the 'ten-twenty-thirty' cent theatre, the nickelodeon and the silent serials: *Star Wars* and the Lucas/ Spielberg collaboration *Raiders of the Lost Ark* (1981) established an alliance between action-adventure and the fantastic that persisted into the 1990s and beyond (*Stargate*, 1994; *The Mummy*, 1999). *Raiders* and its sequels (1984, 1989) self-consciously revived perhaps the action-adventure film's most paradigmatic form, the exotic quest narrative, and this traditionalist genre model was adopted by various imitators including *Romancing the Stone* (1984), *Big Trouble in Little China* (1986) and *Ishtar* (1987). The reappearance of the arch-imperialist Victorian adventurer Allan Quatermain in two lower-budget adventure films (1985, 1987) confirmed that, as Robert Stam and Ella Shohat (1994) among others have noted, *Raiders* also reaffirmed the genre's Orientalist perspective (in a particularly unreconstructed fashion in the first sequel, *Indiana Jones and the Temple of Doom*).

Meanwhile, a second strain translated melodramatic traditions of overwrought emotion and pathos into a novel, parodically masculine action vernacular through a distinct sub-genre of 'hard' action films that emerged into prominence during the 1980s with the success of *The Terminator* (1984) and *Die Hard* (1988). Taking their cue from 1970s urban vigilante and 'rogue cop' films like *The French Connection* and *Dirty Harry* (1971), *Death Wish* (1974), *The Exterminator* (1980) and their sequels, these films translated the lone male adventurer of the action-adventure film into contemporary urban and warzone settings, courting an R rating with extreme and graphic violence. Whereas the action-fantasy cycle solicited a pre-Oedipal wonder, the 'hard' action films expanded *Jaws*' emphasis on a reasserted masculinity and male bonding (in the film's staging of the confrontation with the shark as a rite of passage for the three principal male characters, and its explicit marginalisation of the domestic – coded 'female' – sphere). *Jaws*' climactic personal confrontation between Brody and the shark also established a trend that would be followed more closely by the male action films than by the fantasy-adventures that emerged in the wake of *Star Wars*, which often – as in *Raiders* or *Jurassic Park* – rendered the protagonists virtual bystanders to a climactic visual effects sequence. The protagonists of the 'hard' action films were most often police officers (*Cobra*, 1986; *Die Hard*; *Red Heat*, 1988; *Extreme Prejudice*, 1987; *Tango and Cash*, 1989; *Lethal Weapon*), soldiers (*Rambo: First Blood Part II*, *Missing in Action*, 1984) or paramilitaries (*Commando*, 1984; *Raw Deal*, 1985; *Predator*, 1988), but they owed little to the police procedural or combat genres. Rather, the new male action heroes of the 1980s seemed to many commentators to embody in barely coded form some of the prevailing political orthodoxies of the Reagan era, such as rampant individualism, hostility to 'Big Government' and the valorisation of 'traditional values' (i.e. the restoration of white patriarchal power after the challenges of the 1960s) (see Ryan and Kellner, 1988: 217–43; Britton, 1986; Traube, 1992: 28–66). The 1980s action hero mostly survived in beleaguered isolation – perhaps aided by a sidekick, often a woman or a person of colour – intensified both by the seemingly impossible odds he faced and the endemic flaws in American social and political structures that critically impeded his heroic efforts. In an era when it became the established political wisdom that electoral success was best achieved by running as an 'outsider', it is unsurprising that Federal government agencies are often excoriated as ineffective or outright corrupt. Rambo's betrayal and abandonment by the craven CIA man Crocker in *Rambo: First Blood Part II* (transparently intended as a re-enactment of the film's fantasy 'stab-in-the-back' account of the Vietnam War) is a paradigmatic example. Smugness and incompetence rather than treachery characterise the LAPD and the FBI in *Die Hard*, while political infighting and sclerotic bureaucracy imperil heroic US special forces in *Clear and Present Danger* (1994).

External enemies, however, remained the male action hero's principal antagonists. Reaganite action films like *Rambo: First Blood Part II* and *Rambo III* (1989) as well as the invasion fantasies *Red Dawn* (1984) and *Invasion USA* (1985) vigorously exploited the renewed Cold War tensions and reinvented the diabolical yet fatally unimaginative (compared with the improvisatory genius of his US adversary) Soviet enemy. With the transformation of the Soviet Union during the Gorbachev era and the rapid final collapse of Communism from 1989 to 1991, new villains emerged in the form of 'international terrorists', usually associated with the newly designated 'rogue states' that challenged American hegemony in the Middle East: Libyan terrorists feature in *Back to the Future* (1985) and the *Top Gun* derivative *Iron Eagle* (1986); in *Top Gun* (1986) itself the nationality of the enemy fighters is unstated but they are clearly identified as Arabs. Generic Arab terrorists, first featured in *Black Sunday* (1977), were the antagonists in *True Lies* (1994) and *The Siege* (1998), but *Patriot Games* (1992) and *Blown Away* (1994) feature Irish Republican extremists (carefully disassociated from the IRA in order not to offend sentimental Irish-American identification with the Nationalist cause). The collapse of the Soviet Union allowed for the invention of revanchist Stalinist diehards seeking to restore Communism in *The Package* (1989), *Air Force One* (1997) and *The Sum of All Fears* (2002). A Bosnian extremist maddened by the timorousness of US policy during the Yugoslav war attempts to set off a portable nuclear device in New York in *The Peacemaker* (1997). Globetrotting hired assassins, their paymasters obscure, turned up in *The Jackal* (1997) and *Face/Off*. Extreme rightist groups also occasionally featured, either as home-grown fascists (*Die Harder* or henchmen of the apartheid regime in South Africa (*Lethal Weapon II*). Karl Gruber, the Armani-clad master criminal of *Die Hard*, masquerades as a terrorist and demands the release of obscure political criminals whose names he has read in *Time* magazine as a cover for his straightforward heist operation.

The 1980s 'hard' action picture was dominated by such immobile, muscular action stars as Sylvester Stallone and Arnold Schwarzenegger, and the rather less prestigious Jean-Claude van Damme, Chuck Norris, Stephen Seagal and Dolph Lundgren, of whom a number began their careers as martial arts practitioners (or of course bodybuilders). That three of these stars (Schwarzenegger, van Damme and Lundgren) were European-born and delivered their lines in heavily accented English, tended to support the argument that nuances of characterisation and motivation were being largely sidelined in favour of muscular action in which the male bodies on display seemed as machine-tooled and gleamingly technological as the weaponry and other hardware they deployed. Susan Jeffords (1994) argues that the 1980s saw the rise of a 'hard body' aesthetic as part of a conscious effort to rectify the perceived (literal, figurative and political) 'soft bodies' of the Carter years, a period when (according to New Right mythology) an emasculated America faced collapsing morale at home and eroding prestige abroad. Her argument is apparently strikingly borne out by a novelty in 1980s 'hard' action films, the male hero's repeated subjection to extraordinarily graphic physical privations and torture. Rambo is crucified by sadistic Russians and Vietnamese; John McClane in *Die Hard* is forced to run barefoot across an office floor strewn with broken glass (a subsequent scene shows him extracting shards of glass from the soles of his feet); Murphy and Riggs in *Lethal Weapon II* are subjected to prolonged electric-shock torture; even Rocky Balboa suffers ritual poundings at the hands of mouthy ghetto trash (*Rocky III*, 1982) and Soviet supermen (*Rocky IV*, 1985). The punishment meted out to these male bodies masochistically powerfully mobilises melodramatic tropes of pathos and victimhood to render an inchoate yet pervasive sense of injury on the part of patriarchal white males. Their protagonists' ability to take enormous punishment and come out not just standing but fighting asserts the reaction against the passivity and 'weakness' of the 1960s and 1970s.

BRINGING IT ALL BACK HOME

Jeffords sees the representation of the masculine body in popular culture as a pivotal articulation of national self-identity and goes on to argue that following the reactively violent but successful reassertion of male power in the early 1980s, the later 1980s and 1990s saw a further modification of the image of the male action hero, undertaken from a resecured patriarchal hegemony. During this period, 'hard bodies' like Sylvester Stallone saw their careers decline dramatically from their mid-1980s peak, faced with the rise of less one-dimensional male stars like Harrison Ford, Bruce Willis, Michael Douglas, Tom Cruise, Mel Gibson and Nicolas Cage (more recent additions to this list might include John Cusack, the rejuvenated John Travolta, and the boyish Leonardo DiCaprio). The more flexible personae of the new stars allowed them to dramatise the successful negotiation of male crisis rather than simple displays of military prowess. Marriage, the family and/or parenthood emerged as central preoccupations of the action theme during this period, in films as varied as *Die Hard*, *Terminator 2: Judgment Day*, *True Lies* and *Face/Off* (1997). The action stars of the 1990s were also likely to alternate out-and-out action vehicles with domestically-centred melodramas like *Fatal Attraction* (1987), *Regarding Henry* (1991) and *Eyes Wide Shut* (1999) that permitted a more extensive elaboration of their stressed and embattled masculinities. In a large number of films, 'female' melodramatic tropes of helplessness, sacrifice and emotional crisis transferred themselves wholesale onto their male protagonists. However, whereas in the domestic and family melodramas of the 1950s the stylistic excess through which such pathologies found symptomatic expression had of generic necessity been confined to *mise-en-scène* and performance, in the new action melodrama the massive overkill of the action sequences themselves – as so often noted, often barely advancing the narrative but simply providing opportunities for the repeated statement, on an ever-larger scale, of the same antagonistic situation – expresses the desire for a transformation and resolution of the intractable conflicts generated in the personal and familial contexts. (This complex, its melodramatic roots and its acting-out through the action genre, are all subjected to excoriating satirical treatment in *Fight Club*, 1999.)

The changes in the action film during the 1990s may also relate to its increasing industrial centrality. With the exception of Stallone, none of the 'hard body' 1980s male action stars – not even Schwarzenegger until the very end of the decade – commanded the blockbuster budgets and associated marketing and release strategies associated with the decade's SF-fantasy adventures. They did, however, perform particularly strongly both in home video and foreign markets. By the late 1980s, these markets were becoming increasingly important to Hollywood's profitability and action stars accordingly became increasingly central to studio production strategies. At the same time, however, the enlarged scale of productions featuring these action stars entailed some softening of the often brutal tenor of their earlier vehicles, in pursuit of the wider audience enabled by a PG-13 rating. As agents of this process, action vehicles increasingly relied on humour, cartoon violence and the combat of depersonalised threats arising from elemental natural forces rather than the macho face-off against criminal conspirators.

Thus, supported by the new digital technologies, the late 1990s saw a cycle of natural disaster movies, including tornadoes in *Twister* (1996), volcanoes in *Dante's Peak* and *Volcano* (both 1997), asteroid or comet collisions in *Armageddon* and *Deep Impact* (both 1998), geophysical damage in *The Core* (2003) and catastrophic climate change in *The Day After Tomorrow* (2004). The same technologies made possible the creation of the fantasy-adventure landscapes of the three-part *The Lord of the Rings* (2001–3), the reinvention of the 1950s-style SF monster picture in *Independence Day* (1996) and *Godzilla* (1998), the reimagining of classical civilisations in *Gladiator* and *Troy*, and even the revival of the naval swashbuckler and the pirate film in *Master and Commander* and *Pirates of the Caribbean* (both 2003). While male heroics are central to these films, sexual romance is mostly subordinated to the ongoing concern with parenting. In the great majority of the SF-fantasy vehicles, the Manichean melodramatic model integral to Hollywood narrative from its earliest period is somewhat modified by either the impersonal or the inhuman nature of the threat, producing in some cases a novel and almost abstract moral landscape in which moral qualities are not established and tested relationally, as in historic melodramatic and Hollywood practice, but simply provided with a series of blue-screen environments in which to act themselves out.

BEYOND HOLLYWOOD

As already noted in this chapter, large-scale productions, particularly those produced in Italy, played an important part in the consolidation of the feature film worldwide as the dominant form of narrative cinema before and during the First World War. In the late silent period, well-capitalised European studios like UFA in Germany and Studios Réunis in France periodically supported spectacular productions such as *Metropolis* (Germany 1927), *Les Misérables* (1925–26) and *La Merveilleuse Vie de Jeanne d'Arc* (France 1927). After the Second World War, however, the massively reduced dimensions of European film production as a whole (and the virtual obliteration of the largest national film industry, Germany's) combined with soaring production costs in these heavily unionised industries to ensure that blockbuster productions were a rare luxury. During the Cold War, only the state-run Soviet cinema consistently produced films that could be classed as blockbusters on the postwar Hollywood model (colour, widescreen, epic sweep and scale, etc.) with enormous productions such as *War and Peace* (1965–67) and major historical recreations of subjects from the Great Patriotic War (see Chapter 5). Recently, EU tax regimes have created a more favourable climate for European co-production; however, problems of language translation tend to mean that large-scale pan-European ventures are filmed either in English

(*Enemy at the Gates*, 2001) or in dual-language versions (*Joan of Arc*, 1999). The much larger domestic markets and burgeoning economies of East Asia and the Pacific Rim make supporting indigenous blockbusters more viable, and Berry (2003) and Willis (2003) explore the economics and cultural meanings of the contemporary blockbuster in Korea and China and in India, respectively.

CASE STUDY: *DEEP IMPACT* (MIMI LEDER, 1998) / *ARMAGEDDON* (MICHAEL BAY, 1998)

The release within two months of each other of two films with all but identical narrative premises – the threat of global annihilation by collision with a comet (*Deep Impact*) or asteroid (*Armageddon*) – provoked widespread and derisive comment about Hollywood's imaginative bankruptcy. In fact, the coincidence was not all that surprising. The subject itself was not new, having been depicted in previous special-effects eras in *When Worlds Collide* (1951) and *Meteor* (1980), and according to Bart (1999: 140–3) two other asteroid pictures concurrently in the planning stages had to be cancelled when news broke of David Brown's and Jerry Bruckheimer's rival productions. A principal motivation for all of these projects was the proven market for cinematic devastation on the largest possible scale following the success of *Volcano* and *Dante's Peak* (both 1997) the previous summer season and above all *Independence Day* (1996) the year before that. These films might be seen as extending, with the aid of the new generation of CGI effects, the reach of the disaster films of the 1970s, which bar *Earthquake* typically confined themselves to local catastrophes in skyscrapers, overturned liners and so on. Literal end-of-the-world cinema (in Kim Newman's (1999) phrase) rendered catastrophe global, not local (albeit the affective dimension of worldwide apocalypse was, as we shall see in both cases, to be realised exclusively through normative American subject positions). Thus asteroid collisions were merely one obvious narrative carrier for the proven audience-getter of spectacular annihilation; 1998's other major summer release, *Godzilla* (jokily alluded to in *Armageddon*'s opening sequence), provided a different route to the same end. In fact, 1998 saw a third end-of-the-world film, the low-budget Canadian independent film *Last Night* (not released in the US until 1999), whose localised approach to global extinction, alternating sardonic and poignant vignettes across a small group of characters from different social and ethnic backgrounds as the clock remorselessly ticks down to doomsday – unspecified and indirectly represented but utterly unavoidable – contrasts tellingly with the show-and-tell aesthetic, as well as the classic melodramatic tropes of self-sacrifice and last-minute rescue, that organise both Hollywood blockbusters.

From *Armageddon* (1998). Reproduced courtesy of Touchstone/The Kobal Collection.

As King (2000a: 164–70) notes, although the two films are bound together by their common promise – clearly stated in trailers and poster art – to deliver awe-inspiring spectacular visions of disaster, they are significantly different in some important narrative and affective respects. Produced by Dreamworks SKG, the studio set up in 1994 by Steven Spielberg, Jeffrey Katzenberg and David Geffen on the prospectus of making more 'thoughtful' and 'film-maker-oriented' blockbusters than the existing majors, *Deep Impact* is mildly unconventional in narrative *structure* – following an opening thirty minutes focusing primarily on TV reporter Jenny Lerner (Tea Leoni) with a second half-hour centred on a new group of characters, the team of astronauts tasked with destroying the comet, and then shifting again to a multi-strand narrative dealing with separate (and mutually uninvolved) groups of characters, including President Beck (Morgan Freeman) in the days before the comet impacts. However, its narrative *affect* is noticeably more 'traditional' than its rival, building suspense from the asteroid's first sighting by an amateur astronomer through the dawning public awareness of the threat, and in the second half relying strongly on various sources of pathos (a motif of family separation, however, is common to all strands bar the President's) to personalise and intensify the literally global dimensions of the peril. There are two main action/spectacle sequences in the film, strategically divided between the halfway point – when the astronauts make their initial, unsuccess-ful attempt to blow up the comet – and the climactic sequence when a smaller portion of the comet strikes the East Coast of the USA while the larger, annihilating impact is avoided by the astronauts' sacrificial heroism.

Armageddon, by contrast, although more it has a more conventionally unified narrative centring exclusively on 'maverick' oilman Harry Stamper (Bruce Willis), his team of loveably asocial roughnecks and his daughter Grace (Liv Tyler) – indeed, despite the imminence of global apocalypse the 'world' is represented only by fleeting cutaways to anxious, and finally joyous, crowds of extras in various picturesque and readily placeable locations – in every other regard typifies the relentlessly assaultive, full-on mode of the contemporary action blockbuster. The film opens with a ten–minute effects sequence in which Manhattan is devastated by multiple impacts from what we later learn are outriding fragments flung off the approaching asteroid (subsequent impacts allow the film to offer its other key markets the odd compliment of seeing their own urban centres – Paris, Shanghai – bombarded). Although a few stereotypical 'types' (street hustlers, jiving cab drivers) are sketched into the Manhattan segment to lend it a minimal human dimension (the 'overseas' locations are experienced almost wholly through architectural landmarks), none of them are characters in the narrative; the sequence, delivered in the high-intensity, kinetic style that typifies the entire film, clearly aims to impress or even overwhelm the spectator. The film then introduces its main characters, establishing the broadest of possible character notes (when first seen, Harry is terrorising a shipload of Greenpeace protestors – who can't spell 'polluter' – with golf drives off his rig; upon finding Grace in bed with his protégé AJ (Ben Affleck), Harry stalks him around the rig with a loaded shotgun). Compared to *Deep Impact*, which unfolds over a total of two years (with the principal action taking place over eleven months), both the pace and the time-frame of *Armageddon* are frantically compressed: the approaching asteroid is spotted just a scant fortnight before it is scheduled to hit the earth.

Much more than *Deep Impact*, *Armageddon* appears to typify the action blockbuster's subordination of character development and coherent plot to massive visual overkill. As King (2000a: 166) observes, non-stop spectacle is the rule for the entire last seventy-five minutes (the film's blockbuster dimensions include a running time of 144 minutes), with incident and crisis piled upon one another, less accelerating than accumulating in serial fashion (literally: the succession of cliffhanging near-disasters evokes the silent melo-dramatic serials discussed by Singer (2001): see Chapter 2). Even relatively routine narrative material aims at maximum impact: the gathering of Harry's team (who have mysteriously managed, with no advance word or apparent transportation, to disperse themselves across the continental United States in the 24 hours or less since Harry's departure to NASA) is staged as a series of high-velocity chases and round-ups.

Both films, however, strikingly frame the experience of global annihilation in terms of familial conflicts and their resolution, thus confirming the action blockbuster as a mode of melodrama. *Deep Impact* recalls Griffith in its use of children to generate both pathos and hope: Jenny Lerner sacrifices her place on the network helicopter to safety to a colleague and her daughter while she herself seeks out her estranged father to make a final peace before the tsunami obliterates them both; in a separate narrative strand, parents hand over their newborn child to their teenage daughter Sarah and her boyfriend Leo, who by virtue of Leo's all-terrain motorbike can take the child to (symbolic?) higher ground and form part of the saving remnant that in the film's coda promises to build anew. (Michael Tolkin, the film's co-screenwriter, previously wrote and directed the unsettling Christian apoca-lyptic parable *The Rapture* (1994).) Though superficially similar, *Armageddon*'s focus is different and less overtly moralistic: the principal conflict that is resolved in the film's climax is Harry's acceptance of Grace's relationship with AJ – but since there seems to have been no reason beyond generalised reverse-Oedipal resentment for Harry to disapprove their affair in the first place, this is hardly a major issue (a subordinate plot strand detailing the reunion of a member of Harry's team with his estranged wife is similarly irrelevant). Yet the pathos surrounding Harry's final martyrdom (he remains on the asteroid alone to detonate the nuclear charges manually) is considerably more hysterical than anything in *Deep Impact*, with AJ – for whom Harry has sacrificially substituted himself – bellowing his love for his friend while Grace weeps in Mission Control.

Differences in the degree and nature of the spectacle of disaster are also telling. Both films employ essentially the same narrative device to deliver to their audience both the promised thrill of ultra-large-scale catastrophe and the reassurance of a relatively upbeat ending: since global extinction/the destruction of the planet might be felt to be something of a downer, each film settles for impressive but finally superficial obliteration of discrete portions of the planet's surface by meteorite fragments, while successfully averting the main threat. *Deep Impact*'s climactic tsunami is impressive yet restrained: between the death of Lerner *père et fille* on Virginia Beach and Leo and Sarah's escape up the mountainside, the destruction of the US Eastern seaboard is rendered in a sequence of eight shots, none less than two seconds long, depicting the destruction of New York either in panoramic long-shot or in ground-level medium shots. The tenor of the sequence is as restrained as it could be, given the subject matter, while the absence of any named or even individualised characters lends the sequence a summary, slightly impersonal flavour.

As already noted, *Armageddon* gets its terrestrial destruction in early, thus freeing up the remaining narrative for the individualistic heroics of Harry Stamper's team. (*Armageddon* is a significantly less 'official' narrative than *Deep Impact*: although military and NASA personnel are nominally in charge of the rescue mission, the important drilling and demolition work is subcontracted to Harry's team – who predictably chafe at the uptight military discipline imposed on them during the mission prep – and by contrast with Morgan Freeman's dignified President Beck in *Deep Impact* the President is a noticeably less central and more ineffectual figure, who comes under criticism for slashing the 'object collision' budget.)

By placing the meteorite impacts earlier in the film, Harry's climactic self-sacrifice for the greater good (a sentimental paternal sacrifice shared with not only *Deep Impact* but also *Independence Day*) is more central to the film's climax than the parallel (collective) sacrifice of the astronaut team in *Deep Impact* – indeed, Harry's death arguably supersedes the destruction of the asteroid and the salvation of the planet as the major affective element at the climax of the film. The enormous CGI firestorm and shockwave Harry sets off is accompanied by a montage of images of Grace, tracking both backwards to her childhood and forwards to the wedding Harry will never see, that renders Harry's death a cosmic epiphany transcending the limits of the narrative or even of human comprehension. Thus the ostensibly super-social – the sacrifice of the one for the many – is reoriented to the supremely personal: it is as if *Armageddon*, having thrown every effect bar the kitchen sink at the audience over the course of its 2 hr. 24 min. running time, can conceive of no more spectacular effect – no phenomenon of more global or even cosmic significance – than the death of its own star.

NOTES

1. A comparison of the celebrated chase in *The French Connection* (1971) (which underlines Popeye Doyle's manic obsession with 'getting his man', a compulsion that will eventually have self-destructive consequences) and the car chase through San Francisco that features early in *The Rock* (1996) and has very little bearing of any kind on the main storyline but provides the film with the requisite up-front action sequence, helps clarify the novel structure of the contemporary blockbuster.
2. On the historical adventure film, see Taves (1993).
3. The others were *Made for Each Other* and *Intermezzo*.
4. Motivated in this case by contractual rather than strictly financial considerations, namely the almost simultaneous publication of and sale of film rights to two novels, *The Tower* and *The Glass Inferno*, both portraying catastrophic fires in state-of-the-art skyscrapers.

CHAPTER 11

Genre: Breaking the Frame

This final chapter briefly considers 'non-canonical' genres, questionable genres, or categories of film not typically conceived as generic. Each 'genre' is discussed briefly. The intention in each case is less to argue for its incorporation into or exclusion from the 'canon' of genres, but to explore the new insights or problems thrown out by a speculative identification of these types of film as genre films and reflect them back onto more traditional classifications and approaches. These genres are commonly, though in different ways, 'scandalous' – that is, proposing them as genres to be discussed critically or in academic contexts alongside Westerns, gangster films and the like poses difficulties arising from conventional understandings of, or assumptions about, their/the genre text's subject matter, style and social context(s). Such 'scandalous' genres can hopefully help us to further our critical interrogation not only of standard genre categories – which may prove to have unsuspected affinities with these unconventional neo- or crypto-genres – but also of the practices and structures that underpin the system of film genre as a whole. To reiterate the statement in the introduction to this section of the book, these brief and in some ways speculative discussions are intended to spur further research and enquiry rather than in any sense to produce definitive accounts of the 'genres' in question.

I: DOCUMENTARY

The traditional, literary, concept of genre clearly has a place for documentary and non-fiction film – as distinct from fiction film (similar, and overlapping, large-scale generic categories would include live-action and animated film). But as we know, film genre theory has usually traded in narrower generic categories and has sought to identify specific thematic and narrative consistencies within individual genres as part of the definitional project. This book has followed this practice, while reserving a larger category for 'modes', like melodrama, whose reach seems to encompass several individual film genres, as historically and traditionally conceived.

It is in this sense that documentary-as-genre becomes a scandalous concept. For inasmuch as (fiction) genres entail degrees and styles of *verisimiltiude* – that is, conventionalised, provisional and pragmatically partial *versions* of reality with limited (or, as with some musicals, horror and fantasy films, almost no) pretensions directly to transcribe real-world experience – documentary is on the face of it definitively anti-generic. As a discourse of the real, documentary above all relies on, and is judged by, an explicit profession of encountering reality and being led by it, rather than shaping reality into generically harmonious forms, as Michael Renov summarises:

> (T)he documentary is the cinematic idiom that most actively promotes the illusion of immediacy insofar as it foreswears 'realism' in favour of a direct, ontological claim to the 'real'. Every documentary issues a 'truth claim' of a sort, positing a relationship to history which exceeds the analogical status of its fictional counterpart. (Renov, 1993: 3–4)

Kilborn and Izod (1997: 28) associate this claim on the real with what Charles Peirce has characterised as the 'indexical' aspect of the photographic image – the promise vouchsafed the spectator that what has been captured on the filmic emulsion was *actually present* at the moment of filming (indeed, needed to be present for the image to be produced at all). The technical processes involved in making photographs and cinematography guarantee that the film image is a record of something *real*. Of course, in this sense every fiction film is a documentary: it 'documents' the presence in the pro-filmic space of actors, sets, props and so on. Moreover, the advent of digital technologies such as CGI has allowed for an intensified degree of seamless manipulation of images such that the traditional indexical bond between object-world and image-world is no longer (if it ever was) assured. Brian Winston (1993) and others have suggested that the erosion of this indexical contract have fundamentally challenged traditional understandings of the nature and function of documentary as a form of 'scientific inscription'. Documentary is thus once again characterised as not, in Renov's terms, 'analogical' – *like* life – but closer to or in fact 'real.' Thus unless reality itself harbours generic forms, 'true' documentary must aspire to a status 'beyond genre'.

Yet the history of documentary, from Robert Flaherty and John Grierson to Nick Broomfield and Erroll Morris, refutes such pretensions to a documentary paradigm 'beyond genre'. In fact, even (or especially) at those moments in documentary history when claims for impersonality and non-mediation are most powerfully advanced, there can be clearly seen a conflicting drive towards conventionalised narrative, performative and even iconographic structures that can only be regarded as generic. This is in any case to say nothing of the visual and discursive styles associated with different documentary models that also constitute readily recognisable generic categories (direct-to-camera address by the film-maker, hand-held single-camera set-ups, use of available light and live sound, to-camera interviews, the inclusion of archive footage, etc.).

In his most recent update of what has become a starting-point for much teaching of documentary history and theory, Nichols (1994: 95) posits a classical evolutionary model of generic development through five distinct and successive modal stages, with each stage seeking to remedy the shortcomings of its predecessor. The model starts with the Expository mode in the 1930s and moves through the Observational (1960s direct cinema and *cinema verité*); the Interactive (which relies heavily on participant interviews and in which the spectator may also be compelled to interact with the text by actively engaging in the process of meaning construction, as in the pure archive montage documentary *The Atomic Café*, 1983); the Reflexive (where a self-conscious directorial style enables the act of representation itself to become a/the object of documentary and spectatorial reflection, by foregrounding either the film-maker's own presence, and their encounters with their subjects – as in Michael Moore's *Roger and Me* (1988) – or the process of meaning construction itself, for example Errol Morris' *The Thin Blue Line*, 1987); to the most recent, the Performative (in which the subjective dimension of documentary's 'classically objective discourse' are brought to the fore[1]). As with all such evolutionary accounts (see Chapter 1), Nichols's is open to the standard criticisms of teleology, rigidity and ahistoricism: Bruzzi (2000: 2) points out that Expository documentary's putative supersession accounts for neither the ubiquity of narration-led documentary today nor, conversely, the highly reflexive films of Dziga Vertov and Jean Vigo in the 1920s.

The principal concern of documentary theorists – Bruzzi points out that film-makers, even theoretically informed ones, have been much less exercised about it (and documentary-makers are more likely to be critically aware than many fiction film-makers) – is the inevitable gap between documentary's apparent aspirations to capture reality in an absolutely unmediated form, and the manifest mediations introduced into the documentary artefact by, at a bare minimum, shot selection and post-production, to say nothing of authorial viewpoint and the 'uncertainty principle' of the film-maker's necessary presence in the reality s/he proposes merely to record. A number of well-known documentary theorists (for example, Renov, Nichols) are animated by poststructuralist scepticism about such concepts as 'reality' and 'truth', or at least a conviction that the only 'truths' to be found in the world are plural rather than singular; by contrast, they tend to characterise documentary-makers as naive realists on an endless and chimerical quest for the unattainable goals of absolute immediacy and unvarnished truth. Digital technologies' expanding capacity to produce photo-simulative fictions indistinguishable from 'the real thing' has only intensified such theorists' sense of the collapsing boundaries of truth and fiction and of the unsustainability of documentary's 'truth-claims'. Yet such theories often seem uneasily caught between the logical conclusion of their sceptical premises – that documentary ought simply to be considered as another form of narrative film, its ostensible facticity of no greater or lesser relevance than the historicity of the Western or SF film – and the recognition that documentary remains importantly committed – not least in the perceptions of its audience – to acting in and even upon the real in ways that fiction does not.

In fact, very few documentarians – not just today, but historically – have in reality subscribed to the kinds of realist fundamentalism often ascribed to them. (For that matter, neither did such theorists of filmic realism as André Bazin and Siegfred Kracauer, sometimes charged with providing the intellectual rationale for the 'naïve realism' of documentary film. Their – different – positions related much more to the ethical and political implications of the camera's encounter with physical and social reality as *transcribed* – *not* simply transmitted – by film.) Such accounts seem to identify the generic project of documentary as a whole with the most unguarded claims made by the American 'direct cinema' film-makers of the early 1960s such as Robert Drew and Richard Leacock (*Primary*, 1960; *Crisis*, 1963), D. A. Pennebaker (*Don't Look Back*, 1965) and Albert and David Maysles (*Meet Marlon Brando*, 1965; *Salesman*, 1969; *Gimme Shelter*, 1970). Sometimes, certainly, inflamed by the newly available portable cameras and sound gear, direct cinema did seem to declare itself – to adopt Roland Barthes' phrase – a 'degree zero' cinema, a medium of absolute transparency and communion with the real.

Yet the work of the Maysles Brothers, for example, instantly reveals direct cinema's huge debt to popular narrative forms. *Salesman*, an observational documentary about four Bible salesmen in Florida, seems to invoke the powerful dramatic paradigm of the salesman as contemporary American tragedy – the 'tragedy of the common man', in Arthur Miller's famous description of his celebrated play *Death of a Salesman* (1947) – while *Gimme Shelter* adopts horror film iconographies to render its depiction of the catastrophic 1969 Rolling Stones concert at Altamont even more infernal. (In fact, direct cinema's focus on specific kinds of subjects and personalities – typically, public figures like politicians (Kennedy) or celebrities (Brando, the Beatles) whose own 'performances' of reality structure the viewing experience – generically identifies American *verité* with recordings of the public realm.)

Nor does the work of earlier film-makers who quite clearly mix documentary and fictional elements – for example, Robert Flaherty in *Man of Aran* (1934) – necessarily reflect either lack of sophistication or a failure to achieve notional goals of pure objectivity. (It is worth noting that Paul Rotha's (1936) early taxonomy of documentary used the terms 'naturalist' and 'romantic' interchangeably.)

It may just be that a more general acknowledgement of documentary as a genre can help square the intractably circular arguments in documentary theory around realism and representation. Film genre theory, as we have seen, acknowledges that representational and narrative conventions supply important frameworks for meaning construction. At the same time, the meanings to be derived from an individual text are never exhausted by the conventions within, or against, which it works. For documentary theory, this could point a way out of the ultimately sterile debate that presupposes that the objective of documentary is by some means to access reality – and then preoccupies itself with the ways in which that goal remains forever frustratingly out of reach.

Any generic definition of documentary certainly needs to start by acknowledging the form's fundamental orientation towards the real – and that this aspect neither excludes a rhetorical dimension, yet nor is it purely reducible to rhetorical operations. Documentary, in other words, certainly *wants* its spectator to believe that the multifarious topics with which it engages share a common purchase in historical reality; but this sometimes over-eager insistence on direct access to a reality we know to be necessarily and inescapably mediated ought not obscure our recognition that there *is* after all a historical reality, mediation notwithstanding. Given the obvious problems in establishing a clear semantic basis for the documentary genre (an essentially limitless variety of subject matter and a proliferating set of modes, each with its distinctive visual style), it might be helpful to conceive of documentary as cohering generically in syntactic rather than semantic terms. Nichols (1993: 94) speaks of documentary's 'development of strategies for persuasive argumentation about the historical world'. This search for adequate ways with which to engage with lived reality then constitutes documentary's basic syntactic axis: the various styles, from expository to performative, across which this search is conducted, together supply an evolving – and obviously related and overlapping – series of semantic registers through which 'the real' can be satisfactorily signified.

A genre-based approach to documentary will necessarily regard the reality that is made available to the spectator through documentary practice – like the 'history' of the Western – as ultimately a function of generic convention rather than that which stands somehow outside the film-text altogether (after all, as Jacques Derrida (1976: 158) once famously observed, 'there is nothing outside of the text'). Thus the formal signifiers of immediacy in observational documentary, the semantic conventions of this mode of documentary, mark not only the 'presence' of reality in the text – a 'presence' we recognise as a generic prerequisite – but also the specific ways in which 'reality' is conceived that make such semantic conventions possible and appropriate (in this case, for example, the governing assumption that the object world *does* exist 'outside' of the text whose job is then faithfully to record it). On the other hand, identifying the syntax of documentary, as suggested above, as the interrogation of reality ought to ensure that documentary criticism does not fall back into hermetic formalism (because reality remains a structuring presence in documentary even if it can never be fully apprehended in the text). Understanding documentary syntax in this way also offers grounds for defending the elaborately reflexive, subjective and often artifice-laden work of contemporary 'performative' documentarists from Isaac Julien (*Looking for Langston*, 1988) to Errol Morris (*The Fog of War*, 2003) against Nichols's charge of stylistic excess and a retreat into the charmed circles of the avant-garde.

II: HOLOCAUST FILM

About halfway through Steven Spielberg's 1993 film of Thomas Keneally's novel *Schindler's List*, war profiteer Oskar Schindler confronts a frustrating and incipiently intolerable cognitive and moral crisis: when reminded by Itzhak Stern, Schindler's business manager at the enamelware plant he operates in occupied Poland and the diffident voice of his increasingly restive conscience, that the proliferating administrative euphemisms of his Nazi business partners – 'resettlement,' 'special treatment' and so forth – are in reality merely the thinnest of veils over the reality of industrialised mass murder, Schindler vents on his partner his anger and perplexity at this representational duplicity. 'Dammit, Stern,' he shouts, 'do we need a whole new language?' 'Yes,' replies Stern quietly, 'I think we do.'

However, *Schindler's List* and other – especially, but by no means exclusively, fictional – films about the Holocaust have been widely faulted for, precisely, their *failure* (or refusal) to speak 'a whole new language'. *Schindler's List* is indeed is discursively characterised by the conviction that both the key operative categories of bourgeois fiction and drama in general – individual moral choice, a linear goal-oriented narrative dynamised by dramatic conflict, and so on – and in particular the simplified versions thereof employed by Hollywood genre film, remain adequate to the task of representing events in human history regarded by some as in a sense beyond representation altogether. In fact, the fundamental project of *Schindler's List* is to bring the

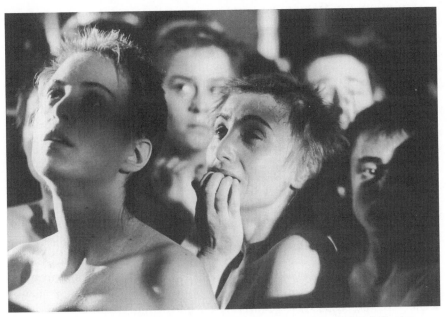

From *Schindler's List* (1993). Reproduced courtesy of Universal/The Kobal Collection.

Holocaust within this century's most normative, universally available and globally comprehended representational parameters, those of the classic Hollywood film, and it is by the legitimacy or otherwise of that project, and its success in carrying it through, that the film has to be measured.

Schindler's List is by some measure the most emphatically and knowingly *generic* of all serious treatments of the Holocaust. That is, Spielberg's film quite consciously sets out to recreate the 'Final Solution' from within the instantly recognisable and comprehensible forms of popular Hollywood genres. For instance, the first thing we notice about *Schindler's List* is that it is in black and white. This is often taken as a documentary affectation: the rendering of the story in monochrome is intended to reinforce the truth claims of the film by invoking the look of contemporary documentary footage of the Second World War. But for the film's anticipated audience, black-and-white footage quite simply provides the correct *filmic* register for a 'Second World War movie': in other words, a set of representational conventions and associations is being quite precisely deployed, wherein black and white connotes 'old movies' at least as much as 'old times'. The opening scenes of the film, which depict, first, the arrival *en masse* of Jewish deportees from the Polish countryside in Krakow, followed by the introduction of Schindler himself in the setting of a German-frequented nightclub in the city, confirm the directive signal of monochrome by their faintly studied classicism (the slightly fetishistic accumulation of period detail, the wreaths of *film noir* shadows, the withheld 'reveal' that keeps the face of Liam Neeson as Schindler concealed from the audience until well into the second sequence) that collectively announces the calculated deployment of a classical Hollywood style and moreover of the classic Hollywood's preferred dramatic engine, the genre film. More specific allusions here include, most notably, *Casablanca* (1943), whose postponement of the introduction of the central character *Schindler's List* consciously imitates: *Casablanca* of course being another wartime parable of the transformation of an individual from profiteering and cynical detachment into passionate commitment to a cause. As the film progresses, the progressive darkening of tone as each new stage in the Holocaust is reached (from ghettoisation, to deportation, finally to mass extermination) is textually marked by another shift in *generic* register. The film abandons the assured classical style of the earlier scenes – which reflect Schindler's own brash early confidence – for the non-classical modes of documentary (including hand-held camerawork that appears to be following the action anxiously rather than framed to receive it) and – notoriously, in the Auschwitz 'shower scene' – of the post-*Psycho* slasher/stalker horror film.

The critical problem posed by this evident generic character relates to critical and theoretical positions that insist on the inescapable singularity of the Holocaust and accordingly – if indeed it is not asserted that the Holocaust is simply 'beyond' depiction, speech and understanding altogether – demand of Holocaust representations that they manifest that singularity through formal disruption of narrative, etc., conventions and – above all – through the abjuration of mainstream representational strategies such as those of genre film. What Holocaust historians call the 'radical incomprehensibility thesis' (the claim that the attempt to understand the Holocaust defeats the procedures of conventional historiography or political economy) finds its echo in a 'radical unrepresentability thesis' which similarly condemns normative representational practices to inevitable failure.

Thus the problematic notion of 'the Holocaust film' as a genre raises ethical questions alongside critical ones. Since the release of *Schindler's List* in 1993 if not well before, the Holocaust has become an established if always controversial subject for historical drama. Indeed, the opening sequence of *X-Men* (2000) – which depicts the future 'Magneto' as a child deportee, using his destructive telepathic powers for the first time as he is separated from his parents at the gates of Auschwitz – suggests strongly that the Holocaust has become increasingly available as a point of reference for genre films well outside the categories of 'serious' historical drama. With pre-existing genres (such as the war/combat film) offering no viable parameters for the representation of industrialised mass murder, Holocaust films have generated their own recognisable representational conventions and narrative templates. Yet there remains a marked critical reluctance to countenance the idea of 'the Holocaust film' – primarily because incorporating the Holocaust into the routinised structures of genre appears to diminish its unique horror by normalising it at the narrative and textual level.

The difficulties entailed by the proposition of a genre, '*the* Holocaust film,' presumptively to be set alongside the detective film, the Western, the musical and so on, relate to the nature of the generic text itself, which by definition entails narrative, iconographic, characterological and conceivably ideological *conventions*; which is further to say normative and – simply by virtue of such normativity – in some measure perhaps affirmative apprehensions of how the world given through the genre artefact to a generic audience is organised. Genre can be seen as a means of ordering the world which by the very fact of that ordering offers its audience the reassuring if circular consolation that the world is, indeed, orderable. In the context of film, this generic orderliness, or orderly genericity, has of course on occasions translated into a more-or-less explicit opposition between (particularly Hollywood) genre film – construed as commodity, the fatally facile pablum of Adorno's 'culture industry' – and the originary apprehension of the authentic, authored artefact, especially in the tradition of the European art film. However exhausted and discredited this opposition has become in critical theory generally, the dichotomy of the generic/normative and the autonomous/exceptional remains a significant presence in critical discussions of narrative and in particular filmic treatments of the Holocaust.

In fact, however, since until quite recently the Holocaust remained largely off-limits to Hollywood cinema, hence as subject matter confined, precisely, to the European art film, the implications of a fully generic approach to the Holocaust have not needed to be fully explored.[2] The fury of many of the responses to the NBC mini-series *Holocaust* (1978) was itself in large measure attributable to that series' historical priority – *Holocaust* was, after all, the first time that 'Hollywood' had attempted to accommodate this subject matter to its existing generic styles. The offence here arguably arose above all from the perception that the Holocaust was indeed being illegitimately accommodated *to* Hollywood norms, rather than what seems to have been a felt imperative that it explode them. It is only in the latter part of the nearly two decades since *Holocaust* was first broadcast that, as one highly visible element in a broad cultural front of creative, commemorative, scholarly and critical concern with the Shoah in Europe and America, the destruction of Europe's Jews has gradually come to feature more regularly if still infrequently in major Hollywood studio productions. Films like *Schindler's List*, *Sophie's Choice* (1982), *Triumph of the Spirit* (1988) and *Jakob the Liar* (1998) are unashamedly and indeed doubly generic: they both trade in existing generic templates like *film noir*, the war movie and soap opera for their initial appeal, and in themselves help trace out the parameters of a still-nugatory new genre.

Against that, it can be argued that rendering the unthinkable conventional allows it to be confronted and acknowledged rather than excluded as untouchable. The Holocaust's emerging 'genericisation' may be seen as insisting, via the *formal* element of generic orthodoxy and convention, on the necessary *continuity* between the quotidian realities of the world we think of as 'ours' and that of the camps. Primo Levi (1988) has insisted that the *univers concentrationnaire* was not a closed universe: if it were, on what basis does one insist on the continuing relevance of the categories of moral responsibility, at least for the perpetrators? How could one, by the same token, even recognise the perverse inversion or evacuation of those categories inflicted on camp inmates – a phenomenon widely remarked in survivor literature? Did the camps not possess to at least some degree, as Trevor Griffiths writes in his play *Comedians*, 'the logic of our world – extended'? (Griffiths, 1975: 63). To the extent that the Holocaust is increasingly seen in historical terms as a potential *within* modernity rather than (as a more reassuring prior interpretative orthodoxy would have it) modernity's Other, the project of adequately reintegrating Holocaust representations within the normative texture of representational convention becomes both more urgent and more problematic: problematic, since at its most extreme (for instance, in some pronouncements of the later Adorno) the regimented assembly-line commodity culture that produces the Hollywood genre film is seen as not only complicit but continuous with the instrumental rationalised modernity that spawned/enabled the Holocaust; yet urgent, since the possibility remains that the Holocaust may be 'refunctioned' through representation to articulate an immanent critique of modernity's own exterminative tendency.[3]

This does not mean, however, that genre forms can be applied unreflectively and in an undiscriminating way to the Holocaust. On the contrary, even the most conventionally generic (which is to say, in terms of Holocaust reception, scandalously *un*conventional) Holocaust films seem to push towards a point at which the spectator is confronted with the difficulty, if not outright impossibility, of portraying *these* scenes in *this* (generic) way, a point marked – like the confusions and contortions of melodrama, or more locally the oneiric distortions that mark out masculine fantasy constructions in *Out of the Past* and other *films noirs* (see Chapter 9) – by extreme textual stress and narrative dislocation. For example, two late 1990s examples of 'Holocaust comedy' – itself of course a massively transgressive category, the most (in-)famous being *Life Is Beautiful* (Italy 1998) – *Train of Life* (France/Romania, 1999) and *Jakob the Liar* (1998) both confront the spectator in their concluding moments with radical narrative reversals and reflexive narrative readjustments. In *Train of Life*, this comes about through the revelation that the whole film has been the memory/fantasy of a camp inmate, possibly a lunatic; in *Jakob the Liar*, through a double ending that substitutes possible redemption for annihilation. Both films seem to pose questions about the desire for optimistic generic resolutions in a narrative context where optimism is unsustainable: their eleventh-hour shift into modernist narrative uncertainty might be construed as an ethical gesture that encourages spectators to reflect on their own motivations for watching Holocaust narratives and their expectations of those narratives.

As an extension of our shared culture into the realm of the unspeakable, then, the genericisation of the Holocaust is marked not – or not only – by the reduction and routinisation of atrocity: it also brings the spectator to that point where cultural signifying practices are split *from within*, where an act of radical and absolute separation is performed upon us by a sudden and as it seems arbitrary scission, a moment which – within the confines of genre, which are what enable us to encounter such appalling historical material in the first place – we experience as an act of violence upon ourselves. Such textual aggression – for example, in the stark tonal/generic shift between sun-drenched, fairy-tale romantic comedy to wartime melodrama in *Life Is Beautiful* – exploits the deceptive security offered by the establishment of a generic locale to communicate to the spectator a sense of radical disorientation when that security is suddenly withheld.

III: PORNOGRAPHY

That pornographic film (which since the mid-1980s has in fact usually meant video) is a genre is hardly debatable. In fact, if film genre is understood in terms of the mass-production of standardised narratives whose well-established conventions supply reliable and repeated pleasures for a regular audience, then porn film could stand almost as a template for genre in general. In all its endless variants, pornography is arguably structured by stronger genre conventions than any mainstream genre, even the Western. Nor, unlike the Western, does it appear in any danger of extinction, in fact quite the reverse: pornographic motifs and allusions have since the early 1990s been rife in Hollywood cinema, whether in films about the sex industry (*Showgirls*, 1995; *Boogie Nights*, 1997) that challenge the grimly negative depictions in such 1970s films as *Hardcore* (1977),[4] sex-centred genre films whose narratives mimic pornographic narrative structures (such as the 'erotic thrillers' discussed in Chapter 9), or simply by incorporating polymorphous sexual content – phone sex (*Girl 6*, 1996), swinging (*Preaching to the Perverted*, 1997; *The Rapture*, 1994), under-age sex (*Kids*, 1995), S/M (*Body of Evidence*, 1993) and so on – whose exploration had previously been confined to porn 'proper'. Meanwhile, an increasing number of independent film-makers have crossed the line that previously definitively separated both upscale 'erotica' and mainstream narrative cinema generally from hardcore pornography, the direct depiction of unsimulated sex acts (*Romance*, France 1998; *Baise-Moi*, France 2001; *Intimacy*, GB 2000; *9 Songs*, GB 2004). This 'pornographising' trend in contemporary film is of course part of a larger mainstreaming of porn imagery and porn itself through 'lad culture' men's magazines, talk shows and so on.

Yet as a socially illegitimate (and quite often extra- or para-legal) form, pornography has more often been the subject of sociological than critical interest. Until quite recently, the idea that pornography could be an object of academic study other than in departments of psychology, sociology or jurisprudence would have been frankly bizarre. In particular, the idea of paying serious critical attention to the formal and stylistic attributes of the pornographic *text* was all but unthinkable. This changed in 1989 with the publication of Linda Williams's ground-breaking study *Hard Core: Power, Pleasure and the Frenzy of the Visible*. Williams argued that pornography had a distinct generic history that both partly recapitulated, but also in important ways departed from, the trajectory of mainstream narrative film. Williams's relocation of porn within the disciplinary context of film studies – which implied that, for example, the structures of pornographic narratives could be classified, discussed and assessed like those of Westerns or musicals – power-fully challenged the operative moral, ethical and legal frameworks in which porn had hitherto been encountered. These included both conservative anti-pornography campaigners whose opposition to pornography was grounded in traditional moral and religious objections to permissiveness and sexual licence, and feminists who regarded pornography as simultaneously a perni-cious expression of phallocentric patriarchal mythologies and a direct spur to further male sexual aggression against women (in other words, as Gertrud Koch ([1981] 1993: 39) notes, finding in porn 'not (like conservatives) the erosion of existing norms but rather their expression and confirmation').

Paying particular attention to constructions for and of the pornographic audience, Williams distinguishes different regimes of pornographic produc-tion and consumption, first a (lengthy) 'primitive' phase where 'stag' films – minimally elaborated depictions of sex acts largely devoid of narrative content – offered a cinema of pornographic attractions to usually all-male audiences in contexts (such as brothels) where the sexual promise the films vouchsafed might be immediately actualised. Porn thus functioned wholly or in part as an adjunct to commodified sexual activity rather than as a sexual commodity in its own right, and was a para-cinematic activity that temporarily colonised other spaces as venues for exhibition. Porn's 'classical' period in the 1970s finds theatrically-released hardcore films, some of them achieving wide distribution and crossing over to mainstream exhibition, with higher production values, more elaborate narratives and careful modulations of tone (for example, the extensive use of comedy) to court a wider and more 'respectable' audience – thus recapitulating, albeit on a different time-frame, the developmental trajectory of mainstream cinema. Williams also finds 1970s porn films less concerned to stimulate desire in the spectator that can (must) be satisfied 'elsewhere' (like the stag films), than themselves to supply textual 'satisfaction' through spectacular concluding large-scale sexual 'numbers'. '(T)he price of manifesting public sexual interest in pornography was the suppression of overt individual sexual responses that were at least possible in the private party atmosphere of the stag film and often solicited by the films themselves' (Williams, 1999: 299). By contrast, 'classic' 1970s porn films like *Behind the Green Door* (1977)

> constructed their arrangement of sexual acts into a climactic satisfaction meant to stand as a visual experience alone. It was the conceit of these narratives ... that the films itself would be so absorbing and satisfying as not to lead the viewer 'on the rebound' back to his or her own body. Indeed, the greater and greater spectacularisations of the multitudinous money shots of this era's pornography seemed determined to prove that the film's visual climaxes were sufficient unto themselves. (*ibid.*)

Such films importantly challenge the perception of pornographic narratives as merely instrumental 'tools' for sexual arousal – though in the book's second edition in 1999, Williams reassesses 'classic' 1970s porn as not, as she first surmised, the genre's most fully-realised form but something of an exception, historically bracketed by the more 'practical' pleasurable applications and interactive sexual/textual engagements of the stag film and video porn (pp. 299–300). The home video revolution of the 1980s, which arguably transformed the economics – but, for the most part, not the aesthetics – of mainstream Hollywood, ended porn film's 'classical' phase, foreclosed on the genre's aspirations to theatrical 'legitimacy' (the object of fond parody in skin-flick *auteur* Jack Horner's ambitions in *Boogie Nights* to make 'real movies'), and returned the consumption of porn to contexts (the private home) that once again promoted spectatorial regimes where porn-watching could be integrated into active sexual pleasure-taking.

In the preface to *Hard Core*, Williams describes the book's origins in a project analysing other film genres in greater or lesser part defined by their somatic affect – their direct address to and impact upon the embodied spectator – a category that also included 'tearjerking' melodramas and horror films. This is a suggestive association inasmuch as those other genres too have, as we have seen, endured critical disapprobation as 'debased' forms appealing to the lowest common (social and perceptual) denominator, only to benefit from a much more favourable reception in contemporary theories of the gendered subject. In Victor Hugo's opinion, whereas tragedy stirred the heart, melodrama rewarded 'the pleasure of the eyes' (quoted in Carlson, 1984: 213). Porn's current rehabilitation as an object of critical analysis can thus be located within the larger context of critical theory's generally expanded interest in forms that through form and/or narrative content challenge conventional viewing positions and the critical categories typically identified with them (see Chapter 7). Not coincidentally, a number of scholars who have written about porn have also contributed important studies of the horror film and/or melodrama, including Williams herself (1983, 1984, 1991, 1998), Carol Clover (1992), Sue-Ellen Case (1989, 1991), Chuck Kleinhans (1978, 1996) and Claudia Springer (1996).

All that said, at first glance porn, its transgressive *content* notwithstanding, would seem to be anything but unconventional in its intense genericity – its attachment to rigid narrative and iconographic procedures that vary less from individual film to film than any mainstream genre. Porn must by definition (and this of course means legally too) feature graphic, explicit and repeated representations of unsimulated sex acts; Williams's *Hard Core* introduced and explained the generic lexicon of 'meat shots' (close-ups of penetration) and 'money shots' (the male ejaculation outside – but usually on – the body of his female partner(s)). In fact, the multiplicity of porn's proliferating specialist sub-genres makes the identification of semantic or iconographic constants surprisingly difficult. Porn can be tender or aggressive, comic or matter-of-fact; its protagonists may be old or young, conventionally attractive or not; production values may be extremely high (as in 1970s porn classics like *Behind the Green Door* or contemporary upscale video porn) or low-rent (in a variety of ways, for different reasons and with different affective modes, as in amateur, 'gonzo' and much fetish porn); and straight, gay, bisexual, transgender and transvestite men and women of course can (and do) perform a bewildering variety of sexual acts and scenarios from the straightforward to the recondite and bizarre. Even nudity is not an absolute given in all porn (for example, in some fetish contexts).

In most cases conventional wisdom would also assume that narratives in porn films are no more than inert (and in the home video age, readily skipped over) 'carriers' for the privileged sex sequences, which in terms both of performance and consumption are essentially autonomous of their narrative contexts. That is, neither the viewer nor the actors maintain any pretence of interest in ostensible characterisations or narrative developments during performances of sex acts that are to all intents and purposes stand-alone textual elements, capable of being, and indeed likely to be, viewed in any or no order with no meaningful diminution of their interest or impact.[5] Even if, as in some 1970s porn, an attempt is made to produced a more integrated narrative, the powerful 'reality effect' of hardcore sex (whose specular, as opposed to purely libidinal, charge is in itself, one might note, socially constructed[6]) is always likely to overwhelm its narrative contexts, as would seem to be borne out by the experience of recent mainstream film-makers who have experimented with including hardcore sex in non-pornographic narratives (see above). Williams, however, argues that porn narratives reveal the genre's underlying syntactic coherence and as such are a good deal more than disposable packaging for sex scenes. For Williams, pornography is 'a genre that is by definition obsessed with visible proof' (p. 230). This accounts for the ways in which the sexual act, and specifically female pleasure, are located as objects of intense narrative curiosity in 1970s porn films premised on 'sexual problems' like *Deep Throat* (1972), *The Devil in Miss Jones* (1974) and *Insatiable* (1978).

This in turn relates back to the tantalising insight allying porn and melodrama: for porn, like melodrama, is arguably also as much a 'mode' as a genre, hence despite appearances and assumptions defined more readily in syntactic than in semantic terms.[7] Porn is generically unified by its emphasis on what Williams calls 'the frenzy of the visible', which may be understood as the programmatic imperative to render on-screen the experience of sexual pleasure in unmistakeable, unchallengeable and even verifiable ways. The most familiar generic marker of this scopophilia is the 'money shot' of straight porn. However, both the female orgasm and fetishistic pleasure pose a problem for the pornographic gaze in their lack of a transparently signifying somatic manifestation.

Pornography poses a particular challenge to conventional notions of generic *verisimilitude* in so far as it is predicated on a fundamental disassociation of its fictive storytelling practices – which are in formal terms usually perfectly conventional – and its ultimate promise to deliver representations which are not *lifelike* but in fact *real*. Porn's specific generic verisimilitude centres on the proposition of a world where libidinal energies are not repressed or sublimated – though they may of course be temporarily frustrated, at least in terms of their attraction to specific objects (a particular partner, orifice or fetish object) – but where, on the contrary, human beings are constantly primed for sexual activity. In this sense, as Williams notes, the porn film's construction of a generic milieu premised on the acting-out and ready grati-fication of sexual desire in 'production numbers' that define the genre parallels both the structure and utopian world of pure expressivity (see Chapter 4) in the integrated musical.

Pornography's structural affinities with not only the musical but that other episodic, spectacular genre, the contemporary action blockbuster, could be used to support an argument for narrative cinemas as a whole to be regarded as 'essentially' pornographic, an argument that some psychoanalytically based theories of spectatorship and cinema's mobilisation of the 'scopic drive' would support. This book has generally questioned the notion of generic 'essences' in favour of a more processual understanding of genres, and it would be perverse now to reintroduce such ideas at the macro-level. Nonetheless, if more modestly we pursue the idea of pornography as a mode, studying the ways in which the pornographic and the melodramatic modes interact in mainstream, narrative dramatic cinema – including within and upon 'canonical' genres – might well prove a rewarding and instructive area for further study.

NOTES

1. Note that Nichols's own definition of the 'performative mode' differs significantly from other constructions of 'performative' documentary – notably Bruzzi (2000) – in light of theories of gender and subjectivity advanced by Judith Butler and others.
2. A comprehensive critical overview of filmic treatments of the Holocaust is provided by Insdorf (2002).
3. Zygmunt Bauman's (1989) *Modernity and the Holocaust* is probably the best-known exposition of the case for the Holocaust as running with rather than against the grain of modernity.
4. Though a film such *8MM* (1999) indicates that the phobic vision of porn as inferno persists, porn's incorporation into mainstream popular culture notwithstanding.
5. Compare the famous non-diegetic shot of the pistol-packing cowboy that could either (or both) begin or end *The Great Train Robbery* (1901) (see Chapter 3).
6. That is, it is the social taboo surrounding graphic imagery that lends hardcore imagery its powerful visual affect: so well-established is the principle of the sex act's unviewability that its inclusion in any narrative not institutionally placed as porn is (presently, at least) transgressive to a degree that challenges the possibility of its narrative integration.
7. On melodrama as genre and as mode, see Chapter 2.

CHAPTER 12

Conclusion: Transgenre?

Towards the end of *New York, New York*, Francine Evans fends off the neurotically aggressive needling of her ex-husband Jimmy Doyle, who has just rebranded her latest hit, *Happy Endings*, 'Sappy Endings', with a half-defensive, half-acquiescent piece of self-deprecation about musicals: 'Seen one, seen 'em all, huh?'

Hopefully, readers of this book will not find themselves agreeing with Francine, either about musicals or about genre films generally. The enormous variety of narratives, visual styles, modes of performance, ideological positions, political implications and forms of spectatorial address evident across the range of films and genres discussed in these pages should have made it plain that both across the system of film genre as a whole, within Hollywood and beyond, as well as between individual genre films in the same generic tradition, seeing one is really nothing like seeing them all. *New York, New York* itself, as a classic work of 1970s 'New Hollywood' genre revisionism, apparently torn between the desire to preserve the bittersweet memories of Hollywood's genre past and the urge to bury them alive, amply testifies to the ways that genres change in complex relationship to changing times and institutional contexts.

Yet Francine is not wholly wrong either: in so far as each individual genre film acts as a summation of and commentary on the totality of its generic predecessors, there is a sense in which when we watch any one genre film, we are if not 'seeing them all' then at least perhaps *sensing* 'them all'. Most genre films are of course neither as consciously nor as explicitly intertextual or directly contestatory of genre traditions as *New York, New York* or other 'revisionist', or critical, genre films of the same period (for example, in the US *Chinatown* and *Pat Garrett and Billy the Kid*, in Europe *Fear Eats the Soul* and *The American Friend*, and many others). Most genre films inhabit their generic identities in ways that are both less intensely self-conscious and less challenging. Yet something like – to adapt Fredric Jameson's famous phrase – a 'generic unconscious' persists within, beneath and around genre texts and sets their horizon of signification whether they are fully conscious of it or not. Some genre images – a stagecoach fording a river, say – are so specifically freighted with generic history that it is hard to imagine a film-maker shooting such a scene without the conscious intention of tipping his hat to John Ford. Others are so absolutely 'generic', transcending the need for a specific textual referentiality – a private eye climbing into a taxi and telling the driver to 'follow that cab' – that their inclusion is equally evocative of the 'essential' (or ideal) genre text that Tzvetan Todorov (1990) suggests theories of genre need to invoke as a heuristic fiction.

A remaining question is what part this genre patrimony plays in contem-porary cinema. The first chapter of this book closed with the suggestion that while 'film genres' – understood as the systematic, routinised production of genre films for a regular mass-audience spectatorship – might be a thing of the past, 'genre films' – individual films working self-consciously with (if not within) established generic tradition(s) – had become if anything an even more important instrument guiding contemporary film-makers and audiences. A glance at current releases in any week of the year will certainly confirm that Hollywood films today are as intensely generic as ever, perhaps even more so. As I write this conclusion in the autumn of 2004, the most recent *Variety* box-office Top 10 includes three horror films, three romantic comedies, two family-audience animated films, an action film and a musical biopic.[1] This list is made up of fairly traditional genres, all with long histories dating back to the classical studio era – although closer inspection reveals some of the characteristic ways in which contemporary Hollywood modifies and renovates these older paradigms: two of these films are remakes (of a 1960s British 'New Wave' romantic comedy and a recent Japanese horror film); two are sequels, including predictably one horror film but also one romantic comedy, a genre that has traditionally been less prone to serial exploitation; both of the animated features are digital rather than traditional cel animations, and both clearly aim at the crossover juvenile/adult market established by such breakthrough hits as *Toy Story* and *The Lion King* in the 1990s; the musical biopic tells the story of a rhythm-and-blues musician, Ray Charles, rather than a figure from Broadway (a biopic of Cole Porter, *De-Lovely*, released earlier in 2004 performed poorly at the box office). Such adaptive features – audience crossover, remakes, influence from other national cinemas, updating of generic conventions (show tunes to R'n'B) in line with changing audience preferences – are wholly consistent with the ways in which Holly-wood genres have historically responded to their changing institutional and social contexts.

Yet this picture should not obscure the important ways in which the 'genericity' of contemporary Hollywood films differs from that of previous periods – notably from either the comfortable (yet flexible) inhabitation of conventions in the classical period or the intense and in some cases politicised revisionism of the 1970s. It seems for example that the energetic contestation of classical genre paradigms as a tool of ideological and generational critique that fuelled Hollywood cinema into the 1980s is a less powerful impulse for the second and third generations of 'movie brat' directors than it was for the first. Indeed, as noted in preceding chapters many of the genres most strongly identified with classical Hollywood have given ground to newer and more flexible forms like horror, SF and the action film. On the basis of the critique of 'evolutionary' theories of genre in Chapter 1, I would obviously argue that these classical genres are not 'dead'. Yet it is also clear that many classical genre paradigms have a much reduced importance to the contemporary film industry and in a number of cases have mutated into other generic contexts. For example, as has been widely noted, as the Western has declined aspects of the frontier myth have generically relocated themselves to the post-*Star Wars* SF and action film. The periodic 'revivals' (that is, renewed production cycles) of the Western (in the late 1980s, mid-1990s and again in 2003–4) often produce films burdened with a somewhat academic, almost heritage tone, carefully evocative of genre traditions and their genre antecedents (for example, Kevin Costner's *Wyatt Earp*, 1994, and *Open Range*, 2003). The classical integrated musical, at least, seems now to be acceptable most often in animated cartoon rather than live-action form. The popularity and relevance of the combat film, in line with the discussion in Chapter 5, seems to fluctuate in line with the general cultural visibility of combat and the military (suggesting its immediate future, at least, looks rosy). It may simply be the increasing – temporal and cultural – distance between contemporary film culture and the heydays of these classical genres that makes their reanimation through critical engagement at once more difficult and less urgent.

An important aspect of 1970s Hollywood's critical engagement with classical genres was the assumed industrial and cultural centrality of the genres in question. By inverting or radicalising the generic paradigms of the Western or the MGM musical, it was possible to comment in a coded yet fairly transparent way both on the irrelevance or bankruptcy of classical Hollywood narratives and on the values sedimented in those generic forms. The diversified contemporary entertainment market militates against such a clear sense of public utterance. The disappearance of classic Hollywood's (notionally at least) relatively homogeneous audience, the multiplication of new genres and sub-generic trends, and the weakening of generic boundaries, all make it far harder to identify, let alone contest, genre-specific hegemonic ideologies.

In a more diffuse way, however, a critical impulse is built into some of the genres and cycles that have come to replace and/or supplement classical genres in the 'New Hollywood' – understood in its broadest sense, to take in the entire period since the transformation of Hollywood in the mid-1960s, and thus covering both the 1960s-1970s 'Hollywood Renaissance' and 'Corporate Hollywood' since the 1980s. Many of these 'new' genres are in fact hybrids, at once renovating and combining older generic traditions and alloying them with new concerns, and in some cases the reorientation of traditional generic coordinates expresses a significant ideological shift. The road movie, for instance, which takes its definitive form in 1969 with *Easy Rider* (1969), incorporates the tradition of the Western as a quite explicit intertext, with the freeway network replacing the freedom of the open range: one shot in *Easy Rider* pointedly frames Billy tinkering with his motorcycle alongside a rancher shodding his horse. Yet while the road movie updates the frontier myth to modern America – deriving ultimately from Jack Kerouac's beat rhapsody *On the Road* – it also frequently shares in the cultural disenchantment that informs contemporary 'end-of-the-line' Westerns. Not only does the highway of necessity channel absolute freedom of movement into particular routes – constraints foreshadowed in the barbed wire Billy runs into in *Pat Garrett and Billy the Kid* (1973) – but many road movies suggest there is in any event noplace much left to go to. Billy and Wyatt in *Easy Rider* journey, counter-canonically, from West to East and from broadening to inexorably and fatally narrowing horizons; as expansive and cosmic as their vision of freedom occasionally becomes, it is portrayed as fundamentally at odds with a contemporary America that is hostile to difference or indeed individualism of any kind, even patriotically directed (early on in the film, Billy and Wyatt are jailed for 'parading without a permit'). A sense of shrinking physical, political and personal horizons forms an important strain of the road movie, to the point where, as Douglas Pye observes of Peckinpah's Western heroes (1996: 18), their 'range of action (is) finally limited in some cases to a choice of how to die', as *Thelma and Louise* (1988) discover amid the familiar desert buttes of the classic Western. A number of serial killer/road movie hybrids films from *Badlands* (1973) to *Henry: Portrait of a Serial Killer* (1986), *Kalifornia* (1991) and *Natural Born Killers* (1994) parodically reduce the 'freedoms' of the road to the freedom of anonymous slaughter in a landscape of depersonalised transience, while teen-oriented road movies like *Road Trip* (2000) evacuate the myth of the American journey of any meaning beyond getting drunk and getting laid.

The blending of diverse genre traditions at work in often complex ways in contemporary film-making indicates that the self-advertised cine-literacy which was such a notable feature of 1970s Hollywood has if anything intensified. Undoubtedly, the transformed modes of film consumption in the last twenty-five years – above all, the impact of home video – have significantly heightened levels of genre awareness among mainstream film audiences. Freed from reliance on the idiosyncrasies of TV scheduling and repertory cinema programmers, students of the Western can now easily view, for example, a wide range of 1930s series Westerns[2] – and even some silents – and make their own estimations of the received wisdom about their stereotypicality, puerility and so on. Even more potentially important for both audiences and film-makers is the expanded access through home video to 'world cinema' beyond either the canons of international art film or the charmed circles of cult fandom – Japanese, Korean, Italian, Mexican and Brazilian horror films, for example, or Hong Kong action films (both contemporary and from the 1960s and 1970s). The ready availability of genre traditions has already transformed the forms of intertextual address typical of genre film today, as Geoff King (2002: 118–28) notes in his discussion of the genre-bending gangster-vampire-Western *From Dusk Till Dawn* (1996).

Rather than the wholesale generic interrogations of the 1970s, established generic conventions are often invoked by individual films today on a localised basis to guide the audience's understanding of a particular dramatic situation or character rather than as an overall narrative paradigm: as noted in Chapter 11, *Schindler's List* (1993) invokes the Warner Bros. wartime 'conversion narrative' (such as *Casablanca*) and *Psycho* (not only in the 'shower scene' but in the ahistorical depiction of Nazi Commandant Amon Goeth's villa as a gabled 'Bates Motel'-style house on a rise) to establish a frame of familiar dramatic reference for grossly unfamiliar narrative material. Such referencing tends to lack the scholarly precision embodied by such 'movie brat' directors as Martin Scorsese (who famously insisted that the kerbs of the Manhattan sidewalk in *New York, New York* be constructed artificially high to match the studio sets of his moving-going youth), and increasingly, the film genres invoked and mobilised in this way are themselves post-classical ones. Contemporary gangster films, for example, are often intensely intertextual, but the references they make are much more likely to be post-classical gangster films – notably the *Godfather* series and Martin Scorsese's 'wiseguy' films, principally *GoodFellas* – than the 'classical' early 1930s cycle. *Kill Bill, Vol. 1* (2003) relies almost exclusively on serial allusions to not only 1960s and 1970s Hong Kong kung-fu films and Italian revenge Westerns of the late 1960s, but also to such New Hollywood pastiches as Brian dePalma's *Dressed to Kill* (1980), itself a fetishistically exact reworking of Hitchcockian tropes and motifs. In this way, proliferating and intensifying generic referentiality does not necessarily lead to an expansion of historical awareness parallel to the historical turn in film scholarship. If anything, the frame of historical reference of genre films has become increasingly foreshortened, while the sheer intensity and density of generic allusion encloses genre films

in an increasingly hermetic circle of reference and counter-reference that can
– in extreme cases such as Tarantino – proceed largely without reference or
obvious relevance to the extra-generic world. This may pose a problem for
traditional genre theory which, as we have seen, has tended to attach
considerable importance to the ways in which film genres and genre films
interact with their social, political and cultural contexts.

From another perspective, however, the changing generic field of play
(and the changing rules of generic production and consumption) return us to
the point where this book began – the realisation that genre, and genres, are
inherently processual. As we have seen, a problem that theories of film genre
and accounts of individual genres have periodically encountered has been
their attempt to make genres seem both more internally integrated and more
consistent than they generally are. Even the most atypically integrated and
consistent genre, the Western, has under the pressure of recent critical
interrogation revealed itself as an interestingly fissiparous and multi-stranded
genre tradition. In that sense, the increasingly transgeneric tendency in
twenty-first-century Hollywood film may represent not the breakdown of
'classical' genre traditions, but the more visible enactment, in transformed
institutional contexts, of those 'post-classical' impulses that have always been
present in the system of genres. At the very least, such developments confirm
that we still have a number of questions to ask about what genres are, what
they do, why and for whom, and that genre in turn still has a great deal to
teach us about how movies work.

NOTES

1. Respectively: *Seed of Chucky*, *The Grudge* and *Saw*; *Bridget Jones: The Edge of Reason*,
   Shall We Dance? and *Alfie*; *The Incredibles* and *The Polar Express*; *After the Sunset*; *Ray*
   (source: *Variety* Weekend Box Office, 12–14 November 2004).
2. For example, all of John Wayne's Monogram Westerns are now available on DVD in
   the UK and USA.

Bibliography

Abel, R. (1998) '"Our Country"/Whose Country?: The "Americanisation" Project of Early Westerns', in Buscombe and Pearson (eds) (1998), 77–95.

Adair, G. (1989) *Hollywood's Vietnam, from* The Green Berets *to* Full Metal Jacket. London: Heinemann.

Adorno, T. W. and Horkheimer, M. (1944) (1972) *Dialectic of Enlightenment*, trans. J. W. Seabury. New York: Continuum.

Aleiss, A. (1995) 'Native Americans: The Surprising Silents', *Journal of Cinéaste*, 21.3: 34–6.

Allen, M. (1999) *Family Secrets: The Feature Films of D. W. Griffith*. London: BFI.

Alloway, L. (1971) *Violent America: The Movies 1946–1964*. New York: Museum of Modern Art.

Altman, R. (ed.) (1981) *Genre: The Musical*. London: BFI.

Altman, R. [1984] (1995) 'A Semantic/Syntactic Approach to Film Genre', in Grant, B. K. (ed.) (1995), 26–40.

Altman, R. (1987) *The American Film Musical*. Bloomington, IN: Indiana University Press.

Altman. R. [1989] (1992) 'Dickens, Griffith and Film Theory Today', in Gaines, J. (ed.) (1992) *Classical Hollywood Narrative: The Paradigm Years*. Durham, NC: Duke University Press, pp. 45–162.

Altman, R. (1996) 'Cinema and Genre', in Nowell-Smith, G. (ed.) (1996) *The Oxford History of World Cinema*. Oxford: Oxford University Press, pp. 276–85.

Altman, R. (1998) 'Reusable Packaging: Generic Products and the Recycling Process', in Browne (ed.) (1998), 1–41.

Altman, R. (1999) *Film/Genre*. London: BFI.

Anderson, J. L. and Richie, D. (1983) *The Japanese Film: Art and Industry*, 2nd edn. Princeton, NJ: Princeton University Press.

Andersen, T. (1985) 'Red Hollywood', in Ferguson, S. and Groseclose, B. (eds) *Literature and the Visual Arts*. Columbus, OH: Ohio State University Press, pp. 183–9.

Aristotle (1911) *The Poetics*, trans. D. S. Margoliouth. London: Hodder & Stoughton.

Arroyo, J. (ed.) (2000) *Action/Spectacle Cinema*. London: BFI.

Auster, A. (2002) '*Saving Private Ryan* and American Triumphalism', *Journal of Popular Film and Television*, 38.2: 98–104.

Auster, A. and Quart, L. (1988) *How the War Was Remembered: Hollywood and Vietnam*. New York: Praeger.

Austin, G. (1996) *Contemporary French Cinema: An Introduction*. Manchester: Manchester University Press.

Avisar, I. (1988) *Filming the Holocaust: Cinema's Images of the Unspeakable*. Bloomington, IN: Indiana University Press.

Bach, S. (1985) *Final Cut: Dreams and Disaster in the Making of* Heaven's Gate. New York: William Morrow.

Badsey, S. (2002) 'The Depiction of War Reporters in Hollywood Feature Films from the Vietnam War to the Present', *Film History*, 14.3–4: 243–60.

Balio, T. (1993) *Grand Design: Hollywood as a Modern Business Enterprise*. Berkeley, CA: University of California Press.

Bart, P. (1999) *Who Killed Hollywood? ... and Put the Tarnish on Tinseltown*. Los Angeles: Renaissance Books.

Barthes, R. (1957) *Mythologies*. Paris: Editions de Seuil.

Basinger, J. (1986) *The Second World War Combat Film: Anatomy of a Genre*. New York: Columbia University Press.

Bauman, Z. (1989) *Modernity and the Holocaust*. Cambridge: Polity.

Bazin, A. (1956) (1971) 'The Evolution of the Western', in *What Is Cinema?*, Vol. 2. Berkeley, CA: University of California Press, pp. 149–58.

Belton, J. [1972] (1991) 'Souls Made Great by Love and Adversity: Frank Borzage', in Landy, M. (ed.) (1991b), 371–9.

Belton, J. (1992) *Widescreen Cinema*. Cambridge, MA: Harvard University Press.

Benjamin, W. [1936] (1970) 'The Work of Art in the Age of Mechanical Reproduction', in Zohn, H. (trans. and ed.) (1970) *Illuminations*. London: Jonathan Cape.

Benshoff, H. M. (1997) *Monsters in the Closet: Homosexuality and the Horror Film*. Manchester: Manchester University Press.

Bergfelder, T. (2000) 'Between Nostalgia and Amnesia: Musical Genres in the 1950s German Cinema', in Marshall and Stilwell (eds) (2000), 80–8.

Berliner, T. (2001) 'The Genre Film as Booby Trap: 1970s Genre Bending and *The French Connection*', *Cinema Journal*, 40.3: 25–46.

Berry, C. (2003) '"What's Big About the Big Film?" "De-Westernising" the Blockbuster in Korea and China', in Stringer (ed.) (2003), 217–29.

Bertens, H. (1995) *The Idea of the Postmodern*. London: Routledge.

Binford, M. R. (1987) 'The Two Cinemas of India', in Downing, J. D. H. (ed.), *Film and Politics in the Third World*. New York: Autonomedia, pp. 145–66.

Biskind, P. (1983) *Seeing Is Believing: or, How Hollywood Taught Us to Stop Worrying and Love the Fifties*. New York: Pantheon.

Biskind, P. (1998) *Easy Riders, Raging Bulls: How the Sex'n'Drugs'n'Rock'n'Roll Generation Changed Hollywood*. London: Bloomsbury.

Bodnar, J. (2001) '*Saving Private Ryan* and Postwar Memory in America', *American Historical Review*, 106.3: 805–17.

Borde, R. and Chaumeton, E. [1955] (1983) *Panorama du Film Noir Américain*. Paris: Éditions de Minuit.

Bordwell, D. (2002) 'Intensified Continuity: Visual Style in Contemporary American Film', *Film Quarterly*, 55.2: 16–23.

Bordwell, D., Staiger, J. and Thompson, K. (1985) *The Classical Hollywood Cinema: Film Style and Mode of Production to 1960*. London: Routledge.

Bottomore, S. (2002) 'Introduction: War and Militarism: Dead White Males', *Film History*, 14.3–4: 239–42.

Bowser, E. (1990) *The Transformation of Cinema, 1907–1915*. New York: Scribner.

Brewster, B. and Jacobs, L. (1997) *Theatre to Cinema: Stage Pictorialism and the Early Feature Film*. Oxford: Oxford University Press.

Britton, A. (1986) 'Blissing Out: The Politics of Reaganite Entertainment', *Movie*, 31.2: 1–42.

Brodnax, M. (2001) 'Man a Machine: The Shift from Soul to Identity in Lang's *Metropolis* and Ruttman's *Berlin*', in Calhoun, K. S. (ed.) (2001) *Peripheral Visions: The Hidden Stages of Weimar Cinema*. Detroit, MI: Wayne State University Press, pp. 73–93.

Brooks, P. (1976) *The Melodramatic Imagination: Balzac, Henry James, Melodrama, and the Mode of Excess*. New Haven, CT: Yale University Press.

Brottman, M. (1997) *Offensive Films: Towards an Anthropology of Cinéma Vomitif.* Westport, CT: Greenwood Press.

Browne, N. (ed.) (1998) *Refiguring American Film Genres: Theory and History*. Berkeley, CA: University of California Press.

Browne, N. (2000) *Francis Ford Coppola's* The Godfather *Trilogy*. Cambridge: Cambridge University Press.

Bruno, G. (1987) 'Ramble City: Postmodernism and *Blade Runner*', *October*, 41: 61–74.

Bruzzi, S. (1995) 'Style and the Hood: Gangsters, American and French Style', *Sight & Sound*, 5 (November): 26–7.

Bruzzi, S. (1997) *Undressing Cinema: Clothing and Identity in the Movies*. London: Routledge.

Bruzzi, S. (2000) *New Documentary: A Critical Introduction*. London: Routledge.

Bukatman, S. (1993) *Terminal Identity: The Virtual Subject in Postmodern Science Fiction*. Durham, NC: Duke University Press.

Bukatman, S. (1997) 'The Syncopated City: New York in Musical Film (1929–1961)', *Spectator*, 18.1: 8–23.

Burton, A. (2002) 'Death or Glory? The Great War in British Film', in Monk, C. and Sargeant, A. (ed.) (2002) *British Historical Cinema*. London: Routledge.

Buscombe, E. (1970) (1995) 'The Idea of Genre in the American Cinema', in Grant, B. K. (ed.) (1995), 11–25.

Buscombe, E. (ed.) (1988) *The BFI Companion to the Western*. London: BFI.

Buscombe, E. (1996) 'Inventing Monument Valley: Nineteenth-Century Landscape Photography and the Western Film', in Petro, P. (ed.) (1996) *Fugitive Images: From Photography to Video*. Bloomington, IN: Indiana University Press, pp. 87–108.

Buscombe, E. and Pearson, R. (eds) (1998) *Back in the Saddle Again: New Essays on the Western*. London: BFI.

Byars, J. (1991) *All That Hollywood Allows: Re-Reading Gender in 1950s Melodrama*. London: Routledge.

Cameron, I. (ed.) (1992) *The Movie Book of Film Noir*. London: Studio Vista.

Cameron, I. and Pye, D. (eds) (1996) *The Movie Book of the Western*. London: Studio Vista.

Camon, A. (2000) '*The Godfather* and the Mythology of the Mafia', in Browne, N. (ed.) (2000), 57–75.

Carlson, M. (1984) *Theories of the Theatre*. Ithaca, NY: Cornell University Press.

Carroll, N. (1982) 'The Future of an Allusion: Hollywood in the Seventies (and Beyond)', *October*, 20: 51–81.

Carroll, N. (1990) *The Philosophy of Horror, or Paradoxes of the Heart*. New York: Routledge.

Case, S.-E. (1991) 'Tracking the vampire', *Differences*, 3.2: 1–20.

Case, S.-E. (1989) 'Towards a Butch-Femme Aesthetic', in Hart, L. (ed.) *Making a Spectacle: Feminist Essays on Contemporary Women's Theater*. Ann Arbor: University of Michigan Press.

Casty, A. (1972) (1991) 'The Films of D. W. Griffith: A Style for the Times', in Landy, M. (ed.) (1991b), 362–70.

Caughie, J. (ed.) (1981) *Theories of Authorship*. London: BFI.

Cawelti, J. (1979) (1995) '*Chinatown* and Generic Transformation in Recent American Films', in Grant, B. K. (ed.) (1995), 227–46.

Chambers, J. W. (1994) '*All Quiet on the Western Front* (1930): The Antiwar Film and the Image of the First World War', *Historical Journal of Film, Radio and Television*, 14.4: 377–412.

Chambers, J. W., II and Culbert, D. (eds) (1996) *Second World War: Film and History*. Oxford: Oxford University Press.

Chapman, J. (1998) *The British at War: Cinema, State and Propaganda, 1939–1945*. London: I. B. Tauris.

Chapman, J. (2000) 'Cinema, Propaganda and National Identity: British Film and the Second World War', in Ashby, J. and Higson, A. (eds), *British Cinema, Past and Present*. London: Routledge, pp. 193–206.

Charney, L. and Schwartz, V. (eds) (1995) *Cinema and the Invention of Everyday Life*. Berkeley, CA: University of California Press.

Chibnall, S. (2001) 'Travels in Ladland: The British Gangster Film Cycle, 1998–2001', in Murphy, R. (ed.) (2001) *The British Cinema Book*, 2nd edn. London: BFI, pp. 281–91.

Chibnall, S. and Petley, J. (eds) (2002) *British Horror Cinema*. London: Routledge.

Clarens, C. (1968) *Horror Movies: An Illustrated History*. London: Secker & Warburg.

Clover, C. (1992) *Men, Women and Chainsaws: Gender in the Modern Horror Film*. London: BFI.

Coates, P. (1991) *The Gorgon's Gaze: German Cinema, Expressionism, and the Image of Horror*. Cambridge: Cambridge University Press.

Cohan, S. (1993) (2002) '"Feminizing" the Song-and-Dance Man: Fred Astaire and the Spectacle of Masculinity in the Hollywood Musical', in Cohan, S. (ed.) (2002), 87–101.

Cohan, S. (2000) 'Case Study: Interpreting *Singin' in the Rain*', in Gledhill, C. and Williams, L. (eds) *Reinventing Film Studies*. London: Edward Arnold, pp. 53–75.

Cohan, S. (ed.) (2002) *Hollywood Musicals: The Film Reader*. London: Routledge.

Cohan, S. and Hark, I. R. (eds) (1997) *The Road Movie Book*. London: Routledge.

Collins, J. M. (1988) 'The Musical', in Gehring, W. D. (ed.) (1988), 269–84.

Collins, J. (1993) 'Genericity in the Nineties: Eclectic Irony and the New Sincerity', in Collins, J., Radner, H. and Collins, A. P. (eds) (1993) *Film Theory Goes to the Movies*. New York: Routledge.

Cook, P. (1978) 'Duplicity in *Mildred Pierce*', in Kaplan, E. A. (ed.) (1978), *Women in Film Noir*. London: BFI.

Copjec, J. (ed.) (1993) *Shades of Noir*. London: Verso.

Corkin, S. (2000) 'Cowboys and Free Markets: Post-Second World War Westerns and U.S. Hegemony', *Cinema Journal*, 39.3: 66–91.

Corn, J. (1986) *Imagining Tomorrow: History, Technology and the American Future*. Cambridge, MA: MIT Press.

Coyne, M. (1997) *The Crowded Prairie: American National Identity in the Hollywood Western*, London: I. B. Tauris.

Creeber, G. (2002) '"TV Ruined the Movies": Television, Tarantino, and the Intimate World of *The Sopranos*', in Lavery, D. (ed.) (2002) *This Thing of Ours: Investigating The Sopranos*. London: Wallflower, pp. 124–34.

Creed, B. (1986) 'Horror and the Monstrous-Feminine: An Imaginary Abjection', *Screen*, 27.1: 44–70.

Creed, B. (1993) *The Monstrous Feminine: Film, Feminism and Psychoanalysis*. London: Routledge.

Crowdus, G. (ed.) (1994) *The Political Companion to American Film*. Chicago: Lakeview Press.

Cull, N. (2002) 'Great Escapes: "Englishness" and the Prisoner of War Genre', *Film History*, 14.3–4: 282–95.

Cuomo, P. N. (1996) 'Dance, Flexibility and the Renewal of Genre in *Singin' in the Rain*', *Cinema Journal*, 36.1: 39–54.

Dallek, R. (1998) *Flawed Giant: Lyndon Johnson and his Times, 1961–1973*. New York: Oxford University Press.

Davis, M. (1991) *City of Quartz*. London: Verso.

Delameter, J. (1978) *Dance in the Hollywood Musical*. Ann Arbor, MI: UMI Research Press.

Derrida, J. (1976) *Of Grammatology*, trans. G. C. Spivak. Baltimore, MD: Johns Hopkins University Press.

Derrida, J. (1992) 'The Law of Genre', in Attridge, D. (ed.) (1992) *Acts of Literature*. New York: Routledge, pp. 221–52.

Dibbets, K. and Hogenkamp, B. (ed.) (1995) *Film and the First World War*. Amsterdam: Amsterdam University Press.

Dick, B. F. (1985) *The Star-Spangled Screen: The American Second World War Film*. Lexington, KY: University of Kentucky Press.

Dimendberg, E. (1997) 'From Berlin to Bunker Hill: Urban Space, Late Modernity, and Film Noir in Fritz Lang's and Joseph Losey's *M*', *Wide Angle*, 19.4: 62–93.

Dimendberg, E. (2004) *Film Noir and the Spaces of Modernity*. Cambridge, MA: Harvard University Press.

Dixon, W. W. (ed.) (2000) *Film Genre 2000: New Critical Essays*. Albany, NY: State University of New York Press.

Doane, M. A. (1987) *The Desire to Desire: The Woman's Film of the 1940s*. Bloomington, IN: Indiana University Press.

Dodds, S. (2001) *Dance on Screen: Genres and Media from Hollywood to Experimental Art*. London: Palgrave.

Doherty, T. (1999) *Projections of War: Hollywood, American Culture, and World War II*. New York: Columbia University Press.

Dukore, B. F. (1999) *Sam Peckinpah's Feature Films*. Urbana, IL: University of Illinois Press.

Dyer, R. (1977) (1981) 'Entertainment and Utopia', in Altman, R. (ed.) (1981), 175–81.

Dyer, R. (1986) (2002) 'Judy Garland and Camp', in Cohan, S. (ed.) (2002), 107–14.

Dyer, R. (2000) 'The Colour of Entertainment', in Marshall and Stilwell (eds) (2000), 23–30.

Eberwein, R. (1998) 'The Erotic Thriller', *Post Script*, 17.3: 25–33.

Ecksteins, M. (1989) *Rites of Spring: The Great War and the Birth of the Modern Age*. New York: Houghton Mifflin.

Eisele, J. (2002) 'The Wild East: Deconstructing the Language of Genre in the Hollywood Eastern', *Cinema Journal*, 41.4: 68–94.

Eisenstein, S. (1944) 'Dickens, Griffith and Film Today', in Eisenstein, S. (1949) *Film Form*. London: Dennis Dobson, pp. 195–234.

Eleftheriotis, D. (2004) 'Spaghetti Western, Genre Criticism and National Cinema: Re-Defining the Frame of Reference', in Tasker, Y. (ed.) (2004), 309–27.

Eley, G. (2001) 'Finding the People's War: Film, British Collective Memory, and World War II', *American Historical Review*, 106.3: 818–38.

Elsaesser, T. (1972) (1991) 'Tales of Sound and Fury: Observations on the Family Melodrama', in Landy, M. (ed.) (1991b), 68–91.

Engelhardt, T. (1995) *The End of Victory Culture: Cold War America and the Disillusion of a Generation*. New York: Basic Books.

Fassbinder, R. W. (1972) (1992) 'Imitation of Life: On the Films of Douglas Sirk', trans. K. Winston, in Töteberg, M. and Lensing, L. (eds) (1992) *Rainer Werner Fassbinder: The Anarchy of the Imagination*. Baltimore, MD: Johns Hopkins University Press, pp. 77–89.

Feuer, J. (1977) (1981) 'The Self-Reflective Musical and the Myth of Entertainment', in Altman (ed.) (1981), 159–74.

Feuer, J. (1992) *The Hollywood Musical*, 2nd edn. London: BFI.

Fischer, L. (1976) (1981) 'The Image of Woman as Image: The Optical Politics of *Dames*', in Altman (ed.) (1981), 70–84.

Flinn, T. (1973) '*Out of the Past*', *The Velvet Light Trap*, 10: 38–46.

Fokkema, D. (1996) 'Comparative Literature and the Problem of Canon Formation', *Canadian Review of Comparative Literature / Revue Canadienne de Littérature Comparée*, 23.1: 51–66.

Foucault, M. (1970) *The Order of Things: An Archaeology of the Human Sciences*. New York: Random House.

Francke, L. (1994) *Script Girls: Women Screenwriters in Hollywood*. London: BFI.

Frayling, C. (1997) *Spaghetti Westerns: Cowboys and Europeans from Karl May to Sergio Leone*, 2nd edn. London: I. B. Tauris.

French, P. (1973) *Westerns*. London: Secker & Warburg.

Frieberg, F. (1996) '*China Nights*: The Sustaining Romance of Japan at War', in Chambers and Culbert (eds) (1996), 31–46.

Fuery, P. and Mansfield, N. (1997) *Cultural Studies and the New Humanities: Concepts and Controversies*. Oxford: Oxford University Press.

Fussell, P. (1989) *Wartime: Understanding and Behaviour in the Second World War*. New York: Oxford University Press.

Gabbard, K. (2003) 'Saving Private Ryan Too Late', in Lewis, J. (ed.) (2003) *The End of Cinema As We Know It?* London: Pluto, pp. 131–8.

Gallafent, E. (1992) 'Moving Targets and Black Widows: *Film Noir* in Modern Hollywood', in Cameron (ed.) (1992), 267–85.

Gallafent, E. (2000) *Astaire and Rogers*. London: Studio Vista.

Gallagher, T. (1986) (1995) 'Shoot-Out at the Genre Corral: Problems in the "Evolution" of the Western', in Grant (ed.) (1995), 202–16.

Gehring, W. D. (ed.) (1988) *A Handbook of American Film Genres*. New York: Greenwood Press.

Geraghty, C. (2003) *British Cinema in the 1950s: Gender, Genre, and the 'New Look'*. London: Routledge.

Gibson, P. C. (ed.) (1993) *Dirty Looks: Women, Pornography, Power*. London: BFI.

Gifford, D. (1973) *A Pictorial History of Horror Movies*. London: Hamlyn.

Gillespie, D. (2003) *Russian Cinema*. London: Longman.

Gledhill, C. (1987) 'The Melodramatic Field: An Investigation', in Gledhill, C. (ed.) (1987) *Home Is Where the Heart Is: Studies in Melodrama and the Woman's Film*. London: BFI.

Gledhill, C. (1994) 'Introduction', in Cook, J., Gledhill, C. and Bratton, J. (eds) (1994) *Melodrama: Stage, Picture, Screen*. London: BFI.

Gledhill, C. (2000) 'Rethinking Genre', in Gledhill, C. and Williams, L. (eds) (2000) *Reinventing Film Studies*. London: Arnold, pp. 221–43.

Godden, R. (1997) 'Maximizing the Noodles: Class, Memory, and Capital in Sergio Leone's *Once Upon a Time in America*', *Journal of American Studies*, 31.3: 361–84.

Gomery, D. (2003) 'The Hollywood Blockbuster: Industrial Analysis and Practice', in Stringer, J. (ed.) (2003), 72–83.

Goodwin, A. (1993) *Dancing in the Distraction Factory: Music Television and Popular Culture*. London: Routledge.

Gorak, J. (1991) *The Making of the Modern Canon: Genesis and Crisis of a Literary Idea*. London: Athlone.

Grant, B. K. (ed.) (1995) *Film Genre Reader II*. Austin, TX: University of Texas Press.

Grant, B. K. (1996) *The Dread of Difference: Gender and the Horror Film*. Austin, TX: University of Texas Press.

Grant, B. K. (1998) 'Rich and Strange: The Yuppie Horror Film', in Neale, S. and Smith, M. (eds) (1998) *Contemporary Hollywood Cinema*. London: Routledge, pp. 280–93.

Greene, E. (1998) Planet of the Apes *as American Myth: Race, Politics, and Popular Culture*. Hanover, NH: Wesleyan University Press.

Grieveson, L. (1997) 'Policing the Cinema: Traffic in Souls at Ellis Island, 1913', *Screen*, 38.2: 139–71.

Grieveson, L. (2005 forthcoming) 'Gangsters and Governance in the Silent Era', in Grieveson, L. et al. (eds) (2005 forthcoming) *Mob Culture: Hidden Histories of American Gangster Film*. Oxford: Berg.

Griffin, S. (2002) 'The Gang's All Here: Generic versus Racial Integration in the 1940s Musical', *Cinema Journal*, 42.1: 21–45.

Griffiths, A. (1996) 'Science and Spectacle: Native American Representation in Early Cinema', in Bird, S. E. (ed.) (1996) *Dressing in Feathers: The Construction of the Indian in American Popular Culture*. Boulder, CO: Westview Press.

Griffiths, A. (2002) 'Playing at Being Indian: Spectatorship and the Early Western', *Journal of Popular Film and Television*, 29.3: 100–11.

Griffiths, T. (1975) *Comedians*. London: Faber & Faber.

Grist, L. (1992) 'Out of the Past', in Cameron, I. (ed.) (1992), 203–12.

Grist, L. (2000) *The Films of Martin Scorsese, 1963–1977: Authorship and Context*. Basingstoke: Macmillan.

Gross, L. [1995] (2000) 'Big and Loud', in Arroyo, J. (ed.) (2000), 3–9.

Grossman, J. R. (1994) *The Frontier in American History*. Berkeley, CA: University of California Press.

Gunning, T. (1990) 'The Cinema of Attractions: Early Film, Its Spectator, and the Avant-Garde', in Elsaesser, T. (ed.) *Early Cinema: Space, Frame, Narrative*. London: BFI.

Gunning, T. (1995) 'An Aesthetic of Astonishment: Early Film and the (In)Credulous Spectator', in Williams, L. (ed.) *Viewing Positions*. New Brunswick, NJ: Rutgers University Press.

Gunning, T. (1997) 'From the Kaleidoscope to the X-Ray: Urban Spectatorship, Poe, Benjamin, and *Traffic in Souls* (1913)', *Wide Angle*, 19.4: 25–61.

Halberstam, J. (1995) *Skin Shows: Gothic Horror and the Technology of Monsters*. Durham, NC: Duke University Press.

Hall, S. (2002) 'Tall Revenue Features: The Genealogy of the Modern Blockbuster', in Neale, S. (ed.) (2002b), 11–26.

Halliday, J. (ed.) (1971) *Sirk on Sirk: Interviews with Jon Halliday*. London: Secker & Warburg.

Hand, R. J. and Wilson, M. (2002) *Grand-Guignol: The French Theatre of Horror*. Exeter: University of Exeter Press.

Hansen, M. (1991) *Babel and Babylon: Spectatorship in American Silent Film*. Cambridge, MA: Harvard University Press.

Hardy, P. (1985) *Horror: The Aurum Film Encyclopedia*. London: Aurum.

Hardy, P. (ed.) (1991) *The Western: The Aurum Film Encyclopedia*. London: Aurum Press.

Hardy, P. (ed.) (1998) *Gangsters: The Aurum Film Encyclopedia*. London: Aurum Press.

Harper, S. and Porter, V. (2003) *British Cinema of the 1950s: The Decline of Deference*. Oxford: Oxford University Press.

Harris, O. (2003) '*Film Noir* Fascination: Outside History, But Historically So', *Cinema Journal*, 43.1: 3–24.

Harris, T. (1999) *Hannibal*. London: Hamish Hamilton.

Hasian, M. (2001) 'Nostalgic Longings, Memories of the "Good War", and Cinematic Representations in *Saving Private Ryan*', *Critical Studies in Media Communication*, 18.3: 338–58.

Hawkins, C. (2000) *Cutting Edge: Art-Horror and the Horrific Avant-Garde*. Minneapolis, MN: University of Minnesota Press.

Heffernan, K. (2002) 'Inner City Exhibition and the Horror Film: Distributing *Night of the Living Dead* (1968)', *Cinema Journal*, 41.3: 59–77.

Heffernan, K. (2004) *Ghouls, Gimmicks, and Gold: Horror Films and the American Movie Business, 1953–1968*. Durham, NC: Duke University Press.

Hennelly, M. M. (1980) 'American Nightmare: The Underworld in Film', *Journal of Popular Film*, 6.3: 240–61.

Herzogenrath, B. (2002) 'Join the United Mutations: Tod Browning's *Freaks*', *Post Script*, 21.3: 8–19.

Hills, M. (2005 forthcoming) 'Ringing the Changes: Cult Distinctions and Cultural Differences in US Fans' Readings of Japanese Horror Cinema', in McRoy, J. (ed.) (2005 forthcoming).

Hoberman, J. and Risenbaum, J. (1983) *Midnight Movies*. New York: Da Capo Press.

Hodgkins, J. (2002) 'In the Wake of Desert Storm: A Consideration of Modern Second World War Films', *Journal of Popular Film and Television*, 30.2: 74–84.

Hopewell, J. (1986) *Out of the Past: Spanish Cinema After Franco*. London: BFI.

Hunter, I. Q. (ed.) (1999) *British Science Fiction Cinema*. London: Routledge.

Hurd, G. (ed.) (1984) *National Fictions: Second World War in British Film and Television*. London: BFI.

Hurley, K. (1995) 'Reading Like an Alien: Posthuman Identity in Ridley Scott's *Alien* and David Cronenberg's *Rabid*', in Halberstam, J. and Livingston, I. (eds) *Posthuman Bodies*. Bloomington, IN: Indiana University Press, pp. 203–24.

Hutchings, P. (1993) *Hammer and Beyond: The British Horror Film*. Manchester: Manchester University Press.

Huyssen, A. (1986) 'The Vamp and the Machine: Technology and Sexuality in Fritz Lang's *Metropolis*', in Huyssen, A. (1996) *After the Great Divide: Modernism, Mass Culture, Postmodernism*. Bloomington, IN: Indiana University Press.

Insdorf, A. (2002) *Indelible Shadows: Film and the Holocaust*, 3rd edn. Cambridge: Cambridge University Press.

Isenberg, M. T. (1981) *War on Film: The American Cinema and First World War, 1914–1941*. London: Associated University Presses.

James, E. (1994) *Science Fiction in the 20th Century*. Oxford: Oxford University Press.

Jameson, F. (1991) *Postmodernism; or, the Cultural Logic of Late Capitalism*. London: Verso.

Jancovich, M. (1992) 'Modernity and Subjectivity in *The Terminator*: The Machine as Monster in Contemporary American Culture', *The Velvet Light Trap*, 30: 3–17.

Jancovich, M. (1996) *Rational Fears: American Horror in the 1950s*. Manchester: Manchester University Press.

Jancovich, M. [2001] (2002) 'Genre and the Audience: Genre Classifications and Cultural Distinctions in *The Silence of the Lambs*', in Jancovich, M. (ed.) (2002), 151–62.

Jancovich, M. (ed.) (2002) *Horror: The Film Reader*. London: Routledge.

Jay, G. S. (2000) 'White Man's Book No Good: D. W. Griffith and the American Indian', *Cinema Journal*, 39.4: 3–25.

Jeffords, S. (1988) 'Masculinity as Excess in Vietnam Films: The Father/Son Dynamic of American Culture', *Genre*, 21: 487–515.

Jeffords, S. (1989) *The Remasculinization of America: Gender and the Vietnam War*. Bloomington, IN: Indiana University Press.

Jeffords, S. (1994) *Hard Bodies: Hollywood Masculinity in the Reagan Era*. New Brunswick, NJ: Rutgers University Press.

Jenks, C. (1992) 'The Other Face of Death: Barbara Steele and *La Maschera del Demonio*', in Dyer, R., and Vincendeau, G. (eds) *Popular European Cinema*. London: Routledge, 149–62.

Jordan, B. and Morgan-Tamosounas, R. (1998) *Contemporary Spanish Cinema*. Manchester: Manchester University Press.

Kael, P. (1965) *I Lost It at The Movies*. Boston: Little Brown.

Kaminsky, S. (1985) *American Film Genres*, 2nd edn. Chicago: Nelson-Hall.

Kane, K. (1988) 'The Second World War Combat Film', in Gehring, W. D. (ed.) (1988), 85–102.

Kaplan, E. A. (1986) *Rocking Around the Clock: Music Television, Postmodernism, and Consumer Culture*. London: Routledge.

Kaplan, E. A. (ed.) (1999) *Women in Film Noir*, 2nd edn. London: BFI.

Kapsis, R. (1992) *Hitchcock: The Making of a Reputation*. Chicago: University of Chicago Press.

Keller, A. (2001) 'Generic Subversion as Counterhistory: Mario van Peebles's *Posse*', in Walker, J. (ed.) (2001b), 27–46.

Kelly, A. (1997) *Cinema and the Great War*. London: Routledge.

Kendrick, W. (1991) *The Thrill of Fear: 250 Years of Scary Entertainment*. New York: Grove.

Kenez, P. (2001) *Cinema and Soviet Society: From the Revolution to the Death of Stalin*. London: I. B. Tauris.

Kern, S. (1983) *The Culture of Time and Space*. Cambridge, MA: Harvard University Press.

Kilborn, R. and Izod, J. (1997) *An Introduction to Television Documentary: Confronting Reality*. Manchester: Manchester University Press.

King, G. (2000a) *Spectacular Narratives: Hollywood in the Age of the Blockbuster*. London: I. B. Tauris.

King, G. (2000b) 'Ride-Films and Film as Rides in the Contemporary Hollywood Cinema of Attractions', *CineAction*, 51: 2–9.

King, G. (2002) *New Hollywood Cinema: An Introduction*. London: I. B. Tauris.

King, G. (2003) 'Spectacle, Narrative, and the Spectacular Hollywood Blockbuster', in Stringer, J. (ed.) (2003), 114–27.

King, G. and Krzywinska, T. (2001) *Science Fiction Cinema: From Outerspace to Cyberspace*. London: Wallflower.

Kitses, J. (1969) *Horizons West*. London: Thames & Hudson.

Klein, M. (1994) 'Beyond the American Dream: Film and the Experience of Defeat', in Klein, M. (ed.) (1994), *An American Half Century: Postwar Culture and Politics in the U.S.A.* London: Pluto, pp. 206–31.

Kleinhans, C. (1978) (1991) 'Notes on Melodrama and the Family Under Capitalism', in Landy, M. (ed.) (1991b), 197–204.

Kleinhans, C. (1996) 'Teaching Sexual Images: Some Pragmatics', *Jump Cut* 40: 119–22.

Klinger, B. (1994a) '"Local" Genres: The Hollywood Adult Film in the 1950s', in Bratton, J., Cook, J. and Gledhill, C. (eds) (1994) *Melodrama: Stage Picture Screen*. London: BFI, pp. 134–46.

Klinger, B. (1994b) *Melodrama and Meaning: History, Culture and the Films of Douglas Sirk*. Bloomington, IN: Indiana University Press.

Koch, G. (1981) (1993) 'The Body's Shadow Realm', in Gibson, P. C. (ed.) (1993), 22–45.

Koepnick, L. P. (1995) 'Unsettling America: German Westerns and Modernity', *Modernism/Modernity*, 2.3: 1–22.

Koppes, C. R. and Black, G. D. (1987) *Hollywood Goes to War: How Politics, Profits and Propaganda Shaped Second World War Movies*. New York: Free Press.

Korte, B. (2001) 'The Grandfathers' War: Re-Imagining World War One in British Novels and Films of the 1990s', in Cartmell, D. et al. (eds) (2001) *Retrovisions: Reinventing the Past in Film and Fiction*. London: Pluto.

Kracauer, S. (1947) *From Caligari to Hitler: A Psychological Study of the German Film*. Princeton, NJ: Princeton University Press.

Krämer, P. (1998) 'Would You Take Your Child To See This Film? The Cultural and Social Work of the Family-Adventure Movie', in Neale, S. and Smith, M. (eds) (1998) *Contemporary Hollywood Cinema*. London: Routledge, pp. 294–311.

Krämer, P. (2004) '"It's Aimed at Kids – The Kid in Everybody": George Lucas, *Star Wars* and Children's Entertainment', in Tasker (ed.) (2004), 358–70.

Kress, G. and Threadgold, T. (1988) 'Towards a Social Theory of Genre', *Southern Review*, 21.1: 215–43.

Kristeva, J. (1982) *Powers of Horror: An Essay on Abjection*. New York: Columbia University Press.

Krutnik, F. (1991) *In a Lonely Street:* Film Noir, *Genre, Masculinity*. London: Routledge.

Kuhn, A. (1981) '*Desert Victory* and the People's War', *Screen*, 22.2: 156–73.

Kuhn, A. (ed.) (1990) *Alien Zone: Cultural Theory and Contemporary Science Fiction Cinema*. London: Verso.

Kuhn, A. (1999) *Alien Zone II: The Spaces of Science Fiction Cinema*. London: Verso.

Laderman, D. (2002) *Driving Visions: Exploring the Road Movie*. Austin, TX: University of Texas Press.

Landon, B. (1992) *The Aesthetics of Ambivalence: Rethinking Science Fiction Film in the Age of Electronic (re)Production*. Westport, CT: Greenwood Press.

Landy, M. (1991a) *British Genres: Cinema and Society, 1930–1960*. Princeton, NJ: Princeton University Press.

Landy, M. (ed.) (1991b) *Imitations of Life: A Reader on Film and Television Melodrama*. Detroit, MI: Wayne State University Press.

Landy, M. (2000a) *Italian Film*. Cambridge: Cambridge University Press.

Landy, M. (2000b) 'The Other Side of Paradise: British Cinema from an American Perspective', in Ashby, J. and Higson, A. (eds) (2000) *British Cinema, Past and Present*. London: Routledge.

Langford, B. (1999) '"You Cannot Look At This": Thresholds of Unrepresentability in Holocaust Film', *Journal of Holocaust Education*, 8.3: 23–40.

Langford, B. (2003) 'The Revisionist Western – Revised', *Film and History*, 33.2: 26–35.

Lavery, D. (2001) 'From Cinespace to Cyberspace: Zionists and Agents, Realists and Gamers in *The Matrix* and *eXistenZ*', *Journal of Popular Film and Television*, 28.4: 150–7.

Lawton, A. (1992) *Kinoglasnost: Soviet Cinema in Our Time*. Cambridge: Cambridge University Press.

Leab, D. J. (1995) 'An Ambiguous Isolationism: *The Fighting 69th* (1940)', in Rollins, P. C. and O'Connor, J. E. (eds), *Hollywood's First World War: Great Adventure or Lost Generation Nightmare?* Bowling Green, KY: Bowling Green University Press, pp. 181–98.

Lembcke, J. (1998) *The Spitting Image: Myth, Memory and the Legacy of Vietnam*. New York: New York University Press.

Levi, P. (1988) *The Drowned and the Saved*, trans. R. Rosenthal. New York: Simon & Schuster.

Lewis, J. (2003) 'Following the Money in America's Sunniest Company Town: Some Notes on the Political Economy of the Hollywood Blockbuster', in Stringer, J. (ed.) (2003), 61–71.

Leyda, J. (2002) 'Black-Audience Westerns and the Politics of Cultural Identification in the 1930s', *Cinema Journal*, 42.1: 46–70.

Loshitsky, Y. (ed.) (1997) *Spielberg's Holocaust: Critical Perspectives on* Schindler's List. Bloomington: Indiana University Press.

Lukow, G. and Ricci, S. (1984) 'The "Audience" Goes "Public": Inter-Textuality, Genre and the Responsibilities of Film Literacy', *On Film*, 12: 29–36.

Lusted, D. (2003) *The Western*. Harlow: Pearson Longman.

Maier, C. (1991) *The Unmasterable Past: History, Holocaust, and German National Identity*. Cambridge, MA: Harvard University Press.

Maltby, R. [1984] (1992) 'The Politics of the Maldjusted Text', in Cameron, I. (ed.) (1992), 39–48.

Maltby, R. (1995a) *Hollywood Cinema*. Oxford: Blackwell.

Maltby, R. (1995b) 'Tragic Heroes? Al Capone and the Spectacle of Criminality, 1947–1931', in Benson, J. et al. (1995), *Screening the Past: The Sixth Australian History and Film Conference*. Melbourne: Le Trobe University Press,

Manvell, R. (1974) *Film and the Second World War*. London: A. S. Barnes.

Marshall, B. and Stilwell, R. (ed.) (2000) *Musicals: Hollywood and Beyond*. Exeter: Intellect.

Mason, F. (2002) *American Gangster Cinema: From* Little Caesar *to* Pulp Fiction. London: Palgrave.

McArthur, C. (1972) *Underworld USA*. London: Secker & Warburg.

McBride, J. (1996) *Steven Spielberg: A Biography*. London: Faber.

McCarty, J. (1993) *Hollywood Gangland: The Movies' Love Affair with the Mob*. New York: St. Martin's Press.

McDonald, K. I. (1992) 'The *Yakuza* Film: An Introduction', in Nolletti, A., Jr and Desser, D. (eds) (1992) *Reframing Japanese Cinema: Authorship, Genre, History*. Bloomington, IN: Indiana University Press.

McIlroy, B. (1998) *Shooting to Kill: Filmmaking and the 'Troubles' in Northern Ireland*. Trowbridge: Flicks Books.

McRoy, J. (ed.) (2005 forthcoming) *Japanese Horror Cinema*. Edinburgh: Edinburgh University Press.

Medhurst, A. (1984) 'Fifties War Films', in Hurd (ed.) (1984), 35–48.

Mellen, J. (1994) 'The Western', in Crowdus (ed.) (1994), 469–75.

Mellencamp, P. (1990) 'The Sexual Economics of *Gold Diggers of 1933*', in Lehman, P. (ed.) (1990), *Close Viewings: An Anthology of New Film Criticism*. Tallahassee, FL: Florida State University Press.

Michelson, A. (1979) 'Dr Crase and Mr Clair', *October*, 11: 30–53.

Miller, M. (2000) 'Of Tunes and Toons: The Movie Musical in the 1990s', in Dixon, W. W. (ed.) (2000), 45–62.

Mitchell, E. (1976) 'Apes and Essences: Some Sources of Significance in the American Gangster Film', *Wide Angle*, 1.1: 22–9.

Mitchell, L. C. (1996) *Westerns: Making the Man in Fiction and Film*. Chicago: University of Chicago Press.

Modleski, T. (1988) 'The Terror of Pleasure: The Contemporary Horror Film and Postmodern Theory', in Modleski, T. (ed.) (1988), *Studies in Entertainment*. Bloomington, IN: Indiana University Press, pp. 155–66.

Mordden, E. (1982) *The Hollywood Musical*. Newton Abbot: David & Charles.

Mueller, J. (1984) 'Fred Astaire and the Integrated Musical', *Cinema Journal*, 24.1: 28–40.

Mulvey, L. (1975) 'Visual Pleasure and Narrative Cinema', in Mulvey, L. (1989) *Visual and Other Pleasures*. Basingstoke: Macmillan.

Munby, J. (1999) *Public Enemies, Public Heroes: Screening the Gangster* from Little Caesar *to* Touch of Evil. Chicago: University of Chicago Press.

Murphy, R. (1989) *Realism and Tinsel: Cinema and Society in Britain, 1939–1948*. London: Routledge.

Murphy, R. (2000) *British Cinema and the Second World War*. London: Continuum.

Murphy, R. and Chibnall, S. (eds) (1999) *British Crime Cinema*. London: Routledge.

Musser, C. (1990) *The Emergence of Cinema: The American Screen to 1907*. Berkeley, CA: University of California Press.

Nachbar, J. (2003) 'The Western: A Century on the Trail', *Journal of Popular Film and Television*, 30.4: 178–84.

Naremore, J. (1995–96) 'American Film Noir: The History of an Idea', *Film Quarterly*, 49: 12–28.

Naremore, J. (1998) *More Than Night: Film Noir in Its Contexts*. Berkeley, CA: University of California Press.

Neale, S. (1980) *Genre*. London: BFI.

Neale, S. (1990) '"You've Got to be Fucking Kidding!": Knowledge, Belief and Judgment in Science Fiction', in Kuhn, A. (ed.) (1990), 160–8.

Neale, S. (1991) 'Aspects of Ideology and Narrative in the American War Film', *Screen*, 32.1: 35–57.

Neale, S. (1993) 'Melo Talk: On the Meaning and Use of the Term "Melodrama" in the American Trade Press', *The Velvet Light Trap*, 32: 66–89.

Neale, S. (1999) 'Genre', in Cook, P. (ed.) (1999) *The Cinema Book*, 2nd edn. London: BFI.

Neale, S. (2000) *Genre and Hollywood*. London: Routledge.

Neale, S. (2002a) 'Westerns and Gangster Films Since the 1970s', in Neale, S. (ed.) (2002b), 27–47.

Neale, S. (ed.) (2002b) *Genre and Contemporary Hollywood*, London: BFI.

Neale, S. (2003) 'Hollywood Blockbusters: Historical Dimensions', in Stringer, J. (ed.) (2003), 47–60.

Neve, B. (1992) *Film and Politics in America: A Social Tradition*. London: Routledge.

Newitz, A. (1995) 'Magical Girls and Atomic Bomb Sperm: Japanese Animation in America', *Film Quarterly*, 49.1: 2–15.

Newman, K. (1999) *Millennium Movies: End of the World Cinema*. London: Titan Books.

Nichols, B. (1994) *Blurred Boundaries: Questions of Meaning in Contemporary Culture*. Bloomington, IN: Indiana University Press.

Nochimson, M. P. (2003–4) 'Waddaya Looking at? Re-Reading the Gangster Genre Through *The Sopranos*', *Film Quarterly*, 56.2: 2–13.

Nowell-Smith, G. (1977) (1991) 'Minnelli and Melodrama', in Landy, M. (ed.) (1991b), 268–74.

Oliver, K. and Trigo, B. (2003) *Noir Anxiety*. Minneapolis, MN: University of Minnesota Press.

Paris, M. (1997) 'Democracy Goes to War: *Air Force*', *Film and History*, 27.1–4: 48–52.

Parrish, M. E. (1992) *Anxious Decades: America In Prosperity and Depression, 1920–1941*. New York: W. W. Norton.

Paul, W. (1994) *Laughing Screaming: Modern Hollywood Horror and Comedy*. New York: Columbia University Press.

Pendakur, M. (2003) *Indian Popular Cinema: Industry, Ideology and Consciousness*. Creskill, NJ: Hampton Press.

Penley, C. (1997) *NASA/ Trek: Popular Science and Sex in America*. London: Verso.

Peterson, C. S. (1994) 'Speaking for the Past', in Milner, C. A., II, O'Connor, C. A. and Sandweiss, M. A. (eds) (1994) *The Oxford History of the American West*. New York: Oxford University Press, pp. 743–69.

Petro, P. (1993) *Joyless Streets: Women and Melodramatic Representation in Weimar Germany*. Princeton, NJ: Princeton University Press.

Pierson, M. (2002) *Special Effects: Still In Search of Wonder*. New York: Columbia University Press.

Pierson, M. (1999) 'CGI Effects in Hollywood Science fiction Cinema 1989–1995: The Wonder Years', *Screen*, 40.2: 158–76.

Place, J. A. (1978) 'Women in Film Noir', in Kaplan, E. A. (ed.) (1978), 35–67.

Poague, L. (2003) 'That Past, This Present: Historicizing John Ford, 1939', in Grant, B. K. (ed.) (2003) *John Ford's* Stagecoach. Cambridge: Cambridge University Press.

Polan, D. (1986) *Power and Paranoia: History, Narrative and the American Cinema 1940–1950*. New York: Columbia University Press.

Prince, S. (1998) *Savage Cinema: Sam Peckinpah and the Rise of Ultraviolent Movies*. London: Athlone.

Prince, S. (ed.) (1999) *Sam Peckinpah's* The Wild Bunch. Cambridge: Cambridge University Press.

Prince, S. (2000) *A New Pot of Gold: Hollywood Under the Electronic Rainbow, 1980–1989*. New York: Scribner.

Pronay, N. (1988) 'The British Post-Bellum Cinema', *Historical Journal of Film, Radio and Televison*, 8.1: 39–54.

Pye, D. (1975) (1995) 'The Western (Genre and Movies)', in Grant, B. K. (ed.) (1995), 187–202.

Pye, D. (1996) 'Introduction: Criticism and the Western', in Cameron and Pye (eds) (1996), 9–21.

Rabinovitz, L. (1998) *For the Love of Pleasure: Women, Movies and Culture in Turn-of-the-Century Chicago*. New Brunswick, NJ: Rutgers University Press.

Rabinowitz, P. (1982) 'Commodity Fetishism: Women in *Gold Diggers of 1933*', *Film Reader*, 5: 141–9.

Rabinowitz, P. (2003) *Black & White & Noir: America's Pulp Modernism*. New York: Columbia University Press.

Raeburn, J. (1988) 'The Gangster Film', in Gehring, W. D. (ed.) (1988), 47–63.

Rattigan, N. (1994) 'The Last Gasp of the Middle Class: British War Films of the 1950s', in Dixon, W. W. (ed.) (1992) *Re-Viewing British Cinema 1900–1992*. Albany, NY: State University of New York Press.

Ray, R. H. (1985) *A Certain Tendency of the Hollywood Cinema*. Princeton, NJ: Princeton University Press.

Reid, M. (1993) (1995) 'The Black Gangster Film', in Grant (ed.) (1995), 456–73.

Renov, M. (1993) 'Introduction', in Renov, M. (ed.) (1993) *Theorising Documentary*, London: Routledge.

Richards, J. (1997) *Films and British National Identity: From Dickens to Dad's Army*. Manchester: Manchester University Press.

Ricketts, R. (2000) *Special Effects*. London: Virgin.

Roberts, A. (2001) *Science Fiction*. London: Routledge.

Robertson, P. (1996) (2002) 'Feminist Camp in *Gold Diggers of 1933*', in Cohan, S. (ed.) (2002), 129–42.

Rodowick, D. N. (1982) (1991) 'Madness, Authority and Ideology in the Domestic Melodrama of the 1950s', in Landy, M. (ed.) (1991b), 237–47.

Rosow, E. (1978) *Born to Lose: The Gangster Film in America*. New York: Oxford University Press.

Rotha, P. (1936) *Documentary Film*. London: Faber.

Rubin, M. (1993) *Showstoppers: Busby Berkeley and the Tradition of Spectacle*. New York: Columbia University Press.

Rubin, R. (2002) 'Gangster Generation: Crime, Jews and the Problem of Assimilation', *Shofar*, 20.4: 1–17.

Rubinstein, L. (1994) 'War Films', in Crowdus, G. (ed.) (1994), 451–8.

Russell, D. J. (1998) 'Monster Roundup: Reintegrating the Horror Genre', in Browne, N. (ed.) (1998), 233–54.

Ruth, D. (1996) *Inventing the Public Enemy: The Gangster in American Culture, 1918–1934*. Chicago: University of Chicago Press.

Ryall, T. (1975) 'Teaching through Genre', *Screen Education*, 17: 27–33.

Ryan, M. and Kellner, D. (1988) *Camera Politica: The Politics and Ideology of Contemporary Hollywood Film*. Bloomington, IN: Indiana University Press.

Sacks, A. (1971) 'An Analysis of the Gangster Movies of the Early Thirties', *The Velvet Light Trap*, 1: 5–11.

Saunders, J. (2000) *The Western Genre: From Lordsburg to Big Whiskey*. London: Wallflower.

Schatz, T. (1981) *Hollywood Genres: Formulas, Filmmaking and the Studio System*. New York: Random House.

Schatz, T. (1983) *Old Hollywood, New Hollywood: Ritual, Art and Industry*. Ann Arbor, MI: UMI Research Press.

Schatz, T. (1993) 'The New Hollywood', in Collins, J., Radner, H. and Collins, A. P. (eds) (1993) *Film Theory Goes to the Movies*. London: Routledge, pp. 8–36.

Schatz, T. (1998) 'World War II and the Hollywood "War Film"', in Browne (ed.) (1998), 89–128.

Schneider, S. J. (ed.) (2003) *Fear Without Frontiers: Horror Cinema Across the Globe*. Guildford: FAB Press.

Schrader, P. (1972) (1995) 'Notes on Film Noir', in Grant, B. K. (ed.) (1995), 213–26.

Schwager, J. (1991) 'The Past Rewritten', *Film Comment*, 27 (January/February): 21–3.

Seydor, P. (1997) *Peckinpah: The Western Films: A Reconsideration*. Urbana, IL: University of Illinois Press.

Shadoian, J. (2003) *Dreams and Dead Ends: The American Gangster Film*, 2nd edn. New York: Oxford University Press.

Shain, R. E. (1976) *An Analysis of Motion Pictures about War Released by the American Film Industry 1939–1970*. New York: Arno Press.

Shindler, C. (1979) *Hollywood Goes to War: Films and American Society, 1939–1952*. London: Routledge.

Sickels, R. C. (2003) 'A Politically Correct Ethan Edwards: Clint Eastwood's *The Outlaw Josey Wales*', *Journal of Popular Film and Television*, 30.4: 220–7.

Silver, A. and Ursini, J. (eds) (1996) *Film Noir Reader*. New York: Limelight.

Simmon, S. (1993) *The Films of D. W. Griffith*. Cambridge: Cambridge University Press.

Simmon, S. (2003) *The Invention of the Western Film: A Cultural History of the Genre's First Half-Century*. Cambridge: Cambridge University Press.

Singer, B. (2001) *Melodrama and Modernity: Early Sensational Cinema and its Contexts*. New York: Columbia University Press.

Singer, A. and Lastinger, M. (1998) 'Themes and Sources of *Star Wars*: John Carter and Flash Gordon Enlist in the First Crusade', *Popular Culture Review*, 9.2: 65–77.

Skal, D. J. (1993) *The Monster Show: A Cultural History of Horror*. London: Plexus.

Sklar, R. (1992) *City Boys: Cagney, Bogart, Garfield*. Princeton, NJ: Princeton University Press.

Slotkin, R. (1998) *Gunfighter Nation: The Myth of the Frontier in Twentieth-Century America*. Norman, OK: University of Oklahoma Press.

Slotkin, R. (2001) 'Unit Pride: Ethnic Platoons and the Myths of American Nationality', *American Literary History*, 13.3: 469–98.

Smith, P. (1993) *Clint Eastwood: A Cultural Production*. London: UCL Press.

Sobchack, V. (1987a) *Screening Space: The American Science Fiction Film*, 2nd rev. edn. New Brunswick, NJ: Rutgers University Press.

Sobchack, V. (1987b) 'Child/Alien/Father: Patriarchal Crisis and Generic Exchange', *Camera Obscura*, 15: 7–34.

Sobchack, V. (1988) 'Science Fiction', in Gehring, W. D. (ed.) (1988), 228–42.

Sontag, S. (1966) 'The Imagination of Disaster', in *Against Interpretation and Other Essays*. New York: Farrar, Strauss & Giroux, pp. 209–25.

Sorlin, P. (1994) 'War and Cinema: Interpreting the Relationship', *Historical Journal of Film, Radio and Television*, 14.4: 357–66.

Spicer, A. (2002) *Film Noir*. Harlow: Pearson.

Springer, C. (1996) *Electronic Eros: Bodies and Desire in the Postindustrial Age*. London: Athlone.

Springhall, J. (1998) 'Censoring Hollywood: Youth, Moral Panic and Crime/Gangster Movies of the 1930s', *Journal of Popular Culture*, 32.3: 135–54.

Stables, K. (1999) 'The Postmodern Always Rings Twice: Constructing the Femme Fatale in 90s Cinema', in Kaplan (ed.) (1999), 164–82.

Staiger, J. (2001) 'Hybrid or Inbred: The Purity Hypothesis and Hollywood Genre History', *Film Criticism*, 22.1: 5–20.

Stam, R. (1992) *Reflexivity in Film and Literature: From* Don Quixote *to Jean-Luc Godard*. New York: Columbia University Press.

Stam, R. and Shohat, E. (1994) *Unthinking Eurocentrism: Multiculturalism and the Media*. London: Routledge

Stanfield, P. (1998) 'Dixie Cowboys and Blues Yodels: The Strange History of the Singing Cowboy', in Buscombe and Pearson (eds) (1998), 96–118.

Stanfield, P. (2001) *Hollywood, Westerns and the 1930s: The Lost Trail*. Exeter: University of Exeter Press.

Storr, B. (1997) *Imaginaires de Guerre: Algérie-Viet-nam, en France et aux Etats-Unis*. Paris: Editions la Découverte.

Street, S. (2002) *Transatlantic Crossings: British Feature Films in the USA*. London: Continuum.

Strick, P. (1976) *Science Fiction Movies*. London: Heinemann Octopus.

Strinati, D. (1995) *An Introduction to Theories of Popular Culture*. London: Routledge.

Stringer, J. (ed.) (2003) *Movie Blockbusters*. London: Routledge.

Swain, J. (1998) 'Bleeding Images: *Performance* and the British Gangster Movie', MA diss. Birkbeck College, London.

Tasker, Y. (1993) *Spectacular Bodies: Gender, Genre and the Action Cinema*. London: Routledge.

Tasker, Y. (ed.) (2004) *Action and Adventure Cinema*. London: Routledge.

Taves, B. (1993) *The Romance of Adventure: The Genre of Historical Adventure Movies*. Jackson, MS: University of Mississippi Press.

Telotte, J. P. (1995) *Replications: A Robotic History of Science Fiction Film*. Urbana, IL: University of Illinois Press.

Telotte, J. P. (1997) *A Distant Technology: Science Fiction Film and the Machine Age*. Middletown, CT: Wesleyan University Press.

Telotte, J. P. (2001) *Science Fiction Film*. Cambridge: Cambridge University Press.

Telotte, J. P. (2002) 'The New Hollywood Musical: From *Saturday Night Fever* to *Footloose*', in Neale (ed.) (2002b), 48–61.

Thomas, D. (1992) 'How Hollywood Deals with the Deviant Male', in Cameron, I. (ed.) (1992), 59–70.

Thomas, D. (2000) *Beyond Genre: Melodrama, Comedy and Romance in Hollywood Films*. London: Cameron & Hollis.

Todorov, T. (1990) *Genres in Discourse*. Cambridge: Cambridge University Press.

Tohill, C. and Tombs, P. (1994) *Immoral Tales: European Sex and Horror Movies, 1956–1984*. New York: St. Martin's Press.

Tompkins, J. (1992) *West of Everything: The Inner Life of Westerns*. New York: Oxford University Press.

Traube, E. G. (1992) *Dreaming Identities: Class, Gender and Generation in 1980s Hollywood Movies*. Boulder, CO: Westview Press.

Tudor, A. (1973) (1976) 'Genre and Critical Methodology', in Nichols, B. (ed.) (1976), 118–26.

Tudor, A. (1989) *Monsters and Mad Scientists: A Cultural History of the Horror Movie*. Oxford: Basil Blackwell.

Tulloch, J. and Jenkins, H. (ed.) (1995) *Science Fiction Audiences Watching* Doctor Who *and* Star Trek. London: Routledge.

Turk, E. B. (1998) *Hollywood Diva: A Biography of Jeannette MacDonald*. Berkeley, CA: University of California Press.

Turner, F. J. (1947) (1986) *The Frontier in American History*. Tucson, AZ: University of Arizona Press.

Twitchell, J. (1985) *Dreadful Pleasures: An Anatomy of Modern Horror*. Oxford: Oxford University Press.

Vardac, A. N. (1949) *Stage to Screen: Theatrical origins of Early Film, David Garrick to D. W. Griffith*. Cambridge, MA: Harvard University Press.

Vernet, M. (1993) '*Film Noir* on the Edge of Doom', in Copjec, J. (ed.) (1993), 1–31.

Vincendeau, G. (1992) '*Noir* Is Also a French Word: The French Antecedents of *Film Noir*', in Cameron, I. (ed.) (1992), 49–58.

Wagstaff, C. (1992) 'A Forkful of Westerns: Industry, Audiences and the Italian Western', in Dyer, R. and Vincendeau, G. (eds) (1992) *Popular European Cinema*. London: Routledge.

Walker, J. (2001a) 'Introduction: Westerns Through History', in Walker, J. (ed.) (2001b), 1–26.

Walker, J. (ed.) (2001b) *Westerns: Films Through History*. New York and London: Routledge.

Walker, M. (1982) 'Melodrama and the American Cinema', *Movie*, 29/30: 2–38.

Ward, L. W. (1985) *The Motion Picture Goes to War*. Ann Arbor, MI: UMI Research Press.

Warshow, R. (1948) (1975a) 'The Gangster as Tragic Hero', in *The Immediate Experience: Movies, Comics, Theatre and Other Aspects of Popular Culture*. New York: Atheneum, pp. 127–33.

Warshow, R. (1954) (1975b) 'Movie Chronicle: The Westerner', in *The Immediate Experience: Movies, Comics, Theatre and Other Aspects of Popular Culture*. New York: Atheneum, pp. 135–54.

Weiss, A. (1992) *Vampires and Violets: Lesbians in the Cinema*. London: Jonathan Cape.

Weissman, G. (1995) 'A Fantasy of Witnessing', *Media, Culture and Society*, 17.1: 293–307.

Wells, P. (2000) *The Horror Genre: From Beelzebub to Blair Witch*. London: Wallflower.

Welsh, J. (2000) 'Action Films: The Serious, the Ironic, the Postmodern', in Dixon, W. W. (ed.) (2000), 161–76.

Wexman, V. W. (1993) *Creating the Couple: Love, Marriage and Hollywood Performance*. Princeton, NJ: Princeton University Press.

White, E. (2005 forthcoming) 'Case Study: Nakata Hideo's *Ringu* and *Ringu 2*', in McRoy, J. (ed.) (2005 forthcoming).

Wierzbicki, J. (2002) 'Weird Vibrations: How the Theremin Gave Musical Voice to Hollywood's Extraterrestrial 'Others' – Electronic Music from 1950s Science Fiction Films', *Journal of Popular Film and Television*, 30.3: 25–35.

Williams, A. (1984) 'Is a Radical Genre Criticism Possible?', *Quarterly Review of Film Studies*, 9.2: 121–5.

Williams, L. (1983) 'When the Woman Looks', in Doane, M. A. et al. (eds), (1983) *Re-Vision: Essays in Feminist Film Criticism*. Los Angeles: American Film Institute, pp. 83–99; also in Jancovich (ed.) (2002).

Williams, L. (1984) (1991) '"Something Else Besides a Mother": *Stella Dallas* and the Maternal Melodrama', in Landy (ed.) (1991b), 307–30.

Williams, L. (1988) 'Feminist Film Theory: *Mildred Pierce* and the Second World War', in Pribram, E. D. (ed.) (1988) *Female Spectators: Looking at Film and Television*. New York: Verso, pp. 12–30.

Williams, L. (1998) 'Melodrama Revised', in Browne, N. (ed.) (1998), 42–88.

Williams, L. (1999) *Hard Core: Power, Pleasure, and the 'Frenzy of the Visible'*, 2nd edn. Berkeley, CA: University of California Press.

Williams, L. R. (1993) 'Erotic Thrillers and Rude Women', *Sight & Sound*, 3.7: 12–14.

Williams, L. R. (2005 forthcoming) *The Erotic Thriller in Contemporary Cinema*. Edinburgh: Edinburgh University Press.

Williams, R. (1973) (1980) 'Base and Superstructure in Marxist Cultural Theory', in *Problems in Materialism and Culture*. London: Verso, pp. 31–49.

Willis, A. (2003) 'Locating Bollywood: Notes on the Hindi Blockbuster, 1975 to the present', in Stringer, J. (ed.) (2003), 255–68.

Wilson, R. (2000) 'The Left-Handed Form of Human Endeavor: Crime Films During the 1990s', in Dixon (ed.) (2000), 143–59.

Wilson, R. G., Pilgrim, D. H. and Tashjian, D. (1986) *The Machine Age in America: 1918–1941*. New York: Abrams.

Winokur, M. (1991) 'Eating Children Is Wrong: The Ethnic Family in Gangster Films of the 80s and 90s', *Sight & Sound*, 1: 10–13.

Winokur, M. (1995) 'Marginal Marginalia: The African-American Voice in the Nouvelle Gangster Film', *The Velvet Light Trap*, 35: 19–32.

Winston, B. (1993) 'The Documentary Film as Scientific Inscription', in Renov, M. (ed.) (1993) *Theorising Documentary*. London: Routledge.

Wollen, P. (1992) *Singin' in the Rain*. London: BFI.

Wood, A. (2002) *Technoscience in Contemporary Film: Beyond Science Fiction*. Manchester: Manchester University Press.

Wood, A. (2004) 'The Collapse of Reality and Illusion in *The Matrix*', in Tasker, Y. (ed.) (2004), 153–65.

Wood, G. C. (1988) 'Horror Film', in Gehring, W. D. (ed.) (1988), 211–28.

Wood, R. (1979) 'An Introduction to the American Horror Film', in Nichols, B. (ed.) (1985) *Movies and Methods, Vol. II*. Berkeley, CA: University of California Press, pp. 195–220.

Wood, R. (1981) *Howard Hawks*. London: BFI.

Wood, R. (1986) *Hollywood from Vietnam to Reagan*. New York: Columbia University Press.

Worland, R. and Countryman, E. (1998) 'The New Western American Historiography and the Emergence of the New American Western', in Buscombe and Pearson (eds) (1998), 182–96.

Wright, J. H. (1974) (1995) 'Genre Films and the Status Quo', in Grant, B. K. (ed.) (1995), 41–9.

Wright, W. (1975) *Sixguns and Society: A Structural Study of the Western*. Berkeley, CA: University of California Press.

Wyatt, J. (1994) *High Concept: Movies and Marketing in Hollywood*. Austin, TX: University of Texas Press.

Young, N. (2000) '"We May Be Rats, Crooks and Murderers, but We're Americans": Controlling the Hollywood Gangster Protagonist during Early World War II', *Irish Journal of American Studies*, 9: 112–28.

Youngblood, D. J. (1996) '*Ivan's Childhood* and *Come and See*: Post-Stalinist Cinema and the Myth of World War II', in Chambers and Culbert (eds) (1996), 85–96.

Youngblood, D. J. (2001) 'A War Remembered: Soviet Films of the Great Patriotic War', *American Historical Review*, 106.3: 839–56.

Zinn, H. (1995) *A People's History of the United States*, 2nd edn. New York: HarperCollins.

Žižek, S. (1993) '"The Thing That Thinks": The Kantian Background of the *Noir* Subject', in Copjec, J. (ed.) (1993), 199–226.

Index